PENGUIN PRESS

New York

2018

Dangerous Mystic

Meister Eckhart's Path
to the God Within

JOEL F.
HARRINGTON

PENGUIN PRESS
An imprint of Penguin Random House LLC
375 Hudson Street
New York, New York 10014
penguin.com

ISBN 9781101981566 (hardcover edition)
ISBN 9781101981580 (e-book)

Printed in the United States of America
1   3   5   7   9   10   8   6   4   2

Designed by Gretchen Achilles

For Beth

Contents

There are those who seek knowledge for the sake of knowledge;
that is curiosity. There are those who seek knowledge to be known by others;
that is vanity. There are those who seek knowledge
in order to serve; that is love.

BERNARD OF CLAIRVAUX (1090–1153)

THE WORLD OF MEISTER ECKHART
circa 1300

Inset map

Hannover
Magdeburg
Berlin
Elbe
VIA IMPERII
Oder
Saale
Elbe
Hochheim
VIA REGI
Weser
Leipzig
Dresden
THURINGIA
Erfurt
Gotha
Tambach
Main
Hof
Prague
Vltava

Scale of miles
40   80

Main map

DENMARK
Baltic Sea
North Sea
Lübeck
Hamburg
Elbe
SAXONY
BRANDENBURG
POLAND
Münster
Bruges
BRABANT
Cologne
Leipzig
THURINGIA
SILESIA
Prague
Oder
English Channel
FLANDERS
HOLY ROMAN EMPIRE
BOHEMIA
HAINAULT
Seine
Paris
Strasbourg
Rhine
BAVARIA
Danube
Allier
FRANCE
BURGUNDY
HUNGARY
Atlantic Ocean
Vienne
Rhône
SAVOY
Po
Venice
Avignon
Bologna
Adriatic Sea
NAVARRE
Florence
PAPAL STATES
CASTILLE
CORSICA
Rome
Tajo
ARAGON
Tyrrhenian Sea
Mediterranean Sea
Ionian Sea

Scale of miles
10   20   30   40

Map by Gene Thorp

Key Names and Terms

ALBERT THE GREAT: aka Albertus Magnus; ca. 1200–80, a Dominican and the greatest German philosopher of his day

AVERROËS: aka Ibn Rushd; 1126–98; Aristotelian philosopher from Muslim Andalusia

AVICENNA: aka Ibn Sīnā; 980–1037; influential Islamic philosopher from Persia

BEATIFIC VISION: In Christian theology, the face-to-face experience of God; highly disputed whether possible before death

BEGUINE: A member of a community of religious women who do not take formal vows

DIETRICH OF FREIBERG: ca. 1250–ca. 1310; Dominican scholar and administrator, also mentor of Eckhart

DISPUTATIO: A formal scholastic debate on a specific theological question

DIVINE BIRTH: aka the eternal birth; according to Eckhart, the direct experience of divine essence in the soul

DIVINE SPARK: According to Eckhart, the piece of divine essence found in every soul

DOMINICANS: aka the Order of Preachers, a religious order founded by Dominic de Guzmán in 1215

ERFURT: Thuringian city and home to Eckhart for most of his life

ESSENCE: In scholastic philosophy, the necessary or defining properties of a thing

FRANCISCANS: aka the Order of Friars Minor, a religious order founded by Francis of Assisi in 1209

FRIENDS OF GOD: Fourteenth-century Rhineland followers of Eckhart's mystical teachings

HEINRICH OF VIRNEBURG: 1245–1332; archbishop of Cologne from 1304 on

INTELLECT: In scholastic terms, the power for conceptual thought, located in the soul

JOHN XXII: Born Jacques Duèz; reigned as pope in Avignon 1316–34

LATERAN IV: Universal church council convened by Pope Innocent III in 1215

LETTING-GO-NESS: Translation of *gelâzenheit*, the necessary precondition to the divine birth

MAIMONIDES: aka Moses ben Maimon; 1135–1204; Sephardic Jewish philosopher from Cordova

MARGUERITE OF PORETE: Beguine author of *The Mirror of Simple Souls*; burned as a heretic in 1310

MECHTILD OF MAGDEBURG: ca. 1208–92; beguine and author of mystical *Flowing Light of Divinity*

MENDICANT: aka friar, a member of one of the "begging orders" of Franciscans or Dominicans

MYSTIC: An individual who has directly experienced the divine or ultimate reality

OPUS TRIPARTITUM: The three-volume theological *summa* planned by Eckhart but never completed

PHILIP THE FAIR: aka Philip IV, reigned as king of France 1285–1314

PRIORY: A mendicant or monastic house, headed by an elected prior

PSEUDO-DIONYSIUS: Anonymous Christian theologian of the late fifth and early sixth centuries; a major source of medieval mystical thought

ST. JACQUES: The Dominican priory in the Latin quarter of Paris

SCHOLASTIC: A "schoolman" trained at a university, typically in philosophy or theology

SENTENCES: The influential four-volume theological handbook compiled by Peter Lombard (ca. 1096–1160)

SPECIES: The scholastic definition of any kind of cognitive representation of a group

SUMMA: A summing up of theological knowledge in one work

HEINRICH SUSO: aka Heinrich Seus; ca. 1295–1360; a prominent Eckhart disciple

TALKS OF INSTRUCTION: Excerpts from Eckhart's discussions with Dominican novices during the years 1294–98

JOHANNES TAULER: 1300–61; a prominent Eckhart disciple

TERTIARY: A layman or laywoman who attaches to a religious order without taking permanent vows

THOMAS AQUINAS: aka the Angelic Doctor; 1225–74; supremely influential Dominican theologian, canonized in 1323

THURINGIA: Landgraviate in central Germany; during Eckhart's lifetime ruled by the Wettin dynasty of Meissen

UNIVERSAL: A common concept, like a Platonic form, whose reality scholastics debate

UNIVOCITY: Among scholastics, a property of words whose meanings are identical; an essential component of "scientific" theology

VIA NEGATIVA: The theological method of "knowing" God by what He is not

Dangerous
Mystic

Prologue

The contrast between the setting and the message could not have been starker. The year was 1318; the location, the cathedral of Our Lady in the German city of Strasbourg, during a typical Sunday morning mass. The man about to speak was Eckhart von Hochheim, better known to posterity as Meister (German for "Master") Eckhart. Some three hundred men and women sat silently in the wooden pews. A few of them whispered Latin prayers while fingering the recently invented prayer beads known as the garland of roses, or rosary. Most waited in an anticipatory hush, focused on the middle-aged priest solemnly seated on the left side of the altar, the top of his head shaved in the distinctive tonsure of monastic orders, the man himself extravagantly robed in the embroidered green vestments of the liturgical season.

During the extended pause for reflection after the gospel reading, some members of the congregation must have let their eyes wander to the surrounding wonders of the magnificent cathedral. For nearly a century, the earlier church, built in a style later called Romanesque, had been slowly transformed into "the French style," known today as Gothic. External flying buttresses and other engineering marvels had enabled the cathedral's builders to shift to tall arches and thin, largely ornamental columns, giving the interior of the church a steep and dramatic thrust upward, toward God. Brightly colored stained-glass windows told stories of the saints and martyrs, while casting rainbow-colored shafts of morning light onto the congregation. The smoke of incense from the mass's opening procession lingered in the streaming sunshine, filling the air with its mildly sweet, otherworldly odor.

Still waiting for the celebrant to address them, some members of the congregation might have surveyed the wall coverings and statuary on the

sides of the nave that also called to mind holy predecessors. The most prominent of these was "Our Lady," the Blessed Virgin Mary, patroness of the cathedral. But not all the images were comforting. Many portrayed terrifying
agonies suffered in the service of God, beginning with the large crucifix
suspended above the main altar. One column—known locally as the Angels
Pillar—reminded those assembled of their own imminent demise and
afterworldly fate. On it were larger-than-life-size figures of the four evangelists, crowned by four angels blowing the trumpets of judgment, with three
angels and a suffering Jesus atop, prepared to pass sentence on departed
souls. In contrast to this unsettling image, the altar glittered with jeweled
reliquaries, each displaying a shard of bone or miraculously preserved body
part of a revered saint, a sight that, though grisly by today's standards, conveyed to the medieval Christian an unmistakable aura of safety and holiness.

The Angels Column from the south transept of Strasbourg Cathedral. The angels
blow the trumpets announcing the Final Judgment of the living and the dead
and the ultimate fate of eternal reward or punishment for every soul.

Finally, Meister Eckhart rose, and all eyes returned to the priest as he
slowly mounted the steps to the pulpit. He was a stranger to most in the
congregation, a specially invited guest, but virtually everyone present knew
of his remarkable reputation. Rigorously trained in the clerical Order of
Preachers, commonly called the Dominicans or Blackfriars, the learned

priest had studied the Bible and theology for decades and served two tenures as a chaired professor at the University of Paris, home to the most esteemed theological faculty in Christendom. He was indisputably a man of great learning, but Eckhart was also reputed to be an especially engaging speaker, one capable of making the wisdom of the ages accessible to even the simplest listener. Most enticingly, according to his admirers, the slightly stooped friar about to address them could guide the truly pious among them to an immediate, personal experience of God Himself.

The biblical text that served as the basis for the sermon was from the book of Wisdom (8:14–15): "For while gentle silence enveloped all things, and night in its swift course was now half-gone, your all-powerful word leaped from heaven, from the royal throne." After translating the verse from Latin into German, the language of his listeners, the preacher proceeded to speak to them in the vernacular about the birth of the Word, a common reference to Jesus's appearance on earth. But Eckhart made no mention of donkeys, stables, shepherds, or angels. The birth that this preacher described was "the eternal birth," God coming to earth not just in the person of Jesus or in the consecrated bread and wine of the Eucharist, but as a palpable presence entering into the soul of any believer who was sufficiently prepared. One did not need the priest to transform bread and wine into the body and blood of Jesus, he explained. One did not have to be a monk or a nun or even an educated person. No, Eckhart insisted, anyone who was spiritually ready could experience the birth of God directly within his or her own soul.

How could this be, most of his listeners must have wondered. To their knowledge, only a very few holy people since the days of the Savior had been blessed with genuine visions or other direct encounters with God. But Eckhart insisted: The authentic experience of the divine he described did not depend on apparitions, special powers, or extraordinary acts of piety. It was not partial to certain holy places or rituals. What the "eternal birth" did require was a proper mental attitude, a soul that had learned to let go of all worldly things, all desires and preconceptions, even the image of God Himself. *The more completely you are able to draw in your powers to a unity and forget all those things and their images which you have absorbed, and the further you can get from creatures and their images, the nearer you are to this and the readier to receive it.* Then, he said—*in the midst of silence*—God would come within your soul.

After speaking for more than twenty minutes, the preacher neared his conclusion. *The Son of the heavenly Father,* he repeated, *is not born alone in this darkness, which is his own: You too can be born a child of the same heavenly Father and of none other, and to you too He will give power.* The key lay in *divesting yourself of yourself and of everything external. And in very truth,* he continued, *I believe, nay, I am sure, that the man who is established in this cannot in any way ever be separated from God. I say he can in no way lapse into mortal sin . . . such people cannot willingly commit or consent to even a venial (lesser) sin in themselves or in others if they can stop it.* The preacher surveyed his audience. *May the God who has been born again as man assist us to this birth, eternally helping us, weak men, to be born in him again as God. Amen.* He turned, walked down the pulpit steps, and made his way to the seat side of the altar. The church remained engulfed in deep silence.

This sermon was unlike any that had ever been heard within the cathedral's walls. After forty years of contemplation and study, the esteemed friar and theologian was taking advantage of his assignment to this important city to preach his spiritual philosophy to the common people. Merely speaking in this way to ordinary women and men about "elevated matters" was remarkable, a practice scorned by most priests and scholars of the time. But more provocative still was the radical message that Eckhart delivered. Although he did not denigrate the external forms of piety around him—indeed he was in the midst of celebrating a mass—Eckhart's focus on the internal, on thought, was highly unusual, perhaps even unsettling to many of his listeners. The church they knew preached that each person's salvation depended on the performance of good works and penitential acts of contrition—yet these were absent from Eckhart's teaching. The church they knew revolved around the veneration of saints and the celebration of sacraments—yet these played no apparent role whatsoever in the internal self-transcendence Eckhart described. The church they knew esteemed monks, nuns, and other contemplatives as closer to God—yet Eckhart preached that direct experience of God was accessible to any true seeker, regardless of social or religious status. More surprising still, he seemed to say that the effect of this divine union was permanent, that it guaranteed the believer who experienced it an eternal state of sinlessness and bliss.

This may have come as inspiring news to the congregation that day, but it was unlike any description of salvation they had ever heard. Although Eckhart himself saw his teachings as completely congruent with those of the church, others within that institution did not. In the years to follow, this learned monk and gifted preacher would eventually see much of his theology condemned by a papal inquisition, his teachings formally suppressed, and his followers dispersed.

Fast-forward seven centuries, however, and Meister Eckhart—after languishing many years in relative obscurity—has emerged as something of a spiritual celebrity. Millions of Roman Catholics and other Christians have claimed the rehabilitated preacher as one of their own, not to mention many Zen Buddhists, Sufi Muslims, Advaita Vedanta Hindus, Jewish Cabbalists, and a wide variety of other seekers who describe themselves as spiritual but not religious. Even many avowed atheists, including Martin Heidegger and Jean-Paul Sartre, have admired the master's speculative philosophy and helped spread his insights among their own generations of disciples. Composers John Cage and John Adams have each written musical works inspired by the teachings of Meister Eckhart. On the Internet, quotations attributed to Eckhart (many of them spurious) proliferate, as do sites devoted to his teachings. More than a hundred publications on his life and teachings (not counting blogs) appear annually, and there are now three international Meister Eckhart societies, as well as two scholarly journals devoted to the once-condemned friar.

In the United States, the works of Eckhart owe much of their recent popularity to the master's namesake, Eckhart (born Ulrich) Tolle, a spiritual teacher and author whose beliefs weave together the medieval monk's teachings with an eclectic blend of contemporary Eastern and New Age concepts. "In essence," writes Tolle, "there is and always has been only one spiritual teaching, although it comes in many forms." That one teaching, Tolle maintains, is nowhere better encapsulated than in the insights of Meister Eckhart, whose key concepts shape his own belief system. Thanks in large part to the massively influential endorsement of Oprah's Book Club, the modern

Eckhart's *The Power of Now* (1997) and *A New Earth* (2005) each enjoyed several months on the *New York Times* bestseller list and together have been translated into thirty-three languages and sold more than ten million copies worldwide. And Tolle is not the only one. Other contemporary spirituality authors—from a wide variety of traditions—make similarly extensive use of the master's various sermons and philosophical writings.

What is it that all these people see in the words of this medieval sage? The most common denominator appears to be an attraction to Eckhart's revolutionary method of direct access to ultimate reality (aka God)—a profoundly subjective approach that is at once intuitive and pragmatic, philosophical yet nonrational, and, above all, universally accessible. Many modern Christian authors, such as the Catholic Richard Rohr—who calls Eckhart "a mystic's mystic"—view his teachings as part of a long and ancient Christian contemplative tradition. Yet while Eckhart's path never opposes or denigrates religious rituals or church authorities, it also does not rely on them. This makes him equally appealing to individuals and groups who reject the Christian notions of both God and the soul. Buddhists and existentialists, for example, appreciate the master's distinction between the artificial "I" or "false self"—the constructed individual identity of each person—and the authentic self, the common nature that we all share. At the same time, Eckhart's embrace of meditation and mindfulness anticipates by seven centuries the popularity of both practices among people of faith and the ever-growing number of New Age seekers, agnostics, and avowed atheists who list their religious affiliation as "none." Marginalized in his own time, Meister Eckhart seems to have been made, in fact, for ours, an age with a penchant for spirituality that is customized, experiential, and doctrine-light.

But in our eagerness to embrace this "forgotten heretic," to find in his teaching the fulfillment of our own needs and to appropriate him for our own uses, we risk seriously distorting the historical man and his thought. The label "mystic," for instance—a concept invented in the seventeenth century—calls to mind a secluded, otherworldly sage, caught up in the throes of divine rapture. But Meister Eckhart was no recluse and never wrote of any special visions, miraculous events, or ecstatic physical experiences. He lived, in fact, as a person immersed in the activities of the external world, a wide-traveling preacher, university professor, confessor, administrator, and diplomat. He saw himself first as a Dominican friar, dedicated to spreading the gospel, and second as a religious philosopher, a scholar determined to bring together all types of knowledge—Christian and pagan, intuitive and scientific, general and personal—and to assemble from them a coherent, comprehensive whole that led back to God.

The divine union he preached did not in fact require any suspension of rational thought nor did it entail any special individual powers. On the contrary, it was the universal accessibility of the experience he described that made him simultaneously popular with his audiences and dangerous to his clerical opponents. The internal transformation itself, he conceded, was difficult to describe with language, and thus appeared "mysterious" to human thinking. But reaching this point was a straightforward matter of intention and attitude, a process described by Eckhart in practical terms. And *the divine birth in the soul*, once achieved, always produced a life devoted to others, not retreat from the world. If Meister Eckhart was a mystic in the modern sense of the word, he was a profoundly antiobscurant, egalitarian, and down-to-earth one.

Similarly, the image of Eckhart as a misunderstood visionary, a man who would have been more at home in our modern progressive era than in his own narrow-minded age, ignores the richness and spiritual dynamism of medieval European society. In fact, Meister Eckhart attracted a significant following in his own day, clear evidence that he was not the lone and disregarded man-ahead-of-his-time we might assume. In fact, many people in the fourteenth century shared his desire for a direct experience of the divine in their lives, beyond what conventional religious practices offered. There were, of course, the thousands of ordinary Christians who flocked to hear his sermons. But many of Eckhart's fellow religious scholars also shared his radical reimagining of "God" and "heaven," as well as his focus on the divinity within each person, what Eckhart called *the divine spark*. What most distinguished him from other theologians of his day was Eckhart's willingness to take the learning of the universities to the pulpit and to teach a practical kind of mysticism that was accessible to all those with the proper intention and attitude. The fact that a papal commission later condemned some of his teachings should not be construed to mean that all or even most of his contemporaries rejected Eckhart's approach to God.

In fact, when we put aside modern misperceptions about medieval Christianity itself, we discover an unexpectedly vibrant period in Western history, when new ideas and practices abounded among a population hungry for more meaningful spiritual experiences. Might that history have unfolded differently if Eckhart's teachings had not been stifled by a church hierarchy fearful of spiritual anarchy? If the few ecclesiastical authorities in question had embraced (or at least not condemned) Eckhart's teachings, could many of the later ecclesiastical abuses that led to the Protestant Reformation have been avoided? With that question, we contemplate a hidden watershed moment and a viable alternate world history. Most aspects of Eckhart's teachings were in fact thoroughly compatible with both Catholic and later Protestant doctrine. How might Christianity today look if the Reformation itself had amounted to what one historian has characterized as "a passing breeze rather than a hurricane"?

Obviously it is just as perilous to separate the man from his times as it is the teachings from the man. An anachronistic Eckhart, however personally satisfying, is a distorted and misleading Eckhart. Before we attempt to adapt his ideas to our needs, we must make a genuine effort to understand their author within the context of his own life and his own world. Most literate people—including those who count themselves among his admirers—know very little if anything about the man himself. Until now, the individual often described as "the most influential mystic in Christian history" has been scrutinized mainly by theologians, philosophers, and German literary scholars, producing a rich but often daunting body of scholarship, focusing overwhelmingly—and often in very demanding prose—on Eckhart's teachings. Among popular authors, the social milieu and biographical aspects of the revered teacher receive even shorter shrift, rendering Eckhart himself a shadowy and ethereal figure, prone to gnomic declarations such as "The eye with which I see God is the same eye with which God sees me." Without any historical context, the master sounds more like a cartoon guru on a mountaintop than an accomplished theologian and philosopher.

Yet Meister Eckhart, like all of us, was the product of a particular place and period. It is meaningless to talk about the "timeless" nature of his teachings unless we first understand which aspects of them were in fact timely—shaped by his own life experiences and environment—and in which ways. We must come to know the vibrant character of his social and intellectual world, his distinctive voice as a preacher and thinker, and the diverse ways that he was understood in his time. Do this and we can't help but better understand his relevance in our own time.

Why has so little been written about Eckhart the man? Perhaps it is because the scarcity of resources available to the would-be Eckhart biographer presents a steep, though not insurmountable, challenge. None of Eckhart's correspondence or personal writings has survived the seven centuries since his death. Certain Latin documents related to his heresy trial have been preserved, providing insight into the points of greatest controversy, but, although there are at least two dozen mentions of him in other documents written during his lifetime, none of these is more than a passing reference. What does remain are Meister Eckhart's own theological teachings. As of this publication, we know of at least 128 authenticated German sermons (plus two dozen more under consideration), fifty-six Latin sermons, three German discourses, seven Latin commentaries, and a handful of short academic pieces, none of them actually written in the master's hand, but instead transcribed by followers who heard him speak, and in some cases approved by Eckhart for publication. This book draws heavily on the outstanding edited collections of Eckhart's Latin and German writings that appeared between 1936 and 2007 (see "Recommended Reading"), as well as the careful scholarship of several generations of Eckhart scholars, particularly during the last four decades.

My approach is both chronological and thematic, combining the key steps in Meister Eckhart's lifelong pursuit of God with the various identities he accumulated over the years: friar, scholar, preacher, and spiritual icon. All four sections of the book have been framed around what I find to be Eckhart's most important concept: *gelâzenheit* (*Gelassenheit* in modern German), a word he coined and that I translate as "letting-go-ness." I devised this intentionally awkward translation to distinguish it from such conventional—but misleading—English renderings as "detachment," "releasement," or "abandonment." The implicit trust involved in "letting go" of desire itself was for

Eckhart the essential precondition to achieving divine union, a realization that he reached only after many years of practical devotion and reflection. Only after he had first learned to let go of the external world (Part I) as well as all of his preconceived notions of God (Part II) did Eckhart feel ready to let go of his very self, including his pursuit of God, and thereby allow God to come to him (Part III). The implications of this realization for organized religion, which he by no means intended to "let go," are described in Part IV.

This narrative of Eckhart's own internal, spiritual evolution is closely interwoven with the story of his experiences in the wider world. Unlike most descriptions of Meister Eckhart—which present his teachings as fully formed, coherent, and static—this chronological perspective allows us to witness the evolution of Eckhart's thinking over the course of his life. How and why did a seemingly conventional young German noble become the radical spiritual thinker of legend, questioning not just much of the orthodox approach to God but the prevailing notion of God itself? First we dive into the dynamic world of thirteenth-century Germany, discovering the origins of Eckhart's lifelong quest and his formative embrace of the Dominican life (Part I). Here we witness his gradual transformation from a traditional spirituality based on external acts to one based on contemplation and mindfulness. His identity as a professional preacher in turn gives shape to his subsequent development as a renowned scholar (Part II), where Eckhart's increasing exposure to philosophical thought eventually moved him toward a still more radically intuitive approach to God and spirituality. Most of these earlier years, until his mid-fifties, were spent in his native Thuringia, based in the Dominican priory at Erfurt. He traveled widely, though, including many years of advanced study in Cologne and Paris, several years of work as an administrator for his order, and three years as a professor at the University of Paris. Part III describes the acclaimed theologian's subsequent efforts to distill his complex and unorthodox ideas into sermons that ordinary women and men could understand. Most of this popular preaching took place in the German cities of Strasbourg and Cologne, during the last quarter of his life. It was the resulting controversy over his provocative teachings there that eventually transformed Eckhart into a spiritual icon, with his admirers and detractors struggling to define his legacy for centuries to come (Part IV).

The spectacular rise and fall of this prescient spiritual teacher carries important ramifications for the perennial debate over religious authority, even today. Church leaders' concerns during Eckhart's lifetime that simple people might misunderstand the master's words and reject all religion may appear at first as mere self-justification for their own authoritarian agenda. Yet as the later Protestant Reformation and subsequent schisms have made clear, the appeal to individual conscience as the ultimate arbiter of spiritual truth invariably leads to ever more interpretations, ever more denominations, ever more religious conflicts. What might a fuller embrace of Eckhart's teachings mean for the doctrine, structure, and rituals of today's Catholic and Protestant churches? For organized religion itself? Eckhart did not consider himself a radical opponent of traditional religion, but his effect on the same remains in dispute. Meanwhile, many modern readers, who prefer a more individualistic approach to spirituality, welcome the skepticism of institutional religious authority that they infer from Eckhart's teachings. But is theirs the type of individual enlightenment Eckhart himself imagined? Is the relativism of today's customized spirituality the inevitable outcome of the subjective approach taught by Eckhart and his modern successors?

It's obvious why fourteenth-century defenders of religious orthodoxy and order considered Meister Eckhart a dangerous mystic. But many twenty-first-century Christian leaders likewise fear the moral relativism and spiritual chaos unleashed by "religionless spirituality." Does a revived Eckhart still pose a threat to established churches or does he offer a bridge between new spirituality movements and older traditions? To answer that question, we must first be willing to see Meister Eckhart with fresh eyes, meeting him again for the first time.

Note on Usage:
All direct quotations from Meister Eckhart have been placed in italics. For the German sermons, I have relied mostly on the excellent English translations of Maurice O'C. Walshe (see "Recommended Reading"), while still

providing in endnotes the sermon number from the standard Middle High German edition (*Die Deutschen Werke*) for those readers interested in consulting the original. Most of my translations from Eckhart's Latin writings come from two works edited by Bernard McGinn: *Meister Eckhart: The Essential Sermons, Commentaries, Treatises, and Defense*; and *Meister Eckhart: Teacher and Preacher*. All other translations from German, French, or Latin are my own, unless otherwise cited. For the purposes of clarity (Eckhart loved ambiguous pronouns) I have capitalized He, Him, and His in references to God the Creator (even though the mature Eckhart rejected any human gendering of the divine except for the convenience of language).

During Eckhart's lifetime, most people reckoned the beginning of the new year at Easter, or some close approximation (e.g., March 25). I have followed the modern dating of the new year as starting at January 1.

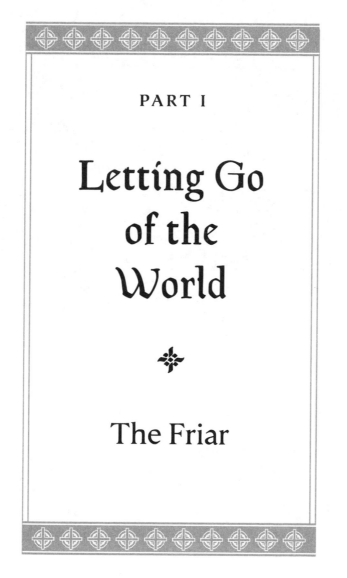

PART I

Letting Go of the World

�֎

The Friar

CHAPTER ONE

The Noble Heart

*Some people are half raised up: they practice one virtue but not
another. Some, ignoble by nature, covet riches. Others of a nobler
nature care nothing for possessions but are bent on honor.*

GERMAN SERMON 25

A World Without Love

Meister Eckhart lived from about 1260 to 1328. By our modern reckoning,
his lifetime straddled the High Middle Ages (ca. 1000–1300) and the Late
Middle Ages (ca. 1300–1500). Of course these concepts would have been
completely alien to Eckhart and his contemporaries, who—like all people
who have ever lived—considered themselves "modern." To enter his world's
notion of modernity and its struggles, we must first unburden ourselves of
most twenty-first-century connotations of the very word "medieval." From
its late fifteenth-century origins, the designation has been mostly pejorative,
lumping together the roughly thousand years following the demise of the
Western Roman Empire. Proponents of the Renaissance and later the Enlightenment particularly delighted in envisioning a "bad" Middle Ages to
contrast with their own notions of human progress: a violent, dirty, and
backward time when superstition and cruelty reigned supreme. Nineteenth-
century Romantics countered with a "good" Middle Ages: an era of simple
and joyous vitality and pageantry, dominated by the virtues of loyalty,

bravery, and courtesy. More recent imaginings—from *Lord of the Rings* to *Game of Thrones*—have creatively combined different aspects of these two stereotypes, but with the same implicit contrast to our own more sophisticated age.

"Medieval," consequently, has today become a synonym for inferior—whether in discussing criminal justice, sanitary conditions, social attitudes, understanding of the natural world, or virtually any aspect of contemporary life viewed as lacking. And certainly in structural terms, the modernity of thirteenth-century Europe more closely resembles the modernity of a twenty-first-century developing country, such as Afghanistan or Somalia: weak central governments, roaming warlords, no clear division between secular and religious spheres, patriarchal social systems, low literacy rates, high infant mortality, and an overall low standard of living.

Yet the material constraints of Eckhart's world did not impair an explosion of artistic, literary, and intellectual creativity. Shorter life expectancies than today's did not prevent parents from loving their children; recurrent natural and man-made hardships did not stop frequent public celebrations of life. Intelligence, if not education, was just as evenly distributed among the population as in any human society. And, as many recent studies of well-being have indicated, happiness and depression do not correlate directly to a material standard of living (and in many instances poorer societies fare better). This is not an endorsement of bad hygiene and pandemic violence but rather an attempt to break free of Western technological determinism that equates material progress with social, psychological, and spiritual development. Eckhart's relatively rudimentary living conditions no more restricted his insights into the human spirit than plentiful food and advanced technology have guaranteed superior understanding to any modern Westerner.

The modernity of Eckhart and his contemporaries differed from our own in another important way, namely their concept of history. Not only was there no medieval era for thirteenth-century Europeans, there was no such thing as an era in terms of anything but political regimes (e.g., "the age of Emperor Charles the Great," aka Charlemagne). Obviously the glories of ancient Greece and Rome were long past, but they did not seem distant culturally. One quick glance at the period's paintings or sculptures of Jesus and the apostles reveals an imagined bygone world that looked indistinguishable from their own, in clothing, movements, and emotions. The Western Roman Empire was still alive and well—albeit dominated by German kings for more than two centuries—and the church founded by Jesus still used Latin liturgies and Roman clerical dress. Individual emperors and popes came and went, but the institutions seemed to remain constant. Above all, no one in the thirteenth century imagined human history in terms of progress—a completely alien notion in a society ruled by the cyclical rhythms of the agrarian year and the liturgical calendar of annual feasts.

This does not mean that they had no notion of social change. To the contrary, most of Eckhart's contemporaries were convinced that their world was becoming worse, was perhaps even on the eve of the Last Days. Of course they were hardly unique in this conviction. It is one of the oldest truisms, repeated ad nauseam by historians, that every society in every age (including our own) perceives itself as declining. Children are growing ever more ungrateful and unruly, youths ever ruder and lazier, adults more selfish and self-absorbed. Politicians are always becoming more corrupt, religious leaders more hypocritical, and businesspeople more dishonest. Whether this broader perspective brings one comfort or despair, the universality of the lament throughout human history is hard to refute. What differs throughout specific cultures and eras—sometimes to a remarkable degree—is the perceived nature and source of that disintegration from a previous golden age. And that is where we start to understand the world of Meister Eckhart and the appeal of his teachings.

The greatest single subject of all thirteenth-century literature, poetry, painting, sculpture, and sermons was love. Again, hardly a unique phenomenon in any human society, but it is the way this topic was portrayed that is most revealing. Love, everyone agreed, was indispensable for happiness in this life and the next. Love between family members, friends, neighbors, and fellow Christians (caritas) was the glue that held society together and helped one in times of trouble. "There is nothing on this earth to be prized more than true friendship," wrote the theologian Thomas Aquinas

(1225–74), echoing a common sentiment. Love and trust between a lord and vassal, between trading partners, between allies of all sorts (*fides*) ensured peace and justice. (Only Jews and Muslims remained outside this exclusively Christian circle of mutual interdependence and charity.) Love of God, the Virgin Mary, and the saints (*religio* or *pietas*) inspired a virtuous earthly life that would end with a heavenly reward. Eckhart's exact contemporary Dante Alighieri marveled at the human network woven by "the love of God, unutterable and perfect . . . the more souls who resonate together/the greater the intensity of their love/and, mirror-like, each soul reflects the other."

Virtually everyone also agreed that love, at the time of Eckhart's birth, was under siege. The perceived breakdown in personal relationships of all kinds threatened not just individual happiness but the social order itself. Knight Wirnt von Grafenberg bemoaned that "the world has changed; its joyousness is in a wretched state. Justice has fled, violence is arising. Loyalty has become brittle, disloyalty and hatred are prevailing. Times have changed completely, and every year it gets worse." "Formerly, the world was so beautiful," sighed the poet Walther von der Vogelweide, "now it is wretched." In a world with weak institutional confidence, personal trust and mutual reliability were indispensable and a world without them was too terrifying to contemplate.

Explanations for the decline of love were myriad, ranging from bad political leaders to irresponsible parents to the direct influence of Satan and his numerous human allies, most notably emboldened criminals, bloodthirsty soldiers, and Jewish financiers. In every instance, culprits placed their own personal gain before the duties of Christian charity, wreaking havoc on the larger society. "Worse morals" was a convenient catchall characterization of social decline, generalizing the blame without offering any specific causation. Some religiously minded people saw their collective suffering as God's deserved chastisement of such widespread sinful behavior, but again focused on selfish individual choices rather than systemic problems. Only one common nonpersonal catalyst emerged in virtually every lamentation about the sorry state of affairs in mid-thirteenth-century Europe: the corrupting and insidious dominance of money.

The Root of All Evil

Money, of course, is as old as human civilization. What was novel in Eckhart's world was the degree to which many of the elements of what we now call "the consumer mentality" had permeated popular attitudes and beliefs. Not since the days of ancient Rome, seven centuries earlier, had money assumed such a prominent role in ordinary Europeans' everyday lives and imaginations. The new ubiquity of cash was above all the product of escalating consumer demand, in turn driven by several generations of steady demographic growth throughout most European lands. The five centuries following the disintegration of the Western Roman Empire—what we now call the Early Middle Ages—had been a period of widespread political and economic instability. Once greater order returned around the year 1000, the population of the continent proceeded to grow steadily, more than tripling by the time of Eckhart, to more than seventy million people.

While this expansion took place over the course of several generations, many dramatic changes would have been evident even within the lifetimes of Eckhart's own parents and grandparents. Just within his own century, the population of German lands—usually defined as east of the Rhine, north of the Danube, and west of the Elbe—surged from eight to fourteen million. Eckhart's home territory of Thuringia experienced at least tenfold growth over the same period, spurred by the "push to the east" that saw hundreds of thousands of German settlers moving into Slavic areas, resulting in the foundation of more than 250 towns east of the Elbe and Saale and nearly 200,000 new communities overall. Human settlements encroached on formerly "vast empty spaces" dominated by wild animals—dense forests, forbidding swamps, sprawling meadows—adapting these "deserts" to their own needs.

Of course the diverse societies of Europe were still overwhelmingly rural—and would remain so well into the nineteenth century. Within German lands, at most one-fifth of the population lived in towns of more than three thousand people, and even among the fifty or so towns passing this threshold, few held more than ten thousand inhabitants. Cologne, where Eckhart would end his long career, was the largest German city, with a population of forty thousand—about the size of contemporary London and one-fifth the size of the sprawling metropolis of Paris. Eckhart's own tiny home village of Tambach, with a population of a few hundred, remained by far the more typical experience for most denizens of premodern Europe for centuries to come.

Yet what they lacked in numbers, urban residents made up for in economic and cultural influence, particularly in giving birth to the new money mentality. The marketplaces that towns and cities provided for agricultural and manufactured goods thrived on the exchange of cash. Both farmers, who brought their produce to market for sale, and urban artisans, who worked for wages, relied on an ample supply of currency. Bankers and merchants involved in long-distance commodities exchanges likewise required still larger amounts of gold and silver for payments, even with the rise of various credit arrangements during the thirteenth century. Growing urban populations also drove the need for expanded investments in infrastructure, leading to large publicly financed construction projects, ranging from roads, bridges, and canals to paved or covered marketplaces and new town halls. And invariably all of this spending accelerated a spiral of more demand for skilled workers, an expanding array of consumer goods, ever more building, and ever more money.

The marketplace of a medieval town, literal and symbolic heart of the growing money economy. Cash was essential to the exchanges of producers and consumers of manufactured and agricultural goods at both the retail and wholesale levels.

Many of these products of thirteenth-century consumer demand remain with us today, most famously the massive castles commissioned by wealthy aristocrats and the majestic cathedrals constructed over the course of generations with church and town funding. The stunning cathedral at Chartres was dedicated about the time of Eckhart's birth; the colossal structures of Notre-Dame de Paris, Strasbourg, and Cologne remained sprawling, multilingual construction sites throughout his lifetime. Other specimens of rising consumerism at the elite level are also still visible in modern museums: magnificent linen and silk mantles trimmed in gold and fur, exquisite rings and necklaces, elaborate customized personal armor. Most of the objects for spending among the rich, though, have passed from memory. We know only through contemporary accounts of the frequent sumptuous banquets that required enormous outlays of cash, even more than knightly tournaments and countless other noble diversions.

By far the greatest expense of the landed aristocracy was the cost of maintaining and expanding a family's own territorial holdings. Soldiers needed to be paid, conquests required expensive military equipment, and other nobles required large gifts to ensure their loyalty, with cash increasingly preferred to real estate. Even allegedly high-minded enterprises such as crusades to the Holy Land could not function on faith alone. "We are in desperate need of money," the emperor Frederick II had lamented more than once in his efforts to organize the sixth crusade a few decades earlier. It was a refrain that future planners of crusades would repeat for centuries to come.

Land remained the most valuable commodity in the thirteenth century, but the newly pervasive influence of money affected some important political and economic changes, what historians used to call "bastard feudalism." Desperate to raise funds for their military ventures and luxurious lifestyles, monarchs and other aristocrats scrambled to monetize many of their seignorial rights. Many converted property holdings and privileges (such as control over certain forests or springs) through rent or sale to banks, corporations, other nobles, or virtually anyone who could pay. In some German lands, feudal dues paid almost exclusively in agricultural produce at the end of the twelfth century had within fifty years shifted to more than 90 percent cash rents. Sometimes entire lordships or high ecclesiastical offices were sold outright, or at least decorously transferred in the company of very large monetary "gifts." Kings and emperors in particular relied on large cash bribes to secure noble support at crucial times, and in turn were occasionally forced to levy taxes on certain sales and products. Towns and marketplaces likewise increasingly turned to public financing to pay for infrastructure costs.

From a twenty-first-century perspective, the new money culture of Eckhart's day was not without some positive developments. The simultaneous expansion of long-distance trade brought an ever greater variety of consumer goods to those same towns, mainly at the luxury end: pepper, cloves, and other rare spices from Asia; exquisite woolen cloth and elaborate tapestries from Flanders; fine linen from Champagne; silk from China; superior leather from Pisa; elegant furs from northern Russia; precious stones from India; pearls from the Persian Gulf. While such items remained out of reach for the great majority of the population, their very visibility helped fuel general consumer desire, spurring greater production of more affordable products such as shoes, tools, and a range of fabrics.

As is true today, money promised to provide more choices and opportunities overall, hence its tremendous allure. The urban marketplace, chief metaphor of twenty-first-century capitalism, embodied that assurance of freedom. Here many individuals, particularly immigrants from the country, converged, hoping to improve their quality of life, typically through unskilled labor. Some sons of newcomers might even enter into craft apprenticeships, providing other opportunities for advancement. Economic independence in German towns gradually translated into political independence from local lords. Finally, as in any society, greater affluence spurred patronage of the arts and, among the artisan and burgher class, stimulated still another sector of the economy, including teachers for both boys and girls (although nothing like modern mandatory schooling). In all these respects, the medieval town seems to deserve its designation by some historians as "the cradle of modernity" (meaning our current version of modernity).

Yet when people in Eckhart's day referred to "urban values," they rarely intended it as a compliment. The potential commodification of everything struck many contemporaries as unnatural and dangerous. Basic human relationships built on trust or kinship, they argued, should be more important than trying to fulfill all the desires and appetites that consumerism had unleashed. What looks to us like individualism—a cherished Western value—looked to Eckhart and many of his contemporaries like selfishness at the expense of communal *caritas* and divine *religio*. Proliferation of money also invariably led to proliferation of theft, robbery, prostitution, and organized crime—further apparent signs of social decay. With a labor force more plentiful than work, unemployment and begging surged, triggering further conflict and divisiveness.

Social change is always unsettling and confusing, even to those who benefit the most from it. In general, the economic status quo seems to have been generally preserved: most thirteenth-century aristocrats in fact prospered amid the new money economy, and rags-to-riches stories of immigrants from the countryside remained rare. Only occasionally might a cash-poor knight on the way down in social status pass an enterprising peasant on the way up. Yet such episodes sufficed to fuel universal uneasiness at the apparent rapidity and scope of cultural transformations under way, in turn giving rise to perceptions of a decline in basic morals and decency, largely tied to the rise of money. "All over the world," mocked the Spaniard Juan Ruiz, "money does marvelous things. . . . Its itch and scab infests the whole earth . . . mak[ing] a lord out of a servant and a servant out of a lord."

Born into this "world without love," a society widely perceived as in steep political and moral decline, the future Meister Eckhart might have grown up consumed in either cultural despair or nostalgia for a lost golden age. Instead, the noble youth from Thuringia would join those who sought to redeem their troubled world and themselves in the process. For inspiration, they looked to their own mythic past, seeking examples of men and women worthy of admiration and emulation. Disdain for personal enrichment was understood; strength, constancy, and courage were indispensable; but the most esteemed common feature of these thirteenth-century heroes was their selfless and unquestioned service to a cause greater than themselves. For Eckhart and other boys of his social status, the search for a higher purpose amid the superficial ephemera of the day continually returned to two heroic types: the brave warrior who sacrificed everything, sometimes including his life, for a sacred cause, and the equally pure and devoted saint, who had likewise renounced the seductions of the material world for a higher love. Both figures directly repudiated the loveless materialism of the day. For a young Eckhart, tales of selfless warriors and intrepid saints were more than nostalgic entertainment: they were lights in the darkness of an increasingly loveless world.

A Noble Childhood

The first written mention of the Thuringian hamlet of Tambach, dated December 13, 1251, appears in the recorded donation of sixty acres of land to the Cistercian monastery at nearby Georgenthal by the Duchess Heilwig von Berka, in the memory of her late husband Dietrich. One of the witnesses present was a knight, "Eckehard de Hochheim," resident in Tambach, serving as *voigt* (district governor, or castellan) of the nearby castle of Waldenfels. By this time, there were perhaps ten thousand "castles" of diverse description in German lands, many of them built during the construction boom of the previous half century. Most were unremarkable structures, far from the massive fortresses or elaborate palaces that word conjures today. No trace remains of the original Waldenfels. Its seventeenth-century successor was a modest structure about forty feet high, built on a bluff overlooking a creek, near a lake known as the Schmalwasser ("narrow water"), about ten miles south of Tambach. Most likely the thirteenth-century version was a rudimentary timber-and-mortar structure typical of such toll outposts, perhaps surrounded by a fence, palisade, or even a moat. By law it could not have been more than three stories high, and even if that substantive it would not have been large, ornate, or otherwise impressive by the standards of the few major structures that have survived from the period.

The knight Eckehard of Hochheim's employer was the patriarch of the Wettin dynasty, Heinrich III ("the Illustrious"), margrave of Meissen and of Lusatia and putative landgrave of Thuringia. Both lord and vassal were considered noble, but they found themselves situated at different ends of a steep hierarchy of nobility that, taken together, encompassed at most 2 percent of the general population. Landgraves such as Heinrich were the equivalent of dukes, a princely status higher than all but kings and emperors. Many of the twenty or so German aristocrats of this level traced their families' privileges back four or five centuries, to the time of Charlemagne—often with the help of fictionalized genealogies.

Eckehard von Hochheim, by contrast, was one of the numerous "new nobles" of the preceding half century known as ministerials, former household servants to kings and other aristocrats who had ascended through governmental work or by virtue of their accomplishments on the battlefield to become both free and noble (although their lords still maintained some prerogatives over them). Ministerials tended to be educated and many worked as stewards, judges, toll collectors, market overseers, treasurers, or heads of mints. Eckehard performed one or more of these duties for Landgrave Heinrich. Some of the new nobles took on still greater administrative roles in their lords' service, while simultaneously accumulating wealth of their own and entering into commercial ventures. Although still viewed warily in older aristocratic circles, ministerials such as the knight Eckehard von Hochheim and his family enjoyed the same privileges and standard of living as most noble households.

Around 1260, the knight's wife gave birth to a son, subsequently baptized with the name of his father. This likely indicates that the younger Eckhart was the oldest boy of the household, but it's possible that older siblings had not survived infancy and that the name—an ancient Teutonic appellation derived from *ekke* ("edge of a sword's blade") and *hart* ("brave; hardy")—remained available. Christian saints' names were not yet common among German nobility. The family's ancestral home in Hochheim, about twenty miles north of Tambach, provided the family name, in the tradition of many nobles of the period. Eckehard and his household, however, resided not in Hochheim or at Waldenfels, which served as an administrative outpost, but rather in Tambach or perhaps in nearby Gotha. Five years later, another document refers to Eckehard as the "previous castellan of Waldenfels," having been succeeded by Bertold von Siebeleben. Thirteen years later, by which time the younger Eckhart had already moved out, the knight was still living in the Tambach area, suggesting a continuing family presence there.

Like most of Germany, Thuringia was a predominantly wooded land, shaded by vast forests of towering beech, spruce, and pine trees. Even today, after centuries of clearance, the region is known as "the green heart of Germany," situated in the center of the post-1990 Federal Republic. At the time of Eckhart's birth, the territory constituted the northeastern frontier between traditionally Germanic and Slavic areas. The hamlet of Tambach, just inside the dense Thuringian Forest, lay only a dozen miles south of the Via Regia, the main east–west highway between Paris and Frankfurt am Main in the west and Cracow and Kiev in the east. Nearby Gotha, a town of some four thousand inhabitants and possibly a residence for Eckhart's family during his youth, saw a variety of merchants, pilgrims, and eastbound settlers pass daily through its gates. Thus while surrounded on all sides by mountain ranges and situated far from the great seats of power, young Eckhart's youthful home was neither socially nor culturally isolated.

At the same time, it's impossible to know how much Gotha and the Via Regia exposed young Eckhart to the wider world. We also know nothing of his mother or siblings, and he would only mention his father four times in the sermons that have survived. The adult Eckhart's tone in these references is consistently affectionate. In describing the powerful attraction of human relationships, he turns to his own experience as a son: *Why do I love my father more than another man? Because he is my father and my* omne . . . *that is my all, my very own.* This is an unusual and unexpected—but apparently genuine—display of familial love for a sermon of the era. Eckhart's point in describing his own filial devotion, however, is to underscore the still greater allegiance to his heavenly Father. [My] *bodily father,* in other words, whom Eckhart loved more than any other man, *is not my real father except for one tiny bit of his nature, and I am distinct from him: he can be dead while I am still alive.* Both Eckehard the father and Eckhart the son were truly offspring of the same divine Father, bound together by nature and affection but equally dependent on their common Creator.

Eckhart also left no record of his experiences as a noble youth in Tambach and Gotha, but the contours of such a life are familiar to us today. Embracing the aristocratic culture established in royal and princely courts, a lesser noble such as the knight Eckehard von Hochheim would likely have employed one or more tutors to school his son in the ways and expectations of his social estate. For Eckhart the son this invariably included training in horseback riding and hunting with hawks and hounds, sometimes at the expense of basic Latin grammar and other book learning. He might have also learned to play backgammon and chess. Some musical literacy was expected and ideally the youth would have developed skill with one or more instruments (although the adult Eckhart makes no mention whatsoever of any musical topic or term). Manners, or courtly etiquette, was another area of careful schooling, particularly among "new nobles" anxious about their precarious status. Aptitude in the social graces clearly served the adult Eckhart well in his work as an administrator and occasional diplomat.

And of course as a typical aristocratic youth, Eckhart became acquainted early on with the various courtly rituals of conspicuous consumption. From a child's perspective, he observed how much time and money noblemen and women spent acquiring colorful, precious fabrics, especially silk and fine wools, often ornamented with expensive gold or silver trimmings or buttons. Aristocratic identity itself hinged on such extravagant self fashioning, with the latest styles always in demand. In Eckhart's youth, noble fashion favored tight-fitting clothing that accentuated the wearer's body—a vivid contrast to the coarse and heavy wool robes he would later wear as a Dominican friar.

In addition to large expenditures for clothing, furnishings, and horses, his father's social status obliged him to spend significant amounts of money on the various social occasions that required copious amounts of food and drink: weddings, knighting ceremonies, tournaments, and of course a great number of religious holidays. When the knight Eckehard hosted such gatherings, sometimes lasting several days, he was expected to arrange and pay for diverse forms of entertainment, possibly including a poetry recital, piping or fiddling, singing, performances by acrobats or jesters, games, or athletic competitions, such as javelin throwing, stone hurling, sword fighting, wrestling, running, or jumping. Finally, like his own lords, a lower noble such as Eckehard regularly displayed his magnanimity in the bestowing of luxurious clothing, precious objects, or other gifts on friends and subordinates. Noble life, Eckhart the son quickly learned, was expensive, competitive, and relentless in its demands of money and time.

A noble banquet from medieval France. These costly gatherings on various occasions signified the host's status and prestige among his peers.

Even years into his life of voluntary poverty as a friar, Eckhart would continue to draw on the language of his aristocratic background in his sermons and writings. In that sense, his self-identification with noble culture never disappeared entirely. Like all of his contemporaries, though, there was no "political" aspect to this noble identity. "Europe" in the thirteenth century did not exist, or rather was known to its inhabitants as "Christendom"—a patchwork of several hundred dynastic territories ranging in size from several thousand square miles to a crumbling manor (designated a "castle" by its proud owner) and its neighboring village. National identity as such was a foreign concept to Eckhart and his contemporaries. Instead this political allegiance consisted mainly of a personal obligation to the local land-owner, typically a wealthy family such as Eckhart's own lords, the Wettins of Thuringia, who continually strove to expand their territorial possessions through marriage, purchase, and war.

"Germany" itself was more than six centuries away from becoming a nation-state; the designation in Eckhart's time served mainly as a loose linguistic one, encompassing the dozens of dialects that peppered the lands in the heart of the European continent. Throughout his life, the Thuringian Eckhart remained deeply cognizant of this linguistic identity, both as a frequent traveler to "lands of other tongues" and in his own preaching, where he translated Latin theological terms and also coined neologisms in his native dialect. Latin remained the language of scholarship, prayer, and often diplomacy, and Eckhart's mastery of it was unquestioned, but German would always provide the Thuringian with a more intimate and comforting personal bond, evident in both his friendships and his popular preaching.

There was admittedly a German monarchy, but its claimants fashioned themselves as Roman emperors above all else, not more accurately specifying "of the German nation" until two centuries after Eckhart's day. The resuscitated Western "Roman" Empire was a hard-fought creation of the Frankish king Charles, known to history as Charlemagne, and remained a contested entity from the time of its proclamation in the ninth century to its dissolution a thousand years later. In theory, the supreme authority of the Holy Roman Emperor, himself elected by seven of the most prominent princes and archbishops, served as a check on the political ambitions of the continent's constantly feuding noble families. He ruled in principle as supreme judge and highest feudal lord over a vast empire of more than 600,000 square miles and roughly twenty million inhabitants, ranging from northern Italy to the Baltic Sea and from France to Bohemia and Silesia in the east. In practice, even the strongest rulers—including Charlemagne himself—spent much of their reigns negotiating with competing nobles to maintain a semblance of peace. By the thirteenth century, the German kingdom had become "a thoroughly feudal monarchy," with an array of nearly twenty "princes" (dukes, landgraves, counts), some eighty high church leaders (archbishops, bishops, abbots), and thousands of other nobles, all proclaiming fealty to the king but still expecting frequent gifts to ensure that allegiance.

But even by the low standards of feudal monarchies, the empire at the time of Eckhart's birth was suffering a profound crisis of political authority. For more than a century, emperors of the Hohenstaufen dynasty had overseen alternating waves of prosperity and political instability. Before, during, and after Eckhart's lifetime, almost all threats to imperial authority and ambitions resulted from long-standing conflicts with the papacy, the other great political power of the day. The long reign of Emperor Frederick II (1220–50), while artistically and intellectually glorious, failed to reverse the slide into political chaos and in some ways accelerated it, especially after continued conflicts with Pope Gregory IX culminated in Frederick's formal excommunication and deposition in 1239. The premature death of Frederick's successor, Conrad IV, in 1254, launched nearly two decades of bloody conflict over the throne, an era later known as the Great Interregnum. By the time all the wearied combatants finally came to an agreement on the elderly Swabian count Rudolf of Habsburg in 1273, the empire itself was saved but at the cost of strong central authority for the remainder of its existence.

The collapse of an already dysfunctional imperial order had wide-ranging political and social repercussions throughout the various duchies, counties, and many smaller territories that made up the empire. In Eckhart's own Thuringia, twenty-five-year-old Albrecht II, also known as "the Degenerate," upon assuming the landgraviate in 1265 swiftly proceeded to drive his own wife into exile (where she died within a few months), foist his three sons on a relative, marry his mistress, and legitimate his two previous children by her. His older sons, aided by their uncle, promptly declared war on the young landgrave, and even succeeded in capturing and imprisoning their estranged father in his own castle—before he escaped and resumed hostilities. Only after another four decades of sporadic violence and destruction did Albrecht ultimately reconcile with his oldest legitimate son Friedrich (the latter's rival half brother having since died), and Thuringia welcomed a new lord, who was himself already involved in another conflict with neighboring Brandenburg.

Of course by modern standards most medieval "wars" are more accurately called feuds. The numbers of combatants in skirmishes and battles were typically reckoned in the dozens and hundreds, respectively, and the numbers of combat fatalities were accordingly low. Prolonged sieges of castles and other strongholds were more common than open-field engagements, lightning raids more frequent than full-scale invasion. Targeted assassinations and lynchings were also familiar tactics. Yet the relatively small scale of the warfare flowing from the absence of a strong central authority did not diminish the profound psychological effect of such instability on the society as a whole. Feuding nobles and their roaming entourages had the same terrorizing effect on local populations as modern "warlords" and their heavily armed bands in today's developing countries.

Marauding troops, in fact, often directly targeted farmers and townspeople to exert pressure on their lord, to generate "protection money" and food, or more simply to satisfy a primal bloodlust. Arson and pilfering of livestock, devastating to small property holders and tenants, were standard military tactics.

The Quest for Honor

Among nobles themselves, the openly cynical nature of all this incessant feuding fed a particular type of identity crisis. Buffeted by the sordid and often petty reality of violence in their day-to-day lives, Eckehard von Hochheim and other thirteenth-century nobles embraced the literature and culture of chivalry with a fervor that yielded a golden age for the genre. The broad appeal of courtly epics, especially among aristocrats themselves, is not difficult to grasp. The exploits of selfless military heroes from the past offered at the very least a welcome escape from the materialism and violence of Eckhart's day, a glimpse of an earlier age when "higher values" mattered. Then, unlike "our current sad times," the epics proclaimed, love, loyalty, and self-sacrifice reigned supreme.

Not surprisingly, the nature of "true nobility" was the topic of endless discussion in the German literature of Eckhart's youth. As a child, he listened intently at banquets and other gatherings as bards dramatically recited heroic epics, sometimes to music. Most of the material troubadours performed was recent, composed by one of more than 130 distinctive German poets in the time of Eckhart alone. Drawing on a tradition dating back more than a century earlier in southern France, German court singers and poets performed not in the Latin of clerics and scholars but in the vernacular of ordinary people and boasted diverse repertoires, ranging from lofty celebrations of pure love to earthy and humorous satires. The one thing uniting the various genres and styles was their common reverence for "true nobility," however elusive the quality proved in real life.

The thirteenth-century flood of noble epics was characterized by three overlapping varieties of the genre, each more highly idealized than the other. The tales most popular with Eckhart and other noble boys were the stories of pagan, Germanic heroes: most famously the *Nibelungenlied* (inspiration for Richard Wagner's nineteenth-century operatic cycle) and the Dietrich Cycle. Like modern accounts of superheroes, these stories inspired various versions and spin-offs that frequently varied in specific plotlines but relied on the same character mythology and themes.

Young Eckhart was evidently also a fan of a second, closely related genre: chivalric romances centered on the court of the legendary King Arthur of ancient Britain. The basic plotline was a foreign import, dating back more than a century to the first narrative account of Arthur's life by Geoffrey of Monmouth and the even more famous romantic dramatizations of Chrétien de Troyes. Like their counterparts throughout Christendom, German noblemen and youths were captivated by the legend of a good and successful ruler surrounded by brave and honest knights united in their pursuit of a just and peaceful society.

The legendary Round Table of King Arthur, with the Holy Grail as a centerpiece. The thirteenth century witnessed numerous variations and offshoots of this chivalric tale of noble comradeship and devotion to a higher purpose.

Based on his subsequent sermons, the chivalric romance that most clearly resonated with Eckhart himself was the most celebrated Arthurian work of the period, perhaps in all medieval German literature: Wolfram von Eschenbach's *Parzival*, a greatly expanded version of Chrétien de Troyes'

Perceval, the Story of the Grail. Parzival was both a coming-of-age tale and a thoughtful exploration of the meaning of "true nobility." Its initially secluded and naïve young protagonist learns the ways of Arthur's court and of battle before embarking on a quest to recover the Grail—in this instance not the holy chalice of Christ but a magical precious stone. Like his pagan counterparts, the Christian Parzival struggles with pride and self-mastery and is not always the victor in his various exploits. Most significantly, he suffers from a profoundly spiritual alienation that is only resolved by his submission to the divine will. The nobility he achieves, in other words, is measured not only in terms of courtly manners and fighting prowess, but in self-sacrifice toward an explicitly religious goal.

Parzival's gradual transformation into a humbler and more compassionate protagonist also involved the love of a strong and beautiful woman—a feature many chivalric romances shared with a third, more sprawling genre of noble literature: courtly love poetry. Whatever the literary form, all focused on a quest for love, a trait shared by some Arthurian romances, such as *Parzival*, but less so with pagan epics. Often this love involves a man's admiration for a woman of high nobility, for both her physical beauty and purity of character, although sometimes the object of desire is lowly born.

Thirteenth-century German celebrations of *minne* (originally "a friendly thought," but by Eckhart's time meaning "love") were also initially imitations of much older French and Provençal traditions. "To love wisely" long remained the ostensible theme of German *Minnesänger*, but by Eckhart's day, poets relied increasingly on allegorical language to blur the boundary between "high," or spiritual, love and "low," or carnal, love. Here too, the overlap with the adult Eckhart's description of his own spiritual journey is significant. As in Wolfram's *Parzival*, chivalric quests of love began with physical desires but during a period of suffering and tribulation evolved to become quests for spiritual redemption. Courtly and hunting terms mixed freely with explicit references to souls, heaven, and salvation. Many "dawn songs," a favorite motif, took the form of prayers to the divine sunlight about to "break through" to the petitioner below—another common Eckhartian image.

Wooing scene from a tale of courtly love. By the time of Eckhart's youth,
the theme of a male pursuer suffering in the name of lady love had
taken on ever greater religious symbolism.

As in any society, noble epics and love poems resonated differently with individual listeners and readers. The combined impact of all three overlapping genres on the imagination and behavior of German nobles of the thirteenth century was nevertheless palpable. Eckhart's contemporary, poet Hugo von Trimberg, complained that most people knew more about epic heroes and their adventures than about the saints and their miracles. Visual representations of Arthurian figures, in paintings and tapestries, easily competed in number with their religious counterparts. Tournaments, those staples of the noble life, increasingly took on Arthurian themes, with re-creations of the famed Round Table or even special grail competitions (i.e., jousts). Professional combatants roamed the tournament circuit of Christendom in the guise of King Arthur or "the new Parzival." Children, especially among nobles, were increasingly named after their parents' literary heroes, including one Thuringian noble from Eckhart's time known as "Conrad, called Parzival."

Not everyone considered the examples of legendary warriors especially salutary for the woes of the day. Hugo of Trimberg expressed the minority opinion that the epics actually exacerbated the worst tendencies of already ambitious nobles: "The way I see it, the teachings of these German books have already cost many a man his life and soul, his possessions and reputation . . . for many a man thinks he would be nothing if he did not become like [Tristan and Parzival]." Most people, however, apparently agreed with the poet Thomasin von Zirclaere that "even if the invented stories are not true, they do show symbolically what every person who aspires to an exemplary life should do." In some ways this courtly model of nobility matched the Christian ideal for all individuals, emphasizing such virtues as humility, generosity, and fidelity. Traditional knightly attributes such as great physical strength and skill in combat, by contrast, obviously remained practically important but carried no religious value.

The most dramatic real-world embodiment of the Christian knight ideal throughout Eckhart's lifetime remained the crusader. Nearly two hundred years had passed since Pope Urban II's initial call to rescue the Holy Land from the infidel, yet the ideal had retained a surprising amount of its vigor among the nobility of Christendom. As a boy, Eckhart heard of the heady launch of the eighth crusade, led by Louis IX of France, perhaps witnessed his own father make some financial contribution, and shared in the widespread dismay when the sainted monarch's death led to the campaign's abortion in 1270. Although fund-raising campaigns continued for years to come, especially in the wake of the 1291 fall of Acre, the last crusader state in Palestine, there would be no more sustained efforts during Eckhart's lifetime, no further opportunities for a young nobleman to fight and die for the faith in the Holy Land.

Yet even in the absence of crusades, Christendom remained filled with crusaders. Thousands of young noblemen, sometimes inspired by heroic epics, regularly joined one of the military religious orders established during the previous century. The most remarkable repurposing of crusader energy took place within the Order of Brothers of the German House of Saint Mary in Jerusalem, more commonly known as the Teutonic Knights. The German Lords, as they were also called, had been founded in Acre to provide hospital services to fellow Germans serving in the third crusade (1189–90). Early in the next century, they were summoned by King Andrew II of Hungary to help fight against the invading Kipchaks. When that alliance quickly soured and Andrew expelled the order, the Teutonic Knights dedicated themselves to a new campaign of nearly five decades to defeat and Christianize the pagan Old Prussians east of the Vistula River. By the war's end, the knights had become a formidable economic and political power, establishing their own state in Prussia before proceeding to do the same in Livonia. Soon they were battling Christian Slavs as well as pagans, earning the wrath of a series of Polish kings.

A Higher Love

The Teutonic Knights' Prussian campaign was still under way throughout Eckhart's youth. The order had established an especially strong presence in Thuringia early on, including castles at Nägelstädt and Mühlhausen in the west and a house in nearby Gotha. Eckehard von Hochheim's social status and political connections frequently brought him into contact with local leaders of the order, who may have regaled young Eckhart with tales of their military exploits.

Yet teenaged Eckhart von Hochheim did not join the Teutonic Knights or any other military order. Like all Christians of the day, he was aware of the crusading ideal's continuing appeal among many of his noble contemporaries. But there are no military terms, concepts, or metaphors in any of his surviving writings. Whether the child Eckhart's enjoyment of the chivalric adventures of Parzival and other knights of the Round Table ever inspired him to consider the life of a crusader is unknown. Even if he was once tempted to join the Teutonic Knights or another military order, it's difficult to imagine the adult Eckhart considering the exploits of literary warriors as more than diversionary entertainment at best.

This did not mean that he remained untouched by the thirteenth-century obsession with the topic of "true nobility." The language and images of courtly literature clearly influenced Eckhart's perception of his own spiritual quest. Like the Minnesingers he knew as a youth, Eckhart the preacher would often rely on allegorical language in describing the soul as a lover or bride. Reason and the Intellect, too, frequently appear as highly idealized— usually feminine—figures from courtly love poetry, with Eckhart employing the same language of unfulfilled desire, in this instance for God Himself. *Knowledge,* he preaches on one occasion, *is a princess, seeking her dominion in the highest and purest realms, and she conveys it to the soul and the soul to nature and nature to all the bodily senses. The soul,* he continues, *is so noble at her highest and purest that the masters cannot find any name for her.*

Most strikingly, the adult Dominican friar, long absent from the courtly life and its pleasures, instinctively used "noble" in the same heightened manner as courtly love poetry. For Eckhart, the term no longer meant just "superior" in the conventional social sense, but also in a moral and spiritual sense. As in a contemporary work such as the *Romance of the Rose,* his later sermons imagine a universal continuum for such virtues as love and mercy, with humans becoming progressively nobler the closer they came to the ultimate, divine *Minne,* or love. Of course the seeker must proceed slowly and with great care. Individual human beings are carnal and thus further from God than angels, but *Humanity in itself is so noble that the highest peak of humanity is equal to the angels and akin to God.* In other words, all humans are naturally endowed with what Eckhart would later call a *divine spark,* and have at least the potential of attaining true spiritual nobility. Their thoughts and actions as flesh-and-blood beings are deemed more or less noble, depending on whether they bring an individual closer to the love object, God.

Eckhart's version of the noble quest was in that sense radically egalitarian, with success based on individual perseverance, not the manners or innate superiority of high social status. It is unlikely to have endeared him to many of his aristocratic peers, but it was a logical extension of the most spiritualized aspects of courtly love poetry itself. What mattered most, for both the Minnesingers and Eckhart, was not the lover's birth status but his desire and the willingness to undergo hardship in attaining the ultimate goal. The path of the true spiritual quest, as Parzival and other literary seekers learned, was solitary and difficult. Like the knight of romances, the Christian in pursuit of his or her love object *must leave the crowd* and learn self-denial in order to become receptive to true love and mercy. *I extol detachment above any love,* preached Eckhart, *because at best, love constrains me to love God, but detachment compels God to love me.* Such complete surrender to the divine will, in Eckhart's view, was a *far nobler* sacrifice than the simple suffering extolled by the poets of courtly love.

This version of the chivalric quest, he preached, was the true meaning of the gospel passage, "There was a nobleman who went out of his own accord into foreign parts and returned home richer" (Luke 19:12). In one of his most telling tracts, entitled simply "The Nobleman," Eckhart recounts at length the prolonged struggle between the "inner man" (noble and spiritual) and the "outer man" (carnal, transient, sinful). Full of scriptural references, "The Nobleman" provides one of the most concise and colorful descriptions of the mature teacher's key insights. It makes no explicit references to the literature of courtly love, yet the affinity is unmistakable. *How could a man know that he knows God if he does not know himself?* The greatest conquest of any life, as all Arthurian heroes learned, is defeat of the foe within. Only then, writes Eckhart, can the Christian seeker obtain the object of desire. That object—symbolized by the riches bestowed upon the journeying nobleman—is nothing less than union with God.

At some point in his youth, certainly before the age of sixteen, Eckhart von Hochheim decided on his own life's quest. Later in life, in his mid-fifties, he compared his chosen path with the other two likeliest career choices of an ambitious youth of his social status: merchant or knight. Both of these professions involved great self-sacrifice and hardship, in the case of the merchant, *frequently go[ing] on long journeys and perilous ways through mountains and valleys, wildernesses and seas, braving robbers and killers of his life and property, enduring great privations of food and drink, sleep, and other discomforts.* Meanwhile, *a knight in battle risks property, body, and soul.* Yet in the end, all of this suffering achieved only the possibility of *a small profit* for the merchant and *fleeting and brief honor* for the knight. The son of knight Eckehard von Hochheim, onetime castellan to the Wettins of Thuringia, aimed much higher, and was more than willing *to endure a little suffering for the sake of God and eternal blessedness.*

CHAPTER TWO

Heroic Christianity

*Nothing is so cheap as heaven, when it is for sale and nothing
is so glorious and precious a possession, when it has been earned.
It is called cheap, because it is on sale to everybody for as
much as he can afford. Therefore a man should give all he
has for heaven—his own will. As long as he keeps any part
of his own will he has not paid for heaven.*

GERMAN SERMON 58

The Path to Heaven

The boy Eckhart likely dreamed of enduring more than *a little suffering* in his
quest for salvation. Reaching heaven, as everyone knew, was a painful
ordeal—much more so for a youth who set his sights on spiritual greatness.
The bloody stories of the ancient martyrs were almost as common as tales of
chivalry in his world. Saints books, sermons, and various paintings and statues all vividly conveyed the agony of Saint Apollonia as her persecutors tore
out her teeth one by one, or the intense suffering of Saints Bartholomew and
Laurence as they were flayed alive. All educated children knew that Saint
Agatha was tortured extensively on the rack and taunted with fire before her
breasts were cut off, or that when Saint Sebastian survived an attempted
execution by arrows, the outraged emperor Diocletian had him clubbed to
death. Accounts of more recent saints were less gruesome but still involved

impressive feats of fasting, flagellation, and tremendous endurance of physical and spiritual trials.

By the time of Eckhart's youth, stories about the apostles and other saints had become a virtual industry, long before the printing press would make these tales even more readily accessible to the reading public. Hunger for edifying (and entertaining) accounts of their exploits appears to have been formidable, spurring a number of popular collections during the thirteenth century. The most famous compilation of saints' lives of the entire Middle Ages actually began to appear in manuscript copies about the time of Eckhart's birth, in 1260. The Genoan Dominican Giacomo da Varazze (better known as Jacobus da Voragine, ca. 1229–98) intended his encyclopedic *Legends of the Saints*, later renamed *The Golden Legend*, as a source book for his fellow Dominicans and other sermon writers. Its colorful stories of more than three hundred saints and their miracles, however, rapidly attracted a number of clerical and lay admirers. At times Voragine's collection more resembles the later *Grimms' Fairy Tales* than a sober supplement to the Bible. Later Renaissance humanists would mock the work's clunky style and naïve credulity, but sermon writers in Eckhart's day found the collection an endless source of reliable anecdotal material.

The common message of the saints' stories to the youthful Eckhart was clear: getting closer to God was a hard-won triumph of spirit over body, a steady resistance of all the physical comforts and temptations this life offered. All quests for holiness were thus essentially internal in nature. Yet the spirit, like the church itself, remained embedded in the material world. And it is these external forms of religion in Eckhart's day that come most readily to the twenty-first-century mind: elaborate rituals, intricate clerical vestments, saints' relics, shrines, and of course the massive Gothic cathedrals that still attract countless photo-snapping tourists. Even more superficially, we imagine popes and bishops ruling the millions of faithful like absolute monarchs, imposing uniform religious standards—which they themselves regularly violated—and ruthlessly punishing dissidents through inquisitorial courts and public burnings. To modern eyes, medieval religious practices—attending mass, receiving the sacraments, collecting holy objects, praying, going on pilgrimage—appear like business transactions, spiritual payments aimed at countering the deficit created by individual sins. We assume that for medieval Christians, the only thing that mattered was the afterlife, and even there the clergy had constructed an intermediate waiting place between heaven and hell known as purgatory, where tainted souls relied on the intercessions of their living friends and relatives—aided by priests—for reduction of their lengthy sentences. In the modern imagination, medieval religion was, in short, an externally practiced, clerically dominated mechanism for getting to heaven. Genuine concern for the internal spiritual life seems virtually nonexistent, an anomaly practiced by a pious few.

Of course this parody distorts a much more complex range of beliefs and experiences, and it is further warped by the hostile filters of the sixteenth-century Protestant Reformation and the still later Enlightenment. Until recently, historians have also been hampered by an overreliance on clerical documents for understanding this largely illiterate society, accordingly exaggerating the role of the hierarchical Church and its leaders in the everyday lives of most people and minimizing the extent of true spiritual yearning across all levels of society. We now know that religion during this period was remarkably diverse in beliefs and practice, varying by region, social status, age, gender, education, individual preferences, and a number of other factors. Not everyone in the "Age of Faith" was pious (by any definition), and among those who were, there could be a stunning divergence in the very interpretation of what piety meant.

All myths have some basis in fact, of course, and in this instance it is the average Christian's reliance on external help—especially priestly and saintly intercession—in ultimately going to heaven rather than hell. This was a lesson imparted to Eckhart at an early age. Since the fall of Adam and Eve, he learned, human nature had been inherently inclined toward selfish and otherwise sinful behavior. Only Christ's incarnation and sacrificial death made some kind of reconciliation with God the Father possible, but even then humans—fatally addicted to sin—required constant counseling and other assistance from the divinely ordained vehicle of God's grace, the universal Church.

While "the Church" in fact comprised the community of all baptized

Christians, only a small proportion of the whole, roughly one-tenth, devoted themselves exclusively to this mission of individual and collective redemption. Known as clerics, or canons, these Church leaders made special vows (typically poverty, chastity, and obedience) that separated them from the remainder of their fellow Christians, the laity. Like his parents and all other laypeople, young Eckhart relied on the mediation of members of the clergy with God, through sacraments and other means. Not until the Protestant Reformation two and a half centuries later would some European Christians talk about "a priesthood of all believers," requiring no intermediaries between the individual believer and the sovereign of the universe.

Christians in Eckhart's day were surrounded with frequent reminders of Christ's agonizing death on the cross as atonement for the original sin of Adam and Eve. Only baptism and other interventions of the institutional church made personal salvation possible, and even then great personal suffering was considered integral to reconciliation with God.

The clergy were in turn separated into two general groups. The first, known as pastoral, or "secular" clergy (because they worked in the world), was charged with administration of the institutional church and spiritual care of the laity. Secular clergy were all men, usually ordained, and included leaders such as the pope, cardinals, and bishops, as well as canons and priests assigned to cathedrals and parishes. Clerics of this kind in theory all reported up the chain to superiors, starting at the parish level with pastors, who were accountable to archdeacons, then bishops, then archbishops, and finally the pope and his court (*curia*).

Popes were powerful political figures as well as church leaders, ruling as princes over a large part of central Italy known as the Papal States. But despite the notable growth of the bureaucracy of the pope's curia during the time of Eckhart, we must not exaggerate the extent of papal authority or centralized control, especially on questions of religious belief or practice. Nor was there any notion of papal infallibility during this time; popes regularly reversed the proclamations of their predecessors on doctrinal matters. The greatest institutional power, rather, remained at the local level, in the hands of the bishops who oversaw large districts known as dioceses, or sees, and both ordained and disciplined all priests within their jurisdiction. Selection and appointment of bishops was thus the most common source of conflict between popes and secular rulers throughout the Middle Ages.

The second type of clergy, known as "cloistered," or "regular," were men and women who lived in closed communities under specific vows and followed a detailed constitution and daily plan, or Rule (Latin *regula*, whence "regular"), usually either the Rule of St. Benedict (ca. 480–543) or that of St. Augustine (354–430). Before the twelfth century, most of these monasteries and convents operated as independent entities, with all authority invested in the head of each house, the abbot or abbess. Between 1100 and 1215, there was an explosion of new regular orders, each comprising several houses collectively governed by a superior general.

Regular clergy also prayed daily for their fellow Christians, offering their own sacrifices and hardships in hope of divine forgiveness and favor. Life within the walls of a monastery or a convent was devoted exclusively to the contemplation and worship of God. Male communities, governed by abbots, defined "work" in a variety of ways (manual, artisanal, academic, liturgical), but all agreed with St. Benedict's ideal of a daily routine balanced between prayer and work, *ora et labora*. Female communities, led by abbesses, tended to interpret work in terms typical for women (washing, cooking, weaving, spinning, embroidery) but also provided opportunities for study between periods of private and collective prayer. Preaching by nuns was nonexistent, except for the instruction of novices, and even monks focused such efforts within the confines of the monastery. Ministry to laypeople, except among the Cistercians, remained a minor part of the monastic vocation.

Together, secular and regular clergy routinely interceded with God on behalf of their lay brothers and sisters. Ordained priests enjoyed special powers, confirmed by the 1215 church council Lateran IV, most notably the ability to forgive sins (in the sacrament of confession) and the ability to transform bread and wine into the body and blood of the Savior (in the sacrament of the Eucharist). They also typically administered the sacrament of baptism to infants (although this could be validly performed by any Christian), blessed various undertakings and special occasions, gave dying Christians a final infusion of grace with last rites, and prayed for the souls of the departed in purgatory. All of these acts, young Eckhart learned, were intended to help compensate for his sins and move him closer to ultimate redemption. None of this activity obviated the need for good deeds and prayer on his own part, but clerical intervention remained indispensable to all salvation efforts.

Like most laypeople, Eckhart's parents and their friends accepted their spiritually inferior status as the price of living in the world amid all its temptations and cruelties. However minimal their understanding of doctrinal matters, virtually everyone knew and accepted their own sinful nature and need for salvation. But the contemplative life remained a rare full-time pursuit for laypeople. Unlike monks and nuns, the great majority of the population had to earn a living, raise a family, struggle with neighbors, and look to their own material interests. Accepting the assistance of religious professionals in exchange for small donations struck most people as a sound proposition. After all, who would be more likely to sway the heavenly judge's ultimate decision, an average sinner whose commitment to the Creator had been less than unwavering or someone who had devoted his or her life to divine service (and was possibly invested with supernatural powers)?

This does not mean that the lay approach to salvation Eckhart learned was entirely passive. There were many options for pious believers to supplement whatever grace they received from the sacraments and other clerical

interventions on their behalf. Alms to the poor, or to any philanthropic endeavor, would surely count in any sinner's favor at the Final Judgment, as
would generous public acts of any kind. Many wealthy individuals accordingly made provisions in their wills for ecclesiastical foundations, such as
hospitals, orphanages, schools, and charities for the local poor. During Eckhart's lifetime, postmortem endowments of annual masses offered on behalf
of departed souls (presumably in purgatory) became increasingly common,
generating opportunities for posthumous intercession while at the same
time providing much-needed supplemental income to local pastors and their
small churches. Over the subsequent two centuries, such commemorations
grew numerous enough to employ several cathedral priests full time to say
daily obit masses in side chapels, or chantries.

All Christians, regardless of income, could also earn spiritual merit from
fasting or other deprivations, as well as more extreme forms of self-
mortification. Punishing one's own body not only supposedly kept carnal
temptations at bay but also represented a self-sacrifice that would be viewed
favorably by the divine judge. The most dramatic example of a meritorious
hardship was the undertaking of a pilgrimage to a regional or distant shrine.
Shrines themselves could range from a simple roadside cross, perhaps with
the statue of a saint, to an ornate cathedral. The site was typically considered
hallowed based on the presence of one or more relics from a saint—a skull,
bones, hair, nail clippings, even in one instance a piece of intestine (also
clothing, shoes, hats, and combs). Even Jesus and the Virgin Mary, though
believed to have ascended bodily into heaven, allegedly left behind many
relics, ranging from vials of Christ's blood and the Virgin's milk to the um-
bilical cord and circumcised foreskin of the baby Jesus. Sometimes a pilgrimage was performed as penance for a great sin; other times it was considered
an act of special piety, perhaps with a specific goal in mind. A pilgrim who
undertook an arduous journey to the famous Spanish shrine of Santiago de
Compostela, for instance, might be rewarded with a healing miracle, the
divine granting of another request, or at the very least much spiritual merit
to be applied at the time of Final Judgment (not to mention several blessed
souvenirs).

The most obvious and ubiquitous self-help for any Christian anxious about his soul was simple prayer, and not necessarily in any sanctified space. Prayer was the principal "public service" offered by monks and nuns, but it was also something anyone in Eckhart's world could do, in a variety of ways for a variety of purposes. Some prayer, particularly liturgical, was aimed at worship, but most prayer, particularly by individuals, appears to have been votive, or specific in intention. A merchant setting out on a journey might pray for safe passage, a farmer for the end of a drought, an adolescent girl for a suitable husband, a mother for the health of her sick child. Prayers on behalf of souls in purgatory were believed capable of reducing the sentence of the sinner in question, not unlike appealing directly to a judge in an earthly criminal case. Other prayers sought less elevated objectives, such as finding a lost object. Few prayers—at least according to the adult Meister Eckhart—were completely selfless, and therein lay the fundamental problem in his eyes.

Even when the prayer was not delivered via a clerical intermediary, young Eckhart is unlikely to have ventured a direct appeal to God the Father, or even to Christ. Just as no commoner would ever dare to petition the emperor himself, the average Christian turned instead to a well-placed intercessor in the heavenly court. Most commonly this was the Virgin Mary, recently proclaimed the "Queen of Heaven." The more emotive religiosity of the thirteenth century elevated Mary, "the Mother of God," as the subject of intense veneration. Countless statues and other images of Jesus's mother emphasized her maternal kindness and generosity, a stark contrast to forbidding portrayals of a stern Creator or Final Judge. During the decades leading up to Eckhart's birth, several devotions had developed around Mary: she now enjoyed her own special prayers and hymns (the Ave Maria and Salve Regina, utilizing the newly developed rosary), her own feast days (Purification, Annunciation, Visitation, Assumption, Nativity, Immaculate Conception), her own churches (Notre-Dame de Paris, among many others), and numerous shrines dedicated to her glory (with numerous attested miracles).

The other frequent recipient of a votive prayer was one of the multitude of saints recognized in the church's liturgical calendar (more than 4,500 by the thirteenth century). The great majority of figures came from antiquity and were male, although the number of recent female saints was on the rise in Eckhart's day. A new papal canonization process in the thirteenth century recognized twenty-two new saints between 1200 and 1275, including the founders of the Dominican and Franciscan orders and the local Thuringian saint, Elizabeth of Hungary (1207–31). In searching for a heavenly patron among this multitude, petitioners were often guided by a saint's geographic origin, name, or traditional area of expertise, such as St. Christopher for travelers or Saints Peter and Andrew for fishermen. Many saints developed their own special followings, or cults (in the medieval sense of the word).

Four years after her death at the age of twenty-four, with great support from the Teutonic Knights, Elizabeth of Hungary was canonized. In addition to more than one hundred miracles, some described in *The Golden Legend*, the saint was credited with feeding the poor and bathing (as well as sleeping alongside) lepers. Her ascetic merits included meekly suffering frequent beatings at the hands of her confessor Conrad, pictured here.

Spirituality in a Materialistic Age

Whether or not young Eckhart prayed to any saints, he could not help but be influenced by their models of spiritual success. But following the path of the saints in the thirteenth century was no easy feat. There were no more deadly persecutions as in Roman antiquity and the dangerous missions to pagan Asia and the Americas remained centuries away. The surest and swiftest path to achieving *eternal blessedness*, if not sainthood, lay not in the piecemeal effort of the layman but in the complete devotion of the monk. Only here, his society told him, in his extended contemplation, might he encounter God directly, and only here, through his various ascetic sacrifices, was he likely to endure the suffering that would allow him to reach his goal.

Eckhart's choice of a religious vocation over military honor, commercial prosperity, or (like his father) government service represented an obvious repudiation of the glories of the world. In this respect he was embracing the Church's long-standing aversion to secular values. Jesus and his apostles had been poor and the Savior himself had often spoken critically of wealth, contrasting the material success of the world with the heavenly rewards of the spirit. Both the martyr and ascetic ideals of the ancient church represented dramatic rejections of earthly desires and possessions. The supreme monastic virtues of poverty, chastity, and obedience represented the best path to spiritual perfection because they recognized the emptiness and futility of their worldly counterparts of wealth, lust, and power. The original Christian ethos was not just neutral about the pursuit of profit and wealth; it was diametrically opposed to it.

At least that was the message preached from the pulpits. In reality, the church of Eckhart's day faced a conundrum with the new money economy. The problem had been simmering for nearly a thousand years, since the disparate, otherworldly, charismatic cult of Christianity was transformed into the official religion of the Roman Empire. During the intervening centuries, the church's new institutional status had frequently come into conflict with the gospels' clear "contempt of the world." Most obviously, as the result of countless donations from the faithful, the pope and his bishops now controlled extensive landholdings and other wealth, collectively more than any of their secular counterparts. Thousands of monasteries and convents, likewise devoted to spiritual poverty, had similarly accrued considerable property. And by the time of Eckhart, the recently reorganized administrative arm of the papacy, the *camera apostolica*, had begun collecting an extraordinary range of tithes and ecclesiastical fees that provided the pope and his curia with the resources not only to run the institutional church, but to maintain a magnificent residence and deploy large armies as needed.

The disjunction between the teachings of the gospels on wealth and the reality of the institutional church struck many of Eckhart's contemporaries as contradictory, even hypocritical and corrupt. Satires such as the *Gospel of the Mark of Silver* and the *Romance of Charity* openly mocked the moneymaking machinery of the papacy, long before the more formidable attacks of Protestant reformer Martin Luther three centuries later. The buying and selling of ecclesiastical offices and privileges, a practice known as simony, posed an even more direct challenge to church teachings on wealth. Though officially condemned, simony was in fact a routine matter for noble families seeking appointments to bishoprics or abbeys, just like the buying, selling, and trading of secular titles. Critics could not imagine a more obvious repudiation of Jesus's original injunction to his followers.

But remarkably no Christians in the thirteenth century questioned the legitimacy of the papacy itself, any more than complaints about tyrannical lords challenged the feudal order at its core. Individual popes could be considered corrupt (and indeed Dante placed most of the pontiffs from his own day in *The Divine Comedy*'s Hell), but that was a different matter from questioning the institution proper. Nor did most people consider money evil in itself. It was the *love* of money, an *individual* failing, that plagued all levels of society, thus requiring *individual* repentance and conversion.

Greed, or avarice, already had a long history as one of the Seven Deadly Sins familiar to all Christians. Some modern historians have argued that during the thirteenth century it became the most prominent deadly sin decried by preachers and other moralists, far outstripping sloth, gluttony, lust, anger, envy, and even pride. Many preachers stressed how the infectious nature of the desire for money—itself the very embodiment of desire—invariably led to other deadly sins, thus earning its oft-repeated characterization as "the root of all evil" (1 Timothy 6:10). Bodily appetites (lust, gluttony, sloth) required ever more money to be satisfied; the desire to accumulate material goods resulted in envy or pride; inability to obtain enough money generated angry conflicts. Often the language used to describe love of money is reminiscent of modern characterizations of addiction. The celebrated quotation from 1 Timothy refers to avarice as a "craving," and Pope Innocent III compared the insatiability of avarice to hell itself, in that "both consume but do not digest."

Avaricious moneylenders, both Christian and Jewish, were considered the epitome of the selfish and loveless behavior promoted by the new consumer culture.

The adult Eckhart shared many of his age's concerns about the pervasiveness of a consumer mentality, particularly among leaders of Christ's church. He too thought in terms of personal rather than institutional problems and solutions. But he also perceived a less obvious and more dangerous cultural transformation under way. Treating money like God was bad enough; treating God like money, he later preached, threatened to undermine the very essence of true religion. The commercial revolution had already experienced alarming success in recasting all human experience in its own image, so that not only manufactured goods, produce, and livestock but also land, water, and the rest of the natural environment were increasingly viewed primarily in terms of their market value. Like the commodification of nature or time (in charging interest), the commercial approach to the divine reduced every interaction with God to instrumentalist terms—what can I give God in order to get what I want?

The adult Eckhart would warn his listeners about succumbing to this mentality of commerce (*Koufmanschaft*), approaching all human and divine relationships in transactional terms. Basing supposedly pious actions on self-interest (*Eigenschaft*) was the opposite of the self-surrender proclaimed in the gospel. In preaching on Jesus's clearing the temple of merchants and money changers (Matthew 21:12), Eckhart would go beyond the obvious criticism of money and greed to get at what he considered to be the fundamentally unchristian assumption of all commerce, namely the desire for personal gain. This attitude afflicted everyone, even "good" people as they sought redemption:

> Who were they who bought and sold there, and who are they still? Take proper note: I will speak now in this sermon of none but the good people. . . . Those are all merchants who, while avoiding mortal sin and wishing to be virtuous, do good works to the glory of God, such as fasts, vigils, prayers, and the rest, all kinds of good works, but they do them in order that our Lord may give them something in return, or that God may do something they wish for—all these are merchants. . . . Anyone who desires something from God is a merchant.

Eckhart's radical interpretation of common antimercantile sentiments stemmed from a broad and profound disenchantment with the values of the new money culture, particularly evident among many nobles and urban residents most exposed to it. As in any commercial expansion, rising material expectations had provoked an antimaterialist counterreaction. Greater financial security and education, particularly in towns, typically spurred greater desire for personal advancement, but also, for many, a yearning for deeper and more lasting bonds with other people and for higher and lasting meaning in their lives. The paramount question was whether they could find such spiritual fulfillment within the strictures of an institutional Church immersed in the politics and business of the day.

The New Apostles

The teenage son of the knight Eckehard von Hochheim was far from the only Christian of his day seeking a pure, unmediated, authentic religious life. In fact, he lived during the second wave of a European-wide spiritual movement. For more than a century, thousands of laypeople of all social backgrounds, alienated by the materialism of their loveless age and dissatisfied with the religious options before them, had been seeking a more intimate awareness of God at work in their everyday lives—more internal, more emotional, more visceral than what they encountered in conventional religious practices. Some historians in fact refer to the period 1100–1300 in Europe as an "axial age in spirituality," comparable in significance to the doctrinal and structural upheavals of the Protestant Reformation era a few centuries later. For the first time since antiquity, significant numbers of laypeople—not just monks or nuns—valued individual subjective spiritual experience over outward piety and sought fulfillment by a variety of new or established means.

Surely, many pious laypeople (including Eckhart) thought there must be a way to combine elements of the active and the contemplative life, a third way between the isolation of the cloister and submersion in the cares of the world. Surely there must be a more direct way to draw closer to God. The result was a stunning array of new, grassroots religious movements, each pursuing its own vision of "apostolic perfection." As in the instance of military religious orders, the new apostolic groups drew their inspiration from stories of past heroes and their exploits. And just as Arthur and his knights suddenly seemed to be everywhere in the art and literature of the twelfth and thirteenth centuries, the apostles and early martyrs experienced a new and unprecedented prominence in the period's sermons, paintings, sculptures, and popular story collections. Like their chivalric counterparts, Peter and the other earliest followers of Jesus often experienced doubt and suffering, but ultimately overcame all obstacles, sometimes with the help of miraculous powers, all the while serving the cause of their Lord and Savior. Above all, they rejected the wealth and fame of the world, joyously embracing the miseries endured for their noble choices. And in the end they were recognized by their divine king with the reward of eternal redemption.

Of course venerating the *vita apostolica* and defining it were two different things. It was also far from a novel concept: both secular and regular clerics saw themselves as heirs to Jesus's earliest followers. Many members of the clergy were accordingly suspicious of the new apostolic movements populated by laymen and -women who had worldly occupations and often spouses and children. Many of these individuals came from propertied backgrounds, making their rejection of consumer values and embrace of "apos-

Monumental sculptures of the apostles, from the central portal of Notre Dame in
Paris. Each carries the attribute or symbol that would allow worshippers to
identify him based on various popular stories about their exploits
before and after the death of Jesus.

tolic poverty" even more dramatic. The people denigrated by some clerical
opponents as "rustics," "idiots," and "illiterates" in fact appear to have been
typically nobles, burghers, former merchants, and occasionally even educated clerics. Like the original apostles, the new apostles deliberately chose
to be in the world but not of the world, sacrificing some but not all of their
personal attachments. In this sense they appropriated what they considered
the best parts of clerical life—the simplicity and poverty of monasticism and
the worldly activity of secular clergy—while emphatically shunning special
vows of any kind. They claimed no special office or authority, calling themselves "simple Christians," "Good Men/Good Women," or sometimes "Friends
of God."

In everyday behavior, the new apostles were often difficult to distinguish
from other pious laypeople involved in traditional charitable and devotional
practices. What most set them apart was their attraction to the written Word
of God (another by-product of the commercial revolution). Relying on either
Latin Bibles or vernacular translations of individual books, mixed groups of
men and women met regularly to discuss the significance of scriptures for

their own paths to God. By the time of Eckhart, there were translations of all or most of the Bible available in many European languages, including his own, Middle High German. Initially priests or other educated individuals took the lead in scriptural readings, but increasingly average laypeople dominated discussions, even preaching publicly to large audiences on religious themes.

To modern eyes, all of these tendencies look, frankly, Protestant, and we might be quick to attribute subsequent clerical opposition on these anachronistic grounds. A few scholars have even called the phenomenon a "medieval Reformation." But the new apostolic movements of the twelfth and thirteenth centuries—with the distinct exception of the Cathars (also known as the Albigensians)—were not schismatic groups with alternate doctrinal agendas. They attended mass regularly, participated in the sacraments, and prayed to the saints for intercession. Popular preaching and Bible reading were not unprecedented, but rather longtime staples of mainstream Christianity, with the latter more limited during Eckhart's day by low literacy rates and the great expense of manuscript Bibles than by any official prohibitions. The new groups were admittedly more egalitarian, even individualist, in their approach to the divine but not necessarily anticlerical.

The chief concern of some bishops and other clerical opponents was organizational chaos and the *potential* for errant teachings, especially among lay preachers. Since we are limited to documents written by such adversaries, it's difficult to know how many people truly claimed to have achieved "evangelical perfection" or "the merits of the apostles" or openly challenged the authority of the formal successors to the apostles—the bishops. The great majority of apostolic movements—again, excepting the Cathars—claimed to follow the precepts of the gospels and apostles, and appear to have been fairly orthodox on doctrinal matters.

Even those clerics more wary of the new apostles conceded that their hunger for spiritual knowledge and experience appeared both genuine and insatiable. One thirteenth-century critic marveled that "men and women, great and small, day and night, do not cease to learn and teach; the workman who labors all day teaches or learns at night. . . . Whoever excuses himself, saying that he is not able to learn, they say to him, 'Learn but one word each

day and after a year you will know three hundred, and you will progress.'"
By most accounts they also appeared saintly, one otherwise unsympathetic
friar conceding, "We know that they suppose this behavior to be virtuous
and do many things that are in the nature of good works; in frequent prayer,
in vigils, in sparsity of food and clothing and—let me acknowledge the
truth—in austerity of abstinence they surpass all other religions."

Of course highly visible, even extravagant, acts of piety could cut two
ways. Clerical observers less sympathetic to such lay movements deemed the
holier-than-thou demeanor an implicit criticism of their own behavior as
well as a trick to attract unsuspecting new members. "Wolves in sheep's
clothing," spewed one especially vituperative opponent, "seducing others by
their false piety." Bernard Gui, the most famous inquisitor of the Middle
Ages, likewise accused the most prominent groups of fraudulent self-
righteousness: "[They] commonly say that they occupy the place of the
Apostles, since they alone imitate their poor, itinerant, and preaching lifestyle." Tellingly, Gui chose not to dispute the new groups' reputations for
pious acts, just their claims to uniqueness and special authority.

And herein lay the greatest distinctiveness of the new apostolic movements and thus their greatest danger in the minds of some church authorities: the desire for a less mediated experience of religious life. Yet even then,
formal marginalization was not inevitable. Only when the Lyons merchant
Valdes (aka Peter Waldo) and his followers, known as Waldensians, defied a
papal prohibition of lay preaching was the group formally excommunicated
in 1184. "One must obey God more than people," Valdes responded, quoting
Acts 5:29 and standing by his conviction that all Christians should be able to
preach freely. From that point on, the so-called Poor Men of Lyons continued their apostolic mission as an underground movement, wandering the
towns of southern Europe, meeting with secret congregations, and occasionally performing penitential rites.

For the first few generations of the new movements, widespread confusion about their orthodoxy allowed most (again, not the Cathars) to operate
in a gray area of popular toleration, or at least indifference. Local priests and
other clerical opponents, frustrated by their own impotence in preventing
the groups' spread, appealed to their superiors for clearer guidance and

decisive actions. At the dawn of the thirteenth century, sixty years before Eckhart's birth, their pleas were finally heard. The diverse apostolic movements still sprouting up across the continent finally collided with the greatest administrator the papacy has ever known, Lotario dei Conti di Segni, who at his ascension to the throne of St. Peter took the name Innocent III (r. 1198–1216).

Innocent III was one of the most powerful and influential leaders in the history of the papacy. His signature church council, Lateran IV, attempted to reestablish firm boundaries between the respective roles and abilities of clerics and laypeople.

Reclaiming the Apostolic Ideal

Trained as a theologian and a jurist, the ambitious thirty-eight-year-old Innocent spent nearly two decades attempting to transform Christendom itself. Most medieval historians consider him the most influential pope since Gregory the Great (ca. 540–604). When not enmeshed in imperial politics or coalition building for the fourth crusade (1202–4), Innocent devoted considerable attention to the question of religious orthodoxy. On the question of the new apostolic movements, the pontiff quickly concluded that a coordinated response was essential. Innocent viewed the new apostolic movements as symptomatic of a more general failure in clerical leadership. Groups like the

Waldensians and the Cathars, he believed, took root among the laity only because of neglect by both the regular and secular clergy, denounced by the pope
as "dumb dogs who do not bark." His subsequent doctrinal reforms accordingly focused primarily on an enhancement of the powers and roles of priests.

In 1215 Innocent summoned more than 1,200 bishops, abbots, and nobles
from around Europe to participate in the assembly thereafter known as
Lateran IV, the most important ecumenical council of the entire Middle
Ages. Under the pope's guidance, the council painstakingly delineated the
respective religious demands on the clergy, establishing rigorous behavioral
standards but also reinforcing their religious authority. The notion of a celibate, politically independent, nonhereditary priesthood was still far from
universally accepted in the parishes of Christendom. Lateran IV reiterated
the clerical ideal sought by the last four generations of religious reformers,
empowering bishops to discipline and dismiss priests who retained common-
law wives or charged fees for the administering of sacraments. At the same
time, Innocent's council elevated the spiritual status of ordained clergy, recognizing their exclusive power to summon Christ to earth in the sacrament
of the Eucharist (transubstantiation) and their ability to forgive sins as His
vicar. Just as crucially, only ordained priests had the authority (and sacred
duty) to preach the gospel and explicate the Church's interpretations of
God's Word.

Above all, Innocent and his successors sought to reestablish a firm
boundary between the religious activities of clergy and laity. Lay piety was
vigorously encouraged, but along the conventional lines of good deeds and
relying on clerical intercession. Spontaneous, loosely organized, lay communities of like-minded Christians did not fit neatly into his conceptualization of these two categories and had a genuinely befuddling effect on church
leaders in general. Often ecclesiastical officials exaggerated not just the perceived threat of a rival "church," but its actual coherence in teachings or organization. Incapable of imagining any communal religious activity outside
of a clearly ordered structure, the average bishop or his theological adviser
frequently perceived more of a full-fledged rival clergy and alternate doctrine than really existed. They also could not resist linking virtually every
contemporary movement deemed suspicious to an ancient (and supposedly

equally well-organized) heresy, such as the fourth-century Manicheans or fifth-century Pelagians. Other times—contradictorily—it was a grassroots movement's very lack of rules and proper authority that raised the specter of radical individualism and religious chaos. Either way, without the steadfast guidance of church tradition, as defined by popes and councils, clerical reformers considered the average Christian at the mercy of a panoply of erroneous and dangerous ideas, many of them both highly contagious and fatal to the soul. Lay apostolic groups who recognized clerical authority were subsequently assimilated; those who resisted were persecuted, particularly with a new legal procedure known as inquisition.

By far the most significant outcome of Innocent's response to the lay apostolic movements—especially for the career of Meister Eckhart—was the birth of two new religious orders that embraced the most prominent features of the earliest groups—poverty and preaching—but required the usual religious vows of poverty, chastity, and obedience, as well as a special oath of obedience to the pope. The new orders, in other words, represented a clerical appropriation of the lay apostles' combination of the active and contemplative lives. Like the lay groups they hoped to supplant, both Giovanni di Pietro di Bernardone (aka Francis of Assisi; 1181–1226) and Dominic de Guzmán (1170–1221) sought to escape the binary of the active/contemplative model of spirituality. Like their Waldensian rivals, they rejected the isolation of the cloister as well as the lukewarm conventionality of much lay piety. Their common and oft-stated ideal was to be in the world but not of the world. Because they and their followers initially lived by begging, they were known as mendicants. Their principal differences from each other, at least in the beginning, were in degrees of emphasis. The followers of St. Francis, who especially valued poverty and humility, called themselves the Order of Friars (Brothers) Minor, but were better known as the Franciscans, or Greyfriars (because of the color of their habits). St. Dominic and his brothers fashioned themselves as the Order of Preachers, based on their chief ministry, and were otherwise known as Dominicans, or Blackfriars (again, based on their clothing). Together, the new mendicant orders would transform not just lay piety movements but Christianity itself. They would also determine the life choices of a certain young nobleman from Tambach.

An imagined encounter of St. Dominic (left) with St. Francis (right). Their so-called mendicant orders straddled the boundary between regular and secular clergy, offering laypeople guidance and devotional options beyond those of their parish priests.

Although Innocent played no direct role in the formation of either the Franciscans or the Dominicans (and actually died six months before papal recognition of the latter), he would have been delighted at the efficient way both orders undercut the appeal of the remaining independent apostolic movements. Both mendicant groups quickly established widespread reputations for upright character and piety. Each established its own constitution and monastic rule, carefully adapted to the needs of their preaching and other worldly ministries. Franciscans and Dominicans in short embodied the very apostolic ideal that many others merely aspired to—endowing them with considerable credibility vis-à-vis heretics and lax parish priests alike. At the same time, their prioritization of preaching addressed many of the lay desires that had given birth to the apostolic movements, bringing the teachings and spiritual experiences of the monastic world to the population of non-clerics. Men and women attracted to the apostolic life could now either join one of the new orders (both had female versions, known as second orders), attach themselves as a lay follower (known as a tertiary), or otherwise conform their everyday lives to the ideals preached. Best of all, from a church leadership perspective, both Dominicans and Franciscans maintained good training and disciplinary control of their friars so as to ensure completely orthodox messages.

The spread of the new mendicant orders had a curiously contradictory effect on lay spirituality. Thanks in part to Pope Gregory IX's 1231 commissioning of several Dominicans as heresy inquisitors—a new title and a still rudimentary procedure—the confusion of the previous era subsided. By the time of Eckhart, the boundaries between officially sanctioned apostolic orders and their heretical rivals were well established, at least among church officials.

At the same time, Dominican and Franciscan preaching in no way dampened the spiritual yearnings of many laypeople, but to the contrary, fanned the flames. Heroic Christianity was a hard idea to kill, and could no longer be contained to monks and nuns, even with the addition of the mendicants. The impact of both orders was especially evident in the cities and towns of Europe, where the friars counseled lay audiences struggling to adapt traditional Christian values to the challenges of the new money culture. Both of the new religious orders arose as reactions against the growing culture of consumerism, but it was the Franciscans who most explicitly defined the apostolic ideal against the values of the marketplace. The earliest followers of St. Francis were as much penitents in this respect as mendicant preachers. Following the example of their founder, they not only forswore all possessions but displayed a deep-seated, almost pathological contempt for money itself.

Dominicans, who called themselves "men of the gospel" (*viri evangelici*), shared the goal of apostolic poverty, but pursued it in what they considered a less theatrical manner than their Franciscan counterparts. Money and wealth were not necessarily bad in themselves, they preached, but presented many temptations that often led to sinful desires and actions. Many Dominican (and some Franciscan) theologians devoted enormous amounts of energy to developing sophisticated interpretations of such concepts as just price and usury, or charging interest for a loan. Ordinary Christians should not seek wealth, scholars wrote, but neither should they be ashamed of it, especially if they spent it in generous ways, such as the support of mendicant missions.

The sermons and counseling of preaching friars fed the lay hunger for spiritual fulfillment beyond the usual devotions and sacraments offered by the church, but otherwise offered few new options. The new orders did not resolve, for instance, the active-contemplative dilemma for most laypeople, who at most might attempt the halfway life of a Franciscan or Dominican tertiary: attending daily mass or other devotions, participating in scriptural readings and discussions, fasting or self-flagellating, or perhaps even living part time at a convent. Others might seek spiritual fulfillment through an active life of caring for the sick, assisting with burials, caring for the poor, and a wide range of other charitable activities. Voluntary religious associations offered still another devotional option, particularly in cities, with or without the oversight of a member of the clergy.

Eckhart thus came of age in a world still enthralled with the apostolic ideal and still searching for greater spiritual fulfillment. The majority of his lay contemporaries ultimately satisfied themselves with their existing religious options. But for the noble youth from Tambach, tales of the saints and martyrs represented direct challenges to a life of self-sacrifice that he could not resist. The only remaining question was which form his own path of heroic Christianity would take.

CHAPTER THREE

The Dominican Way

*Why am I more glad that something good happens to my brother
or to myself rather than to another? Because I love my own more
than another's. But if I love him as myself, as God's commandment
ordains that I should love God, then it will seem all the
same to me whatever the commandment says.*

GERMAN SERMON 74

A Call to Glory

The thirteenth-century Dominican cloister of Erfurt is one of the city's fortunate few medieval buildings to have survived nearly eight hundred years of religious upheaval, urban renovation, and modern aerial attacks. An Allied bomb dropped on November 26, 1944, destroyed most of the city's Franciscan church, fewer than a hundred yards away, but Eckhart's longtime home escaped untouched. The church and cloister buildings now belong to the Evangelical (Lutheran) diocese but the layout of the former Dominican compound has remained unchanged. The spacious refectory, with its stunning spired ceiling and numerous lofty windows, has been fully restored, as has the adjacent chapter room (still used for meetings) and its neighboring library/sacristy chamber (now a children's nursery). The sprawling attic dormitory remains exposed to thick-beamed roof rafters, as it was in the thirteenth century. The magnificent Gothic church, which today dominates the

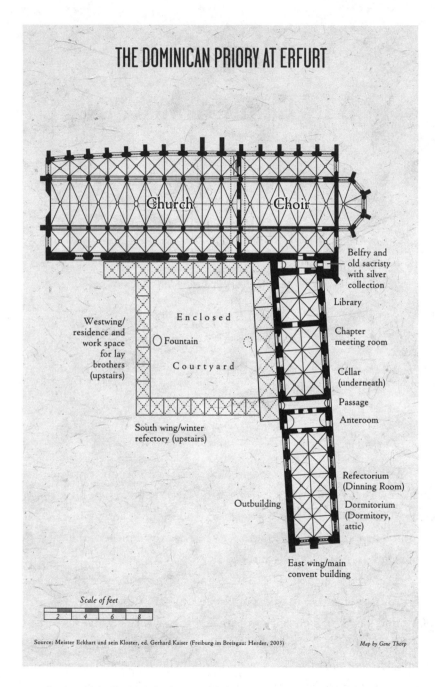

THE DOMINICAN PRIORY AT ERFURT

Church

Choir

Belfry and old sacristy with silver collection

Library

Enclosed

Westwing/ residence and work space for lay brothers (upstairs)

Fountain

Courtyard

Chapter meeting room

Cellar (underneath)

Passage

Anteroom

South wing/winter refectory (upstairs)

Refectorium (Dinning Room)

Dormitorium (Dormitory, attic)

Outbuilding

East wing/main convent building

Scale of feet

2   4   6   8

Source: Meister Eckhart und sein Kloster, ed. Gerhard Kaiser (Freiburg im Breisgau: Herder, 2003)

Map by Gene Thorp

Layout of the Dominican cloister of Erfurt. Amidst his frequent travels and reassignments as an adult, Eckhart spent more of his life here than anywhere else. In that sense, it was his home from his teenaged years until his death.

surrounding landscape, was still under construction during Eckhart's time, with the choir and high stone altar only fully roofed a year or two before his arrival. The cloister's courtyard, roughly sixty by eighty yards, remains enclosed on all four sides, preserving for modern visitors the sense of an entirely self-contained and independent world.

Sometime around the age of fifteen (ca. 1275), with his father's permission (and, possibly, encouragement), Eckhart von Hochheim entered into this alien community. With a population of more than twenty thousand, Erfurt was Thuringia's biggest city, at least five times larger than Gotha, which lay about a day's journey west by foot along the Via Regia. Erfurt also intersected the principal north–south artery of the region that linked the Baltic seaports with the Italian city-states of Venice and Florence, thus drawing significant traffic of people, livestock, produce, and especially manufactured goods. Unlike the provincial village and regional town of his youth, the "gateway to the east" was a cosmopolitan community, thriving on all kinds of trade, particularly textiles and woad (the most popular source of blue dye until the sixteenth-century proliferation of Indian indigo). The town—or more precisely, the Dominican cloister within it—would be Eckhart's home for most of the next forty years. He lived here longer and more continuously than anywhere else during his lifetime.

Eckhart's first extended exposure to the Dominicans had likely come a few years earlier, either in the order's house at nearby Gotha or at the priory in Erfurt, some thirty miles from his home in Tambach. By then, the Order of Preachers had enjoyed nearly a half century of growth in Thuringia, beginning with their 1229 arrival in Erfurt, just fourteen years after Dominic received papal approval for his new religious order. During the subsequent two generations, the Dominicans rapidly established communities throughout the towns of the area, including the house in Gotha. By 1270, when ten-year-old Eckhart might have begun attending the Erfurt school, the original order of some twenty loosely coordinated houses scattered across the continent had transformed itself into a powerful network of more than thirteen thousand friars in twelve provinces. The expansion had been so rapid that a few brothers from the earliest days of the order who had known St. Dominic personally were still around in Eckhart's time.

Like their Franciscan competitors, the Order of Preachers was in constant recruiting mode. The Erfurt priory's Latin school, located in the heart of the city and attended by hundreds of students, offered an especially rich hunting ground. Noble youths like Eckhart were favorite targets, but most students with his background remained intent on secular careers in business or politics. A religiously inclined individual of Eckhart's social status also had many options among the various religious orders, not to mention a possible career as a bishop or even cardinal. The Dominicans' reputation for rigorous educational standards gave the order a distinct edge with middle-class and noble parents, who typically held worldly ambitions for their sons. The resulting pedagogical arms race with the equally ambitious Franciscans led a series of popes, bishops, and superiors to repeatedly prohibit the poaching of pledges from other religious orders but clearly such mandates were difficult to enforce. Just a decade before Eckhart's own decision to join the Dominicans, the order also lowered its official age of admission from eighteen to fifteen, again prompting outrage from their rivals, the Franciscans.

Sometime—perhaps regularly—during his studies at the Erfurt Dominican school, the teenage Eckhart would have heard a vocational pitch along these lines (taken from one of the order's preaching manuals). The life of a Dominican preacher was "an excellent and noble work," more necessary, pleasing to God, useful, and personally profitable (in a spiritual sense) than any other human profession. Whereas knights fought for personal glory or gain, "preachers are also called soldiers of Christ . . . for they make war on the errors against faith and morals, which are opposed to the rule of their Sovereign." Preachers were also more useful than "carpenters, stonecutters, masons and other workers of this kind, for they are charged with constructing in the hearts of men a house exceedingly pleasing to God." They were likewise "happier and more fearless" than merchants, for "they carry on their spiritual trade through the land, exchanging their wisdom for precious acts of faith and numerous good works."

Eckhart's Dominican teachers would also not have hesitated to extol the superiority of their calling to that of their fellow religious residing in monasteries and convents. Paraphrasing Gregory the Great on the virtues of preaching, his recruiter would lament that

> There are some who, endowed with excellent qualities, reserve all their ardor for contemplation, and who refuse to work, through preaching, for the salvation of their neighbor. They love the quiet of the hidden life, and shut themselves up in their meditations; but if judged strictly, they will be found responsible for having omitted much that would have been profitable if done among men.

The preaching of a single friar, the recruiter would remind young Eckhart and his classmates, could reach many people, as seen in two sermons of St. Peter where the apostle claimed to have converted three thousand and five thousand people respectively (Acts 2:41 and 4:4). The Savior himself spent more time preaching than praying and at his ascension gave the Great Commission to "go into the whole world and preach the gospel to every creature." The apostle Paul likewise claimed preaching as his chief vocation—"For Christ did not send me to baptize but to preach" (1 Corinthians 1:17)—as did all of the Church Fathers.

Finally—and this would be the clincher for certain self-confident and ambitious teenage boys—preaching was difficult and thus not for everyone. The world needed strong and effective preachers, but very few were up to the challenge. "Preaching is such a noble art that one cannot fulfill it in an honorable and fruitful manner without overcoming the most serious difficulties. But how success is to be envied and praised!" Those few brave souls willing to take up the challenge of this divine calling would gain "a particular glory," earning them "the joy of angels and the anger of demons."

Why did young Eckhart in fact choose to enter the Dominican order? The Cistercian cloister at Georgenthal lay only a few miles from Tambach and nearby Gotha offered other options, including a Franciscan house. Here the implicit themes of Eckhart's later writing offer some insight. The celebrated rigors of the mendicant life promised an institutionally endorsed type of heroic Christianity in a society that celebrated the great men of days past and lamented the mercenary selfishness of its own time. Preaching God's Word offered a seemingly more useful and nobler purpose than either the contemplative life or worldly careers—two recurrent motifs in Eckhart's later sermons. Above all, the Dominican path promised the most exciting intellectual prospects of any vocation the future scholar could have pursued. Perhaps Eckhart's lifelong spiritual quest began in these early years, spurred by the mentoring of a friar at his school or by the boldly inspirational sermon of a Dominican recruiter.

Not all noble and patrician families were pleased by a son's choice of a vocation in either mendicant order. Joining the secular clergy at least promised the possibility of political prominence, as well as material rewards. Dominicans and Franciscans, by contrast, rarely rose to the rank of bishop, with some notable exceptions. The most famous Dominican of all time, Thomas Aquinas, met fierce resistance from his own noble family upon announcing his vocation, with his brothers even kidnapping and imprisoning the would-be friar for two years before relenting. Nonetheless, the Dominican strategy of concentrating recruitment efforts on schools and universities paid off. Unlike Franciscans, who counted many peasants and lower-class individuals in their number, Dominican friars were far likelier to come from literate, urban, and even noble backgrounds—like the young aristocrat from Tambach.

Upon his application to enter the order, possibly as early as 1275, Eckhart was examined by a panel of three brothers at the Erfurt priory. Often the interview process included an informal walk through the cloister's garden with a senior member of the panel conversing with the prospective friar in Latin about his life, studies, and aspirations. Star pupils such as Eckhart sailed through this part of the process, while candidates displaying inadequate Latin or emotional immaturity were turned away at this point. Following the panel's recommendation, all of the brothers in the house of roughly fifty members voted on his admission, with the prior reserving the right of final approval. The new postulant then began a probationary period of six months, during which his participation in the life of the community was greatly restricted. Only after the prior and other brothers were satisfied with the would-be friar's seriousness and stability was he allowed to proceed with his solemn vows of poverty, chastity, and obedience, and begin life as a Dominican friar.

On the appointed day, young Eckhart was escorted by the novice-master, along with other postulants, to a full chapter meeting of the house and instructed to prostrate himself before the prior, with his arms folded beneath his chest. The ensuing initiation ceremony began with a ritual question from the prior, "What do you seek?," to which Eckhart had been briefed to answer, "God's mercy and yours." The prior then interrogated the postulant before his future brothers about any possible impediments (being too young or already betrothed, holding outstanding debts, or suffering from bad health) and his willingness to endure the many hardships of Dominican life "for God and for the Kingdom of Heaven." Upon Eckhart's clearly audible assent, he was then stripped down to his undergarments and robed in the habit of a Dominican friar.

Following more prayers and a blessing with holy water, Eckhart and other novices then joined their new brothers in a procession through the cloister to the priory's church, marching two by two and singing "Come, Holy Spirit." As the song concluded, Eckhart and his fellow novices again prostrated themselves before the altar and remained immobile during a new sequence of psalms and prayers until instructed by the novice-master to rise and approach the prior, who received each of them with an embrace and a kiss on the cheek. The novice-master and other friars quickly joined the prior in embracing their new brother, after which the assembly retired to a celebratory meal in the refectory. Unlike some orders, the Dominicans did not change an initiate's name; the castellan's son from Tambach would hereafter be known as Brother Eckhart.

Cultivating the Habits of Devotion

During Brother Eckhart's novitiate of a year and a day, he received general character training and began to memorize dozens of hymns, psalms, and prayers, including the fixed-hours devotions known as the daily office, required of every Dominican. He was assigned a slightly older brother as a daily companion, or *socius*, who trained him in the essentials of Dominican life. His companion gave him a tour of the cloister grounds, showing him where to sit and how to behave in the choir during worship, how to modulate his voice and gestures in different settings, and how to enter the refectory two by two, bowing to the prior and then assuming a seat at a table, but not too close to his neighbor. He learned to keep his face veiled by his cowl, or hood, at all times until he had fully entered a room. He was introduced to the *vestarius*, or stock-master, who supplied him with shoes, leggings, straw for his bed, and other essentials. Within the first week, he also met the house librarian, who gave him parchment and pen so that he might write out his general confession. By the end of the week, the novice Eckhart was expected to be able to perform the house's daily routine of prayers and other activities without a misstep.

He was also expected to dress himself properly in his habit—a task that wasn't as simple as it may sound. The most visible sign of Brother Eckhart's new identity, this distinctive set of clothing in black (to symbolize penance) and white (to symbolize purity) would serve as his daily uniform for the next sixty years. Like all Dominicans, Eckhart would don as the base of his habit a white tunic that stretched from his shoulders to his ankles. This was girded by a leather belt, then covered by a white scapular—two long strips of cloth from his shoulders to a little before his knees and elbows, with an opening for the head. To this he attached a black cowl and then placed over his head a black mantle, or cloak, that was sewn together at the breast. Fashioned entirely of unfinished and undyed wool, the habit was, by intention, rough against the skin (also hot during summer) and even ill brothers were forbidden to wear smoother, more soothing linen. Undergarments were also woolen and some brothers chose (for penitential reasons) to exacerbate their physical discomfort with hidden hair shirts or thin ropes tightly bound around their waists. His belt could hold only one knife, a handkerchief, and a paternoster chaplet, or rosary. Unlike many Franciscans, Dominicans were permitted to wear shoes, albeit of modest style. Finally, in the manner of all monks, the new brother would have the crown of his head shaved, leaving him with a narrow band of hair, "about three fingers wide." He was not allowed to wear a hat.

During his first years as a Dominican, Eckhart's pursuit of God was conducted mostly within the confines of the Erfurt priory. He did not leave the priory unescorted during this time and certainly was not permitted to preach or beg. The largely autonomous community of some fifty men and youths, perhaps a third of them lay brothers not under vows, provided the novice with a distinctive combination of structured religiosity and intellectual freedom. Like all monastic orders, the Dominicans lived by a strict daily routine, in this instance based on the Rule of St. Augustine, in which each day began with *Matins* prayer service in the church at midnight (two a.m. in the winter). After an hour or so of reciting the first divine office, Eckhart and his brothers enjoyed a few more hours of sleep or private prayer before rising at sunrise for the *Lauds* prayers, a major office celebrated in the church. The remaining duties of the day—a combination of prayer, physical labor, and studying—were interspersed among the daily office's hours of *Terce* (midmorning), *Sext* (midday), *Nones* (midafternoon), and concluding with the major evening office of *Vespers*, followed by supper, a chapter meeting, the day's last prayer at *Compline*, and three or four hours of sleep before rising again for *Matins*. The chanting of each office's psalms and Bible passages, initiated by a sacristan's bell ringing, followed an annual liturgy. While the content of prayers varied and the timing was adjusted to seasonal variations in sunrise, the schedule itself remained inviolable. Visiting Benedictine

Jesus is greeted by two friars as a guest at a Dominican hospice.

monks noted acerbically that the Dominican style of chant was brisker than in their own monasteries, but reciting the priory's structured prayers—including weekly recitation of the nine-lesson Office of the Dead—still required a great deal of the young friar's time and attention.

As in conventional monasteries, Eckhart's superiors believed that the shaping of internal character began with the externals of physical discipline. Once the rigors of the friars' daily routine engendered habits of body, habits of mind could then follow. The novitiate thus focused on the essentials of liturgical prayer and personal discipline. First Eckhart and his fellow novices learned the order's Marian devotions, such as the Salve Regina and Office of the Blessed Virgin. Once these were mastered, he was then expected to memorize the entire Dominican psalter, containing the various psalms and prayers for the day's liturgical hours. He enjoyed full access to all of the library's liturgical books, allowing him to learn still other parts of the divine office as well as various hymns. The focus on rote memorization of such devotions might strike some modern readers as monotonous and not especially spiritual, but the novice-master and his fellow brethren considered outward conformity to the community's routine worship a virtue in itself.

Eckhart's community also cultivated obedience and humility through more direct means. The novice-master met regularly with his charges as a group to discuss their personal struggles. All brothers in the priory, from novice up, practiced regular confession, ideally every day, meeting one-on-one with a confessor and with the entire brotherhood at evening chapter meeting. As a novice, Eckhart learned that a proper confession must include three sacramental elements: full acknowledgment of specific sins in thought and deed; the expression of genuine contrition or remorse; and "satisfaction" for the offenses in question, by prayer or some ascetic penance. Many Dominican houses provided penitential whips, which brothers applied to one another's bare shoulders at the conclusion of daily compline or to the shoulders of an individual brother who had been found guilty by the chapter of some particular transgression. Confessors often prescribed lengthy fasting or other types of deprivation as penance, and some brothers sometimes imposed these trials upon themselves. Whatever Eckhart's own youthful experience of such practices, he would later criticize flagellation and other intentional suffering, saying they were more often an impediment than an aid to true contrition and detachment.

During his novitiate year, Eckhart's daily routine was dictated by the demands of the divine office, his Latin lessons, and whatever tasks were assigned him—serving as doorkeeper or reader of scriptures during compline, for example, or simply running errands. His world was small in geographical terms. Most group activities took place on the ground floor, which included the refectory and chapter room. The second floor contained an assortment of private cells, small classrooms, artisanal spaces, and study spaces, with the dormitory occupying the attic space.

Although the young friar's day was likewise divided into small compartments, each with a clearly designated purpose, the priory's communal life was designed to provide time (and space) for various forms of individual contemplation and intellectual development. Brother Eckhart spent long periods every day in silence, punctuated by common worship, classes, and the chapter meeting each evening. At least two periods of each day were explicitly devoted to solitary prayer or study, time that he might pass in the relatively well-stocked library, the priory's serene rear garden, the complex's inner courtyard with the sounds of urban life just beyond the cloister's walls, the priory's newly dedicated church, or in many other private, enclosed spaces. As an advanced student in his early twenties, he would be exempted from the major hours of divine office and enjoy still more hours of silent reading, writing, and contemplation. He might even be granted one of the priory's small but private cells as a study, with its own table, window, and sometimes a cot.

In these early years, of course, Eckhart slept in the spacious attic dormitory with the other brothers on their hard wooden beds, softened only by an occasional matting of straw or wool. This was typical of the priory's decidedly egalitarian ethos. All brothers were expected to participate in daily communal prayer and to vote on a variety of administrative and disciplinary issues. The prior retained many prerogatives in the daily running of the community, from assigning preachers and confessors to hosting visitors in the guesthouse. But he also remained subject to the collective will of his brothers, who reviewed him annually and could always appeal controversial decisions to superiors. With brothers assigned to one of thirty-two standard positions—ranging from subprior or novice-master to cobbler or gardener—some sense of hierarchy was inevitable within the priory's walls. Overt signs of status or preferential treatment, however, could provoke disciplinary action from the prior or community as a whole.

The seemingly contradictory blend of authoritarianism and democracy was nowhere more evident than during the two daily meals, one at midday and one before evening compline, or evening prayers. The brothers first cleaned their hands in the lavabo (Latin, "I wash") basin in a small corridor between the church and the library, then proceeded single file through the length of the cloister to the refectory, where upon entering they bowed to the crucifix mounted above the prior at the head table on their right. Finding a seat at one of the wooden tables lining the outer walls of the dining chamber, Brother Eckhart waited for the prior to deliver the initial blessing, and then watched as servers brought at least two cooked dishes to each table. All brothers, even the sick and elderly, ate the same food and drank the same wine. On feast days, a third dish or, on special occasions, pastries might be served, but even then meals remained strictly vegetarian. Other than his place of honor, perhaps seated next to a visiting dignitary, the prior enjoyed no special privileges and ate his meal in shared silence as the day's scripture passage was read for the assembled friars. The egalitarian spirit of the Dominican community made a deep and lasting impression on the noble Brother Eckhart, who throughout his life would remain wary of the larger society's celebration of hierarchy and prerogatives, especially in spiritual matters.

Bending the Bow

His novitiate year complete, Eckhart was finally able to participate fully in the most distinctive components of the Dominican vocation he had chosen: learning and preaching. The daily prayer and discipline of St. Augustine's Rule remained essential to shaping humble and contrite hearts, but the main business of the Order of Preachers lay outside the walls of the priory. Before the younger brothers could be entrusted to preach the Word of God to the wider world, however, they submitted to a rigorous course of study, usually requiring at least four years. In the words of one of the order's most famous leaders, Hugh of Saint-Cher (d. 1263), "first the bow is bent in study, then the arrow is released in preaching." Without learning, preaching would miss its target; without preaching, learning would be a useless skill.

Since its earliest days, the Dominican Order had required that every priory maintain a "school" taught by a lector, or professor, assisted by a university-educated "bachelor," and overseen by a student master (for disciplinary matters) and a visitor (official examiner). All were fellow brothers of the same priory, interacting daily with their charges, which in a provincial house of Erfurt's size might consist of as many as two dozen younger friars. The curriculum they taught was the most rigorous in Christendom, drawn up twenty years previously by a distinguished commission headed by Albert the Great and Thomas Aquinas, two of the most formidable scholars of the entire Middle Ages. Eckhart and his fellow students attended three or four lectures daily, not counting reviews led by a "brother repeater." Their academic year, as in universities, typically began on Michaelmas (September 29) and ended on St. John the Baptist's day (June 24).

Once his command of Latin grammar was judged adequate, Brother Eckhart began his mandatory *studium artium* (liberal arts study) with three years of logic. Like all Dominican houses, Erfurt's school offered at least two or three logic courses at any given time. First the young friar attended lectures on Porphyry's *Introduction* to Aristotle's *Categories*. This third-century work (written by a fervent anti-Christian) was the most important primer of the day for learning how to use such basic philosophical terms as genus and species, property and accident, and how to apply those concepts in arguments. All of his future fame as a scholar would hinge on his attaining absolute fluency in this lingua franca of contemporary intellectuals. He then proceeded to the *Categories* itself, a fifteen-chapter text from Aristotle's *Organon* that enumerated all the possible kinds of things that can be the subject or the predicate of a proposition. If the thing in question is a horse, for instance, it is a subject when considered as a whole (all its attributes), and a predicate when it "participates in" or is derived from an antecedent subject (e.g., animals). After mastering Aristotle's ten categories of subjects—substance, quantity, qualification, relation, place, time, attitude, condition, action, affection—the budding scholar was able to classify all remarks that could be made about any object, from the pen he was using to take notes (length, weight, color, in his hand, etc.) to angels, souls, or God Himself.

During his early studies in logic, Eckhart was also exposed to the works of the ancient Christian philosopher Boethius (ca. 475–ca. 526), another bulwark of thirteenth-century higher education. Expounding on the categories and methods of Aristotle and Plato, Boethius explored the mechanics of logic on subjects such as the three types of arguments: those of necessity (e.g., the sun will or will not come up tomorrow), of ready believability (the sun will come up tomorrow), and sophistry (the sun will not come up tomorrow). In the great philosopher's *De topicis differentiis*, Eckhart further learned most of the rules of rhetorical engagement that would serve him well in his future academic career. Here, for instance, he first encountered such basic dialectical tools as the syllogism: the most famous example being the series of statements that a) All men are mortal; b) Socrates is a man; c) Socrates is mortal. Just as important, instruction in the priory gave Eckhart the chance to develop his logical and rhetorical skills in regular disputations, or debates, with other friars. Unlike typical monastic learning, which prized rote memorization above all, the Dominicans thrived on argumentation, teaching their younger brothers from the beginning of their studies how to persuade others through their words—obviously an indispensable skill for a preacher, even more so for the future university professor Eckhart would eventually become.

Brother Eckhart's early training in logic and rhetoric was complemented by rudimentary instruction in the essentials of the faith. As we might expect of a learning culture based on memorization, this consisted of familiarizing himself with various spiritual taxonomies: the four cardinal virtues, the fourteen corporal and spiritual acts of mercy, the eight beatitudes, the seven deadly sins, the ten commandments, the seven sacraments, and of course various creedal articles of faith (one God, the crucifixion and resurrection of Christ, the forgiveness of sins, etc.). Here the novice-master and other senior brothers aimed to equip their young counterparts with simple guidelines for their own spiritual lives. The Erfurt priory also offered two daily theological lectures, one on a book of the Bible and one on the *Four Books of Sentences* of

Peter Lombard (d. 1160), a twelfth-century compilation of authoritative pronouncements of the Church Fathers and other theological notables. Typically, the professor, or lector, would deliver the biblical lessons and the
bachelor the lectures on the *Sentences*. The latter class was directed mostly at
younger students, but all brothers were expected to attend the daily lectures
on the Bible until they were too old or infirm.

Eckhart's mastery of the *Sentences*, like his skills in Aristotelian logic, was
an essential part of his training as a future academic. In the century since its
compilation, Lombard's systematic overview of excerpts from the Bible and
Church Fathers had become the standard textbook for all theologians—a
distinction it would retain even among sixteenth-century Protestant reformers such as Luther and Calvin. In the tradition of other twelfth-century glos-
sators, or theological commentators, Lombard's goal had been to make a
coherent whole out of diverse passages and interpretations on such topics as
the trinity, creation, and the sacraments. His "sentences" consisted of relevant pronouncements of Christian authorities from Paul and Augustine to
contemporary scholars on the orthodox interpretation of a vast range of doctrinal questions, from free will and predestination to the consensual nature
of marriage. Even when Thomas Aquinas and other thirteenth-century
theologians began composing their own theological summaries, or *summae*,
the *Sentences'* stature as the preeminent primer on Catholic theology remained unquestioned.

Lectures on Lombard's *Sentences* provided Eckhart with his first experience in the sophisticated practice of scriptural interpretation, or exegesis.
Most crucially for his own religious thinking, he learned how to move from
the *sensus historicus,* or literal sense, of Bible passages to various spiritual
senses that revealed certain "deeper truths" of the reading in question. The
allegorical, or metaphorical, interpretation of a scriptural passage, for instance, viewed the people and actions described in a symbolic manner, together conveying an essential spiritual truth. The moral, or tropological,
reading of a text, as in one of Jesus's parables, provided a lesson for right living today. The anagogical sense of the same passage revealed some prophetic
insight into the end times and Final Judgment (including heaven, purgatory,
and hell). Each of the four interpretations, according to his teachers, pointed

in a different direction: the literal backward to the past, the allegorical forward to the future, the moral downward to the present day, and the anagogical upward to the heavenly. Each sense was true, Eckhart learned, but not readily apparent to the casual reader, hence the need for a trained preacher. A reference to Jerusalem, for instance, might historically refer to the Judean city, allegorically to the church, tropologically to the soul, and anagogically to heaven. As an adult, Meister Eckhart would preach that beyond the literal/historical meaning of "Now the serpent was more subtle than any of the beasts of the earth," (Genesis 3:1), the Bible

> *teaches us very clearly about three things, although in parabolic fashion: First, the natures of things, second, the nature of our intellect and how it knows; and third, moral instruction regarding everyman's escape from or fall into sin, as well as the punishments that lead sinners back to virtue and virtue's Lord.*

According to St. Jerome (347–420), translator of the authoritative Latin Bible known as the Vulgate, "each and every sentence, syllable, letter, and comma in God's writing is replete with meaning." The exegetical power to extract those multiple meanings that Brother Eckhart learned as a young friar would prove indispensable in his future theological work.

Of course advanced interpretation of this nature required thorough familiarity with the Bible itself, the main focus of Dominican education. Everyone in the Erfurt priory encountered the scriptures multiple times during the course of a day: as they chanted psalms in the chapel, as they listened to the lector's daily lessons, as they ate their meals accompanied by public recitations, and of course as they sat in private reading and contemplation during free time. Erfurt's library possessed multiple copies of the sacred scriptures, sometimes simply called "The Truth," although not perhaps in the form we are used to today. Jerome's Vulgate was not the only Latin version in circulation during the thirteenth century, and many vernacular translations of certain books and passages were also commonly available.

Just a decade before Eckhart's birth, the theological faculty at the University of Paris had attempted to dispel any confusion—at least among scholars—with a standardized version of the Vulgate, largely based on the

Correctoria composed by Hugh of Saint-Cher and other Dominican scholars. Even then, any Bible used by Eckhart resembled a premodern version of a hypertext, with the main text accompanied by two sets of glosses, or annotations: the *ordinaria*, essentially explanatory footnotes, placed in the margin or at the bottom of the page; and brief *interlinearis*, definitions or pronunciations, situated between the lines of scripture themselves. Typically drawn from the writings of the Church Fathers, such explications assisted all readers, especially professional sermon writers, in interpreting difficult passages, but could also constrict alternate interpretations (although not in the case of the confident Meister Eckhart).

The most significant transformation of the Bible in Eckhart's day was the division of the various canonical books into the chapters and verses familiar to modern readers. This single innovation, taken for granted today, made finding and using key scriptural passages dramatically simpler, thus allowing the future Meister Eckhart and his fellow theologians to navigate an otherwise massive text with relative ease. A new series of biblical concordances—likewise a staple of modern scriptural scholarship—further

A medieval Bible with interlinear glosses, supplemented by the personal notes of a studious reader.

aided theologians and ordinary Christians in their attempts to explore the text thematically. Here too, Dominicans led the way, most notably Hugh of Saint-Cher's regularly revised and expanded 1235 concordance, which contained alphabetical lists of numerous terms, followed by his own chapter/letter method of location. Without such refinements, the extensive scriptural cross-referencing that theologians of the day relied on for evidence would have been dauntingly difficult and time-consuming.

Releasing the Arrow

The Dominican hunger for learning had been a hallmark of the order from its earliest days. The order's original coat of arms even prominently displays a book at its center. Outside observers of the early Dominicans frequently commented on this distinctive aspect of their piety. The French bishop Jacques de Vitry (d. 1240) expressed genuine admiration that "each day they attend lectures on the Scriptures given by one of their own. That which they have diligently heard they then on holy days present to the Christian faithful through the ministry of teaching."

This ministry of teaching, Dominicans frequently reminded others and themselves, remained the entire justification for the learning itself. In the words of the original 1220 constitution: "Our order is recognized as having been specially instituted from the beginning for preaching and the salvation of souls, and our study should be principally and ardently directed to this end with the greatest industry, so that we can be useful to the souls of our neighbors." Half a century later, Humbert of Romans (1200–77), fifth master general of the Dominicans and himself a university graduate, reiterated the primarily practical end of all Dominican learning. "Others apply themselves to the study of holy writings but if this study has not preaching for its end, of what use is it?" Saving souls remained the goal; knowledge, even theological, was merely the means to achieving that goal. This frequently repeated admonishment against sterile or self-serving learning would continue to weigh on Eckhart throughout his life.

The original mission of Dominic and his followers had been to combat false and dangerous preaching, especially by Albigensians and Waldensians. Popular and knowledgeable orthodox preachers, as subsequent church leaders learned, were much more effective weapons against heresy than inquisitorial proceedings. Even in Eckhart's day, when the most notorious heterodox movements were in retreat, this corrective function remained central to Dominican preaching. Like their counterparts in any Christian era, the friars confronted countless uneducated preachers or self-proclaimed prophets who continued to spread their own particular religious messages, sometimes attracting groups of followers that we might call cults. The spectrum between unquestionably orthodox and indisputably heretical preaching remained remarkably broad and ambiguous, leaving many people who thought of themselves as faithful Catholics genuinely confused about what the church actually taught. And here lay the special niche of the Order of Preachers.

The most stirring proclamation of the Dominicans' sacred mission came from their retired master general, Humbert of Romans, shortly before Eckhart entered the order. In *On the Education of Preachers*, Humbert repeatedly stressed the urgent necessity of their joint endeavor: "Were there no preachers, men would not think of heavenly truths and soon their hearts would become as parched land." Preaching, in other words, not only "gains entry for souls into heaven more quickly and more surely, so too it prevents their fall into hell . . . through ignorance." Only such loving guidance could help "those who, because of their simplicity, do not understand anything of the spiritual order and who lead a purely animal existence . . . slaves of their passions." The preacher's words served as a light to those poor souls "groping in the dark."

The most famous preacher of Eckhart's day was the Franciscan Berthold of Regensburg. Although some theologians complained about Berthold's reliance on fantastic stories and mere performance at the expense of a substantive religious message, the friar enjoyed a reputation during his lifetime as the finest German preacher ever. His sermons, even admirers conceded, focused less on doctrine than on simple sin and repentance. And Berthold did favor colorful stories about both evil people and saints, sometimes employing popular songs or catchy rhymes. But he was undeniably popular and—based on various conversion stories—effective. He was in that sense one of the first mass evangelists: according to his contemporary biographer, the animated preacher frequently attracted open-air crowds of up to 100,000. In 1263, Berthold's reputation earned him a special commission from Pope Urban IV to preach against Waldensians, during which he traveled throughout Germany, including Thuringia, and even to Paris, where he was received by King Louis IX, the future St. Louis.

The Dominican approach to preaching was to combine the popularity and accessibility of Berthold's method with rigorous doctrinal training and a greater focus on substance. The ultimate goal remained to move listeners to feel remorse over their sinful lives, but the message needed to be delivered in a precise and deliberate manner, without digressions. A misunderstood or unclear sermon might be worse than one never given at all, giving rise to new confusion and errors. "Dangerously vulnerable to misinterpretation" would in fact be an accusation that the future Meister Eckhart's opponents would apply to his own sermons.

The thirteenth-century professionalization of preaching, mainly at the hands of Dominicans, represented a pivotal moment in the history of Christian evangelization, comparable only to the development of new mass media technologies in the sixteenth and twentieth centuries. It was also unprecedented. Obviously spreading "the good news" of Christ had always been at the heart of the church's mission, but systematic training of preachers had been nonexistent before the arrival of the mendicant orders. For most of the previous millennium, clerics wishing to improve their own oratory might have consulted Augustine's *On Christian Doctrine* or the influential *Book of Pastoral Care* composed by Pope Gregory the Great in the sixth century. But not until Pope Innocent III, himself a renowned preacher, called for a revival of the "art of preaching" *(ars praedicandi)* did the mendicant orders, and to a lesser degree secular clerics, begin to adopt a systematic approach to the practice.

The result was an explosion of preaching manuals and reference works, many of them available to Eckhart in the library of the Erfurt priory. Thirteenth-century Dominican authors alone produced more books than all of the Latin Fathers of antiquity combined. In addition to Humbert's own general preaching manual, the young friar had access to the seasoned

Dominican's more hands-on guide to sermon preparation that provided out-lines for more than one hundred sermons, each tailored to a different specific audience, as well as an additional one hundred sermons categorized by occasion. Jacobus da Voragine, compiler of *The Golden Legend*, supplemented his compendium of saints' lives with an equally exhaustive collection of more than five hundred complete sermons. By the time Eckhart began his studies, the spread of both alphabetized indexes and Arabic numerals had made possible a variety of new reference works for sermon writers, searchable by key terms, by place in the liturgical calendar, or by purpose (e.g., wedding, funeral, public dedication).

Other preaching aids offered the inexperienced sermon writer further comfort, most notably several collections of *exempla*, or thematic anecdotes. This new genre drew heavily on the rhetorical writings of the great Roman orator Quintilian (d. ca. 118), who in turn had scoured ancient literature for useful parables, tales, legends, fables, and anecdotes. Christianity's greatest authority on preaching, Gregory the Great, especially valued the emotive force carried by simple stories of joyously converted sinners, or conversely, of the agonies suffered by unrepentant evildoers. Detailed descriptions of the violent deaths and subsequent hellfire suffered by greedy tax collectors or money lenders were especially popular with audiences. Material of this sort was the lifeblood of popular preachers such as Berthold of Regensburg, and young Dominicans were encouraged to make use of relevant *exempla*—in moderation. Shortly before Eckhart came to the Erfurt priory, the Dominican Stephen of Bourbon published his *Tract on Various Preachable Materials*, containing more than 2,900 such colorful and dramatic vignettes. If the Erfurt library didn't own a copy of this exceptionally popular work, it most certainly had Humbert of Romans' own collection of 228 *exempla*, essentially "greatest hits" drawn from Stephen's work.

The priory's library offered still other resources for Brother Eckhart as he composed his first sermons. A successful preacher, he was taught, needed not just a firm grasp of scripture, but also a deep understanding of the "study of creatures," a category of knowledge that included history, the laws of the church, the mysteries of religion, and experiences from one's own life. Among Dominicans, the most reliable guide to the world of the Old and

New Testaments was the *Historia Scholastica* of Peter Comestor (d. ca. 1178). Combining scriptural accounts with other ancient sources, particularly writings of the Hellenized Jew Flavius Josephus, Comestor's work gradually became the Middle Ages' most popular narrative of life in the ancient world. Finally, for questions of moral theology, the young friar could turn to any one of a number of new penance manuals—another burgeoning genre of the thirteenth century that most likely began with the formidable work of his fellow Dominican Raymond of Peñafort (1175–1275), a volume mandated for all Dominican libraries.

Even the authors of such manuals and reference works stressed that homiletics remained at its heart a practical art. A successful sermon writer, Humbert advised, did not follow any formula, but instead skillfully combined appropriate amounts of material from this wealth of reference sources with his own knowledge and personal experience. The successful preacher was in that sense like a gracious banquet giver:

> Every good preacher should first be practical, like a host who prepares food of good quality for his guests. Secondly, he should use moderation, even in practical things; for everything found in a grocery cannot be used by a host. And thirdly, he should use words which are convincing, just as at a banquet guests are served not only food of good quality, but also food that is well prepared and pleasing to the palate.

A preacher who focused too much on one topic was like "a host who only serves one dish at a table." Nor should the preacher "dwell too long on the less important points, which should be passed over lightly." Preachers who took an inordinate pride in style "are like a host who is more concerned with the beauty of a dish in which food is served than the food itself." The guest, or sermon hearer, should come away perfectly sated, neither bloated nor starved.

Brother Eckhart also learned other performance "tricks of the trade" from his more seasoned fellow preachers. "The manner of delivery," Humbert counseled, "should be neither fast nor slow," and the aspiring preacher must develop clear diction, know the intricacies and resources of language, and preferably develop "a voice with a definite resonance." Eckhart was also advised "to use a different style according as his authority is little or great; if his authority is slight then he should preach with humility, if his authority is greater he has the right to express himself with more severity." Since the earliest Eckhart sermon we have was delivered in his mid-thirties—with great authority—we can't judge whether the young friar heeded this particular admonition.

Finally, both Hugh of Saint-Cher and Humbert of Romans stressed that a preacher needed genuine enthusiasm to arouse a lumbering and often resistant congregation. Moderate the voice to create desired effects, they counseled, and change facial expressions for emotional impact. At the same time, most preaching manuals warned against too much theatricality, too many extravagant gestures or wordplay that, in the words of one author, make a preacher seem more like a comedic performer than a man of God. In contrast to Franciscan preachers, who were openly encouraged to be "jesters of God," in the manner of their freely emoting founder, Dominicans generally showed disdain for such flashy displays as the crusade preacher Robert of Lecce's gimmick of ripping off his Franciscan habit at a dramatic moment in his sermon and revealing a full suit of armor underneath. But restraint was more easily counseled than practiced, especially for an inexperienced friar eager to please.

Perhaps the most valuable preaching advice the young friar received, or at least what is most evident in his later sermons, was to pay attention to his audience, both in preparation and delivery. The ultimate goal of all Dominican preaching was to produce a specific emotional reaction, most commonly remorse for sinful living, which in turn yielded a new intention to live a life more pleasing to God. Fostering a penitential heart was thus just the first part of the mendicant preacher's job: confession, contrition, and penance had to follow. The role of confessor was a central part of the ministry of all Dominican friars, Eckhart included. Sermons that merely informed or entertained were judged failures by the order's standards, regardless of how much acclaim they received. "As the seed is planted in preaching," wrote Humbert, "the fruit is harvested in confession."

As a beginner, Brother Eckhart likely hewed closely to the instructions

he received in the Erfurt priory. Even his mature sermons follow the standard Dominican form of starting with a biblical passage in Latin, translating
it into the vernacular, then proceeding to reveal multiple layers of spiritual
meaning within. In these early years, especially before his university training, these interpretations were likely cautious, drawn from the preaching
manuals he was taught to consult. Later, as his sermons became more daring in content, he still remained attuned to audience reception, filling his
preaching with metaphors and occasionally colorful examples, all delivered
in simple language for a theologically unsophisticated audience. His points
are typically enumerated and his sermons are generally brief. No comments on his voice or performance have survived, and while he was never
the successful mass preacher of Berthold's standing, he clearly developed a
significant following in later years.

The adult Eckhart's greatest violation of his youthful training was probably his deliberate focus on complex, abstract, and sometimes confusing topics. Many preaching manuals quoted St. Augustine's admonition that "those
who cannot be understood without difficulty should never be commissioned
to instruct the people; or at least only in rare instances and in cases of urgent
necessity." Most authorities on preaching considered thematic and theological sermons of the kind favored by Meister Eckhart inappropriate for uneducated lay or female religious audiences, where personal conversion should
always be the objective. Yet in Eckhart's mind, he was bringing sinners
closer to God, just not in a fire-and-brimstone manner. Likely he took comfort from the reassurance of Augustine, one of his personal heroes, that "It is
worth far more to be less understandable, less pleasing, less moving, than to
say what is not true and what is not just." Eckhart also apparently had a
higher opinion of the intellectual capabilities of his audiences, particularly
among the religious women he encountered.

Above all, Brother Eckhart heard repeatedly during his studies, effective
preaching depended on experience and aptitude, two qualities he could not
acquire from a book. At some point during his first few years in the Erfurt
house, the prior granted him permission to preach to his Erfurt brothers.
Once he reached the age of twenty-five and had studied theology for at least
a year he was permitted to preach within the surrounding territory, again

depending on the approval of both the prior and the priory's chief preacher, known as the *limitator*. Reaching this level was not guaranteed to all friars; Dominican superiors noted that Jesus himself waited until the age of thirty to begin his public ministry and that no one without sufficient theological preparation or personal maturity should preach outside the priory's walls. Twenty-five was also the minimum age of ordination as a priest, a requirement for all Dominican friars, though we don't know exactly when Eckhart received holy orders.

After more experience and at least two additional years of theological study, the young friar was finally able to seek the provincial chapter's permission to preach not just in Erfurt's *praedicatio* district, but anywhere within the province. In the case of Teutonia, this meant a large area the size of modern England. We know nothing of Eckhart's preaching trips during these years, but can be sure that they offered a very different experience from life in the priory. Like students off to college for the first time, many young Dominican friars in their late twenties found the experience liberating—to a worrying degree, according to some of their superiors. Humbert of Romans recounted his own experience of those young friars who "are always eager to travel to get away from the discipline of the cloister, like children who run away from school." Many new preachers at this stage in Brother Eckhart's life were apparently less motivated by missionary zeal than by desires to eat better, visit relatives, or simply see the world. Excursions from the priory were not pleasure trips, his superiors stressed, and the ascetic standards of the Rule still applied in the outside world:

> A good preacher should not trouble himself about finding the lodgings where the hospitality is exactly to his taste; he should not turn aside from places where he could do good because he fears to find poor hospitality there; nor should he carry with him provisions in defiance of the rule; he should carefully avoid suspected houses; he should learn to be content with a little; he should leave behind him a good reputation; nor should he be a burden to his hosts; he should show them gratitude; he should hold no bad feelings against those who refused to receive him.

Dominican life on the road was supposed to be hard and unpredictable, an intentional expression of faith in God's providence. Traveling light, with few provisions, Brother Eckhart and his companion were unlikely to be the targets of the many highwaymen roaming the region, but they were reliant on the kindness and generosity of strangers. Dominicans were, after all, begging monks. Whatever the constraints or challenges of these early trips, Eckhart's sermons in Erfurt and elsewhere represented his first visible achievements as a member of the Order of Preachers. The long stretched intellectual bow was finally letting loose arrows aimed at the hearts of his fellow Christians. The community at Erfurt also provided him with a spiritual and emotional home for the rest of his life. In the eyes of many brothers, he was already a success. But in Eckhart's own eyes, his personal pursuit of God had barely begun.

CHAPTER FOUR

The Right State

We are the cause of all our hindrances. Guard yourself against
yourself, then you will have guarded well.

GERMAN SERMON 5A

The Pursuit of Holiness

Spiritual perfection, the goal of every Christian monk and nun, has always
been an elusive quarry. St. Benedict of Nursia (ca. 480–547), author of the
most influential monastic Rule in history, envisioned the seeker's journey as
a twelve-step program (literally) in humility, beginning with observance of
the Ten Commandments and ending with "that perfect love of God which
casts out fear, by means of which everything he had observed anxiously before will now appear simple and natural. He will no longer act out of the fear
of Hell, but for the love of Christ, out of good habits and with a pleasure derived of virtue." Frequently, the spiritual odyssey was imagined as an ascent
up a ladder to God, with climbers often getting stuck, slipping a few rungs,
or even falling off altogether.

The monastic pursuit of spiritual perfection was simultaneously a communal effort and an intensely personal struggle. External structures and enforced behavior—the daily routine of prayer and work, ritualized devotion,
and penance (often corporal)—were intended to discipline carnal desires

The Ladder of Divine Ascent, a twelfth-century icon from the Monastery of St. Katherine, Mount Sinai. Some climbing monks are assaulted or felled by demons, while all are urged on in the perilous journey by angels and saints to be received in heaven by an awaiting Christ. Spiritual perfection is a slow, methodical, and deliberate process of self-improvement.

and provide a fallow field in which God's grace could grow and blossom. Self-reflection and introspection naturally played important roles in this process as well, but the core assumption of the communal life of monks and nuns was that both peer pressure and peer assistance were crucial in developing true humility, and thus finding God. With the exception of a few remarkable saints, individuals were assumed too inherently weak and selfish to attempt such a treacherous spiritual journey on their own.

In the fall of 1294, nearly two decades after Eckhart had entered the Erfurt priory, his brothers there elected him as their leader. He was only in his mid-thirties. Although most of the preceding twenty years are shrouded in darkness, we know that the Erfurt priory remained his home throughout this period, even while he studied for several months or even years at the Dominican houses in Cologne and Paris. An exceptionally bright and confident young man, he likely also accompanied superiors to annual synods or other destinations. In his preaching and confessor duties, he interacted regularly with many laypeople as well as religious women. The practical, worldly dimension of his work was well developed and his election as prior appeared as a harbinger of future professional success in the order. But what of his personal pursuit of God?

While prior of Erfurt, Brother Eckhart composed a confident statement of his personal understanding of spiritual perfection. The work, known as the *Talks of Instruction*, is the most extensive surviving document we have from this early period in his life. Delivered between 1294 and 1298 as a series of discussions with young friars, it provides our first glimpse into Eckhart's own spiritual journey to that point. At the same time, it shows him at work as a preacher and counselor, two roles that he would continue to play throughout his life. Unlike members of the contemplative orders, Dominicans bore the double burden of striving toward spiritual perfection while also translating their own spiritual growth into useful advice for others. It was a dual role that Eckhart would cherish throughout his life.

What, then, did Brother Eckhart, the new prior of the Dominican house of Erfurt, believe about the pursuit of God at this point in his life? The manuscript that has come down to us consists of twenty-three chapters, which an early editor arranged under three themes: obedience, sin and repentance, and struggles of the spiritual life. We don't know if Eckhart approved this highly traditional organization for his talks, we do know that he sought to preserve and even promulgate the work, which was widely circulated during his lifetime. The most important theme of Eckhart's mature spirituality— *letting-go-ness*—plays a central role even at this early stage, albeit in a conventional, monastic form. Several other key components of his later sermons—such as the *divine spark* and the nature of God or the soul—are entirely absent from the *Talks of Instruction*. Yet this book of advice for junior colleagues is as close as we will get to an Augustinian *Confessions* for this stage of his life.

Above all, for a thirty-something Eckhart, the successful spiritual life meant getting in *the right state* of mind. This was not in itself a novel notion and in fact provided the very justification of monastic life, where detachment from the goods and cares of the world was intended to free the individual to focus exclusively on God. An attitude of what Eckhart already called *letting-go-ness* was essential in all ascetic pursuits, so that God's grace might take the place of various worldly attachments. Fame, power, wealth, and sexual gratification all needed to be recognized as empty and ultimately futile objects of desire, impeding true spiritual progress.

Eckhart, however, took this attitude much further, including even the very good works and penitential acts intended to promote detachment—an apparently unprecedented interpretation. Too often, he preached to his young charges, we focus more on the acts themselves than the intentions behind them. *People should not worry so much about what they have to do; they should consider rather what they are. If people and their ways were good, their deeds would shine brightly. . . . Do not think to place holiness in doing; we should place holiness in being, for it is not the works that sanctify us, but we who should sanctify the works.*

The spiritual life, according to Brother Eckhart, was an internal transformation aided by external means, not the reverse. He supported the Rule's routine and outward discipline as means to break the self-will, the conventional monastic goal, but also believed that brothers needed to focus more attention on their own state of mind. True obedience to the Rule and to the abbot, extolled by Eckhart as *the virtue to crown all virtues*, represented more than an act of external conformity; it was an internal *letting-go* of will itself. *In true obedience there should be no trace of "I want so-and-so," or "this and that," but a going out of your own.* Obedience, in other words, was a fully detached state of mind, far more elevated than the actual deeds commanded.

For the sake of his youthful and inexperienced audience, raised with conventional notions of piety, Eckhart made his point explicit: *[God] is little concerned with our works, but only with our state of mind in all our works, that we love Him in all things.* The prior's apparent diminishment of conventional acts of piety should not be misunderstood; it was their perception as bargaining tools with God that he explicitly rejected, not their value as spiritual aids:

> *Many people think they are performing great works by outward things such as fasting, going barefoot, or other such things which are called penance. But the true and best penance is that whereby one improves greatly and in the highest degree. . . . This penance is truly a state of mind lifted into God away from all things, and in whatever works you find you can have it most, and have it from those works, do them the more freely; and then, if any outward work should hinder you, whether it be fasting, watching, reading, or*

whatever else, you can safely leave that alone without worrying about failing
in any penance. . . .

Acts of penitence undertaken without this shift in attitude could in fact have
a deleterious effect, *drag[ging] down into ever greater sorrow and plung[ing] a*
man into such distress that he is ready to despair, and then the repentance remains
painful and he gets no further: nothing comes of this.

Accordingly, the spiritual seeker had to be consistently mindful and careful to avoid an idolatrous attitude toward his own acts of piety.

Skillful diligence is required for this, and in particular two things. One is
that a man has shut himself off well inwardly, so that his mind is on its guard
against the images without. . . . The second is that he should not let himself
be caught up by his internal imagery, whether it be in the form of pictures or
lofty thoughts, or outward impressions or whatever is present to his mind. . . .

This *letting-go* of all images and concepts would form an important part
of Meister Eckhart's mature teaching on divine union. Known by scholars as
negative or apophatic (from Greek "to deny") theology, this approach to the
divine seems inherently impossible to most people. How can one think of
God or heaven without any images or concepts? Trying to get a sense of the
divine from negations—God is not really a being; He does not really exist in
time; He is not really a He—appears befuddling, even if one accepts their
truth. Negative theology is admittedly a difficult concept that Eckhart will
elaborate on only after additional scholarly training and reflection. In this
early context, his passing reference to the practice merely extends the conventional notion of detachment beyond its conventional ascetic limits:
letting-go of all preconceived ideas about holiness as well as one's very will.

To the astonishment of his young listeners—and likely the discomfiture
of some of his older brothers—Eckhart even turned his sights on the contemplative life itself:

People say, "Alas, sir, I wish I stood as well with God or had as much devo-
tion and were as much at peace with God as others are, I wish I were like

them, or that I were so poor," or, "I can never manage it unless I am there or
there, or do this or that; I must get away from it all, or go and live in a cell or
a cloister."

Rather than seize an opportunity to extol the virtues of monastic life,
Brother Eckhart instead challenged the inherent superiority of the contemplative life unless one is *in the right state.*

In fact, the reason lies entirely within yourself and with nothing else . . . rest-
lessness never arises in you except from self-will, whether you realize it or
not. Though we may think a man should flee these things or seek those
things—places or people or methods, or company, or deeds—this is not the
reason why methods or things hold you back: it is you yourself in the things
that prevents you, for you have a wrong attitude to things. Therefore start
first with yourself, and resign yourself.

Even isolation within the friary was not in itself spiritually enhancing.

I was asked, "Some people shun all company and always want to be alone;
their peace depends on it, and on being in church. Was that the best thing?"
And I said, "No!" Now see why. He who is in a right state, is always in a
right state wherever he is, and with everybody. But if a man is in a wrong
state, he is so everywhere and with anybody.

Concerned that some of the young brothers might misunderstand him—
a problem that would continually haunt Eckhart as a preacher—the prior
quickly added, *as I have often said, when we speak of "equality," this does not*
mean that one should regard all works as equal, or all places or people. That would
be quite wrong, for praying is a better task than spinning, and the church is a nobler
place than the street. That said, the emphasis must always be on the intention,
with the outward act or physical setting of secondary importance.

Opening Up to Grace

Eckhart's radical redefinition of spiritual detachment would remain a part of his preaching throughout his later life. His more innovative and expansive notions of *letting-go-ness*, however, had only begun to develop at this point. Drawing closer to God required an arduous effort of the seeker's will, even though he also acknowledged that the end goal is the *destruction of self*. One chapter of the *Talks*, likely titled by a later editor, was called "How the Will Can Do All Things, and How All Virtues Rest in the Will, Provided Only That It Is Just." This was perhaps a logical corollary to Eckhart's emphasis on intentionality, but it would be a source of embarrassment to him in later years, when he had come to believe that the intellect was a far more reliable guide to God than the will.

Even at this point in his life, Eckhart acknowledged that *in all his acts and in all things a man should consciously use his reason*, but he immediately clarified that *this requires much diligence, demanding a total effort of our senses and powers of mind*. His audience of spiritual beginners was not taught self-emptying, in the fashion of his later followers, but self-mastery. *This above all is necessary: that a man should train and practice his mind well and bring it to God, and then he will always have divinity within.* Everyday temptations and obstacles should each be welcomed as spiritual exercises aimed at achieving this goal.

Virtue, Eckhart taught, was a habit of mind that gives value to our actions, not the reverse. The most important thing, the prior told Erfurt's young friars, was to make a genuine effort, no matter what the obstacles or chance of success. Since it was the state of mind that mattered most to God, not the external act, intention to do good (or evil) was likewise more important than the act itself. *If you have a true and proper will, you can lack nothing, neither love nor humility nor any other virtue.* Complacency was not an option for the genuine spiritual seeker:

> *If a man is not drawn to any work and does not want to undertake anything,*
> *then he should force himself into some activity, whether inward or outward*

(for a man should not be satisfied with anything, however good it may seem or be) so that, when he finds himself oppressed or constrained, it may appear rather that that man is worked than that he works; thus he may learn to co-operate with his God.

This submission, according to Eckhart, was the central paradox of the spiritual quest: in applying one's own intentions to good actions, the individual will gradually gives way to the divine will, thereby becoming *perfect and right*.

The focus on purity of heart and intention is reminiscent of chivalric tales, as is the prior's exhortation: . . . *the greater and fiercer the struggle, the greater and more glorious the victory and the honor of victory.* But even here Eckhart refused to valorize external or internal suffering except as a necessary part of spiritual evolution. First, he reassured his audience that God was with them in the midst of their ordeal. *However great the suffering may be, if it comes through God, then God suffers first from it. Indeed, by the truth that is God, there was never so tiny a pang of sorrow that befell a man, not the least little discomfort or inconvenience, but if he placed it in God, then it would pain God incomparably more than that man, and incommode God more than the man himself.*

Second, he relieved them of their unrealistic self-expectations: *People may well be daunted and afraid because the life of our Lord Jesus Christ and the saints was so severe and painful, and a man cannot endure much of this or does not feel compelled to it.* But St. Paul, he claimed, reassures us that *not all people are called to God by the same route* (1 Corinthians 7:24). In the instance of the martyrs and other saints, *our Lord gave them this way and also the strength to do it, so that they could follow this way, and he was pleased with them for all this, in which they should profit best. For God has not bound man's salvation to any special mode.* If acts of great physical endurance were not one's calling, they should not be attempted. Even the command to follow Jesus did not apply *in all respects. Our Lord fasted for forty days, but no one should take it upon himself to follow that. Christ performed many works in which he intended that we should follow him spiritually but not physically.* Underscoring his central theme, Eckhart repeated, *As I have often said, I consider a spiritual work more valuable than a physical one.*

Once more the prior reminded his spiritual beginners that it was the inner state of mind resulting from physical or psychological suffering that mattered, not the pain itself. Spiritual strife was necessary to let go of all attachments, leaving the seeker bereft of all comfort except one: *God in His faithfulness often permits His friends to succumb to weakness to the end that whatever support they might lean on or cling to may give way . . . he wishes to be their sole support and security. Great hope and trust in God,* according to Eckhart, was *the sign of perfect love.* This was the objective of all external discipline, all good acts, and all prayer—to make room for God's grace in the heart. This was also the natural desire of God's love: *Wherever a man in obedience goes out of his own and gives up what is his, in the same moment God must go in there.*

This divine compulsion would remain a distinctive part of Eckhart's spiritual philosophy in later life, challenged by some of his critics who thought it denied the Creator's absolute freedom. For Eckhart, though, mercy was at the heart of the divine essence. God, he stressed, fervently wants to forgive, not to punish, and is always looking for opportunities to reunite with His creatures. *When a man stands right above sin and turns completely away, then our faithful God acts as if that man had never fallen into sin, and will not let him suffer for a moment for all his sins. . . . Provided He finds him now ready, He pays no regard to what he was before. God is a God of the present.* For young friars raised with imposing images of a stern final judge, Eckhart's merciful God must have seemed a startling revelation. In fact, the prior reassured them, *the more and the greater the sins, the more immeasurably glad and the quicker God is to forgive them, the more so since they are more hateful to Him.*

Already at this early stage in his own intellectual development, Eckhart spoke of a hidden God, always present but often unperceived. *In the right state of mind, the good will cannot miss God. But the mind's perceptive faculty sometimes misses Him, and often thinks God has gone away.* Anticipating his listeners' question, he posed it for them: *What should you do then? Do exactly the same as if you were in greatest comfort; learn to do the same when you are in the greatest distress, and behave just as you behaved then.* His advice was not "fake it until you make it," but rather, keep trying and don't despair. Finding the hidden God *requires zeal and love and a clear perception of the interior life, and a watchful, true, wise, and real knowledge of what the mind is occupied with among things and people.* What today would be called mindfulness, he reminded his charges,

A sixteenth-century Bavarian sculpture of God the Father—closer to Eckhart's beneficent and enthusiastic forgiver of sins than most stern medieval portrayals.

cannot be learned by running away, by fleeing into the desert away from outward things; a man must learn to acquire an inward desert, wherever and with whomever he is.

This early and unique reference to an *inward desert* would also become a major theme in Eckhart's later sermons. At this stage, though (and perhaps mainly because of the inexperience of his listeners), he remained surprisingly wary of promoting divine union and other mystical experiences. There are, he told his audience, two kinds of direct experiences of divine assurance of eternal life:

> *One is when God tells a man Himself or through an angel or shows him by a special illumination. This happens seldom and to few. The other kind of knowledge is incomparably better, and this often comes to people who have perfect love. It is when a man's love and intimacy with God are such that he has such perfect trust and security in Him, that he cannot doubt and is thus quite assured, loving Him without distinction in all creatures.*

This assurance, he made plain, *is far greater, more perfect, and truer than the first, and cannot deceive us,* unlike the other, which might be *a false illumination.* Experiencing and acting on love was also far more important than any personal enjoyment of God's presence.

As I have said before, if a man were in an ecstasy as St. Paul was (2 Cor. 12:2–4), and if he knew of a sick person who needed a bowl of soup from him, I would consider it far better if you were to leave that rapture out of love and help the needy person out of greater love.

It's difficult to know how much the young prior's cautious attitude toward mystical experiences reflected the audience of the *Talks of Instruction*. His later sermons, following many years of scholarly study, not only showed more openness to such direct encounters but actively promoted them. There was only one exception at the early stage in Eckhart's thought and it was a highly conventional one: receiving the Eucharist. More than eighty years had passed since Lateran IV had confirmed the doctrine of transubstantiation, that the bread and wine of the mass, when properly consecrated by an ordained priest, took on the essence of Christ's body and blood (while retaining the external form, or particulars, of bread and wine). Ingesting a consecrated host was thus not merely a symbolic gesture but a direct, institutionally sanctioned, physical experience of the divine. And while obviously mediated by a member of the clergy, the sacramental experience remained open to all.

Eckhart's descriptions of receiving the Eucharist in fact often sound like an early, more orthodox version of what he later described as a less formal, less mediated divine experience. First there was the innate feeling of unworthiness before the Creator of the universe: *But you might say, "Alas, sir, I feel so bare and cold and lazy that I dare not face our Lord!" I reply, All the more need for you to go to your God, for by Him you will be enflamed and set afire.* Next there was the preparation, considerably less demanding and more conventional than achieving *letting-go-ness*: *Whenever a man wishes to receive the body of our Lord, he may well approach without undue worry. But it is seemly and very profitable to confess first, even if one has no pangs of conscience, for the sake of the fruits of the sacrament of confession.* Of course genuine contrition for sins was necessary, but the *right state of mind* need not be fully formed.

Again, Eckhart anticipated the reservations of some of his listeners about a genuine divine union: *"How can that be? I can't feel anything?"* and *"How can I believe in higher things as long as I do not feel in such a condition, but feel myself imperfect and prone to many things?"* Proceeding without complete

A priest says the words of consecration that transform the essence of the host and wine into the essence of the body and blood of Christ. This was the most awe-inspiring moment of the mass, later followed by some members of the congregation ingesting consecrated hosts. Frequent communion remained rare in Eckhart's day.

understanding or notable sensation, he reassured them, in fact helped bolster one's faith.

Finally, there was Eckhart's description of the experience itself, also foreshadowing later formulations but still fairly general and uninformed by mystical literature:

> There was never so close a union [as that of the soul and God], for the soul is far more closely united with God than are body and soul, which make up a man. The union is far closer than when a man pours a drop of water into a vat of wine, for that would make water and wine—but this is so turned into one that all creatures could never find out the difference.

It is tempting to look for other signs of Eckhart's mature spiritual philosophy in this early work, but we must be alert to his more conventional goals in this setting. His passing mention of *an inward divinity* was never developed except in the usual sense of an individual conscience, with the intellect serving as a reliable guide. And only our awareness of his later focus on *the divine spark* within each person lends apparent significance to his isolated reference to *a light shin[ing] in the darkness, and then we are aware of it*. In fact, in the context of his advice to young friars, these words spoke only to the guiding light provided by God's grace in the midst of a seeker's internal turmoil and suffering.

It was this focus on an internal battle that most distinguished Eckhart's early description of the spiritual quest from his mature understanding. The heroic Christian, like the truly noble knight of romances, was one who willfully overcame his worldly attachments and ultimately conquered himself. Adversity was to be welcomed and even temptation and sin had their uses in reaching the ultimate goal. *You should know that the impulse to wrongdoing is not without great benefit and use to the righteous*, especially compared to *a man subject to no weaknesses*. The seeker who struggled with temptation *deserves far more praise, his reward is much greater.*

Eager to press his point, Eckhart employed the dramatic and hyperbolic language for which he would become famous (and infamous to some): *Inclination to sin is not sin . . . [and it even] makes a man ever more zealous to practice virtue strongly; it drives him by force to virtue and is a sharp lash which compels a man to mindfulness and virtue, for the weaker a man finds himself to be, the more he should arm himself with strength and victory.* Willingness to sin, he conceded, is sin, but at one point he even boldly proclaimed that *in fact, to have sinned is no sin if one regrets it.* Provocative words like these, spoken by a prior to his youthful charges, undoubtedly startled his listeners, as he intended. Yet even if some friars misunderstood his main point about the centrality of remorse, the prior, Brother Eckhart, risked no dangerous consequences. In later life, the public preacher Meister Eckhart would enjoy no such immunity.

For all his innovative interpretation of the monastic ideal, Eckhart's description of spiritual transformation remained markedly conservative. *Letting-go* did not yet apply to the daily striving that characterized the monastic life. What was most remarkable about Eckhart's thinking at this point was the consistent focus on a subjective path to the divine. Good works and all other external experiences were only valuable to the degree that they helped a particular seeker let go of worldly attachments and adopt *the right state of mind*. Amid the unrelenting enforced conformity of the daily Rule, he reassured young friars that there was no universal path to God, *who gives every man according to what is best and most fitting for him. Whatever God then sends him, let him take it direct from God, regard it as best for himself, and be fully* content. *Though later on some other way may please him better, he should think, "This is the way God has sent you," and accept it as the best.*

Eckhart warned young friars about spiritual competition, a particularly invidious and unproductive peril of monastic communities: *"Do not bother yourself about what condition or way of life God gives anyone. If I were so good and holy that I were to be elevated among the saints, people would talk about it, and speculate whether it was a matter of nature or grace, and get confused. They were wrong to do that. Let God work in you."* "Know thyself," the ancient Delphic maxim, was the essence of Brother Eckhart's advice to his audience of spiritual beginners. That self is the chief obstacle to drawing closer to God and its denial the key to true spiritual fulfillment. *It all depends on that. Observe yourself, and wherever you find yourself, leave yourself: that is the very best way.*

The Promise and Peril of Learning

Self-knowledge and humility were also at the heart of Eckhart's other surviving work from this period. But whereas the *Talks of Instruction* focused on what he had learned thus far in his spiritual journey, the brief Easter sermon of 1294 served as a manifesto for what he had yet to discover. At the very time that Prior Eckhart was counseling his young charges, he had already begun to move beyond the wisdom gained from life in the cloister to the wisdom of the ages—the scholarly work that would dominate the next stage of his life. Following many years of study in Cologne, Strasbourg, and Paris, he had spent the academic year of 1293–94 as a second bachelor, or beginning graduate student, at the theology faculty of the University of Paris, the preeminent institution in Christendom. Near the conclusion of his stay, on April 18, just five months before assuming the priorship of Erfurt, Eckhart had delivered a sermon that presaged this next phase in his spiritual journey.

As with the *Talks of Instruction*, the audience consisted of fellow Dominicans, but there the similarities end. In this instance, an audience of older and more intellectually sophisticated fellow Dominican friars (and perhaps a few educated laymen) elicited a startlingly different style. While in residence at the Paris Dominican house of St. Jacques, the young scholar had been invited to present the Easter Sunday homily at the house's adjoining church. Eager to show off the fruits of his academic training to that point, Eckhart ascended the pulpit to deliver a Latin address that could not have lasted more than thirty minutes. It was probably not the only sermon he delivered during his year at the St. Jacques priory, but it is the only one that he thought worthy of preserving.

Unlike the free-flowing observations and advice of his *Talks of Instruction*, the Easter sermon was linguistically precise, meticulously structured, and packed with external references. Following the standard Dominican model for an academic homily, known as the *sermo modernus* style, Eckhart began with two scriptural excerpts touching on his theme, in this instance Christ as the sacrificial lamb. As in all of his Latin and German sermons, the verses in question—here 1 Corinthians 5:7–8 on Christ as the Passover bread and Luke 15:32 on the return of the prodigal son—served as general pretexts for a message delivered on multiple levels. The young friar then stated his protheme, or introduction, followed by a prayer and further explanation of his purpose, also known as an antetheme. The remainder of the sermon consisted of several subthemes, all carefully enumerated, which eventually culminated in a restatement of the principal theme and a prayer for divine sustenance. Throughout the sermon, Eckhart displayed his ability to enlarge on the central theme (*dilatatio*), employing many other intratextual quotations from the Old and New Testaments that highlighted his creative interpretations and other scholarly skills.

This early academic effort, much less accessible to the average listener than the *Talks of Instruction*, provides us with our first glimpse of a budding scholar, already well versed in the ancient Church Fathers and Aristotelian philosophy, and eager to be part of the intellectual revolution then under way at the University of Paris. His frequent name-dropping of both pagan authors (Ptolemy, Hermes Trismegistus, Avicenna) and Christian authorities (particularly St. Augustine) was more than mere academic posturing; something significant was at work. To be sure, Eckhart aimed to impress the scholarly brothers in attendance with his erudition, but the sermon itself was at the same time his announcement of what would become a lifelong

intellectual project: the formation of a genuine philosophy of religion, a formidable undertaking that aimed to bring together all forms of wisdom,
Christian and pagan alike. It was the same spiritual quest that he described
to his charges at Erfurt, but the "scientific" methods of modern academic
theology would provide him the means to bring a greater intellectual coherence and depth to his own personal experiences and insights. This was a
path already trodden by his order's most gifted thinkers, and one that boded
well for Eckhart's future prominence beyond Erfurt.

On the surface, the Easter sermon celebrated the sacrificial death and
resurrection of the Savior, the focus of the day's liturgy and the central mystery of the Christian faith. At the same time, Eckhart spoke at length about
the sacrament of the Eucharist, the reenactment of that sacrifice whereby
Christ returns to the community of the faithful in the consecrated bread and
wine of the mass. As in the *Talks of Instruction*, the young friar expressed his
wonder at the *unbelievable* ensuing moment of divine union, available to any
true believer. *The more deeply a soul receives this sacrament, based on humility,
the more receptive she is for God.* Here again the direct experience of the ineffable appeared in conventional form, following the conventional preparation
of a humble and contrite heart. The pursuit of God described, despite the
learned elaborations, appears no different from the spiritual pilgrimage described in any parish church of the day.

Just below the surface, however, lay another agenda that most of Eckhart's audience would have recognized. A brief reference to the mystery of
the Trinity provided him with an opportunity to discourse on the meaning
of humility in one of the very capitals of Christian learning. Every wise man,
the young scholar boldly preached, knows the limits of his own knowledge.
Even the pagan Ptolemy taught that *"whoever is the most humble among the
wise is the wisest among them."* Albert the Great, the preeminent Dominican
intellect of the age and a personal hero to Eckhart, likewise *often said, "This
much I know, if I know anything, that we all know little."* Unlike the self-assured
Cicero, introduced by Eckhart at the outset of his sermon, the true Christian
scholar was a humble man, seeking not knowledge of things, but knowledge
of self—the same central theme as in the *Talks of Instruction*.

Clearly Brother Eckhart felt ambivalent about his entry into the world of scholarship. He could not deny that it offered him exciting opportunities to continue his pursuit of God in ways not available in the cloister. Yet he was also already aware of the seductiveness of higher learning, its tendencies to make its acolytes proud, even arrogant. Perhaps he was also struggling with his own ambitions within the academic world, pondering a theological career of great acclaim. His subsequent election as prior in Erfurt offered another source of temptation, with whispered intimations of rising in the leadership of the order, perhaps even to the supreme position of master general itself. Certainly he had the intelligence and apparently the personal skills necessary for success in both career tracks. The world of scholarship offered an intellectual pursuit of God during an exceptionally dynamic and exciting period in Christian thought. The life of a leader in the Dominican order promised less stimulating work but greater direct service to his fellow friars and their communities during a crucial time in the order's history.

The decision on which path to pursue, Eckhart could console himself, was not his but rather that of his superiors, and ultimately of God Himself. Fortunately—as he would find out over the next twenty years—the two paths were also not mutually exclusive. But which would best facilitate his personal pursuit of God? Here he would find himself pulled inexorably toward the famed University of Paris. There, amid the greatest theological minds of the day, Brother Eckhart would eventually abandon the notion of spiritual progress as a willful endeavor of self-discipline and embrace ever more radical notions of both the soul and its true object of desire, the elusive divine Creator Himself.

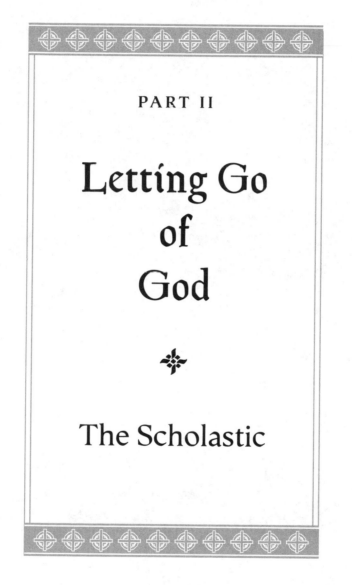

PART II

Letting Go of God

✦

The Scholastic

CHAPTER FIVE

The Science of God

What is truth? The truth is such a noble thing that if God were able to turn away from truth, I would cling to truth and let God go; for God is truth, and all that is in time, and that God created, is not truth.

GERMAN SERMON 25

The World of the University

When Eckhart arrived at the University of Paris in 1293, a year before being named prior of his monastery in Erfurt, he was already a rising star in the Order of Preachers. Graduate study in theology was the most competitive and demanding of all the higher degrees, typically requiring at least fifteen years of study—including three or four years of undergraduate work—to attain the title of "Master," the equivalent to the modern "Doctor." Advanced degrees in law and medicine, by comparison, were usually completed in only ten and six years respectively. The demanding track of the self-proclaimed "queen of the sciences" obviously required a significant investment of time and money. Bishops and heads of religious orders predictably selected only the most intellectually gifted among their brethren to pursue serious theological study in Paris, men identified as future administrative leaders or perhaps even professors themselves. For the great majority of Dominican friars, three years in their own house's *studium artium* would be the extent of their formal education, supplemented of course by daily lectures on the Bible and whatever private reading they wished to pursue. At most one in ten Dominicans went on to some form of higher learning, and the roughly fifteen-thousand-member order annually sent only two friars— men judged to possess "a vast capacity and a great aptitude for grasping sciences of this sort"—to attend classes at the University of Paris in preparation to receive the distinguished and relatively rare title of "master of theology."

Eckhart's 1293–94 stay in Paris was not his first encounter with the city. Unfortunately we don't know the number or duration of previous stays, which would have occurred between 1277, when Eckhart was in his late teens, and 1286, when he was in his mid-twenties. During the intervening years, the still youthful friar had completed at least six additional years of theological study at Dominican houses, most likely in Erfurt and at the order's advanced institute, or *studium generale*, in Cologne. By Eckhart's time, there were at least seven of these advanced programs throughout the provinces, and the house at Cologne enjoyed a reputation as the most vibrant theological community after the era's preeminent universities in Paris and Oxford.

As the now thirty-three-year-old Eckhart approached Paris's Saint-Denis gate once more, he must have recalled the great cultural shock of his initial encounter with the city years earlier. First, there had been his unprecedented youthful foray out of "the lands of the German tongue." Traveling more than four hundred miles from Erfurt by foot—friars were forbidden to journey by horse—would have required at least three weeks, perhaps twice that long. Typically, Dominican friars journeyed in pairs, with each *socius* looking after the physical and spiritual welfare of the other. A young friar such as Eckhart would never have been permitted to make such a trip without at least one older companion along. The brothers would have traveled light, with few provisions, relying on the generosity of those they met along the way for food and shelter. Of course they could count on support from fellow Dominicans, but this was a more haphazard prospect than we might expect. Even though the order boasted more than 590 priories scattered throughout Europe, most of these were in cities; establishments in the sprawling countryside were less common. Further complicating matters, as the brothers moved into territories beyond their native Thuringia, they would encounter

German dialects so different from their own as to be unintelligible, and, eventually, non-Germanic languages including a variety of regional French dialects. In these foreign lands, not only would Eckhart and his companions have difficulty communicating their basic needs, they would be unable to preach for donations, except in Latin, a language typically spoken only by some nobles and those affiliated with the church.

Even now, a decade or more after Eckhart's first visit, Paris remained a metropolis like none the friar had seen elsewhere. The sheer size of the city and its environs far eclipsed that of Cologne, the largest urban center he had known to that point. Earlier in the century, Philip Augustus had undertaken a major public works program to accommodate the city's burgeoning population of fifty thousand, including newly paved thoroughfares, two new bridges across the Seine, and an encircling town wall nearly three and a half miles long, with ten gates and seventy-five defensive towers. The king also continued construction on the famed cathedral of Notre-Dame, begun in 1163 (and still incomplete at the time of Eckhart's death thirty-five years later).

Paris, ca. 1500, viewed from the south. The left bank, home to the university, is at the bottom of the image. The still-unfinished cathedral of Notre Dame is on the island at the center.

Meanwhile, the city had continued to grow exponentially and, by the time of Eckhart's arrival, encompassed an urban center of more than a thousand acres and a population of nearly 200,000, making it the largest metropolis in Christendom. Most of the demographic growth occurred on the Right (or north) Bank of the Seine, home to the shipping wharves, markets, and banks of the city's thriving economy. The Left (or south) Bank was dominated by the university and was thus called the Latin Quarter, as all instruction, and much of the nonacademic conversation among students and professors, who came from all corners of Europe, occurred in Latin. Both Louis IX and Philip IV made further efforts at urban planning, but the city Eckhart knew remained crowded, noisy, dangerous, and dirty, with visitors often complaining about the pervasive stench of excrement and other refuse tinged with the ubiquitous odor of burned charcoal and wood.

Like Erfurt and Cologne, Paris was home to many who were foreign-born—some merely passing through, others longtime residents—who filled the streets with languages, foods, and apparel from every part of the known world. Most of the city's denizens worked in some sort of commerce or manufacturing. In addition to the large merchant houses and banks, there were more than a hundred different trade guilds, comprising more than 1,300 distinct professions, from goldsmiths to tanners. As in many modern cities, the contrast between rich and poor was stark, with the top 1 percent holding three quarters of the community's wealth and 70 percent of the population too destitute to pay any taxes at all. Most strikingly, especially from a modern perspective, at least a tenth of residents—roughly twenty thousand people—enjoyed clerical status of some sort. This included some eight thousand undergraduates at the university, most of whom were only temporarily considered "religious," but also thousands of monks, mendicants, parish priests, and religious women. As in most urban centers of the era, the day's rhythm was set by church bells that announced the eight monastic hours, and all business was conducted according to the liturgical calendar, with its dozens of public feast days.

The University of Paris, less than a century old but already famous, contributed mightily to the cosmopolitan nature of the city, drawing thousands of students, all male, to pursue undergraduate or graduate degrees.

The great majority of these were in their late teens or early twenties and were technically considered clerics, which entitled them to a kind of diplomatic immunity vis-à-vis local secular authorities. In reality, the character of the university was distinctly practical and worldly. Their monastic tonsures and mandatory gowns notwithstanding, undergraduates were much more likely to be ambitious future professionals than prospective preachers or pastors. Even at the graduate level, classes and degrees often exhibited what one modern historian calls "a vocational emphasis," focusing less on the leisurely contemplation of a classical education than on skills that would fuel career advancement in government, medicine, law, or ecclesiastical administration.

As a return visitor to the university, Eckhart was already familiar with the structures of academic life. Most of his daily activity would have centered on the Left Bank, where professors and especially students were ubiquitous. And they came from everywhere. Officially, the undergraduate student body was divided into four "nations": Picard (primarily made up of students from the Netherlands), English (which also included Germans and Scandinavians), French (made up of students from most regions of France, as well as those from Spain and Italy), and Norman (whose members came exclusively from northwestern France). Classes were conducted entirely in Latin, and residential halls similarly prohibited vernacular tongues in an effort to minimize factions and gossip. Despite the use of paid informers and other disciplinary measures, young men tended to congregate along linguistic lines. Perhaps fortunately for the enhancement of Eckhart's Latin, German speakers constituted a tiny minority of the student body, far outnumbered by peers from England, the Netherlands, and of course France.

During his first sojourn at the university, the young Eckhart was no doubt shocked by the undisciplined living of many students, some as young as fourteen and experiencing full freedom for the first time. Although college statutes repeatedly condemned the frequenting of taverns and "dishonest places," the goliards, or young satirist poets, wrote odes to the vices of "dice, wine, and wenches." Not surprisingly, in student letters that survive from the era, young scholars spent most of their ink requesting more money, ostensibly for food, clothes, rent, and books. In the town-and-gown tradition that has survived to this day, Parisians relied on and often exploited the huge numbers of young men with money in their pockets, yet also deplored the violence and disorder that frequently ensued. A few decades earlier, one particularly destructive student riot, starting with a bar fight, had resulted in several severe injuries and at least one student death. Outraged university masters went on strike for two years until townspeople made further provisions for student safety. As in college towns today, drunken disturbances of various sorts erupted weekly, sometimes daily, particularly during such rowdy winter feasts as St. Nicholas (December 6), when a student was elected bishop for a day, and the particularly notorious Feast of Fools on New Year's Day. The French king Philip Augustus marveled at the aggressive instincts of Parisian undergraduates, exclaiming that they surpassed even those of his knights.

Wealthy families leased entire houses for their sons, staffing them with tutors and servants to keep the young men in classes and out of trouble. The great majority of undergraduates, lacking such resources, rented rooms in houses, or colleges, run by masters or other scholars. Here the university charged the adults with enforcing discipline and helping to identify "putrid members" or "fictitious scholars and hangers-on." The most common offenses ranged from sneaking food out of the kitchen or bringing uninvited friends to dinner to "keeping women or pets in their rooms." Most violations entailed a fine of money or pint of wine; the ultimate punishment of expulsion was kept in reserve. Poorer students slept five or six to a room, and some were even forced to find lodging in a tavern or bordello, with no supervision whatsoever.

The worldly, even materialistic nature of the university and its denizens presented a stark contrast to the plain and regimented life of monks who came to study or teach in Paris. Dominicans and other mendicant orders accordingly strove to cultivate separate enclaves within the larger community for their own students. Eckhart and his fellow friars, for instance, were required to reside at the Dominican house of St. Jacques, located near the southern wall of the Left Bank. Originally a pilgrim hospice dedicated to St. James, the priory served as the primary base for Dominicans in France, who became known as Jacobins. (Not until the much later French Revolution was the name associated with the political club that had taken over the building.) In theory, the Paris priory might house as many as 110 undergraduates each year, but in fact most provinces never sent their full quota of young friars to the university, and the actual number of these "externs" might be only half that.

While excused from choir and some other typical obligations, friar students still followed the Rule in their daily routines, rising at midnight to pray and again before sunrise, eating all meals in house, and retiring to bed by eight p.m. Some of their classes were even held within the walls of St. Jacques itself. As an undergraduate, Eckhart had usually been accompanied to outside lectures or debates by his Dominican *socius* (probably a fellow German), presumably so that each might help the other avoid the temptations surrounding them. Of course, the young friars couldn't completely avoid interactions with secular clerics or laypeople, but they lived a carefully restricted version of the university experience enjoyed by most students.

The Dominican "in but not of the university" approach for its students and teachers naturally generated some tensions with other members of the university as well as townspeople. Since their arrival in the 1220s, mendicants in general had assumed ever more prominent roles in academic life. Their distinctive lifestyle and allegiances, meanwhile, continually put them at odds with the secular clerics who dominated the administration and faculty. When both Dominicans and Franciscans refused to take oaths of obedience to university statutes in 1253, decades of animosity finally burst into the open, culminating in the formal expulsion of mendicant lecturers and students. Friars were routinely assaulted in the streets with impunity, excrement and straw were dumped on them from upper windows as they passed by, and the Dominican house of St. Jacques was even attacked with arrows. After a few years, university administrators lifted the ban, largely under pressure from Pope Alexander IV. Of the fifteen faculty chairs in theology, the university allotted six to be split among five mendicant orders, with two of those going to Dominicans. Of course the formal settlement did little to address collegial or popular resentment of mendicants, a constant source of tension throughout Eckhart's numerous residencies in the city.

Even as a double outsider—Dominican and German—the young friar could not have avoided immersion in the dominant academic culture of Paris. Judging from his brilliant successes and frequent return to the university over the years, it was a way of life he found—at least initially—intoxicating. As an undergraduate, he had attended daily lectures on the seven liberal arts, composed of the *trivium* (grammar, rhetoric, and logic) and the *quadrivium* (arithmetic, geometry, music, and astronomy). As in every subject, classical Roman and Greek authors provided the substance of lessons. The *trivium*, for instance, relied heavily on Donatus (fourth century) and Priscian (fifth century) for teaching Latin grammar, and Aristotle (fourth century BCE) for logic—all works that Eckhart had already encountered during his earlier studies in Erfurt and Cologne. The *quadrivium* featured Aristotle's *Metaphysics*, *Nicomachean Ethics*, and *libri naturales* as standard texts, along with Euclid's *Geometry*. None of Eckhart's subsequent treatises or sermons reflects any interest in the *quadrivium*, but he was undoubtedly well versed at a fundamental level in all four subjects.

Now a lecturer as well as a graduate theology student, Eckhart still began his typical class day at the monastic hour of *prime*, roughly six a.m., delivering a lecture that lasted two to three hours, after which a "student master" summarized the professor's main points in a *repetitio*. At the lowest level, professors lecturing to classrooms full of undergraduates made no pretense of "knowledge production." Their task was essentially that of knowledge transmission. A professor would read long excerpts from the writings of past "masters," particularly Aristotle and St. Augustine, to students from his chair (*ex cathedra*) and explicate the text. Good lecture notes, bolstered by weekly reviews with student masters, provided the key study resources for subsequent oral exams. Given the great cost of parchment, many undergraduates supplemented their own scribblings—crammed to fill every available space on the sheet—with various eight-page book excerpts, known as *peciae*, produced by the scores of copyists working in Paris. College libraries obligingly maintained unbound copies of the most important textbooks, allowing students to borrow individual *peciae* for copying.

Passive reception of traditional wisdom, however, was by no means the sole defining feature of medieval academic culture, even among undergraduates. The scholarly life also had an intensely interactive, often combative

A university lecture. The professor reads from a classical text, occasionally adding
his own interpolations. Medieval scholastics considered themselves dwarves
standing upon the shoulders of giants. They could only see a bit farther
because of the monumental work of their ancient predecessors.

character. Eckhart might have detected hints of rival interpretations among
his professors during their lectures, but the true arena of academic competition was the open *disputatio*. In a disputation, the lecturer would put forward
and defend against all comers "a proposition open to doubt," such as "Adam
and Eve were created mortal" or "It is never permissible to tell a lie." Candidates for a bachelor's degree were required to participate in at least five of
these frequent public events per year. In an ordinary disputation, the *quaestio*
was chosen by the presiding master; in a less frequent and extemporaneous
version, known as the *quodlibet* ("what you please"), the question would
come from the audience. During each two-day debate on a given thesis, masters, lecturers, and a few bold undergraduates would gather in a lecture
room or auditorium and present alternate positions based on their quotation
and interpretation of acknowledged sources. Speakers were often accompanied by loud groups of supporters, sometimes known as "sects," and the
overall atmosphere was not unlike that of a joust, with many students and
teachers attracted as much by great feats of memory and nimble oratory as
by the definitive *determinatio*, pronounced at the end by a presiding regent

master. More than the lecture hall, the disputation, especially in its *quodlibet* form, was where academic reputations were made or destroyed. Thomas Aquinas, to take one outstanding example, participated in more than five hundred ordinary disputations during a two-year period, all delivered to overflowing auditoriums. His *quodlibet* appearances, one in Advent and one in Lent, were openly festive occasions, with all lectures and other classes suspended for the duration.

Dwarves on the Shoulders of Giants

What was not entirely clear to contemporaries outside the university and remains fundamentally elusive for many modern observers is that members of this scholarly culture were not merely arguing for the sake of mental exercise and academic posturing (although there was a fair amount of that too, especially during public disputations). Eckhart and other advanced theological students believed they were living in an exceptionally dynamic period of intellectual exploration, epitomized by the rise of "speculative theology," a field pioneered by Peter Abelard in the previous century. Speculative theology went far beyond the usual issues of morality and ethics to explore profound metaphysical questions about the nature of God and human existence. The very notion that one could question and investigate spiritual matters in a rationalist, "scientific" manner remained revolutionary and controversial. Yet by the time of Eckhart, this unprecedented Christian project of philosophical discovery was in full force. Thus, in addition to disputing the nature of sin and virtue according to the Church Fathers, some professors introduced their advanced students to metaphysical debates about the soul, the intellect, and—most significant for Eckhart's subsequent career—the nature of God.

By far the greatest influence on the budding theologian's thinking was the towering figure of Albrecht of Lauingen, better known as Albert the Great (ca. 1200–1280), a fellow Dominican and a fellow German. Historians still debate whether a passing reference by Eckhart—*Albert always said*—indicates that the two men became personally acquainted during the older man's final years in

Cologne. During Eckhart's formative years, the scholar known as "the wonder and miracle of our time" was regularly quoted by contemporaries—especially Dominicans—as an equal of Aristotle, enjoying during his own lifetime "authority which no man has ever had in doctrine." In the words of a later chronicler, "if he had not been, Germany would have remained an ass." Even Albert's most famous student, Thomas Aquinas, didn't attain as great a level of acclaim until many years after the latter's death in 1274.

Albertus Magnus, aka Albert the Great, the most revered
German scholar of Eckhart's day.

The polymath Albert had been recruited as a young man to the order by Dominic's direct successor, Jordan of Saxony (ca. 1190–1237). As in Eckhart's case, superiors quickly recognized the future theologian's exceptional leadership and intellectual abilities. He was the first German Dominican to become a master of theology at the University of Paris; Eckhart would be one of the last. Also like Eckhart, he served as a German provincial for the order and taught theology at Dominican houses. Most crucially, Albert became a central figure in the thirteenth-century debate over the use of pagan philosophy in Christian scholarship. In 1248, despite much internal resistance, he established the first Dominican *studium generale* at Cologne and proceeded to incorporate Aristotle and pagan philosophy into the order's theological curriculum in 1255.

The European recovery of Aristotle during the previous one hundred years was the most important intellectual development of the era we now know as the Middle Ages. Greek philosophy had been a foundational component of all higher learning during the Roman Empire, but most of that knowledge was lost—along with a great number of Greek texts—following the Western Empire's decline. Byzantine and later Islamic scholars continued to study and debate Plato and Aristotle, but in the West only a small number of Greek manuscripts remained, dutifully copied (but not necessarily understood) by a handful of monks. At the beginning of the twelfth century, just two of Aristotle's works (*Categories* and *On Interpretation*) had been translated into Latin, and Plato's *Timaeus* was the sole representative of his own corpus. Three more centuries would pass before the remainder of Plato's works would be known in the West. Aristotle, by contrast, was about to become the most dominant intellectual figure in all of Christendom.

Between 1150 and 1300, more than forty-two books of Aristotle's were translated into Latin. Most of the new publications came from the translations and commentaries of Islamic philosophers, whose rediscovery of the Greeks in the eighth century had ignited a golden age that was just beginning to wane. The Latin version of *Metaphysics*, for instance, was based on a translation of Avicenna (Ibn Sīnā; ca. 980–1037), perhaps the greatest of a distinguished series of thinkers. At the same time, these Muslim philosophers' own sophisticated analyses themselves became part of the Aristotelian corpus of the thirteenth century. The 1230 Latin version of the *Commentary on Aristotle's Metaphysics* by Averroës (Ibn Rushd; 1126–98), another influential author, would become as well known as Aristotle's original book.

The impact of Aristotle in Eckhart's time is hard to overstate. While many scholars, such as Albert, delighted at the insights of the philosopher on such a vast array of subjects, just as many feared the deleterious effects of Aristotelian thought on Christian faith. Learned opposition to the interweaving of philosophy and revelation dated back to the earliest days of Christianity and would continue well beyond the time of Albert and Eckhart. During the thirteenth century, the most frequent objection concerned the relevance or practicality of speculative theology itself, a discipline occupied with such metaphysical issues as the origin of the universe, the nature

A medieval portrayal of Aristotle,
aka the Philosopher.

of God, and the attributes of the soul. Theology, such critics argued, was for
pursuing good morals and righteous living, not—as Dominican master general Humbert de Romans put it—for "seeking to know the incomprehensible, which cannot be clearly understood either by philosophical reasons or
from holy scripture . . . learning things curious and subtle but of little use."

Even more alarming to these critics, some contemporary admirers of
Aristotle appeared to accept certain claims of "the" Philosopher that contradicted scripture and church tradition. In 1270, just fifteen years after the introduction of Aristotle's writings into the undergraduate curriculum, the
archbishop of Paris, Étienne Tempier, struck the first blow for conservatives,
condemning thirteen such propositions allegedly found in the writings of
"radical" Aristotelians, known as Latin Averroists, because of their admiration for the Muslim philosopher. The young and popular Siger of Brabant,
for instance, appeared to argue that truths derived from religious revelation
could coexist with truths derived from philosophy, even when they seemed
to contradict one another. Christians should accept in faith, he argued, that
God created the universe, even though Aristotle logically proved the absence of such a beginning. Looking for reputable allies, Siger invoked the
ostensible endorsement of the long dead but highly respected Jewish philosopher Maimonides (Moses ben Maimon; 1135–1204), who had conceded that
"something might be impossible in the realm of nature and yet possible in
the supernatural realm."

Obviously this was an unsustainable position, yet the new movement
continued to attract many enthusiastic supporters. Dominican theologians

attempted to find a safe middle ground, arguing that natural philosophy and Christian faith were not only compatible but overlapping and complementary. As the great Thomas Aquinas explained, while some Christian teaching had to be accepted on faith, many truths were knowable through unaided reasons. The controversy over using Aristotle in theology raged on, however, including a second, more comprehensive condemnation of the Averroists in 1277. Not until Eckhart's return to Paris in 1293 had the rancor of his undergraduate years eased, with the incorporation of ancient and recent pagan works mostly accepted among academic theologians.

As a graduate "Reader in Sentences," Eckhart's own lectures focused exclusively on theological questions related to Lombard's *Four Books of Sentences* and the Bible, seemingly safe and uncontroversial topics. Building on his earlier work as a young friar in Erfurt, the more mature Eckhart moved from passive reception of Lombard's points, or *distinctiones*, to an active investigation of specific questions. Lombard himself had actually conceived of his collection as a theological casebook, intended to spur informed conversation—an invitation Eckhart eagerly accepted.

Logic, a component of all undergraduate training, lay at the heart of the dialectical method employed by thirteenth-century theologians. The goal was to extend knowledge on a subject by means of inference from certain authoritative texts as well as from common knowledge. Whether in an oral disputation or on the page of a *summa*, Eckhart and other theologians of his time believed that adversarial debate, the practice of arguing both sides of a question, would demonstrate the truth or falsehood of any statement. After stating a question—for instance the initial query of Aquinas's *Summa Theologica*, "whether sacred science (i.e., theology) is a science"—a debater would begin with the principal objections to an affirmative response, providing evidence for each ("It would seem that sacred science (i.e., theology) is not a science because . . ."). In written format, the author would then rebut his own objections, first stating his thesis ("On the contrary . . ."), then giving evidence in support of that thesis ("I answer that . . ."), then making specific replies to each objection. Although the ostensibly true conclusion did not necessarily satisfy all listeners or readers, consensus emerged on some points, allowing scholars a sense of intellectual progress.

No records survive of Eckhart's lectures from this year, but a later collection, preserved in the Erfurt priory, suggests that a mixture of old and new questions intrigued the young theologian. "Whether theology is a science" (i.e., provable by rational means) continued to be a relevant issue throughout Eckhart's life, as did various questions about the Trinity, the subject of Book I of Lombard's *Sentences*. Typically, a lecture would focus on a question raised by one of the chapters, such as "Whether it is to be granted that God generated Himself" or "How God can be said to be able to do all things, since we can do many things which he cannot do" (such as be mistaken, sin, die, etc.). The Erfurt collection suggests that Eckhart often used the *Sentences* as a launching pad for metaphysical questions of more current academic concern, principally about the intellect, the will, and the soul. And while the *Sentences* relied overwhelmingly on one Church Father in particular—St. Augustine—theologians of Eckhart's generation were far more likely to employ broader scriptural support, thanks to the more accessible format of the Bible, as well as the various non-Christian sources that had come to prominence during the century that had passed since Lombard composed his work.

Eckhart's new academic position allowed him to continue his pursuit of God among the most brilliant theological minds of his day. It also represented a significant career step within the Order of Preachers, enabling him to teach as a principal lector of philosophy at any Dominican house in Europe once he left Paris. His privileges would thereafter include a private study, a research assistant, an allowance for food and clothing, and—perhaps most significant—exemption from all pastoral and administrative duties. In practice, very few Dominicans were permitted to pursue full-time academic careers—Aquinas being the most notable exception—and Eckhart, despite his status as a lector, would in fact be called upon to devote more time to preaching and performing administrative functions once he left Paris and returned to priory life. There are indications that he continued to harbor academic ambitions for at least another two decades, but if he resented their consistent curtailing by the demands of his order, those thoughts are lost to history.

He also recognized that at the University of Paris he was still closer to the

bottom of the hierarchy than to its top. His "Second Bachelor" status was a
step up from undergraduate and "Bible Reader," but still below "Student
Master" (essentially a teaching assistant), which required an additional year
of study, and "Principal Lecturer," which required yet another year. Although Eckhart would eventually attain the status of master (the equivalent
of a modern Ph.D.), the path to that degree must have appeared daunting
and uncertain to the young second bachelor: in addition to the six years of
arts study Eckhart had already completed in the *studium generale* of various
Dominican houses, he would need to complete eight more years of advanced
theological study, including the current academic year. The university typically waived the six-year residence requirement for Dominicans and other
mendicants, so some of this demanding work might be completed back in
Germany, but even then he stood little chance of reaching this goal before
the age of forty.

Eckhart's inferior status among the intellectual aristocracy of Paris was
undoubtedly challenging in other ways. Those very few scholars who attained the vaunted status of master enjoyed considerable power within the
university, leading to a widespread reputation among those below them for
arrogance and caprice. Outside of the academic world, resentment could be
even more palpable, especially toward the admittedly elitist theological faculty. Alvarus Pelagius, a member of the papal curia a generation after Eckhart, skewered the insider culture of professors who "despise simple persons
who know how to avoid faults of conduct better than those of words," choosing instead "to teach useless, vain, and sometimes false doctrine . . . they try
to say what is subtle, not what is useful, so that they may be seen of men and
called rabbis, which is especially reprehensible in masters of theology."
Sometimes outsider resentments were prompted by a more fundamental
anti-intellectualism. Francis of Assisi thought that book learning of any sort
inevitably "puffed up" an individual: When one of his novices asked permission to purchase a psalter, the saint replied, "After that you'll want a breviary. And when you have that, you'll sit in your chair like a prelate and say
to your brother: 'Fetch me my breviary!'"

Whatever personal slights and indignities Eckhart suffered during the early stages of his own academic career, his regular return to Paris suggests that at some point he made his peace with the hierarchies and injustices of university life. His subsequent promotions and other rewards likewise indicate that he became adept at its particular mix of genuine intellectual curiosity and personal ambition. And even a sincerely humble young friar would have had difficulty suppressing his pride in the high degree of success Eckhart would eventually enjoy in this arena, an intellectual accomplishment far beyond the abilities of almost all his fellow Dominicans. How could he not feel a surge of satisfaction upon hearing one of his professors, Henry of Ghent (1217–93), tell promising young scholars that it was far better for a young doctor to use his gifts at the university than to squander them in a parish church? Was not scholarship also a sacred and noble vocation?

Cracking the Celestial Code

There was also the sheer intellectual excitement around speculative theology in Eckhart's university days. To understand what a charged experience this represented to many intelligent seekers, we must suspend most preconceptions about the medieval scholastic endeavor. Since the inception of the university, it has been common to portray the theological work of "the schoolmen" as petty squabbling over unknowable abstractions. Long before the pejorative characterizations of Martin Luther and other Protestant reformers, even during Eckhart's own time, outsiders like Alvarus Pelagius mocked both the jargon and abstractness of professional theologians' debates. Much as today, when a fine point of no apparent real-world significance is dismissed as "academic," most people in Eckhart's time spoke of arguing "in the manner of the schools" to describe quibbling over irrelevant subtleties. There is no known record of an actual scholastic debate on how many angels could dance on the head of a pin (an invention of the later satirist François Rabelais), but the absurdity of both the question itself and the image of a roomful of professors fervently attempting to resolve it has come to emblemize an entire intellectual culture.

From the perspective of Eckhart and his professors, however, they were "scientists" engaged in cutting-edge research on a question of monumental importance—the very nature of reality. Their big questions still preoccupy us today: Why is there something instead of nothing? How does the universe work? What is the place of humans in that universe? With the academic rigor and bold imagination that characterize today's theoretical physicists, they systematically accumulated evidence and built scholarly consensus, all inspired by the goal of achieving a comprehensive outline of human knowledge and—even more exciting—a unifying theory. The intellectual level of their debates and the intense scrutiny applied to all arguments easily matched the cerebral exchanges of a modern MIT conference or Caltech symposium. To grasp the points of contention among scholastic theologians, let alone their very language, required years of specialized training, as well as a tremendous capacity for abstract thinking—an ability to temporarily suspend understanding of "the real world" and engage in prolonged thought experiments that often relied on purely speculative objects and categories.

The guardians of church doctrine from the pope on down may not have understood the specifics of most scholastic arguments, but they were eager to cite scholarly consensus in making pronouncements that suited their own beliefs and goals. The Eucharistic doctrine of transubstantiation, for instance, endorsed by the Council of Lateran IV in 1215, relied on Aristotelian notions of universal essence (which changed from bread and wine to the body and blood of Christ even while the external appearances, or "accidents," remained the same). Most laypeople were even less likely than ordinary clerics to comprehend the subtleties of the schools, but they indirectly experienced the consequences of such debates in the everyday administering and veneration of the sacraments.

At the same time, the *scientia* ("way of knowing") of Eckhart's theology professors was obviously not the same as the science of modern researchers. There is of course a fundamental difference in the nature of proof, but an even bigger difference between the two approaches was the scope of their respective ambitions. Whereas today's cosmologists limit themselves to the material universe and remain officially agnostic on spiritual matters, scholastic theologians took it upon themselves to come up with theories that also encompassed the nonmaterial universe, including God, angels, and the soul. This new quest for a spiritual-material unified theory was controversial in its own time. As is true today, many believers of Eckhart's era saw the two spheres of knowledge—material and spiritual—as overlapping at best, but believed that each relied on essentially different ways of knowing and different sources for evidence. What gave these theological theorists the confidence to undertake such a bold and unprecedented endeavor?

The answer, in a word, is Aristotle. In order to explain something as complex as the universe, speculative theologians needed to break it up into parts and give the parts some kind of order based on mutual relationships. Grafting the dominant concepts and terms of natural philosophy (i.e., natural science) onto theological questions provided Eckhart and his contemporaries with a well-established method of observation, analysis, comparison, and generalization. Aristotle's most basic taxonomy, for instance, which distinguished between the substance, or "essence," of all things and those nonessential traits of individual things called "accidents," allowed thirteenth-century theologians to discuss and categorize all created things, living or inanimate, material or spiritual.

For instance, every discernable "species" of everything in creation, from angels to rocks, was believed to possess an essential nature, defined by a combination of certain attributes. Scholastics referred to this essence as the universal of the species (similar to the Platonic "form"). The universal chicken, for instance, was feathered, warm-blooded, reproduced by laying eggs, and so forth. By various logical means, a scholastic might then distinguish between the essential traits of the universal "chicken" and the secondary, or "particular" traits of distinctive varieties or families of chickens, such as coloring, size, or other aspects of physical appearance.

By the time of Eckhart's study in Paris, this understanding of universals had become the norm among speculative theologians. There was still room, however, for disagreement on whether universals existed in reality. Some scholars believed that universals were part of God's creation but remained essentially abstract ideas from which material examples flowed. For so-called Realists, though—including both Aquinas and Eckhart—universals were real entities in themselves, albeit directly knowable only to God. Everything else in creation—material or spiritual—flowed from this divine constellation of universals.

Thirteenth-century theology was thus a science in the Aristotelian sense, in that it was internally consistent in terms and eminently logical. The integrity of the scholastic system relied on univocity ("one meaning"), a "pure" and constant language like mathematics. Yet as disputations over even the pivotal concept of universals demonstrated, this degree of consensus proved elusive. Many of Eckhart's professors also recognized the challenges inherent in applying Aristotle's categories to spiritual matters. Generalizing about chickens and other poultry is one thing (the favored example of Eckhart's teachers was actually how individual horses participated in the universal "horseness"). Using the same technique to understand the essence of "love" or "the soul" was an endeavor of a completely different order. The even more audacious prospect of reaching back from any particulars and universals to understand the uncreated Creator Himself struck some scholars as hubristic, even blasphemous. Yet whatever the risks, for most members of the Paris faculty of theology—including the young Eckhart—the potential to unlock mysteries of this magnitude was what made the entire project worth the while.

In his studies as a second bachelor, Eckhart learned that there were two generally accepted ways to demonstrate the truth of a philosophical claim about God or any aspect of creation, material or spiritual. The first, called *propter quid* ("on account of which"), was a fact deduced from an indisputable truth. In many instances, this was a priori information attainable to humans only through divine revelation, usually via scripture, and preferably elaborated on by St. Augustine or another Church Father. The most frequent scholastic example was the triune nature of the Godhead—not something that human beings could adduce from the natural world, but once revealed, a truth that could be rationally explored, at least to a certain degree. The second method of demonstration scholastics named *quia* ("because" or "that"), meaning knowledge induced from observed phenomena. One could observe the commonalities of all chickens in the world and thereby come closer to understanding the universal chicken—or tree or human or rock.

Or, to take the most famous example, while humans cannot know God directly, they can induce God's existence by observing various effects in nature. Aquinas actually began his *Summa Theologica* with five such *quia* or "natural" proofs of God's existence: from motion (since rest is the natural state of things, a universe in motion requires a prime, unmoved mover), from efficient causation (since every effect requires a cause, one can work backward from any effect in nature and must eventually arrive at a prime cause), from contingency (a universe of completely contingent beings could not exist; a prime being is necessary), from degrees (all things have degrees, including perfection, which must have a pinnacle), and from the governance of things (the universe reflects intelligent design).

The scholastic method of Eckhart's day was simultaneously traditional—relying on authoritative texts (*auctoritates*) and Aristotelian logic for proof—and innovative, often juxtaposing the wisdom of past masters and Christian teachings in creative ways. What had changed most from the eleventh-century beginnings of scholastic thought to the time of Eckhart's own work at the university was a much greater tendency of theologians to cite pagan and even contemporary scholars as authoritative alongside the Church Fathers of late antiquity. Frequently this approach produced contradictory, even paradoxical results, leading to the bitter disputes for which the theological schools were famous.

Many of those conflicts stemmed from the inevitable incompatibility of even limited empiricism with official dogma. "Authority is the weakest form of proof," Aquinas professed, yet he repeatedly invoked it to support the claims in his own *Summa*. Reason and revelation were compatible, he argued, but they were not interchangeable. When human reason concluded, for instance, that "three persons in one God" was an inherent contradiction, and thus an impossibility, revelation and faith must come to the rescue with the doctrine of the Trinity. Even such a vocal proponent of incorporating the methods of natural philosophy was forced to concede that theology as a whole ultimately relied on divine revelation and was thus more of a *propter quid* science derived from self-evident truths than a purely Aristotelian project of inductive reasoning based on observation. To the twenty-first-century mind, this reliance on revealed truth would disqualify theology as a science

at all and make its claims—including the very existence of God—impossible
to prove at best, at worst, patently false. Not so for Aquinas and his fellow
scholastics, including Eckhart, who found theology's basis in divine revelation reassuring, the equivalent of having the answer key to a set of perplex-
ing problems. This confidence in the powers of human perception and
reason, fortified by the revealed truths of the Bible and the divinely inspired
teachings of the Christian tradition, gave Eckhart and his fellow speculative
theologians hope (their critics said hubris) that they actually might reach up
toward the mind of God.

One protracted debate from Eckhart's day provides an illuminating example of the strengths and weaknesses of the scholastic method, as well as
its internal logic. Virtually every theologian of Eckhart's time, including the
Dominican friar himself, at some point took part in the lively discussion of
angels. Why this apparent obsession with the theological subfield known as
angelology? Certainly angels were a well-embedded part of Christian tradition, inherited from Judaism, and prominent throughout the Old and New
Testaments. Another reason scholastic theologians felt compelled to write
about angels is that they simply never met a question they could resist trying
to answer. This propensity attests to the insatiable curiosity and optimism of
their inquiring minds and helps explain their frequent digression into exceptionally speculative questions of interest only to specialists (hence the
angels-on-the-head-of-a-pin stereotype).

There was, however, a more significant motivation at work, based on the
scholastic conceptualization of the universe as a hierarchical great chain of
being, with God at the top and inanimate objects at the bottom. The proximity of a thing—human, animal, rock—to God determined how much of
God's essence that thing shared. The closer on the chain one got to the Creator, in other words, the closer one got to understanding Him. For example,
any especially saintly person was thought to be closer to God than the average Christian, and this belief gave rise to its own category of scholarly study,
known as hagiography. But if a speculative theologian wanted to get even
closer to the divine essence, the better option was a scientific examination of
angels.

Angels were created beings, like humans, but noncorporeal, like God.

They were, according to scholarly consensus, not eternal like God but they also weren't temporal like humans. Their status was unquestionably far above that of humans, who suffered from the temptations of the flesh and other limitations, but they remained distinct beings from the Godhead. This middle status between God and humans made angels an irresistible subject of study. According to Aristotelian logic, if one could define distinctions at the top of a hierarchy, in this instance between God and the angels, it inevitably helped explain similar phenomena, albeit in debased form, that occurred at a much lower level, such as that of humankind. Angelic love, to take one example, provided both a point of aspiration for humans and a crucial conceptual link between divine love and human love in the scholastic conception of a hierarchical universe.

Theologians carefully avoided arguing that God had been compelled to create angels, since that would be an infringement of His absolute freedom. But Thomas Aquinas, who devoted a significant section of his *Summa Theologica* to the subject, openly admitted that "the perfection of the universe"—as scholastics understood it—"requires the existence of an incorporeal creature," that is, angels. What he and another prominent angelologist, the Franciscan St. Bonaventure (aka the Seraphic Doctor), called "beings of pure intelligence" were indispensable components of their scientific model, a kind of medieval Higgs boson particle. Unlike modern physicists, though, scholastics did not build elaborate machinery to establish the existence of their theoretical link; they turned, as always, to the usual written authorities, which they interrogated with a rigorous sense of higher purpose.

Most of the groundwork for thirteenth-century angelology had been laid in the six centuries following the death of Christ. Both Paul and Augustine wrote about angels as divine servants and aspirational models for humans. Several later fathers—most notably Ambrose (ca. 340–97), Jerome (ca. 347–420), Gregory the Great (ca. 540–604), and especially Pseudo-Dionysius (sixth century)—actually enumerated nine angelic orders, each endowed with a specific heavenly function.

The major intellectual work at Eckhart's University of Paris, however, was less concerned with a seating chart of heaven than with various metaphysical and physical questions prompted by angels' unique status in creation between God and humans. Why and where, specifically, did God create angels? Do they have form and matter? What does it mean to be ageless and sexless? To have a spiritual body? Do angels speak with their mouths or in some other way? If they don't have bodies, can they exist in a certain place, or be in several places at once? Are angels capable of joy or other emotions? Can they see the future? There was virtually no question Eckhart's professors could resist asking about angels, impelled by their hierarchical model of creation and the Aristotelian tools of analysis and debate now at their disposal. And in the process, of course, they would also learn more about those above and below angels in the hierarchy of creation, that is, about God and humankind.

As always, passages from the scriptures and Church Fathers often provided evidentiary support, but both the questions and their answers were constrained by the core assumptions of the scholastic system. Because scholastic consensus taught, for instance, that individuation—creation of an individual from a universal—required matter, the only logical conclusion was that each of the hundreds of millions of noncorporeal angels had to be its own species. A few scholars proposed a nebulous kind of "spiritual matter," but no scholastic would have questioned the starting assumption about individuation (or universals), leaving a befuddled Godfrey of Fontaines (ca. 1250–1309) to agree with the conclusion but concede that such a plurality of angelic species was "difficult to understand." In this instance and in countless others, the science of God, in other words—despite its rigorous logic and insights—proved itself an elaborate construct built on faith, not just in Christian doctrine but in the Aristotelian method itself.

Eckhart was an eager participant in this inspired project of discovery, yet he was also attuned early on to the dangers of hubris among his fellow explorers at the university. Naturally he encountered some arrogant senior academics, impervious to criticism and ripe for rebuke in the name of humility. But as his Easter sermon from 1294 indicates, Eckhart was concerned with something beyond mere academic courtesy, a more fundamental notion of scholarly humility. As he explained, the writings of Aristotle and all philosophers provided many useful tools for understanding God's creation, but reason alone could lead to some flawed conclusions—as the Averroists had discovered twenty years earlier. Like his contemporary the English monk Roger Bacon (ca. 1220–92), Eckhart believed that a Christian philosopher should think of his task as "correcting Aristotle through a pious and reverential interpretation."

As a junior and later senior scholar, Eckhart would continue to employ the dominant academic language and methodology of the day in his pursuit of God. And later, in the German sermons where he questioned church teaching to the point of near heresy, he would consistently rely on the phrases and terms of the scholastic world model—including many references to angels. Gradual dissatisfaction with the limitations of academic discourse would never lead him to abandon his youthful faith in the accumulated wisdom of prophets and masters before him, or his confidence in rational exploration. Whatever its flaws, the university was a place where ideas about God were taken seriously. In that sense, the alien academic community Eckhart first encountered years earlier would become a home and refuge to him, second only to the Erfurt priory itself.

It was, in fact, his duty to that first home that would compel the young friar to leave Paris in the summer of 1294. The order had called him to return to Erfurt to serve as head of the priory. Now thirty-four and recognized by the university as a second bachelor, he put aside—at least for the moment—the life of the scholar. Taking up the few travel provisions allowed and accompanied by a small band of brother Dominicans, Eckhart walked back through the Saint-Denis gate and turned his steps toward Erfurt.

CHAPTER SIX

Master of Learning

Now a master [i.e., Aristotle] says no man is so foolish that he does not desire wisdom. Why, therefore, do we not become wise? Much is required for this. The main thing is that a man must pass through and transcend all things, and the causes of things, and a man becomes weary of this, and so man stays in his pettiness.

GERMAN SERMON 10

A Scholastic Mind

One late summer evening in 1302, Eckhart was again in Paris, this time the focus of great attention. After an interval of four years as prior of Erfurt and four additional years during which his activities are lost to history, the now middle-aged friar had finally reached the pinnacle of academic learning—installation as a master of theology in the premier faculty of Christendom. The solemn ceremony of induction required two days, beginning on the first evening at vespers (roughly seven p.m.) in the priory of St. Jacques. All other lectures and disputations had been suspended that day, so that the theology masters and bachelors (graduate students) could make final preparations for a *disputatio* in Eckhart's honor.

Four debate questions had been circulated among the group eight days earlier. (Unfortunately, no record of these questions has survived.) After a brief introduction by the most senior master, teams of masters and bachelors successively debated the first two questions, allowing the guest of honor to formulate his own response to each. At the conclusion of the last debate, the presiding master made a few remarks about the teaching of sacred scriptures, then closed with a bit of wry commentary on Eckhart himself, something akin to a modern roast.

On the morning of the second day, around ten a.m., all masters and bachelors of theology again assembled at St. Jacques. Eckhart sat in the center of the dais, with the chancellor of the university on his right side, along with all the senior masters, and the presiding master on his left, together with the junior professors. At a signal from the chancellor, all the young men about to receive their bachelor's degree came forward and presented their sworn testimony to Eckhart, who accepted their oaths on behalf of all the masters. Then the presiding master rose and reverently set the traditional cap of learning on Eckhart's head, saying, "I place on you the magisterial biretta in the name of the Father, of the Son, and of the Holy Spirit."

Surviving records don't indicate whether this ritual was followed by loud acclamation from the assembled scholars or a moment of reverential silence. While Eckhart remained standing, the chancellor rose and solemnly proclaimed the new master's right to teach. After Eckhart's brief inaugural lecture (also no longer extant), the students and bachelors debated the third and fourth questions, followed by dialogues between the senior and junior masters, with Eckhart ceremoniously deciding which team's argument had carried the day. Finally, the newest member of the theology guild led a joyous procession to a feast in his honor, which might have lasted the rest of the day and would include a second lecture by Eckhart, as well as more disputations. Henceforth his Latin-speaking colleagues would address him as Magister (Master) Eckhart. To the German speakers in his homeland he was Meister Eckhart, the name by which he would come to be known to subsequent generations the world over.

For the next three academic years, Meister Eckhart was to hold the St. Giles chair as regent professor of theology at the University of Paris, a position of great honor previously occupied by both Albert the Great and Thomas Aquinas. Having already served as prior of Erfurt for four years, Eckhart was being groomed by the Dominican master general as a future

leader of the order. There were only two regent professorships allotted annually to foreign Dominicans, and in recent years the honor had gone almost exclusively to Italian friars. The last German to receive the chair before
Eckhart was one of Albert's most eminent pupils, Ulrich of Strasbourg, who
unfortunately had died en route to Paris twenty-five years earlier.

Eckhart's summons to the prestigious professorship thus represented not
just a personal triumph but a victory for his entire province. His responsibilities included lecturing daily on one book of the Bible (apparently he chose
Genesis), presiding over a weekly disputation, and preaching every Sunday
at St. Jacques or elsewhere. He was also expected to serve on bachelor examination panels with three fellow masters. In return, the university provided
him with two graduate teaching assistants who handled all communications
and negotiations with undergraduates, including the payment of fees. As a
Dominican, Meister Eckhart was exempt from the usual university taxes
and his living and book costs were assumed by the St. Jacques priory, where
he resided.

What of his continuing pursuit of God? Although only a few disputation
questions and one sermon survive from Eckhart's first academic year as a
master, he was clearly still intent on the same intellectual project he had
announced during his Easter sermon eight years earlier at St. Jacques: the
construction of a philosophy of Christianity, arrived at by combining the
wisdom of both pagan and Christian thinkers. This was in fact an endeavor
shared by several of his fellow Dominican theologians. Albert the Great had
been one of the first and strongest advocates of a new metaphysics, as was
his student Thomas Aquinas, who so masterfully interwove Aristotle and
Augustine, philosophy and theology, in his *Summa Theologica*. When the
archbishop of Canterbury and other church leaders throughout Europe
lauded the 1277 Parisian condemnation of the Averroists, the Dominicans of
Cologne had pronounced it a mere local decision and continued to investigate scripture with a more moderate combination of reason and revelation
in the tradition of their common mentor Albert.

The most important direct Dominican influence on Eckhart, however,
was not Albert or Aquinas but Dietrich of Freiberg (ca. 1250–ca. 1319). A decade older than his protégé, Dietrich followed a career path very similar to

Eckhart's, including coursework at the *studium generale* of Cologne from 1267 to 1270 (possibly under Albert himself), further theological study at the University of Paris from 1272 to 1277 (overlapping with Aquinas), a brief stint as lector at the priory of Trier (1280–81), and twelve years as a lecturer in Paris. He met and got to know Eckhart when they both lived in the St. Jacques house, during the younger man's year of study in 1286–87, if not earlier. In 1293, Dietrich was elected provincial of Teutonia, whereupon he immediately appointed Eckhart to a graduate lectureship in Paris. A year later, he approved the election of the young friar as Erfurt prior, guaranteeing that he would see Eckhart at least twice a year at provincial and general meetings.

Dietrich of Freiberg's influence on Eckhart went far beyond his promotion of the younger man's career in the order. He read the same texts as his protégé, and was likely the person who introduced Eckhart to some of them, particularly Neoplatonist works. He embraced the same scholastic method and expressed himself in a precise (and dry) Latin similar to that in the younger man's scholarly writings. (By contrast, Eckhart's German sermons ring with rhetorical flourishes.) Most important, Dietrich's conception of reality itself, including the relationship of the individual soul to the divine essence, profoundly shaped Eckhart's own thinking.

Like most speculative theologians, Dietrich sought a unifying theory for the material and spiritual worlds. He differed in some significant ways, however, from his fellow Dominican Aquinas, and he passed some of that skepticism about the Thomist model on to Eckhart. The most important way in which the mentor and his acolyte differed was their ultimate intellectual goal. While Dietrich's writings on the Beatific Vision (a direct experience of the divine) clearly influenced Eckhart, the older man looked more to an intellectual appreciation of all creation through natural philosophy. Light, he believed, was the key to a universal theory encompassing both the material and spiritual realms, and Dietrich subsequently devoted far more attention to theories of optics, including a famous treatise on rainbows. Eckhart, meanwhile, continued to pursue a subjective experience of God, with learning playing a supportive role.

His pursuit of that goal, however, remained entrenched in the culture of scholasticism. As a regent professor of theology, Meister Eckhart had to follow the conventional rules of argumentation or risk accusations of irrational—or worse yet—unscholarly behavior. Accordingly, Eckhart's disputation questions were (unlike his German sermons) terse, dialectical, and full of scholastic jargon. He wielded such concepts as universals, species, distinctions, and accidents with confidence and careful qualifications. Logic, not rhetorical eloquence, was the prime scholastic aesthetic; mastering its established vocabulary and methods was essential if Eckhart wanted his arguments to have bearing on the larger controversies debated by his peers.

The influence of scholasticism was not limited to form and style. The regent professor likewise embraced that other conceptual foundation of speculative theology: the great chain of being. Like his mentor Dietrich, Eckhart framed his arguments around three hierarchical levels of being: intelligences (God and the angels), human souls, and bodies (including human bodies and the animal world). All creatures, he believed, possessed something of the divine essence and were thus linked with one another, albeit in graduated ranks determined by their respective proximity to the Creator. *Nature*, he wrote, *does not make a leap, but descends in an ordered process or progressive order by degrees, and in the smallest steps possible.* In a later sermon, Eckhart acknowledged that this interconnectedness of all creation was not a recent or even a Christian idea:

> *Pagan masters say that God has so ordered all creatures that one is always above the others, and that the highest touch the lowest and the lowest the highest. What these masters have declared in obscure words, another states openly, saying that the golden chain is pure and bare nature, which is raised up to God and which relishes nothing that is outside of Him, and which touches God. Each creature affects the other, and the foot of the highest is set on the crown of the lowest.*

Like his fellow theologians, Eckhart relied on the great chain of being to construct unified theories of reality. But the interconnectedness of all creation was more than an abstract philosophical concept to him; he frequently expressed awe at the beauty of the whole. As he wrote in a later reflection on

A late medieval portrayal of the great chain of being, with plants and animals furthest from the Divine Creator, humans above them, and angels closest.

this period of his life, *I used to wonder . . . whether I should be asked why one blade of grass is so unlike another; and as it happened, I was asked why they are so different. Then I said it is more marvelous that all blades of grass are so much alike.* His own spiritual affinity with all the interconnected parts of creation also provided him great comfort, as he explained in a later German sermon: *If I were in a wilderness alone and was afraid, the presence of a child would dissipate my dread and give me courage, so noble, so joyous and mighty a thing is life itself. And failing a child, even a beast would comfort me. . . . Likeness gives strength in all things.* This likeness, he would preach, is not mere similarity but a shared divinity, and extends to all of God's creation. *The masters say all creatures are striving to bring forth and to emulate the Father. . . . [I]f God had not previously begotten something that was uncreated that [thing] bore within itself the images of all creatures.*

Eckhart also accepted but adapted the conventional authoritative texts of the day to his purpose. Like virtually all academic theologians of his time, he possessed a thorough knowledge of the philosophical works of Aristotle and his medieval commentators. In the academic works that have survived,

Meister Eckhart makes more than two hundred explicit references to "the Philosopher" and thirty-one direct mentions of "the Commentator," Averroës. But the two non-Christian masters he most admired were the Persian polymath Avicenna, whom he explicitly cited 102 times in his Latin works, and the Jewish philosopher Maimonides, known to Eckhart as "Rabbi Moses," whom he directly quoted 119 times. Together with several Neoplatonist authors (to be encountered in the next chapter), these two towering figures provided Eckhart with creative ways to talk and think about the ineffable Creator and his creation, as well as the individual soul's return journey to God, a topic of particular concern. By comparison, Thomas Aquinas—the pride of the Dominicans, who was on the cusp of becoming a preeminent theological authority (not to mention a saint)—merited only sixty-five explicit mentions.

The most important intellectual and spiritual inspiration for Eckhart throughout his life was Augustine, whom he quoted directly nearly three times as often as Aristotle in his Latin works. The new regent professor had been steeped in many of the saint's works from his days as a lecturer on the Augustine-heavy *Sentences* of Peter Lombard. By the time of his elevation to master of theology, Eckhart had become an expert on Augustine's writings, especially his cherished *Confessions*. "Let me know Thee who knowest me, let me know Thee even as I am known" are words that resonated deeply with the German friar, nine centuries after they were written—words that he himself might have written. In the bishop of Hippo's lifelong struggle toward God Eckhart recognized his own passionate pursuit of the Creator, although Augustine described his journey in a much more emotional fashion than the more circumspect professor would ever embrace. Only the Bible itself outranked Augustine as an authority in Eckhart's Latin writings, and even there, he usually fell back on an Augustinian reading of the passage in question.

The profound kinship between the two men was especially evident in Eckhart's approach to biblical exegesis, or spiritual interpretation of biblical passages. Like Augustine, he compared the richness of sacred scriptures to *the deep sea*. But without guidance, even the clever and pious reader risks drowning in the vastness of the Holy Writ. The Bible, according to Eckhart, is not a collection of logical demonstrations or natural philosophy (*scientia*) but rather, borrowing the words of Maimonides about the Old Testament, *a book of spiritual wisdom* (*sapientia*). Every passage, he believed, had two basic levels: *the plain meaning [or] the surface of the letter [and other meanings] hidden beneath the shell*. His commentary on the first line of Genesis, for instance, contained seven philosophical explanations and ten points on the moral meaning of the verse "In the beginning God created Heaven and earth." This plurality of truths beneath the shell or surface led Eckhart to again exclaim, *I am astonished that Holy Scripture is so full, and the masters say they are not to be interpreted barely as they stand: they say that if there is anything crudely material in them it must be expounded, but for this parables are necessary.*

In parables, virtually every word had multiple meanings, many of them *hidden beneath sensible figures* and requiring special diligence and insight on the part of the reader. God deliberately made the surface meaning more accessible, with the hope that deeper understanding would eventually follow. Like his master Augustine, Eckhart believed that the meaning offered "in a most humble style of speaking . . . arouses the attention of those who are not light-hearted."

In admitting his fondness for using ambiguous symbols and paradoxes in his own writing, Eckhart explained, *I do this to arouse the more skilled readers to seek better and richer explanations of the theological, natural, and moral truths hidden behind the form and surface of the literal sense, both in the few passages I briefly treat and in the many others I omit.* Again quoting Augustine, who called the Bible a "book of mysteries," he compared extraction of this multifarious *mystical understanding* of parables to *bringing honey forth from the depths of the honeycomb or rubbing the ears of grain with our hands to find the hidden kernels. No one,* he reiterated, *can be thought to understand the Scriptures who does not know how to find its hidden marrow—Christ, the Truth.*

Of course Eckhart's method did not guarantee that every reader would find the same meanings. He conceded as much, noting that often the same scriptural *words [have been] interpreted in different ways by different saints,* as well as by distinguished Jewish scholars, such as Maimonides. But unlike those who feared such diversity of interpretation, Eckhart reveled in the astounding variety of ways that God's revelation could assist readers on their respective spiritual journeys. In fact, in his own works, he frequently provided multiple interpretations of a single line of scripture so that fellow Christians might learn to consider a wide range of possible meanings. As he wrote in the conclusion to his commentary on the gospel of John: *Please note that the preceding words have been interpreted in many ways so that the reader can freely take now one and now the other as seems useful to him. I use the same method of multiple exposition in many of my commentaries.* As the prior Brother Eckhart had preached to young friars in his *Talks of Instruction*, there was no one universal path to God. Moreover, *since the literal sense is that which the author of a writing intends, and God is the author of the holy scripture, as has been said, then every true sense is a literal sense . . . every truth comes from the Truth itself.* Here, as in many of his own scriptural interpretations, Eckhart was following his favorite authorities, Augustine and Maimonides. God's truth was so powerful, they all believed, that it could potentially reach anyone reading the Bible, *even if the [human] author he is reading [had] not grasp[ed] it.*

Eckhart's lifelong dedication to both usefulness and subjectivity in his own pursuit of God consequently led him to make eclectic—some might say arbitrary—choices of which biblical texts to explicate. Like his hero Augustine, he favored books that he thought had the most interpretive possibilities, particularly Genesis (which he wrote about twice), Exodus, Wisdom, and the gospel of John. He showed no interest in narrative or history or broader context in general. His *Commentary on John*, for instance, focused intensely on the Prologue ("In the beginning was the Word . . .") but omitted nearly the entire life and passion of Jesus. His especially copious *Commentary on Exodus* used only fourteen of the book's forty pericopes, or subsections. Some modern scholars have argued that Eckhart treated the Bible as a "hypertext," with his own complex system of intertextual references, pasting together various fragments that served his argument. Certainly, a general disregard for context was common among speculative theologians (including Aquinas), but Eckhart took this tendency to new lengths, actively encouraging diverse and subjective readings—as long as they resonated with larger truths.

The Dialectical Path to Truth

As with his *Talks of Instruction*, given a few years earlier, it is mainly in hindsight that we perceive Eckhart's more radical tendencies in the writings he produced during his time as a regent professor in Paris. In most respects, he was still thinking and writing like a typical scholastic, albeit one consumed by a personal spiritual quest. His three surviving disputations from 1302–3 accordingly reflect his ongoing pursuit of God, but couch it in the context of the leading scholarly debates of the day. Now that he was a member of the theological guild, Eckhart intended to further bolster his intellectual reputation by proving both his mastery of relevant terms and concepts and the distinctiveness of his own scholarly project. In short, he sought to make his own mark as a theologian, and the surest way to do that was to weigh in on the contentious issues of the moment.

For more than twenty years, the most controversial topic among speculative theologians had been the relationship between existence (*that* something is) and essence (*what* something is). Resolving this question could yield one of the first principles that scholastic metaphysics relied on for a variety of scientific deductions. If existence and essence were distinct from each other, for instance, which had priority? If they were the same, what was the relationship between God, who had no beginning, and humans, who did? Without any preexisting essence, some argued, humans must first exist and then derive their essence from God (a kind of medieval existentialism).

As in the twentieth-century debate on the relationship between time and gravity, a lot of contingent questions hung in the balance. Plato had argued that all living things shared the same essence, but this posed problems for Christian philosophers who believed that each human soul—and its path to salvation—was distinct. Aristotle, by contrast, thought it meaningless to distinguish between the existence of a thing and its essence. Instead, he preferred to speak of the difference between primary and secondary substances—or, in scholastic terms, between universals, the perfect form of each thing, which had always existed, and particulars, the countless individual iterations of each thing, which came into being at a certain time and exhibited a particular constellation of the essential qualities of the universal.

The debates Eckhart participated in at the University of Paris mainly focused on whether there was a real or merely a formal distinction between existence and essence. For example, during Eckhart's previous stay as a lector, the Augustinian monk Aegidius Romanus (ca. 1243–1316) engaged in a number of famous debates on the subject with Master Henry of Ghent, who claimed there was no distinction at all between the two. Thomas Aquinas, by contrast, argued that the distinction was real, that is, existence and essence were two different principles of things that could be separated—and that existence came first. In the years following his death, this Thomist position was taken up by a number of his fellow Dominicans.

Again, the terms and the arguments of the debate were highly technical; it is less important to grasp the specifics than the intellectual stakes. Eckhart's entry into the fray during his year as a regent professor is represented by two surviving disputation questions: *Are Intellect and Being identical in God?* and *Is an Angel's Understanding, as it denotes an action, the same as his existence?* In both instances, Meister Eckhart's response was no, but his reasoning was quite different from that of his revered Dominican predecessor Aquinas. In the first disputation, he actually turned Brother Thomas on his head, accepting the real distinction between existence and essence, but boldly refuting six of the Angelic Doctor's arguments for the priority of existence. According to Eckhart, *understanding,* which he identified as an aspect of essence, *is superior to existence and belongs to a different order.* Thus God's understanding, or His thinking, preceded His existence; by thinking, God brought Himself into existence so that His own being was the first of all created things. *I am no longer of the [Thomist] opinion that God understands because he exists, but rather that he exists because he understands. . . . God is intellect and understanding and understanding itself is the foundation of His being.*

This was not an earlier version of Descartes' famous *cogito ergo sum,* which was meant as a proof of the thinker's existence. Eckhart did not doubt the existence of God or humans and thus did not seek to prove it. Rather he sought to reverse Aquinas's existential argument—God thinks because He is—and argued instead that, for God as well as for humans, thinking *is* the act of being. He was heavily influenced by Dietrich in this approach, but the new master went further than his mentor, proposing pure thought itself as the reason for and substance of reality, the cause of all things, including time and space. This argument was not mere theological sparring for Eckhart; its purpose was intensely practical and personal. In the idea that pure thought is both the cause of God's existence and the essence of His being, Eckhart had found the key to his own lifelong pursuit of God. For if God is thought, and some small part of God exists in the essence of every human being, then human thought offers a direct connection to the Creator. The intellect provided the link he had been searching for.

Eckhart's favoring of the intellect stemmed from a Dominican tradition going back to Albert—hardly surprising in a religious order that so esteemed learning. It was also the subject of a secondary, ongoing debate between Dominicans and Franciscans over whether the intellect or the will is the primary pathway to God. These terms are not as self-evident as they appear. Intellect, for example, was considered to be compatible with reason but was not the same thing. The closest modern equivalent would be "intuition." As Thomas Aquinas explained, "Intellect is the simple (i.e., indivisible) grasp of an intelligible truth, whereas reasoning is the progression towards an intelligible truth by going from one understood point to another. The difference between them is thus like the difference between rest and motion or between possession and acquisition." Aquinas believed the intuitive way of knowing to be a more reliable pathway to God than reason, but cautioned that many divine truths remain beyond the grasp of either type of human thought. For Dietrich and his protégé Eckhart, however, intellect was much more than a pathway to God—it was a direct experience of the divine mind. Intellect in individual humans, they argued, was the shared part of divine essence that was able to recognize itself and its Creator.

Similarly, the term "will" denoted more than simple desire to the mostly Franciscan scholars who argued for its primacy over the intellect. God, they pointed out, wants humans to love Him but He wants it to be a free choice. Accordingly, the will is the choice, freely made, to love God, and, because of that love, to follow God's ways. The supreme example of this was Christ's own willingness to suffer and die on a cross—a choice freely made out of love for God that resulted in the salvation of the world. Will and choice also lay at the heart of medieval Christianity. In the minds of most clerics and laypeople alike, understanding the ways of God was difficult, if not impossible, and—in the end—less important than choosing to perform the concrete acts of love and devotion that would ensure personal salvation.

Sometime during Eckhart's regent professorship, he entered into a public disputation on this subject with the holder of the Franciscan regent professorship, Gonsalvo of Spain (ca. 1255–1313). The question they addressed was a typical scholastic offshoot of the larger issue: "Is the praise of God in heaven more excellent than the love of God in this life?" Gonsalvo argued that love (which was expressed through the will) was more important than praise (which was a result of knowing God). Eckhart asserted that intellect held preeminence over being, and being over love and free will. Love, he said, represented a mere striving toward God, while through the intellect, a believer experienced God directly. Eckhart's position in the debate put him in the odd situation of seemingly denigrating the love of God, yet he refused to waver. Will and love, he argued, focused on God's attributes rather than His essence and thus remained inferior to the intellect, which yielded a direct experience of God:

> Will and love fall on God as being good, and if He were not good, they would ignore Him. Intellect penetrates right up into the essence without heeding goodness or power or wisdom, or whatever is accidental. It does not care what is added to God, it takes Him in Himself, sinks into the essence and takes God as He is pure essence. Even if He were not wise nor good nor just, it would still take Him as pure being.

One of the preacher Eckhart's favorite metaphors compared God to a naked man in his dressing room, completely exposed, stripped of all his adornments and protective clothing. Intellect embraced the man himself; love (or the will) remained obsessed with the fine garb the man has cast off: Goodness is a cloak under which God is hidden, and will takes God from under the cloak of goodness. If there were no goodness in God, my will would not want Him. In this way, Eckhart explained, love was not only inferior to knowing, it held the seeker back from actually encountering God. *Love infatuates and entangles us in goodness, and in love I remain caught up in the gate, and love would be blind if knowledge were not there. A stone also possesses love, and its love seeks the ground.*

Putting aside Eckhart's premodern understanding of gravity, his main point is clear: in the pursuit of God, go straight to the source, without intermediaries or attributes. In a departure from Eckhart's view during his priory days that discipline and willpower were key to the pursuit of God, the scholastic Eckhart now identified the intellect as both the source of God's being and the only direct and reliable human connection to the essence of that being. Freedom of will was still real, he conceded, but it would be pointless without knowing God and His truth.

A Masterwork for the Ages

Eckhart's participation in scholastic debates during the 1302–3 academic year helped the new master crystallize his thinking on the two mysteries that were most important to him: the nature of God and the connection between God and humans. By the end of his tenure as regent professor, a new and coherent theology had begun to emerge. While clearly drawing on the tradition of Albert and Dietrich, the interpretations of the friar from Erfurt already displayed many of the distinctive traits for which he would become famous. The coalescence of his diverse thoughts and experiences into a system marked a significant turning point in his spiritual quest. It would be several years before Meister Eckhart took the still bolder step of preaching on how to put his understanding of the divine-human bond into practice. Instead, he poured himself into a project that most successful scholastics attempted but only a select few achieved: writing a scholarly magnum opus, or *summa*, that would elevate him to the ranks of the theological giants.

To understand the irresistible appeal of the *summa* among academic theologians, consider these lines from the introduction to Lombard's *Sentences*, a work all scholastics knew intimately: "In this brief volume, we have brought together the sentences of the Father and the testimonies apposite to them, so that one who seeks them shall find it unnecessary to rifle through numer-

ous books, when this brief collection effortlessly offers him what he needs."
Lombard's work served that inspirational purpose for many generations, but
soon other scholars were attempting to build on the *Sentences* or even improve upon it. Alexander of Hales (ca. 1185–1245), aka the Unanswerable Doctor, authored the first major commentary on the *Sentences*, itself a *summa*,
but was unable to complete the magnum opus before his death. While his
fellow Franciscans revered and continued his work, Alexander's reputation
had waned by the end of the thirteenth century, with his massive volume
mocked by Roger Bacon (1214–92) for being as heavy as a horse and full of
errors. Like Albert and Dietrich, Bacon (aka the Miracle Doctor) looked to
natural philosophy for a unifying metaphysical theory, although he decried
the great deference accorded Albert as an unprecedented "monstrosity,"
given the latter's indirect and incomplete knowledge of Aristotle.

To Bacon's disappointment, his own attempt at a universal vision received
little attention among contemporary theologians, especially compared with
the brilliant and influential Franciscan scholar Duns Scotus (ca. 1266–1308).
Admirers and enemies alike considered Scotus the most philosophically
talented theologian of the day. His *summa*, framed as a commentary on
Lombard's *Sentences*, aimed to surpass all previous works on the subject,
including the esteemed four-volume commentary of his fellow Franciscan
Bonaventure. Like Eckhart, Duns Scotus sought a theory encompassing
God and all His creatures, for "unless being implies one single concept, theology will simply perish." Eckhart encountered Scotus during his regent
professorship, when the Scotsman came to Paris to lecture on the *Sentences*.
We don't know the nature of their personal relationship, but the two men
shared many beliefs about the divine essence, even though they disagreed
about its distinction from existence. Later in that academic year, Scotus was
expelled from the university for siding with Pope Boniface VIII in his feud
with King Philip IV of France over the taxation of church property. Within
five years, Scotus was dead at the age of forty-two, his much-anticipated but
incomplete *summa* surviving mainly in lecture notes and disputation questions from his time at Oxford and Paris.

Sometime during this academic year, Meister Eckhart resolved to write
his own *summa*. Of course the competing achievement foremost in his mind

John Duns Scotus, considered by most scholastic
peers to be the most talented theologian in
Eckhart's day.

was the magisterial *Summa Theologica* of his fellow Dominican Aquinas. Aquinas's reputation outside the Order of Preachers was still far from the universal acclamation he enjoyed in later Catholic tradition. Duns Scotus, for one, clearly considered Henry of Ghent a more formidable intellectual rival than Aquinas, even though he had more in common with the anti-Aristotelian Henry. Among Dominicans, however, the thirty-year-old magnum opus had already taken on canonical status: Aquinas's *summa* was *the summa* Eckhart needed to surpass, or at least challenge. Yet if he disagreed with the Angelic Doctor on any point, the argument still needed to be couched in respectful, if not reverential, terms.

Like Aquinas, Meister Eckhart presented his prospective work as an aid to theological beginners. His goal, he claimed, was *to satisfy as far as possible the desires of some of the diligent friars who already for a long time with pressing requests had often asked and compelled me to put in writing what they used to hear from me in lectures and other school activities, and also in preaching and daily conversations.* For Eckhart, all intellectual endeavors needed to have some practical justification of this sort. His objective remained the one he had announced in his Easter sermon nine years earlier: a philosophy of Christianity that allowed the seeker to see behind the curtain of perceived reality and know God directly.

Also like Aquinas, Eckhart relied on a supposedly seamless combination of Christian revelation and natural philosophy, although his preferred

St. Thomas Aquinas, holding his *Summa Theologica* and flanked
by his pagan predecessors, Plato and Aristotle.

sources more closely followed the Aristotelian interpretation of Maimonides
than that of his Dominican predecessor. The scope of the German master's
ambition is evident in his remarkable claims about thoroughness:

> By way of preface, it should be noted beforehand that I have gone through the
> Old and New Testaments in order from beginning to end and I have written
> down whatever came to me then and whatever I remembered I said about the
> interpretation of these authoritative texts at any time. Not to be long-winded,
> I have taken care to abbreviate or to omit completely most of it, especially so
> that the better and more useful interpretations that the saints and venerable
> teachers, particularly Brother Thomas [Aquinas], have written are not ne-
> glected. On a few occasions I decided merely to note where their interpreta-
> tions are to be found.

Eckhart's foundational premise of unifying all knowledge likewise
echoed the confidence of Aquinas and all members of the Dominican tradition of Albert:

> What the philosophers have written about the natures and properties of things
> agrees with [the Bible], especially since everything that is true, whether in

*being or in knowing, in scripture or in nature, proceeds from one source
and one root of truth. . . . Therefore, Moses, Christ, and the Philosopher
[i.e., Aristotle] teach the same thing, differing only in the way they teach.*

In rare instances of conflict, he added, obviously the opinions of pagan masters, *who knew only by the light of nature*, should always give way to the words
of *saintly masters, who knew by a much higher light. My intention*, Eckhart wrote,
*is the same as in all my works—to explain what the holy Christian faith and the two
Testaments maintain through the help of the natural arguments of the philosophers—*
not the other way around, as with the Averroists.

Also like Aquinas, Eckhart conceived of his own *summa* as a three-part
work, and that in fact became its name: the *Opus Tripartitum*. The planned
scale of the work, described by Eckhart at the end of his year in Paris, was
breathtaking. Whereas the entire *Summa Theologica* of Aquinas comprised
512 questions (subdivided into 2,669 articles, with more than 10,000 objections), Part I of the *Opus Tripartitum* alone would contain more than twice
that number of theological propositions, divided into fourteen tracts on
paired conceptual opposites: 1. Being/Nothingness; 2. Unity/Multiplicity; 3.
Truth/Falseness; 4. Good/Bad; 5. Love/Sin; 6. Virtues/Vices; 7. Whole/
Parts; 8. Common/Particular; 9. Upper/Lower; 10. First/Last; 11. Ideal and
Unformed/Private; 12. Why something is/What something is; 13. Highest
Essence (God)/Nonessence; 14. Substance/Accident. Part II would contain
disputed questions, like most traditional *summae*, and Part III would com-
prise various "expositions," namely systematic commentaries on all the
books of the Bible, followed by a collection of sermons.

Even by the standards of scholastics, famed for their love of systemiza-
tion, Eckhart's ambitions for the *Opus Tripartitum* were unprecedented. Unlike the authors of other *summae*, including Aquinas, he envisioned a holistic,
organic approach to his philosophy of Christianity. First he would resolve
most of the current disputes about first principles—a formidable (some would
say impossible) task in itself. Then he would proceed to address more specific
questions according to the findings of Part I, taking on many of the positions
staked out by Aquinas and other rivals. Finally he would expound on the
practical truths found in both the philosophy he has described and scriptures

themselves. Eckhart knew that completing a work of this magnitude would require several years, perhaps the rest of his life. This, he decided at the end of his regent professorship, would be his practical contribution to the pursuit of God: a universal metaphysics of Christian morality.

Eckhart's 1303 announcement of his massive project included the first thesis for Part I, the first question for Part II, and the first commentary for Part III, whereby he demonstrated his method. The first thesis, in Part I, propounded what he now considered his central insight into the divine nature: God is pure intellect and pure being and everything else in creation emanates from Him. God was not *a* being or *the most powerful* being; God was *being itself* (*esse ipsum*). Humans and other creatures had no existence without Him. As in one of Eckhart's favorite metaphors, creatures were like the image of a face in a mirror; take the face away and the image disappears. *An image is not of itself or for itself; it is solely that thing's whose image it is, and all that it is belongs to that.* Humans have no existence of their own apart from God. This new interpretation actually reversed one of his arguments from earlier that year, in which he posited that if creatures are essentially being, then God is a nonbeing, or beyond being. This new position—*God is being*— would be the one that Eckhart ultimately embraced, expounding on it later that fall in the first of a series of sermons and lectures on Ecclesiastes to his fellow German Dominicans at their annual provincial chapters.

As promised in the general prologue, Part II of the *Opus* then proceeded to build on the proposition established in Part I with specific questions, following the order established by *the* Summa *of the illustrious and venerable friar Thomas of Aquino*. The first question, "whether God exists," thus became a *self-evident* four-point demonstration, since God had already been established as existence or being itself, and if God didn't exist, nothing existed. *Everything that exists*, in other words, *exists through existence, and existence is God*. Part III accordingly picked up the same four points of Part II in its commentary on Genesis 1:1 ("In the beginning . . ."), drawing extensively from Eckhart's lectures and notes from his regent professorship. As interpreted by the master, scriptures further demonstrated the truth of what he had written in Parts I and II about the nature of God and existence.

For the *Opus Tripartitum* to prove useful in the way its author intended, it would need to be succinct rather than comprehensive. Even so, Eckhart's confidence in the originality of his contribution is remarkable:

> *All of this would seem to require an ocean of words, but two factors lend to brevity, as far as this is possible, and tighten up the work: first, because the explanations here are very seldom found elsewhere, and some topics scarcely at all; second, because in the Book of Questions and Book of Commentaries I treat piecemeal and concisely only a few matters.*

St. Augustine, the master claimed, favored this same selective approach, and Eckhart's own work merely provided a modern, systematic, and scientific amplification of the hallowed Father's insights. Since the *Opus* would *simply touch upon a distinction in the text and some noteworthy matters arising from the text under discussion. . . . It will be left to the experienced reader to delve further into Scripture to harmonize it.*

Studious brothers, not casual lay or clerical readers, were the master's intended readers, and even this select audience had to proceed carefully to grasp the *new and rare things* that the *Opus* would reveal. Contrary to the accusations of Eckhart's later critics, anxiety about being misunderstood or accused of unorthodox statements always weighed heavily on his mind. In introducing the *Opus*, he warned readers that *at first glance some of the following propositions, questions, and expositions will seem monstrous, doubtful or false*, but he simultaneously reassured and admonished them that *it will be otherwise if they are considered cleverly and more diligently.*

Meister Eckhart completed his first year as regent professor confident that he had at last found his life's work. The magisterial *summa* he envisioned would provide an unprecedented metaphysical foundation for all Christian beliefs and morality. His "utterly original" attempt to surpass both Thomist and Franciscan systems would put forward a new theology (God is intellect) and a new anthropology (intellect is part of uncreated divinity and present in all humans). Eckhart must have known that many of the brethren for whom he was supposedly composing the *Opus Tripartitum* would find much of the massive work beyond their understanding. But at least he could be confident that his ideas would make their mark in the schools and in the

theological faculties of Christendom, where his new composition might supplement, and perhaps eventually supplant, the *summae* of Aquinas and
Bonaventure. Naturally it would have been unseemly for any theological
author, particularly a Dominican friar, to admit such worldly ambitions for
his own efforts. But the scope alone of Eckhart's *Opus* left no doubts about
how high he was aiming.

CHAPTER SEVEN

Knowing the Unknowable God

Where is this [hidden] God? It is just as if a man were to
hide himself and then to give himself away by clearing his throat.
God has done the same. No man could ever have found God,
but He has revealed His presence.

GERMAN SERMON 79

The Limits of Reason

Meister Eckhart's dreams of intellectual immortality had no sooner taken shape than they confronted the stark reality of a friar's duty to his order. During the three decades since Eckhart entered the Dominican priory at Erfurt, the order had continued to grow significantly in German lands, now claiming at least 3,500 male members and perhaps 2,500 nuns. During May of Eckhart's regent professorship, Dominican leaders decided to break off part of the German province of Teutonia to form a new province, Saxonia (Saxony). By the end of the following month, the new master had left Paris, with two years still remaining in his regent professorship. It's possible that Eckhart, like Duns Scotus, got caught up in the political controversy between Pope Boniface VIII and King Philip the Fair that resulted in so many university masters being banished from the city. More likely, the Dominicans decided to create a new province with one particular experienced leader and distinguished scholar in mind as its chief administrator. Three months later, in September 1303, the first provincial chapter of Saxony met in Erfurt and elected Meister Eckhart its leader.

The new province contained forty-seven male houses and seventy female convents. Its geographical scope was vast, encompassing Holland, Frisia, Westphalia, Hessia, Saxony, Thuringia, Brandenburg, Mecklenburg, Pomerania, and the Baltic. Eckhart's new position required him to be "prayerful and respectful" of his predecessors and their traditions, while also undertaking many personal inspections and instituting reforms as needed. As a Dominican provincial, Eckhart oversaw all liturgical practices in his jurisdiction and was charged with maintaining discipline "in a just and fraternal manner." Usually such oversight involved counseling, interventions, and "gentle" corrections. Sometimes disobedient or "dangerous" brothers needed to be relocated or, in rare cases, imprisoned. Eckhart handled all internal relations among Saxony's priories, as well as external contacts with other Dominicans from the master general on down. He was the province's chief diplomat, responsible for maintaining good relations and supervising legal arrangements with bishops and other secular clergy, with Franciscans and other orders, with nuns and tertiaries, and with local lay leaders, both noble and bourgeois. The provincial also managed all the order's property in his district, maintaining and supplying existing houses, negotiating to establish new ones, and overseeing all major purchases and donations. The cumulative responsibilities of the job required nearly constant travel, often over great distances.

The Dominicans had a long history of scholar-administrators, dating back to Dominic himself and continuing to Eckhart's own mentor, Dietrich of Freiberg. With four years of previous administrative experience under his belt and new status as a master of theology, the middle-aged Eckhart was embarking on a path that could well lead to his becoming master general of the entire order. Clearly the academically talented scholastic must have also possessed some notable leadership skills. Not only were no complaints registered against him during his tenure as provincial—remarkable given the size of his province—but just four years later, in 1307, he was elected to an additional office: general vicar of Bohemia, charged with restoring order to the especially unruly province. Apparently the new general vicar's house-cleaning went well, as no further complaints circulated about Bohemia and the province was allowed to elect a new provincial a year later. The new leader's unsteady tenure, however, required Eckhart to remain in his oversight role for another three years, until Bohemia's long-serving former provincial Brother Zdislav was persuaded to return to his post.

With his administrative success in both Saxony and Bohemia, Eckhart seemed destined for higher office within the Dominicans. But this was not to be. Instead, the Order of Preachers had a new diplomatic mission for Meister Eckhart: another term as regent professor at the University of Paris. A second term as regent professor was a distinct honor, one previously granted only to the great Aquinas. Eckhart undoubtedly merited the distinction, but his Dominican superiors had an eminently practical motive for the assignment as well.

In 1311, Paris and all of Christendom were still reeling from the aftershocks of the French king Philip the Fair's single-minded obliteration of the Knights Templar. The Templars had been the most famous and most successful military order to emerge from the crusades. During the thirteenth century, their victories on the battlefield began to be surpassed by their prowess as bankers, which was rivaled only by certain Lombard and Jewish houses. After despoiling both of these groups, in 1291 and 1306 respectively, Philip turned his attention to the impregnable Templar fortresses within his own kingdom. Employing a series of intermediaries, he accused the Templars of various blasphemies, including a secret initiation ceremony that culminated in new recruits spitting on the crucifix and later committing sodomy. On October 13, 1307, the king ordered the Templars' grand master, Jacques de Molay, arrested along with several of his brethren as "enemies of the faith." Critics of Philip's bold action noted that the king remained heavily in debt to the Templars for his recent English wars.

Aymericus de Piacenza, the master general of the Dominicans, who resided in the order's house in Paris, was commissioned by Pope Clement V to examine Philip's charges against the Templars. After a brief investigation, he had the temerity to find the knights innocent. This outcome did not sit well with the king, who demanded Aymericus resign as inquisitor, then resumed his campaign against the Templars by other means, including pressure on the pope to support him. Following this embarrassing incident, the Order of Preachers required a friar with proven diplomatic skills and a stellar academic reputation to help revive the Dominicans' status in Paris, especially at the university. Eckhart was the ideal man for the job.

A contemporary portrayal of the burning of Grand Master Jacques de Molay
and other Templars in Paris, 1314.

Seven years had passed since Eckhart's previous professorship in Paris. Although he had continued to work on his *Opus Tripartitum* during that time, progress had been slow amid all his travel and administrative work on behalf of the order. Eckhart's second regent professorship in Paris offered him the time and resources to make significant progress on the *Opus*. Ironically, it was at just this point that his ambitious intellectual pursuit of God appears to have hit a deeply troubling impasse—namely the outer limits of human reason. It was a paradox that Aquinas too had discovered during the composition of his own *Summa*: "Man reaches the peak of his knowledge of God when he realizes that he does not know Him, understanding that the divine reality surpasses all human conception of it." Shortly before his own death, in fact, the Angelic Doctor had experienced a deeper understanding of the divine that "made everything I had written seem as straw." For Aquinas and Eckhart, all human perceptions, however logical, remained limited by the derivative and subsequently partial nature of our understanding. As Eckhart had explained back in 1303, *[God]'s knowledge is the cause of things, whereas our knowledge is caused by them. Consequently, because our knowledge is dependent upon the being by which it is caused, with equal reasoning it is itself dependent on God's knowledge.* Human reason, like humans themselves, was a creation, a dim reflection of God that could only point to the infinite, not truly or fully convey its essence. Rational thought was accordingly limited by its own very partial experience of the universe. In other words, any speculation about God and the infinite involves not just what former U.S. secretary of defense and philosopher Donald Rumsfeld once described as known unknowns but also unknown unknowns—countless realities beyond our ability to even imagine them.

For some theologians, such a disheartening challenge to a cherished project might have triggered a cascade of professional and personal crises. It's possible that the philosophically gifted Eckhart experienced doubt and anxiety upon reaching the limits of his rational pursuit of God. If so, he nonetheless remained an active participant in the learned debates that were the hallmark of scholastic life during his new tenure in Paris, arguing such questions as "Does motion without a terminus imply a contradiction?" and "Did the forms of the elements remain in the Body of Christ while Dying on the Cross?"

There are other reasons to conclude that Eckhart's uncertainty about the future of his Christian philosophy project was not personally devastating. Over the past several years, the master had become increasingly intrigued by an alternate way of knowing God—the intuitive or "mystical" approach embraced by his spiritual father, Augustine. According to Eckhart, Augustine had grasped that theologians were always trying to balance the understanding of God offered "through a glass darkly" by reason with other wisdom obtained more directly by nonrational experience of the divine. Now Eckhart decided that knowing God intuitively from within was no longer merely a complementary method to knowing God from without through rational inquiry, but was in many important ways superior to it. The master never completely abandoned his philosophical work, but he increasingly acknowledged its inadequacies, particularly in reaching his own ultimate goal of achieving direct experience of the divine.

Recognizing the divine in oneself, and in the universe, offered Eckhart a direct experience of God that was much more satisfying than any rational-ized model. But how exactly did this intuitive approach to God work? Was reason an aid to this different kind of knowing, or should it be disregarded entirely (if such a thing were possible)? Should one engage in specific spiri-tual practices? Meditate on certain scriptural passages? The pastoral Eckhart had offered his monastic charges practical advice about how to pursue God, but the scholastic Eckhart concluded that such a pursuit was doomed until one abandoned all preconceptions about God Himself. The God most Chris-tians thought they knew was not the true God. To know the uncreated Cre-ator directly required first unknowing the human-created God, a process known to theologians as the *via negativa*, or negative way.

Unknowing God

Eckhart first indicated his attraction to the *via negativa* in a sermon deliv-ered a decade earlier, at the St. Jacques priory—appropriately enough—on the feast of St. Augustine (August 28), in either 1302 or 1303. While still praising scholarly pursuit of divine wisdom, "the golden vessel, encrusted with every kind of precious stone" (Ecclesiasticus 50:10), the new master proposed a notably different definition of the theologian's quest for wisdom from that of his Easter sermon of 1294. His inspiration, Eckhart claimed, was Augustine himself, whom he characterized as *a good theorist, an outstanding logician, and a superb ethicist*. Ethics, which Eckhart for the first time declared synony-mous with theology, drew its insights from different sources than the other philosophical branches of mathematics and physics. Unlike the natural sci-ences, theology sought *to see more deeply the ideas of things in the divine mind, before they proceed into the physical world.*

Yet when it came to the highest things, Augustine agreed with Plato that "it is impossible to say anything about God, and how difficult it is to find Him." Here Eckhart explicitly proposed the negative way to God described by Boethius and Pseudo-Dionysius as offering the best point of departure. He also quoted extensively from Augustine's *Confessions* on the effect of ex-periencing the divine light directly, leading to higher understanding, practi-

cal grace in overcoming temptations, as well as occasionally prophetic
insights or ecstasy of the spirit. Reason was not to be despised, but in the end
it was less reliable than direct, intuitive knowledge of God, which Eckhart
variously compared to cooling snow on hot desires, the gentle dew of a ver-
dant valley, the refreshment of an intoxicating wine or soothing oil, a puri-
fying fire, a reassuring light in the darkness, and a mighty wind.

Unfortunately, direct experience of the divine light was usually blocked
by reason itself, which had constructed its own ideas about the divine. Eckhart had long opposed the anthropomorphic images of God that remained
common even among highly educated people. The Creator of the universe
was not an old man with a beard, or even a man, and imagining God with
any human attributes inevitably caused confusion and harm. Twenty years
earlier, Prior Eckhart had lectured his young charges that *a man should not
have, or be satisfied with, an imagined God, for then, when the idea vanishes, God
vanishes! Rather, one should have an essential God, who far transcends the thought
of man and all creatures. Such a God never vanishes unless a man willfully turns
away from Him.*

But what did an essential God look like? Human minds have great difficulty thinking of any sentient entity without an image, even an abstract one.
Here Eckhart's many years of study offered an intellectual starting point:
negative theology, a school of thought endorsed by both Augustine and Maimonides. Negative theology is the process of knowing God from what He is
not, of unknowing all the attributes we might previously have assigned to
God. The *via negativa* required first disposing of, or at least suspending,
some basic ways of rational thinking. Yet, paradoxically, Eckhart believed
that only this path provided hope for a rational pursuit of God.

Eckhart's espousal of negative theology grew steadily during the ten
years between his two regencies in Paris, making him increasingly wary
of attempts to make affirmative statements about God based on His creation. Like most of his colleagues, he had long rejected equivocation, or applying human terms such as "good" or "just" to God, but other affirmative
methods had previously held some appeal for him. Arguing from cause, for
instance—favored by Aquinas—permitted theologians to know the Creator
through His actions, such as a hierarchical ordering of the universe, or His

fashioning of humans in His own image. Eventually Eckhart agreed with Maimonides, however, that statements about God inferred in this manner were *unsuitable, improper, and not in keeping with the truth.* The same was true about positive statements based on analogy and metaphors, which Eckhart himself often used, albeit cautiously and with qualifications. Eckhart even rejected reasoning by eminence—a method he had favored earlier—in which one tried to describe the nature of the divine by imagining ever greater degrees of virtues, such as goodness, or of powers, such as understanding. The human mind, he concluded, remained hopelessly limited by its own "creaturely" concepts, leaving only the *via negativa:*

> *Know that whatever you add by way of negative names with respect to the Creator, you come nearer to grasping Him and will be closer to Him than the person who does not know how to remove from God the perfections and attributes that have been proven to be far from Him.*

Embracing negative theology required a radical demolition of the most basic human preconceptions about reality itself, a process Nicholas of Cusa (1401–64) later called "learned ignorance." Maimonides, the most formative influence on Eckhart's thinking in this respect, began with the Socratic axiom, "The one thing I know about God is that I do not know Him." Like the ancient Athenian, the Jewish sage believed that negative theology could not guarantee absolute truths, but it could help us to be less wrong. Specifically, Maimonides posited in his *Guide for the Perplexed* that there were four basic mental categories that had no relevance to God and consequently distorted all human understanding of Him: corporality, mutability, privation, and similarity. Eckhart streamlined this list of rational barriers to three fundamental notions: time (which included mutability), corporeality (or space), and multiplicity. In other words, anything that most of us can imagine exists in time and space, and is distinct from something else. God, by contrast, exists outside of time, throughout and beyond space, and is one with all creation. He is totally other, *outside and above every genus.* Our concepts of time, space, and distinctiveness do not apply to this unique entity, which Eckhart had already identified as pure thought and existence (one of the few affirmative statements about God he thought possible). Only the negative way of theology, which strips away what God is not, allows us to come closer to understanding what God is.

Take our common notion of temporality. Even after all of the modern theorizing about the elasticity of space-time, most of us still tend to think of time in linear terms, with one thing happening before or after another. Eternity is often imagined as just a really long time, with the notions of "no beginning" or "no end" used more for emphasis than with any genuine understanding of what such words actually mean. Yet according to Eckhart, *Nothing is so firmly opposed to God than time. Paul [in Ephesians 5:8] means not just time, but clinging to time; he means not just clinging to time but contact with time: not only contact with time but even a smell or savor of time—for just as where an apple has lain the smell lingers, so you must understand it with time.*

What would happen, he asks, if we attempted to suspend this human perspective on time and imagine the universe from God's perspective, what philosophers called *sub specie aeternitatis* ("under the aspect of eternity")? *Some people ask how a man can do the work that God was doing a thousand years ago and will be doing a thousand years hence. They cannot understand it. In eternity there is no before and after. Therefore, what God did a thousand years ago, and what he does in a thousand years, and does now, is all but a single act.* From the divine perspective, in other words, there is no past and no future, only *one present Now.*

Eckhart knew that *the Eternal Now* was virtually inconceivable for most human minds. He recounted being asked, *"What was God doing or what kind of life did he lead when he was alone before creation?,"* and he conceded that *untaught people falsely imagine that some delay or suspense intervened when time did not exist.* To God, however—and thus in reality—*all that happened a thousand years ago, the day that was a thousand years ago, is in eternity no further off than this moment I am in now; or the day which shall be a thousand years hence, or in as many years as you can count, is no more distant in eternity than this moment I am in.* Distinctions in time and development, key to human understanding, remain antithetical to the divine perception of *Now.* In eternity, *being and youth are in it the same, for eternity would not be eternal if it could become new and were not always so.* The eternal *Now*, according to Eckhart, was the meaning of the scriptural phrase "fullness of time," and should be the true objective of any meaningful pursuit of God. Breaking free of the sensory world of cause and effect, change, and other temporal constructs might be impossible for most humans, but the aspiration to do so might at least provide direction for those seeking to grasp the divine perspective.

Human concepts of physicality and space likewise hindered even an approximate understanding of what or where God is. Eckhart had no truck with a sky god or even an outer space god. *If I were asked where God is, I should reply, "He is everywhere." If I were asked where the soul is that dwells in Love, I should reply, "She is everywhere." . . . Thus God is one All without everything.* Borrowing a popular Neoplatonic metaphor, the master compared God to a circle with no circumference, where the center is everywhere. Preaching in a Dominican church, possibly in front of a painting of the Trinity enthroned in heaven, Eckhart playfully asked, *Where are we to look? . . . Where is Christ sitting? He is sitting nowhere. Whoever seeks him anywhere will not find him.*

Heaven itself was also not how most people imagined it. *Heaven is at all points equidistant from earth . . . untouched by time and place.* It was also, he added, *so vast and so wide that if I told you, you would not believe it. If you were to take a needle and prick the heavens with it, then that part of heaven that the needle point pricked would be greater in comparison to heaven and the whole world, than heaven and the world are compared with God.* Like perceiving the *Eternal Now,* imagining a God and a heaven of such vastness was beyond the capability of most finite minds. (Just as well, since the purpose of negative theology was not to provide a new way of imagining God but to deconstruct all such images that the rational mind might create.)

Eckhart's third mental barrier to imagining God is perhaps the most difficult to understand. Humans exist in a world of multiplicity, perceiving various individual things at all levels, all distinct from one another. Our reason knows only parts and boundaries and degrees of separation, and thus we imagine God in those terms. But God has no distinctions: *He is utter simplicity, pure unity.* On the great chain of being, God is *the One, both male and female, odd and even,* the unity of the reality from which the created many emerged. His indistinctiveness and unity never change (change being a temporal concept in itself), meaning that *God is in all things. The more He is in things, the more He is out of things: the more in, the more out, and the more out, the more in. I have often said, God is creating the whole world now this instant.* This apparent lack of distinction between God and His universe is not pantheism, as some of Eckhart's critics later charged, but what scholars today call panentheism. Pantheism considers the divine and the universe identical; panentheism sees the entire material cosmos infused with a transcendent divinity, known to Eckhart as *the One.*

Grasping the master's point on this question requires distinguishing between the One—absolute unity and intellect—and numbers themselves. In calling God *the One,* Eckhart was referring not to the number one (a human distinction) but

> . . . *the source of all numbers . . . a number that is numberless, one without oneness, or more properly, one which is above oneness. . . . We must understand that the term "one" is the same as indistinct, for all distinct things are two or more, but all indistinct things are one. Furthermore, there is an indistinction that concerns God's nature, both because He is infinite, and also because he is not determined by the confines or limits of any genera or beings.*

Imagining God as one being is a fundamental distortion, he argues, as erroneous as perceiving the Trinity as three persons, based on human perception of numbers and distinctions. Any apparent contradiction between God's unity and the Christian doctrine of the Trinity stems purely from human lack of imagination. Consequently, *everything that is said or written about the Holy Trinity is in no way really so or true. . . . Hence the Psalm text, "Every man is a liar"* [Psalms 115:11]. *It is true, of course, that there is something in God corresponding to the Trinity we speak of and to other similar things.*

In one of his most difficult passages, Eckhart returned to the meaninglessness of distinctions for God:

> *For anyone who could grasp distinctions without number and quantity, a hundred would be as one. Even if there were a hundred Persons in the*

A conventional late medieval portrayal of the Divine Trinity, here crowning the Virgin Mary Queen of Heaven.

Godhead, a man who could distinguish without number and quantity would perceive them only as one God. . . . Unbelievers and some untutored Christian people wonder at this, and even some priests know as little about it as a stone: they think of three like three cows or three stones. But he who can make distinction in God without number or quantity knows that three Persons are one God.

Sadly, as in discussions of eternity and infinity, the power to make distinctions without number or quantity remains an elusive human skill. Yet without it, according to Eckhart, all discussions of God remain meaningless.

By now we are experiencing deep sympathy with the *unbelievers* and *untutored Christian people* unable to grasp the master's finer points. That would not have surprised Eckhart, given the inherent limitations of human language itself. Put simply: *God is unnamable to us because of the infinity of all existence in Him.* All attributes we would apply to God are what Aquinas called "creaturely concepts," profoundly inadequate in representing His "diverse perfections." Eckhart continues in typically provocative style:

God is nameless because none can say or understand anything about Him. . . . If I now say God is good, it is not true; rather, I am good, God is not good. I will go further and say I am better than God: for what is good can become better, and what can become better can become best of all. Now God is not good, therefore he cannot become better. And since He cannot become

*better, therefore He cannot become best; for these three, good, better and best
are remote from God, since He is above them all.*

Neither is God wise, just, or true; rather He is the active principles of wisdom, justice, and truth. *If you think of anything He might be, He is not that. No
distinction,* Eckhart insists, *can exist or be understood in God Himself.*

The only true proposition we can make about God in language is "God
is" (*Deus est*). This was the burning bush's response to Moses's query about
the divine name: "I am who I am." As Eckhart explains, *"Shaddai" signifies
that God is Existence itself and that his essence is Existence itself.* It is *a name that
is not really a name,* yet it conveys one of the few truths about divine nature
that the human mind is capable of understanding. In this sense, Eckhart
agrees with Avicenna that *we may as well say "Being" instead of "God."* Otherwise, he counsels, *we should learn not to give God any name . . . for God is above
names and ineffable.*

Confounded by the utter inadequacy of human expression, Eckhart in
fact decided that *every word that we can say of it is more a denial of what God is
not than a declaration of what He is.* Here he was sharing the conclusion of his
spiritual father, St. Augustine, who had lamented that *whatever we say of God
is not true, and what we do not say of Him is true.* Eckhart also agreed with
Pseudo-Dionysius, author of a celebrated work about the names of God, who
wrote that *the finest thing one can say about God is to be silent from the wisdom of
inner riches.* Therefore, the master counseled his audiences,

> *. . . be silent and do not chatter about God, because by chattering about Him
> you are lying and committing a sin. Nor should you [seek to] understand
> anything about God, for God is above all understanding. One master says:
> "If I had a God I could understand, I would no longer consider him God."*

Eckhart's advice to his listeners did not prevent him from continuing to
talk about God in his own sermons and academic writings, but he did appreciate the resulting conundrum for a theologian. Like Augustine, he recognized that even declaring God beyond words or images was itself an internal

contradiction: *The more one tries to speak about the ineffable, the less one says about it as ineffable.* Yet as a member of the Order of Preachers, Brother Eckhart's mission was not silent contemplation of the divine wonder but helping others find their way to God. His biblical predecessors grappled with the same dilemma. The prophets, Eckhart preached, *fell silent and were tongue-tied,* utterly incapable of conveying the vastness and sublimity of what they encountered, yet *it sometimes happened that they did turn outward and speak, but owing to the incommensurability of the truth they lapsed into gross matter and tried to teach us to know God with the aid of lower, creaturely things.*

Finding Our Way Back to the One

Eckhart's frustration with the inadequacy of *lower, creaturely things* when he spoke about God led him to two conclusions. The first was that human language and concepts could at best only point toward the infinite, and always inadequately at that. There was only one unambiguously true statement one could make about God: that He (i.e., existence) cannot not exist. Put differently, since existence exists, God is necessary. This tautological statement, based on the self-evident fact that there is existence, provides *the purest form of affirmation and the fullness of the term affirmed.* The existence of the One, source of all created things, negates the negation of nonexistence, for *outside of God there is nothing but—nothing!* This was Eckhart's version of the mathematical formula $-1 \times -1 = 1$.

Even then, the master remained wary, warning that *anything we ascribe to [God] except pure being, encloses Him,* limiting His absolute freedom and unity. *He is as high above being as the highest angel is above a midge. I would be as wrong to call God a being as I were to call the sun pale or black. God is neither this nor that.* It would be better, Eckhart advised, to think of God as *pure nothing* (or rather no thing), for *he is neither this nor that; if you think of anything he might be, He is not that. He is being above all being; He is beingless being,* or more simply, *He is beyond all speech.*

The second conclusion Eckhart drew from the inadequacy of human language to convey the essence of God was that the only way to truly know

God was to experience Him directly. Only intuitive recognition allowed the human mind to transcend the limitations of rational perception and description. Here the ancient authority Eckhart most relied on was not Aristotle, but the Philosopher's own mentor, the sage Eckhart called *that great priest*: Plato. Most of what the German Dominican and his contemporaries knew of Plato, however, came to them secondhand: Only the first part of Plato's *Timaeus* dialogue was available in Latin translation to Eckhart. While this provided him some direct familiarity with Plato's cosmology, he relied more on the interpretations of the Philosopher's teachings by his two most prominent later disciples, Plotinus (ca. 205–ca. 270), founder of the movement today known as Neoplatonism, and Proclus (412–85). Scholars today debate the fidelity of Plotinus—and Proclus in particular—to Plato's original teachings, but this distinction was unknown to Eckhart, who in fact cited Proclus more frequently than either Albert the Great or Aquinas.

Proclus's ideas arrived in the thirteenth century in various forms. First there was the *Book of Causes*, a collection of thirty-one propositions on the nature of the universe and God, available only in a twelfth-century Latin translation of a ninth-century Islamic version of the lost Greek original. *The Book of Causes* enjoyed wide acclaim, particularly within the Dominican Order, and by 1255 it had become a part of the University of Paris curriculum. About the same time, a Latin translation of Proclus's *Elements of Theology* appeared, complemented by a Latin version of the *Book of the Twenty-four Philosophers*, supposedly written by the ancient Egyptian sage Hermes Trismegistus. Here several Procline ideas emerge from the lips of various wise men of old, each positing a different enigmatic definition of God.

Eckhart's embrace of Neoplatonic philosophy in his own pursuit of God was in fact part of a long tradition among Christian thinkers he admired, beginning in antiquity with Augustine, Boethius, and Pseudo-Dionysius, and continuing all the way up to his own time with Albert the Great and Dietrich of Freiberg. Virtually all theologians since antiquity, for instance, had accepted Augustine's identification of the gospel of John's "Word made flesh" (1:14) with the Platonic *Logos* that ordered the universe. The Church Father even went so far as to detect "the book of the Platonists" in the first eleven verses of John's gospel, Eckhart's favorite New Testament book.

The Neoplatonic intuitive approach to "knowing" God had an especially profound impact on Albert the Great and the German Dominicans who followed him, including Eckhart. In 1265, Albert's disciple Hugh Ripelin of Strasbourg published the master's various "mystical" writings in the collection *Compendium of Theological Truth*. The great man's interpretations of Paul, Augustine, and Pseudo-Dionysius on divine union sent heavy ripples throughout the Order of Preachers. Even Aquinas, the supposed champion of "Christian Aristotelianism," was deeply influenced by Albert's Neoplatonism, citing Pseudo-Dionysius in his *Summa* more often than the philosopher himself. Eckhart and his fellow Dominicans naturally differed on specifics, but all accepted Albert's general adaptation of Platonic cosmology and its privileging of intuition, which, unlike reason, provided an infallible way of "knowing" God.

The basis for this confidence was simple. According to Albert's version of the Platonic teaching of emanation, all human souls—or at least the most important part of them—were in fact divine in essence. These souls were themselves the result of a primordial big bang, or what Albert and his followers called a boiling-over (*bullitio*) of the Godhead into the divine Trinity, followed by a creation (*ebullitio*) of the universe, flowing out into time and space. One image in circulation among Christian and Jewish philosophers of Eckhart's day was that of sudden expansion from a dense point of light, not unlike the singular density postulated by modern physicists. In Eckhart's mind at least, creation was simultaneous, not the laborious process described in the first chapter of Genesis:

> *Do not imagine that God, when he made heaven and earth and all things, made one thing one day and another the next. Moses describes it like that, but he really knew better: he did so for the sake of the people who could not conceive or grasp it any other way. All God did was this: He willed, He spoke, and they were!*

Nor, wrote Eckhart, was this Neoplatonic vision of the universe's origin in conflict with the laws of Aristotelian science as interpreted by the

Averroists. God's intellect did indeed create only one thing at a time—the entire universe!

During this process, tiny pieces of the divine essence were scattered throughout the cosmos within creatures. This is what Eckhart meant when he argued that human beings had only virtual existence, borrowed from God. *Creation is the production of things from nothing*; or put differently, *the giving of existence after non-existence.* There was only existence (God) and non-existence; take away the face in the mirror (God) and the reflection (the human soul) is lost. Fortunately for humans, the act of creation endowed every person with what Christians called the *imago dei* ("image of God"), providing every soul with an innate guide back to its source. The terrestrial pilgrimage was thus a story of the soul's rejoining its Creator, a gradual reversal of the spiritual big bang.

How did this return journey (*reditus*) work for individual souls? Surprisingly, most scholastic theologians did not address this topic, preferring to leave ordinary Christians to conventional means of individual purification, such as penance and good works. For Eckhart, by contrast, this was *the* topic. Like his spiritual father Augustine, he believed that the human soul was *created as if at a point between time and eternity, which touches both. With the higher powers she touches eternity, but with the lower powers she touches time.* While the *lower powers* faced toward the world, the *higher powers* possessed a "mind's eye" that provided access to the divine mind, albeit in a limited capacity. Intuition was in fact one function of this mind's eye: it was the soul recognizing, or remembering, its divine origins.

Following the Dominican tradition of Albert, Eckhart identified this mind's eye within the soul as the Intellect, which encompassed both intuition and reason. The highest part of this Intellect, what academic theologians called the active intellect, provided direct access to the divine, whereas the potential or passive intellect merely received guidance from the superior active intellect. Like Albert, Eckhart actually believed in a collective of active intellects, each with a corresponding passive partner rooted in the sensory world. But unlike Albert and Dietrich of Freiberg, Eckhart argued that it was through the passive intellect that the soul was joined with God, *in unity, not like in likeness.* God came to the passive intellect through its divine *spark* (*vünkelîn;* or Latin *synderesis*), which did not require reason or any other intermediary in order to grasp God *in his pure essence.* This part of the intellect, in fact, had *no actual existence of its own*—it was God Himself, and the human act of intuition was that part of God recognizing Himself.

The Intellect, like all of creation, was always being irresistibly pulled back to its divine source, like a metal filing drawn to a gigantic magnet. This was a fact of existence for Eckhart, a kind of spiritual electromagnetic or gravitational force:

> *You must know that all creatures strive and work naturally to become like God. The heavens would not revolve if they did not pursue or seek for God, or a likeness to God. If God were not in all things, nature would cease operation and not strive for anything; for, whether you like it or not, and whether you know it or not, nature secretly and in her inmost parts seeks and aims at God.*

In another evocative metaphor, Eckhart compares the pursuit of the divine to an insatiable appetite, where *God, as infinite Truth and Goodness and Existence, is the meat of everything that is, that is true and good. And he is hungered for. They feed on him, because they exist, are true, and are good; they hunger, because he is infinite.* Reason and the will remain susceptible to lesser, carnal appetites, but the Intellect knows that it can be satisfied only by God; all else is vile in comparison.

But how exactly did the Intellect or *divine spark* work? On this question some of Eckhart's most revered philosophical forebears remained silent. Maimonides, like many Aristotelian-oriented scholars, looked down on "mystical" pursuits, such as the Cabbalistic practices of his contemporary Rabbi Moses ben Nahman (aka Nahmanides; d. 1270). Most scholastic theologians also avoided discussions of the inner spiritual life, with a few notable exceptions, particularly among the German Dominicans. Thus Eckhart again relied heavily on Albert and especially Dietrich of Freiberg in his early attempts to describe the gradual process he called *letting-go* through which the Intellect might achieve a moment of illumination and perhaps even divine union. In his Latin writings, however, the master seemed noticeably

reluctant to discuss this key question in detail, perhaps because he anticipated hostility from his academic audience, perhaps because he had not yet
clearly formulated his ideas on the subject.

Only in his German sermons, mostly from the period after his second
regent professorship in Paris, would Meister Eckhart begin to speak at
length about the actual process through which the soul might achieve re-
union with its Creator, an experience known to theologians as the Beatific
Vision or Divine Union. Most scholastics agreed with the apostle Paul that a
"face to face" encounter with God was normally reserved for the afterlife,
despite the extrasensory experiences described by Paul himself and by Augustine. The divine light was simply too powerful for the human mind, in
Augustine's opinion. Eckhart agreed—in most instances—that the human
experience of God was partial and distorted. *Is there then*, he lamented, *no
way of seeing God quite clearly? Yes*, Eckhart replied to his own question, but
the master would not fully explore the specifics of achieving the divine
union until his popular sermons after leaving the university.

The same reluctance was evident in his first tentative mention of the
most radical and distinctive new component in his theology: the explosive
notion of a common ground (*grunt*) of reality from which both God and
human souls emanated. Building on Augustine's notion of a *fundus animae*
(foundation of the soul), Eckhart ventured still further than his Dominican
mentors had dared, when discussing the universality of the active intellect.
God the Creator, he claimed, was distinct from *the hidden darkness of the eternal Godhead, which is unknown and has never been known and shall never be
known. God and Godhead are as different as heaven and earth*, he intuited, in the
same way *the inner man* (soul) is superior to *the outer man*, although *God is
loftier by many thousands of miles*. The key point was that God Himself was
not the ultimate source of the soul, but rather also emerged from the nameless *ground*, becoming "God" through the act of creation.

Meister Eckhart rarely mentioned this radical concept in his academic
writings, and when he did the full implications were not yet developed. In
the *Commentary on Exodus*, for instance, composed as part of the *Opus Tripartitum*, the discussion of God's timelessness contains a startling comment,
made in passing: *When someone asked me why God had not created the world*

earlier, I answered that He could not because He did not exist. . . . God's speaking is His making, and also unlike us His speaking is the cause of the entire work and of all its parts.

In a later vernacular sermon, Eckhart was less guarded and more explicit about the common origin of both God and the individual soul. He daringly described a primordial state, before creation itself, where the essence of the individual soul existed without a Creator.

> *When I yet stood in my first cause, I had no God and was my own cause: then I wanted nothing and desired nothing, for I was bare being and the knower of myself in the enjoyment of truth. . . . But when I left my free will behind and received my created being, then I had a God. For before there were creatures, God was not "God": He was That which He was.*

The effect of such a statement on his audience must have been considerable. The master concluded his discourse with one of his most shocking and oft-repeated pleas.

> *I pray to God to make me free of God, for my essential being is above God, taking God as the origin of creatures. For in that essence of God in which God is above being and distinction, there I was myself and knew myself so as to make this [earthly] man. Therefore I am my own cause according to my essence, which is eternal, and not according to my becoming, which is temporal.*

Meister Eckhart's theatrical flourishes aside, this triangulated notion of the ground, God, and the soul was remarkable. More than any of his other insights, the master's recognition of an ultimate origin and destination beyond God Himself transformed his lifelong spiritual pursuit. Eckhart now believed that the soul's journey toward union with the Creator was more complicated than the conventional vertical ascent he and other theologians had long espoused. The more apt analogy, he decided, was an excavation within the quiet of the soul, in which

Intellect forces its way in, dissatisfied with goodness or wisdom or truth or God Himself. In very truth it is as little satisfied with God as with a stone or a tree. It never rests; it bursts into the ground whence goodness and truth proceed, and seizes it in principio, in the beginning where goodness and truth are just coming out, before it has any name, before it burgeons forth, in a much higher ground than goodness and wisdom.

The simple ground, again only described in vernacular sermons, was a *silent desert into which no distinction ever peeped, of Father, Son, or Holy Ghost.*

Eckhart realized the dangerous implications of such a radical position and accordingly refrained from such explicit declarations during his time in the institutional heart of Christian orthodoxy. His broader championing of the intuitive pursuit of God, on the other hand, while controversial, was not without precedent (both Augustine and Albert had embraced similar ideas). Members of the world of disputations were accustomed to master theologians proposing innovative positions, usually in the hope of making a name and establishing a following. Intellectual experimentation was the very stuff of the academy and virtually every argument was open to vigorous debate.

Privately, Eckhart knew that his embrace of intuition as the surest way to God generated profound questions. Was this a path open only to an enlightened few, as most Neoplatonists believed, or a universal route that might be made available to all through a common, perhaps even teachable, approach? Was philosophical understanding needed for this inner journey? More unsettling still, what about the Church and its sacraments—might even these be unnecessary? From his perch atop the academic mountain, Meister Eckhart pondered the significance of his hard-won insights for the future course of his life.

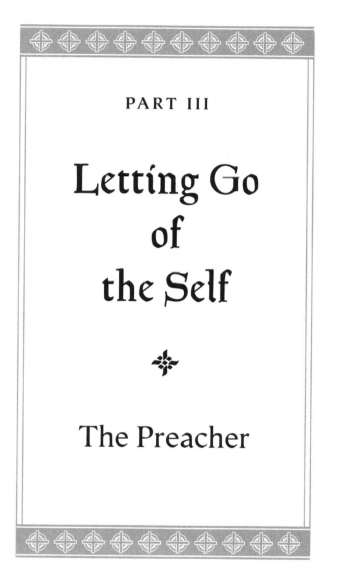

PART III

Letting Go
of
the Self

✦

The Preacher

CHAPTER EIGHT

Pernicious Females

I thought of something recently: if God did not want what
I wanted, then I should want what He does.

GERMAN SERMON 9

The Religious Women's Movement

By any conventional measure, Meister Eckhart at age fifty-three had achieved an impressive level of professional success. An esteemed theologian and influential leader within his order, he could have expected to spend his remaining years rising into the upper reaches of the Dominican hierarchy and enjoying ever greater public recognition. Most of his fellow Dominicans knew him for his administrative and scholarly achievements and would have likely imagined him known to posterity as a master general of the order or an esteemed theologian, a worthy successor to Albert and Aquinas. Eckhart's personal pursuit of God had also matured. It now encompassed both rational and intuitive approaches to the ineffable and drew on the work of a variety of pagan and Christian fellow seekers. Granted, some of his theological notions were startling, but if he had continued to write mostly in Latin and address only fellow male scholastics and friars, his reputation would never have been in jeopardy. It is also likely that most of us today would never have heard of him.

Fortunately, God—as Meister Eckhart would have said—had other plans for him. The master's greatest fame would not be for his administrative work or even for his scholarship but for his popular preaching. This was not a development the lifelong academic would have foreseen at this point in his life. Eckhart was obviously a capable preacher but so were many friars; not once was he singled out as a remarkable orator, on the level of Berthold of Regensburg or the later Bernardino of Siena (1380–1444). Like all Dominicans, he had preached throughout his career, but in these later years he made the radical decision to put aside the conventional sermon topics his order prescribed for popular audiences. Instead, he resolved to translate his own innovative religious philosophy into terms that any genuine aspirant, regardless of rank or education, could understand.

Spiritual egalitarianism to this degree represented a profound departure not only from Dominican practice but also from the elitism of his fellow Neoplatonists and most other scholastics. For this decision, Eckhart was both rewarded and punished. Ordinary people began to flock to his sermons, delivered in the vernacular rather than Latin, convincing Eckhart that there was a significant popular appetite for sermons of greater spiritual substance. But this very popularity simultaneously exposed him to the wrath of some jealous fellow clerics and the suspicion of certain powerful church leaders who would eventually prosecute him for heresy.

What inspired Eckhart to take this unconventional path? In part, he considered his popular preaching merely the fulfillment of his vocation as a Dominican friar, bound always to be "useful." His increasingly intuitive approach to divine union also somewhat dampened his enthusiasm for the scholastic project of discovery. But more than any other factor, it was a midlife reassignment, possibly at his request, that created the circumstances for his new focus on preaching. In Strasbourg the master encountered a particular appetite for his ideas among religious women—nuns in orders and laywomen known as beguines—that would define the remainder of his career, shaping both the form and the content of his preaching, while simultaneously drawing him into the sights of their common enemies in the church hierarchy.

Who were these beguines and where did they come from? In effect, they were the last remnants of the grassroots apostolic movements of the previous century. By 1300 the heretical Cathars lay on the verge of extinction and the Waldensians had been successfully marginalized and contained. But the lay appetite for a more authentic spiritual experience remained keen, especially among women. One sign of this was the phenomenon of the God House (*Gotzhaus*), an all-female religious community made up of lay-women from every social class who lived together, often in a residence donated by a wealthy member. Numbering in the hundreds, God Houses had begun to appear in the late 1100s and, by Eckhart's time, could be found in cities across the continent, with a particular concentration in northern Germany and the Netherlands. The resident women, known as beguines (possibly a pejorative term from "Albigensian"), sought a life of simplicity and prayer without vows or clerical oversight. They embraced apostolic poverty and an enhanced spiritual experience, but did not preach. Thanks to the beguines' refusal to proselytize and their generally orthodox views, church authorities seldom censured them as they had other lay apostolic movements of the time.

A fifteenth-century portrayal of a beguine.

Under the more restrictive atmosphere created by Pope Innocent III and Lateran IV in the early thirteenth century, however, many God Houses began to seek religious and secular patrons. During the subsequent decades, some became formally affiliated with male religious orders, taking religious vows and assimilating into female second orders, such as the Franciscans' Poor Clares (named after their founder St. Clare, 1194–1253). By the time Eckhart himself joined the Dominicans in the 1270s, the Order of Preachers had reluctantly agreed to assume responsibility for fifty-eight convents, forty of them within the German province of Teutonia. Within twenty-five years that number would more than double, to 141 houses across Europe and 65 in Teutonia.

Even with the startling growth in female religious orders, the appeal of independent, lay beguinages remained extraordinary. By 1300, for example, the largest German city, Cologne, was home to 169 beguinages, each housing anywhere from a handful to sixty or more women. With numbers like these, beguines had a significant urban presence, making up 5 to 10 percent of the city's total population of forty thousand (which also included more than a thousand nuns in orders). Many west German and Dutch towns experienced a similar growth in female religious communities, which slowly spread to the countryside as well. Despite this expansion, requests to join these communities—usually distinguished by a white cross painted on the main door—far exceeded the space available. Some houses began to require dowries or other property for entrance, a common practice among formal religious orders. Others turned to the property owners of their localities for donated buildings or deathbed bequests. Virtually all supported themselves through weaving, spinning, laundry, cleaning, and other work.

The communal focus, however, remained explicitly religious. Each house followed its own set of rules, similar to those in a monastery or convent. The goal was to pool the group's work and income, so that each of the "sisters" would have sufficient time to attend mass, hear sermons, read, and pray. Typically the women wore plain white, brown, or gray tunics and head coverings—similar to those worn by nuns and thus a frequent source of confusion and controversy. Again, unlike mendicant friars or the wandering lay preachers known as beghards, beguines did not engage in street begging or public preaching. Whether or not the affiliation with a male order was formal, Dominican and Franciscan friars were frequent visitors, serving as confessors, counselors, and preachers. The sisters themselves ranged in age from young women still considering marriage to elderly widows. The communities were apparently dynamic in membership, with some women joining for a short time and others eventually entering convents and making formal vows. Sometimes whole houses would convert to regular Dominican or Augustinian convents.

Beguinages remained the major outlier of the apostolic life movement, flummoxing the binary lay-clerical thinking of most church leaders. The papal legate Gilbert of Tournai, while preparing a report on the movement for the 1274 Second Council of Lyons, readily admitted that he couldn't figure out whether to call them "nuns" or "laywomen." Not all members of the church hierarchy found such lay religious associations troubling. The prominent canonist Hostiensis (d. 1271) acknowledged that "in the wide meaning, a 'religious' is so called who lives holily and religiously in his own house, even though not professed . . . such a one is called a 'religious' not because he is tied to any specific rule, but on account of his life, which he leads more strictly and holily than other secular people."

Like other lay apostolic movements, beguines inevitably encountered some detractors who dismissed them either as "pious fools" or "pernicious females." At one end of the spectrum they were condemned for practicing "easy religion" and at the other end for being too curious about religious "subtleties and novelties." Nikolaus of Bibra, a poet in Eckhart's Erfurt, was careful to distinguish between good beguines, who "worked day and night," and bad beguines, who "connive under cover of a false religious leisure, wandering through the localities, consorting with students and monks." When Pope Nicholas III bestowed one local house with the privilege to deal in wool and cloth, Bibra sniped that "now they have blankets to cover their loose lifestyle." Many of the derogatory comments sprang from simple misogyny; a house of women without male supervision could never be a good thing in many people's eyes. Yet until the fourteenth century, the most common attacks were not on beguines' orthodoxy, but on their sincerity, and such criticism did nothing to slow the proliferation of new God Houses across Europe.

Still, so many financially independent women, unaccountable to any higher church authority, was in itself troubling to many church leaders. It didn't help, from the perspective of bishops and their clergy, that both Dominicans and Franciscans thrived as confessors to such female communities and encouraged their growth. During Eckhart's years as provincial of Saxony, clerical attacks on beguines escalated in both frequency and intensity. Not long after assuming office in 1306, Strasbourg bishop Johann I of Zürich began accusing several beguines and beghards of unspecified heresy. Some of the women satisfied the bishop with solemn oaths of orthodoxy; many more fled the city. A brave few resisted the episcopal action and were handed over by Johann to the secular arm, empowered to impose sanctions ranging from fines to banishment to execution. Fortunately for the beguines in custody, civic authorities sympathized with the local Dominican friars who intervened on their behalf and got the charges dismissed.

The following year, the newly consecrated archbishop of Cologne, Heinrich II of Virneburg—an adversary Eckhart himself would come to know well—threatened all beguines in his diocese with excommunication if they didn't give up wearing habits and living in separate communities. Three years later the archbishops of Trier and Mainz followed suit, although enforcement in each instance remained spotty and ineffective. General suspicion of unorthodoxy or misbehavior (not to mention pervasive misogyny) rarely provided specific grounds for disciplinary action. What clerical critics of beguines desperately needed was a clear and irrefutable link to heresy. They didn't have to wait long for this dream to be realized.

Hiding Under the Cloak of Holiness

In late 1308, royal officials in Paris arrested Marguerite Porete, a fifty-eight-year-old beguine. Her crime was the obstinate refusal to recant any of the supposedly heretical claims made in her book, *The Mirror of Simple Souls*. Marguerite had already been admonished for this offense several years earlier by Bishop Guy II of Cambray, who had forced her to witness the burning of her manuscript. Undaunted, she rewrote the book, adding six chapters, and submitted it to three theologians for approval. This time, upon her arrest she was handed over to William of Paris, close adviser to King Philip the Fair and general inquisitor of France.

Marguerite, in William's view, was a "pseudo-woman" who had written a book "filled with errors and heresies." In 1310, he formed a commission of twenty-one renowned theologians to review the evidence against her. There were at least three grounds for this surprising thoroughness. First, William was a scholastic, educated at the University of Paris and committed to expert evaluation of any theological question. Second, Marguerite was no country bumpkin, but an educated noblewoman from the county of Hainault (in what is today northeastern France). She wrote well in prose and poetry and displayed an impressive familiarity with both courtly love literature and academic theology. She addressed sophisticated ideas about God and love in an eloquent Old French, making her teaching more accessible and thus potentially more dangerous than the polemics of a common rabble-rouser. The third reason for William's deliberate and rigorous approach was that Marguerite had been repeatedly identified as a beguine (although some modern historians remain unconvinced that she truly was). If William could persuade his clerical colleagues to condemn this well-spoken beguine for her unorthodox beliefs, it might prompt the church to suppress all beguines on grounds they were linked to heresy.

The Mirror of Simple Souls was a subtly subversive work. On one level it appeared to be a typical allegorical romance of the period, with the questing soul portrayed as a young princess in love from afar with the magnificent King Alexander the Great. This sly reversal of the usual distant lady as love object was just the first of Marguerite's manipulations of familiar themes. In 139 chapters, some quite brief, the dialogue between the Soul and Love (also feminine) is joined at various times by other allegorical figures, including Light of Faith, Divine Reason, Holy Spirit, Graciousness, and Errant Will. In her quest for the divine, the Soul learns about seven progressively higher levels of grace, each bringing her closer to ultimate joy. She eventually achieves the goal of self-annihilation in the fifth stage, followed by a sixth stage of rapture, in which the Soul becomes completely passive, with no independent cares and no concern for good works. Finally, in the seventh stage, achieved only in heaven, the Soul becomes fully immersed in divine love, or God.

What most concerned William and his fellow inquisitors—aside from the apparent claim of becoming God—was Marguerite's obvious contempt for many of the external acts of piety she dismissed as part of "Holy Church the Lesser." Contrary to "Holy Church the Greater," guided only by divine love, the worldly version of Christianity was dominated by "peasants of grace" and "merchants of the spirit," who focused on asceticism and other external works, rather than the internal life of the spirit.

Marguerite's belittling of Reason also undoubtedly irked her clerical interrogators, all of them highly educated scholars. "Men of theology and scholars such as they/will never understand this writing properly," she warned, guided as they were by "Reason, who understands only the obvious and fails to grasp what is subtle." "You take the straw and leave the grain," she chided them, "because your understanding is too base." Fortunately, during the course of *The Mirror*, Reason eventually realizes her own limitations and gladly swears allegiance to Love and Faith as "her liege lord and for this/Always she must herself abase." Even then, Marguerite concedes that "in the whole of a kingdom one could not find two creatures who were of [such a] spirit," and even if one could, they would have great difficulty communicating the truth of God's love to those "gross wits" not so illuminated.

It's possible that some of William's panel of experts might have had greater sympathy for Marguerite had they read her work in its entirety. Instead, in typical inquisitorial fashion, they reviewed only the fifteen seemingly heretical sentences that William had extracted from *The Mirror*, without any broader context provided. It did not take the commission long to decide the heterodoxy of a statement such as "[annihilated] souls . . . do not make use of [the Virtues], for they are not in their service as they once were; and, too, they have now served them long enough, so that henceforth they may become free." This was pure antinomianism in the theologians' minds, maintaining that sufficiently enlightened people had ascended beyond the demands of normal Christian morality. Marguerite did not help herself by refusing to testify in her defense, while some questionable witnesses for the prosecution eagerly contributed damning assessments.

On April 11, 1310, the theological commission unanimously condemned Marguerite Porete and her book as heretical. On June 1, 1310—a year before Meister Eckhart's arrival in Paris—she was burned at the stake in the Place de Grève (today known as the Place de l'Hôtel de Ville). Even a hostile chronicler acknowledged that Marguerite met her fate with considerable dignity and composure, moving many spectators, among them high-ranked nobles, to open weeping.

Lingering questions about the status of beguines came to a head the next year at the Council of Vienne, convened on October 16, 1311. After first resolving the question of the Templars' guilt (to King Philip's satisfaction), the council turned to the subject of "women, commonly called beguines who, although they promise no obedience and neither renounce property nor live in accordance with an approved rule," wear religious habits and associate with nuns, friars, and priests. Rather than rely on the usual clerical complaints of dissolute living among beguines, the resulting decree, known as *Ad Nostrum*, proceeded directly to the greater danger of heresy. "Some of them, as if possessed by madness, dispute and preach about the highest Trinity and the divine essence and in respect to the articles of faith and the sacraments of the Church spread opinions that are contrary to the Catholic faith." There were, the council conceded, some good beguines, but there were also many bad ones "hiding under the cloak of holiness" and holding "perverted views" (*opinione sinistra*), with which they "deceive many common people and lead them into diverse errors." Good beguines, *Ad Nostrum* decreed, should disband and return to their parishes as ordinary laywomen; bad ones should be excommunicated and otherwise punished.

Specifically, the council condemned "an abominable sect of malignant men known as beghards and some faithless women known as beguines in the Kingdom of Germany." Few if any beguines were members of a new "Free Spirit" sect—only first identified by Pope Clement the year before—but many did help spread "godless and bad lessons." The heretical teaching of this mostly imagined cult drew its main inspiration from Paul's declaration that "where the spirit of the Lord is, there is freedom" (2 Corinthians 3:17). Here the text of Marguerite Porete's *The Mirror* proved especially useful, providing many tenets that supposedly had gained greater currency in the wider population and were endangering numerous souls. *Ad Nostrum*'s first two articles, for instance, adamantly refuted "that someone in the present life can acquire so great and such a degree of perfection that he is rendered completely without sin and is not able to advance further in grace," and that "upon having attained the degree of this kind of perfection a person does not have to fast or pray, because then sensuality is so perfectly subject to spirit and reason that a person can freely give the body whatever pleases it."

Ad Nostrum was arguably directed more at beghards, wandering male preachers, than beguines, and the decree did not yet conflate the latter with the Free Spirit heresy. The guilt by association, though, was sufficient for many opponents of religious women, most notably the archbishops of Strasbourg and Cologne, who reignited their campaigns to close down beguinages. One modern historian has characterized the period between the Council of Vienne and the Council of Constance (1415) as "a hundred years' war against beghards and beguines." As in all wars, as Eckhart would himself discover, that campaign would entail considerable collateral damage.

A New Calling in Strasbourg

Sometime toward the end of Meister Eckhart's second year as a regent professor in Paris, Berengar of Landora, recently elected master general of the Dominicans, approached the scholar with a new mission. The priory in Strasbourg, the order's second most important German house (after Cologne), was in crisis. Its deepest and most long-standing conflict was with the secular clergy of the city, who had regularly quarreled with the friars since their arrival nearly a century earlier. Twice—from 1261 to 1263 and between 1287 and 1290—the bishop and his clergy had persuaded the town council to expel the Dominicans from the city. In the second instance, only a papal interdict, suspending all religious services in the city, forced Strasbourg's magistrates and secular clergy to relent. Twenty years later, the Strasbourg priory maintained a fragile truce with the bishop and his clergy, often jeopardized by local Franciscans, who were among the Dominicans' most vocal critics.

Much of the clerical conflict in Strasbourg centered on competition over lay donors. Parish churches, like mendicant houses, relied heavily on voluntary contributions for both maintenance and expansion of their operations. "Message control" was another significant source of strife. Dominicans and

BEGUINE HOUSES IN STRASBOURG

Circa 1300

◆ Houses of Beguines

Map by Gene Thorp

Scale of feet

400   800   1,200   1,600

Augustinians

Ill River

St. Mark

St. Peter
the Elder

All Saints

Franciscans

St. Peter

St. Thomas

Dominicans

St. Clara

St. Nicholas

Place Broglie

Cathedral

Ill River

St. Mary
Magdalene

St. Stephen

St. Clara on
the Werde

Ill River

St. William

Source: Dayton Phillips, *Beguines in Medieval Strasbourg: A Study of the Social Aspect of Beguine Life* (Jackson, TN: Edwards Brothers, 1941).

other mendicant friars were supposed to obtain episcopal approval for all preaching within their jurisdiction, especially at parish churches, but in practice oversight of sermon content and delivery (even among secular clergy) was virtually nonexistent. Eckhart and his fellow friars routinely preached to all types of audiences, not only at their own churches, covering a range of religious topics. Discordant or even dangerous sermons, from a bishop's point of view, could be as threatening to the diocesan church as lost revenues.

But the most pressing issue was "the religious women question." The Council of Vienne's issuance of the antibeguine *Ad Nostrum* in the spring of 1312 significantly exacerbated local tensions for Strasbourg's Dominicans. Two-thirds of the city's eighty-five God Houses lay within a quarter mile of the order's priory, with the friars (and their Franciscan rivals) generally providing pastoral services to the women. Parish priests and cathedral canons, already suspicious of the female communities, considered the mendicants' activities further evidence of their encroachment on the secular clergy's sphere.

Their champion was the man who a few years earlier had reignited the campaign against the beguines, Bishop Johann I of Zurich. Like most high-ranking churchmen, Johann was a career politician, not a theologian. Unlike most of the ecclesiastical elite, however, he was lowborn (even illegitimate) and had risen through the ranks in close personal service to King Albrecht I and the house of Habsburg. He was also unusual in the sense that concern for his church duties occupied almost as much time as political machinations. Educated at the University of Bologna, Johann devoted considerable energy to enforcing clerical discipline, through multiple synods and strict punishments. Order and hierarchy reigned as his supreme values. Multiple communities of several hundred beguines—abetted by the mendicants—indisputably threatened both.

Eckhart, in the opinion of his superiors, was the perfect emissary to defuse the order's tensions with the clergy of Strasbourg, particularly on the beguine question. The decision had little, if anything, to do with his theological views or scholarly reputation; it was his more practical skills that appealed to the order's leadership. Since his appointment twenty years earlier as prior of Erfurt, the friar from Thuringia had accumulated an impressive administrative résumé. During nearly eight years as provincial of Saxony, he had dealt regularly and directly with princes, cardinals, bishops, and a variety of other nobles. His shared background with society's privileged few undoubtedly helped on such occasions. He was likewise exceptionally well connected within the Order of Preachers, where he knew most, if not all, of the Dominican leadership personally, either from shared time at the university or from his attendance at general and provincial chapters held in locations throughout Europe.

Most relevant to this newest assignment, Eckhart had extensive experience in dealing with civic officials and members of the secular clergy. In addition to frequent interventions in local conflicts involving Saxony's seventy existing houses, the provincial had overseen the negotiation and founding of at least four new male convents and three new female convents. (The first, and most straightforward, was his father's testamentary donation for a new Dominican convent in Gotha, upon the aged knight's death in May 1305— our only documentary evidence of the elder Eckehard's passing.) In most instances, securing princely and papal approval for the new priories—often a challenge in itself—was inevitably followed by prolonged discussions with local officials who remained wary of Dominican expansionism. Attempts to establish a new Dominican priory at Dortmund, for example, had failed three times until Eckhart obtained the backing of Emperor Henry VII and similarly assuaged local leaders' concerns (and even then, local tensions resurfaced after Eckhart's departure, with the Dominicans eventually forced out of the city in 1330). By the time he left office in 1310, Eckhart had become known in the order as a man who got things done.

Did Eckhart suggest or even volunteer for this assignment? The details of this monumental transition in his life and career are shrouded in mystery. We don't even know exactly when he left Paris—sometime after June 1313— or when he arrived in Strasbourg—sometime before April 1314. Clearly the subsequent decade in Strasbourg represented a significant personal move for the friar, who had spent most of the previous forty years based at the priory of Erfurt. Although he had visited the Strasbourg house on multiple occasions, most of the priory's hundred-some residents were strangers to him. The easy camaraderie of the Erfurt house, or to a lesser degree St. Jacques in Paris, gave way to an unfamiliar environment, by no means hostile but still unfamiliar and perhaps unsettling for a man in his mid-fifties.

Eckhart first appears in Strasbourg's records as a witness to a property donation on April 14, 1314. He is listed as "Master Eckhart, professor of sacred theology." A similar document two and a half years later names him as "Brother Eckhart, vicar general" of Teutonia. Whenever this formal appointment by the master general came, it gave him wide-ranging powers among the Dominicans in Strasbourg "to investigate, to punish, to absolve, and to reform." His successes and failures in this mission are largely hidden from the historical record. Conflicts between the city's secular clerics and Dominicans did not disappear entirely, but the initial years of Eckhart's residence did witness an apparent de-escalation in confrontational rhetoric. Surviving deeds and other financial records indicate that the former provincial's fund-raising and persuasive abilities remained sharp, giving the Strasbourg Dominicans an ever firmer foothold in the city and its environs. Most tellingly, his superiors chose to keep him in place during a ten-year period when men of Eckhart's capabilities and stature were in high demand throughout the order. In December 1322, he was still in Strasbourg, and still described as vicar general.

Meister Eckhart's most lasting and visible impact in his new home would be on the Dominican men and women he instructed—possibly as an official lecturer, unquestionably as a much-revered senior colleague and preacher in his sermons and private conversations. The Strasbourg *collegium* was one of the most highly regarded programs within the order, attracting exceptionally bright (and ambitious) young men from Alsace and further abroad. Its cohorts, officially capped at an annual enrollment of twenty-three, included two of Meister Eckhart's most famous disciples, Johannes Tauler and Johann of Dambach. The two professors resident during the master's early years in the priory, Jean Picard of Lichtenberg and Heinrich of Lübeck, were both resolute Thomists, unlikely sympathizers with Eckhart's Neoplatonic leanings. Yet whatever differences of opinion emerged, there is no mention in chapter documents of open confrontations with the master general's newly resident emissary, fresh from his second regent professorship in Paris.

Pastoral care of nuns, or *cura monialium*, constituted a key component of the vicar general's charge, rendered even more timely by Bishop Johann's antibeguine campaign. The city of twenty thousand was home to eight Dominican convents, each housing more than a hundred nuns, and eighty-five beguine houses. Many secular clerics clearly resented the influence that the friars exercised over these women, serving as preachers, counselors, and confessors. What angered the bishop and his clergy even more was that many Dominican men continued to protect and serve Strasbourg's beguine communities, despite the explicit prohibition of Vienne's *Ad Nostrum*. Some of the city's oldest beguinages—Turm, Offenburg, Innenheim—remained under the explicit supervision of the Dominican priory. Boundaries between the order's official tertiary (lay) branch and beguines were also quite porous, as were the divisions between nuns and beguines in general, with some of the latter eventually embracing life in the convent under a rule. Eckhart and his fellow friars might have avoided visiting beguinages themselves (as mandated by *Ad Nostrum*), but they could not prevent beguines from coming to any of their churches, hearing their sermons, and participating in other activities of the spiritual community.

Eckhart had counseled and preached to religious women for at least twenty years, since his days as prior at Erfurt and later as provincial of Saxony. His surviving German sermons include offhand mentions of visits to convents in Cologne, Colmar, Zurich, and the Lake Constance region. In the wake of Marguerite Porete's execution and the Council of Vienne's *Ad Nostrum*, this pastoral role took on a new urgency, especially for the man sent by his order to defuse the escalating conflict in Strasbourg. Some historians in fact believe that Eckhart's principal mission in the city was to rein in some of the more controversial opinions of its religious women, beguine and nun alike. Certainly the master from Erfurt was not one to shy away from correcting what he considered harmful ideas and practices. What he did not anticipate was how much preaching to Strasbourg's religious women and laypeople would shape him and his own spiritual pursuit.

Divine Suffering

Meister Eckhart was familiar with Marguerite Porete's celebrated case and almost certainly had access to parts or all of *The Mirror*. He knew witnesses for the defense, especially his longtime colleague Godfrey of Fontaines, as well as many members of the investigating commission, including both his future Dominican superior, Berengar of Landora, and his contemporary from Erfurt, the Augustinian Eremite Heinrich of Friemar the Elder. Most significantly, he co-resided with William of Paris, the inquisitor himself, at the St. Jacques friary from 1311 to 1313. Eckhart's opinion of *The Mirror* is more difficult to assess. His own German sermon on Matthew 5:3 ("Blessed are the poor in spirit . . .") matches up closely with chapter 24 of Marguerite's book, and like her he consistently downplayed the role of asceticism and other external acts in drawing closer to God. *The Mirror's* criticism of Reason likewise resonated with the master and his increasingly intuitive pursuit of God. At the same time, Eckhart remained a scholastic at heart and likely bristled at her full-scale dismissal of philosophy and higher learning. He also clearly disagreed with her seemingly elitist notion of divine union and withdrawal from the world.

The most important question, and the one most difficult to answer, is what he made of her attempts to circulate such a potentially dangerous description of the divine pursuit among the wider public. Eckhart's fellow theologian Godfrey of Fontaines had marveled at the deep and subtle wisdom of *The Mirror*, but also cautioned that it should be used carefully, "for the reason that [many readers] might abandon their own way of life and follow this calling, to which they could never attain and so they might deceive themselves, for it is made by a spirit so powerful and trenchant that there are only a few such, or none." Meister Eckhart apparently concurred with this assessment and took great care never to mention Marguerite by name or to quote from *The Mirror*. At the same time, he also likely agreed with Godfrey that "none should doubt that this seed ought to bear holy fruit for them who hear it and are worthy." Was his own preaching on the subject in Strasbourg an attempt to continue Marguerite's work in a more orthodox manner?

The piety that Meister Eckhart encountered among Dominican nuns and beguines in fact showed few signs of infection by the alleged "Free Spirit" heresy. To the contrary, the devotional practices of the Rhineland's religious women is better characterized as hyperorthodox, in the instance of some mystical virtuosi taking conventional church teachings about penance and the other sacraments to extreme levels. Speculative mysticism, of the kind practiced by both Marguerite Porete and Meister Eckhart, likewise remained rare in these houses. More commonly, the pursuit of divine union involved great physical suffering and special visions—just the opposite of Eckhart's contemplative approach.

While female mystics remained an exceptional minority among nuns and beguines, their extravagant penitential practices and achievements made a profound impression on their sisters. During his lifetime, Eckhart witnessed a boom in the number of accounts by and about religious women claiming mystical experiences. The new trend—not coincidentally—paralleled the dramatic spike in women entering convents and beguinages and signaled a new degree of self-confidence among female spiritual seekers. More than a century earlier, the forthrightness displayed by the noble abbess Hildegard of Bingen had been rare; her fellow mystic and correspondent Elisabeth of Schönau (not highly born) claimed that an angel had repeatedly beaten her until she agreed to reveal her own visions.

The period 1250–1350, by contrast, was awash in written accounts by religious women in the forms of spiritual diaries (especially "sister books" kept by individual cloisters), hagiographies composed by male admirers (some of them Dominicans), and allegorical dialogues, such as Marguerite Porete's *Mirror.* Many of the latter relied heavily on the language and imagery of courtly love. As in such secular works, the central metaphor in every case was the quest, typically for the experience of ultimate love and unity with the divine. The main difference was that the seeker, the soul, was female and the love object, usually Christ, was male (although sometimes both He and Divine Love were also female—an even more interesting transformation).

Just as in the instance of chivalric romances, the public appetite for tales of these women's spiritual journeys appeared insatiable. This did not mean that such writings were universally accepted as valid. The beguine

Mechthild of Magdeburg (ca. 1208–92) knew that the authority of any female author was automatically suspect. "Ah Lord," she sighed, "if I were a learned, religious, man" (such as Eckhart), others might more readily accept such claims to divine experiences. Instead she adopted the familiar tack of acknowledging herself as "a fool, a sinful and poor being in body and in soul." When, in the course of one of her visions, she implored God to entrust his truths to some "wise people," He responded that it was her very humility that had led Him to choose her: "One finds many a master wise in the scripture who in himself, in my eyes, is a fool." Even then, Mechthild knew that her writings might be subject to "ill-willed interpretation" at the hands of spiteful "Pharisees." Her conundrum was distressing: "Now I fear God, if I keep silent, and I fear ignorant people, if I write. Most dear people, what can I do about it that this happens to me, and has often happened?" "I was warned about this book," she confided, "and people told me that if it were not protected, it could be thrown on the fire." Like many other women experiencing divine visions, the German beguine relied on the shared authority of a male cleric, in this case her Dominican confessor and scribe, Heinrich of Halle.

Mechthild's work, *The Flowing Light of Divinity*, was known to Eckhart long before his arrival in Strasbourg. The similarities that Mechthild's revered *Flowing Light* shared with Marguerite's condemned *Mirror* are striking. Both works describe the ascent of the soul to a mystical union with God. Both favor dialogues between the Soul and various figures, and employ the allegorical language and style of the courtly love genre, alternating between poetry and prose. The ultimate goal for Mechthild appears to be the same as for Marguerite: self-annihilation. In describing the divine union, which Mechthild calls "receiving God's greeting," she clarifies that "[n]o one can or should receive this greeting unless one has gone beyond oneself and become nothing. In this greeting I want to die while living. The blind holy people can never ruin this for me. These are those who love and do not know." Mechthild, like Marguerite, knew because she had experienced God herself. Her book, like *The Mirror*, might even provide a guide for those enlightened few who were able to understand and follow.

Brigitte of Sweden (1303–73) receiving a divine revelation from heaven, which she passes on to two mendicant biographers. Visions and other godly communications were common among late medieval female mystics.

But the differences between the two works are even more instructive, particularly in terms of Eckhart's subsequent responses to both. Mechthild, separated from Marguerite by two generations and hundreds of miles, had stayed markedly closer to the conventions of courtly love. Much of *The Flowing Light's* seven books and 267 chapters is occupied with wooing and dancing, ecstatic consummation and painful separation. Mechthild takes the bridal imagery made popular by Bernard of Clairvaux a century earlier to new heights. The Soul is a "full-grown bride," who longs to share the marriage bed with her Divine Lover, and accordingly strips naked in "the secret chamber of the invisible Godhead." Joining her beloved, "[t]he narrower the bed becomes, the closer they embrace. / The sweeter the kisses taste on my lips, the more longingly they look at one another." Ultimately,

[A] blessed stillness
That both desire comes over them.
He gives himself to her,
And she gives herself to him.
What happens to her then—she knows—
And that is fine with me.

Mechthild was also more clearly orthodox than Marguerite. Whereas Marguerite envisioned a difficult but steady spiritual journey to self-annihilation (seemingly bringing freedom from good works), Mechthild's ascent to God was gradual, full of "great torment," and occasionally yielding fleeting moments of ecstasy. In all his years of working with beguines and nuns, Eckhart regularly encountered this common linkage between extreme asceticism and heightened religious experiences. As with their male counterparts, communities of religious women sought to cultivate detachment from the body and an *imitatio Christi* through daily acts of self-mortification. The seasoned friar knew many of these practices from his own experiences in the Erfurt priory: fasting, sleep deprivation, physical work to the point of collapse, refusal to succumb to illness, and so on. He was also familiar with the frequent recourse of many brothers and sisters to self-flagellation, a penitential act that also supposedly curbed the appetites of the flesh. In some convents and beguinages, extreme versions of these and other "holy exercises of virtue"—such as carrying a cross of nails on one's back—often reached the point of alarming other sisters. Lack of food, drink, and sleep, aggravated by intentional self-isolation, led some women to deep despair and the brink of suicide. Yet almost all of the individuals singled out for pious biographies during Eckhart's lifetime described such willful acts of self-annihilation as necessary preparation for their intense spiritual experiences.

Food played a particularly significant role in the piety of religious women. This is not surprising, given the stereotypical role of women in preparing meals, but deciding when and what to eat also represented a particular kind of physical autonomy among female mystics. Denied the priesthood, holy women could nevertheless experience the suffering of Jesus through remarkable fasts and other painful ordeals. As the *Book of Twelve Beguines* explained, fasting also intensified the soul's insatiable hunger for God. Beatrice of Nazareth found this divine hunger so overwhelming that she frequently experienced choking and other tortures. Fortunately, the consecrated Eucharist allowed fasting women to "eat God," and be filled with the divine presence. Again, these were not heterodox events (or simple cases of anorexia nervosa) but rather intensifications of orthodox practices, such as Fri-

Christ hanging the bride, representing annihilation of the self,
in a fourteenth-century manuscript on divine love.

day and Lenten fasts or the Feast of Corpus Christi, a newly sanctioned
devotional practice focused on the consecrated host.

According to most written accounts of famed religious women, God not
only welcomed feats of great mortification but rewarded them with revelations and moments of ecstatic divine union. Only when self-will had been
weakened or destroyed through intense suffering could a soul experience
the "turn" (kêr) that opened it to rapture in the Holy Spirit. The visions accompanying these divine encounters might then occur at any time. The beguine Hadewijch of Antwerp (d. ca. 1260), like many religious women, was
often seized by the divine spirit during mass, particularly at elevation of the
consecrated host. The liturgical calendar and nearby statues clearly influenced the nature of visions, with appearances of the baby Jesus and Blessed
Virgin more common during Advent and Christmas, the suffering adult Jesus during Lent and Easter. The figure of Christ played a central role within
convents and beguinages, with various ascetic acts aimed at re-creating the
Passion and agonies of the Savior. (On rare occasions, holy women contem-
plating the crucified Savior's five wounds, or stigmata, were rewarded with
the same marks on their own bodies.) The Man of Sorrows was as often the

focus of female visions as was the Divine Lover—resulting in a profoundly Christocentric form of mystical encounters among religious women.

Such extreme practices and dramatic successes inspired both wonder and individualistic competition. Most accounts of famous religious women accordingly emphasized that the awe-inspiring feats described should not be attempted by readers. A century earlier, for instance, Christina of Saint-Trond (aka Christina the Astonishing; 1150–1224) had become famous for whirling like a Sufi dervish when in divine ecstasy, then climbing (some witnesses said levitating) up to church rafters, roofs, and nearby trees. The theologian Jacques de Vitry described how the holy woman tried to replicate the torments of the damned in hell by putting herself in ovens, plunging into boiling water (and suffering no visible injuries), having herself lashed to mill wheels and hanged on the gallows, or lying in open graves. In Eckhart's day, the Premonstratensian nun Christina of Hane died at the age of twenty-three after subjecting her sexual organs to such extreme tortures that even her pious biographer blanched. Another contemporary, Christina of Stommeln (1242–1312), allegedly suffered many years of diabolical torment in response to her own acts of self-mortification, ranging from being physically torn apart at night by demons (and reassembled in the morning by angels) to dodging the flying excrement thrown at her and her visitors by the same evil spirits.

Of course examples of such extreme asceticism remained rare, as they had in the days of the ancient desert fathers and mothers. And again, the goal of written accounts was to inspire wonder, not imitation. Christina—Vitry stressed—was a remarkable individual, a living example of divine power at work, but not a role model. What was most significant was that other religious women revered the central value of physical suffering and sought to emulate it in more moderate fashion.

From Pursuer to Pursued

Eckhart's reaction to such aspirations among the religious women he encountered was predictable. Long before his arrival in Strasbourg, he had decided that all external acts of piety—particularly the dramatic feats of such "living saints"—needed to be approached with the greatest caution. Ascetic practices were not in themselves harmful. Given his own emphasis on internal piety, he even anticipated the question during one of his sermons:

Now you might ask, "Ought anyone so placed [in contemplation of the divine] to practice penance? Does he lose anything by dropping penitential exercises?" Pay attention. Penitential exercises, among other things, were instituted for a particular purpose: whether it be fasting, watching, praying, kneeling, being disciplined [scourged], wearing hair shirts, lying hard, or whatever it may be, the reason for all is because the body and flesh are always opposed to spirit.

The body is often too strong for the spirit, he acknowledged, *and there is a real fight between them, an unceasing struggle.* The spirit was *an alien* in this world and needed all the help it could get, *but*—and this was a key distinction—*if you would capture and curb [the flesh] in a thousand times better fashion, then put on it the bridle of love.*

As Prior Eckhart had lectured his novices twenty years earlier, intentions mattered far more than deeds. Now he told his listeners, including various religious women, *[i]t is great foolishness when many a man fasts much, prays and performs great works and spends his time alone, if he does not mend his ways, and is impatient and angry. He should find out his greatest weakness, and devote all his energy to overcoming that.* The true seeker's goal was to establish true humility, and in that respect ostentatious works of self-denial were just as likely to feed self-pride as to dismantle it. It was external suffering that needed to be offered up and replaced with internal devotion.

Involuntary pain and suffering was another matter. About the time of his arrival in Strasbourg, Eckhart explicitly addressed the question of personal loss in his *Book of Divine Comfort.* The work was most likely composed for the Habsburg noblewoman Agnes of Austria (1281–1364), whose husband, King Andrew III of Hungary, had died in 1301, and whose father, Albrecht I, king of Germany, was assassinated by his own nephew in 1308. Inspired by Boethius's famous *Consolation of Philosophy,* Eckhart focused on the mental tribulations resulting from *misfortunes occurring to outward goods . . . to our relatives and dearest friends . . . and to ourselves: dishonor, hardship, pain of body, and heart's distress.* His stance was typically Augustinian: pain and suffering are inevitably part of the fallen human condition and ought not to be sought out—but in the end God can always bring good out of evil. His advice to Agnes, and to all of his listeners, was to embrace not the spiritual and physical pain of misfortunes but rather the divine grace that inevitably accompanied them. *There is solace for every sorrow,* he reassured his audience, *no hardship or loss that is without some comfort.*

In the tradition of Augustine and Seneca, Eckhart also saw involuntary suffering as a divine means of self-liberation, bringing the realization that *all suffering comes from love and attachment* to other people, things, and the body, not the misfortunes themselves. Weighed against the rewards of eternal life, earthly troubles should even be embraced: *probably no one can be found who is not fond enough of some living being to gladly do without an eye or be blind for a year, if at the end of it he could have his sight again and if he could thus save his friend from death.* Seneca counseled that *a man should take all things as if he had wished and prayed for them,* to which Eckhart added *if [a man] is perturbed by outward mishaps, then truly it is right and proper that God has permitted him to suffer this harm, for he wanted and thought to be just and yet was upset by so small a thing.* Returning to his recurrent theme of developing a proper mental attitude, Eckhart came to the Stoic conclusion that *the good man should never rail at loss or sorrow: he should only lament that he does lament them, and that he is aware of his own wailing and lamentation.*

Eckhart also remained leery of the out-of-body experiences claimed by some exemplary nuns and beguines as well as their self-inflicted agonies. Here too the master worried about the self-promoting dimensions of many private visions and secret moments of rapture. His own deep antipathy to images of the divine also made him wary of their vivid descriptions of God and heaven, not to mention their claims of intimate conversations with Christ, Mary, and various saints. Such "corporeal" and "spiritual" experiences, even if genuine, were vastly inferior to a purely intellectual encounter of the divine, without means. *Some people want to see God with their own eyes as they see a cow, and they want to love God as they love a cow.* Crude efforts of this nature were bound to fail, because *you love a cow for her milk and her cheese and your own profit.* He did not go as far as Gregory of Nyssa or Pseudo-Dionysius, denying the very possibility of such visions in this life, but neither did he follow many contemporaries in their enthusiastic embrace of the most famous female mystics of the day.

What spiritual advice did the master provide to the many nuns and beguines he encountered in Strasbourg? Rather than proscribe these communities' common valorization of suffering, Eckhart applauded these female audiences' desire for divine union while offering them an alternate vision of it—one based not on mortification, but on contemplation, not on self-isolation and competition, but on a communal project of spiritual progress. The best example he knew of such internalized seeking was the famed Cistercian convent at Helfta (about fifty miles from Erfurt), founded by the count of Thuringia and in Eckhart's youth directed by the formidable Gertrude of Hackeborn (1232–91). According to one admiring chronicler, Gertrude

> would read sacred scripture very eagerly and with great delight
> whenever she could, requiring her subjects to love sacred readings
> and often recite them from memory. Hence, she bought all the good
> books she could for her church or made her sisters transcribe them.
> She eagerly promoted the girls to learn the liberal arts, saying that if
> the pursuit of knowledge were lost they would no longer understand
> sacred scripture and the religious life would perish.

As he had advised his Erfurt novices twenty years earlier, Eckhart urged the religious women and laypeople in his Strasbourg audiences to reconsider their fervent ascetic pursuit of God. External means might help in the earliest stages of spiritual development but—like scholastic philosophy—were incapable of reaching God in themselves. More often they led to confusion and frustration. *Whoever seeks God in a special way gets the way and misses God, who lies hidden in it. But whoever seeks God without any special way gets Him as He is in*

Himself. God is not to be sought in isolation from the world—as was common among cloistered women—or in any human activities. *[I]f a man thinks he will get more of God by meditation, by devotion, by ecstasies, or by special infusion of grace than by the fireside or in the stable—that is nothing but taking God, wrapping a cloak around His head and shoving Him under a bench.* God is not to be sought at all, Eckhart now decided. Letting go of all desires, even the desire for God, was the only true way to prepare oneself for experiencing God.

Meister Eckhart's advocacy of spiritual submission likely resonated with the readers of female mystics, who wrote freely of being "taken" by the divine spirit. "We think that in the Eucharist we eat God," explained Hadewijch, but actually "He eats us." We are not the pursuers, we are the pursued; God initiates contact with the soul when the time is right. Some male religious writers identified themselves as "women" only when they spoke about their own carnal failings, but Eckhart's sermons positively embrace the traditionally female trait of passivity. *Wisdom,* he explains, *is a maternal name, for a maternal name has the property of passivity, and in God we posit both activity and passivity: for the Father is active and the Son is passive, this being the characteristic of being born.*

Female audiences undoubtedly welcomed the master's rejection of his age's misogyny. *When God made man, he made the woman from the man's side, so that she should be like him. He did not make her from the head or the feet, so that she would be neither woman nor man to him, but so that she should be his peer.* Just like men and women, he preached, the active and passive powers of the soul were complementary equals, each essential to achieving divine union. Obviously, *a woman and a man are unlike, but in love they are alike*; dwelling on their differences only brings *bitterness* and *no peace.* All humans, regardless of gender, possessed these complementary powers of the soul and all were capable of knowing God directly. When preaching on the perfectly humble man (*homo*), for instance, Meister Eckhart made clear that *we use the word* homo *for women as well as for men,* even though many of his fellow scholastics *refuse it to woman because of her weakness.*

It's not clear how much of an impact Meister Eckhart's preaching made on the religious women he encountered. His version of the pursuit of God ran counter to the spiritual thinking and experience of most nuns and beguines. One Dominican sister, Anna of Ramschwang, described how she had consulted Meister Eckhart during his visit to her cloister of St. Katharinenthal, asking him the significance of her vision of the Christ child. His response was not recorded, though Anna did note in apparent disappointment that the master spoke "in an elevated way [about] highly incomprehensible matters." Elsbeth of Beggenhofen, the subprioress of Ötenbach, similarly sought Eckhart's advice about her spiritual experiences and was told that *no earthly wisdom can grasp it; it is purely a work of God,* and that her ascetic practices were *of no help unless one submits in free letting-go-ness to God's true command and receives [Him].* Eckhart's discouragement of spiritual competition and external devotions possibly came as a relief to Elsbeth and some of her sisters, but as a source of anxiety to others. The ascetic regime, after all, at least offered a clear and defined path to God. After Eckhart's death, his disciples Johannes Tauler and Heinrich Suso had considerable success in spreading their version of the master's teachings among religious women, but how much fruit Eckhart's own attempts bore is more difficult to say.

On the other hand, Eckhart's encounter with the nuns and beguines of the Rhineland appeared to reinforce his own emerging conviction that pursuit of divine experience should not be an esoteric endeavor. Their genuine hunger for divine experience, he told them, was admirable; their reliance on either extreme suffering or visions was misguided. Instead he proposed a more accessible third way, between the elitist contemplative approach of Marguerite and that of the spectacularly suffering "superwomen" of popular religious literature. The path to experiencing God was open to all, the master preached, not just to an enlightened or self-mortifying few. Unlike most of his fellow scholastics, who considered all women, like uneducated men, incapable of higher spiritual understanding, Eckhart moved toward an ever more universal approach to divine union. But if neither gender nor learning was a barrier to the experience he preached, what then was the value of learning itself? This posed an uncomfortable question for the lifelong scholastic, one he never completely resolved.

CHAPTER NINE

Master of Living

Better one master of life than a thousand masters of learning;
but no one learns and lives before God does.

SAYING 8

The Restless Intellect

Preaching in Strasbourg confirmed Meister Eckhart's sense that there was a genuine popular appetite for his message. Audiences full of friars, religious women, and laypeople began to perceive the revered Dominican not just as a "master of learning" (*Lesemeister*), but as a "master of living" (*Lebemeister*). Eckhart in turn addressed his listeners with an unprecedented level of intellectual respect—not as distracted children in search of entertainment and sensation but as adult fellow seekers:

> [T]here is not one of you who is so coarse-grained, so feeble of understanding, or so remote but he may find this joy within himself, in truth, as it is, with joy and understanding, before you leave this church today, indeed before I have finished preaching: he can find this as truly within him, live it, and possess it, as that God is God and I am a man.

And the content was potentially explosive. Practical, everyday mysticism available to any genuine seeker was a startlingly radical notion for any society, let alone the deeply hierarchical world of Eckhart's day. That it might be pursued with minimal reference to external rituals or acts was even more revolutionary.

At the same time, the master had not completely abandoned his scholarly ambitions, at least for the still incomplete *Opus Tripartitum*. He brought the working manuscript of the *Opus* with him to Strasbourg, as he did in all his travels, but he does not appear to have made much progress. The only Latin works he might have written during this time were the *Commentary on John* and the *Book of Parables in Genesis*; if there were other commentaries or treatises they have not survived. Most historians believe that he abandoned the project sometime during his fifties, while in Strasbourg. In a few sermons, he mentions keeping a notebook, but these and other notes apparently contained ideas for his sermons rather than for his forlorn magnum opus. How could such an ambitious project—his life's work as he initially imagined it—launched just a decade earlier with such enthusiasm and hope come to such an ignominious end?

The likeliest explanation is his long-standing, uneasy relationship with higher learning. Like all Dominicans, Eckhart had preached his entire adult life, more than thirty years by this point. Whenever his consuming pursuit of God and simultaneous deep love of learning veered away from the practical goals of the Order of Preachers he became visibly uncomfortable, even slightly defensive. Academic debates over such rarefied topics as the nature of angelic motion did not square easily with the order's down-to-earth mission of offering comfort, knowledge, and salvation to actual human beings. Time and again during his university days Eckhart admonished himself and his fellow academics against the perils of scholarly hubris. And during the years he worked on the *Opus Tripartitum*, the master made frequent strained—and ultimately unsuccessful—attempts to present it as a practical work that would be useful for his fellow friars.

Throughout the previous two decades he had spent in the upper reaches of university and Dominican leadership, Eckhart had repeatedly reminded himself and his listeners of the necessity of humility in all actions. *Humility is a root of all good. . . . I said in the schools of Paris that all things shall be accomplished in the truly humble man.* Now, surrounded by audiences of novices, nuns, beguines, and laymen, he returned to the theme with a renewed sense of purpose.

> *That is true humility, that a man should concern himself with nothing of that which he is . . . whether by doing or leaving undone, but wait upon the light of grace. The knowing what to do and to leave undone is true humility of nature.*

Was it humility that persuaded Eckhart to leave his magnum opus undone in order to devote his energies to other work he felt divinely called to do? Or had he reached a theological and professional dead end in his work on the *Opus* and decided to make a virtue out of necessity by leaving it incomplete and embracing the role of preacher instead?

Eckhart's ambivalence about the scholastic project in general was not a sudden development. At least since his second professorship in Paris and most likely well before that, his growing appreciation of intuitive approaches to God corresponded with a growing frustration at the limitations of rational inquiry. Without a more experiential way of "knowing" the divine, Eckhart began to suspect that philosophical pursuit would remain endlessly unsatisfying. As he told one lay audience,

> *so long as the intellect does not find true being and does not penetrate to the ground, so as to be able to say, 'this is this; it is such and not otherwise,' so long does it remain in a condition of questing and expectation; it does not settle down or rest, but labors on, seeking, expecting, and rejecting.*

The intellect never rests in this life, he concluded. And even whatever knowledge is gained remained suspect and ultimately inferior.

> *The light of the sun is little compared to the light of the intellect, and the intellect is little compared to the light of grace. Grace is a light that transcends and soars above everything that God ever created or could create. Yet the light of grace, great as it is, is little indeed compared with the divine light.*

In embracing the way of intuition and negative theology, Eckhart had already called into question all so-called scientific knowledge of God. *There is no way man can know what God is. But one thing he does know: what God is not. And this a man of intellect will reject.* More specifically, this was an interpretation many men of intellect at the University of Paris rejected. While libraries today overflow with the manuscripts of scholarly commentaries from this period, only a few scattered notes remain from Meister Eckhart's lectures there. The Neoplatonic modification of Thomist philosophy that he and his mentor Dietrich proposed found few supporters or disciples, at least not in Paris (back in Germany was another matter). His own philosophical project was not attacked so much as ignored—an even worse fate among scholars. In part, this was the by-product of a recent retrenchment of many Dominicans around the *Summa* of Aquinas, which in 1309 they officially declared as canonical for the order.

Eckhart was not alone in his views. Other members of the younger generation, most notably the Franciscan William of Ockham (ca. 1287–1347), had likewise begun to question the overall scientific unity of theology claimed by Duns Scotus. Their attacks focused not just on the conclusions of their fellow theologians but on their methods—specifically assumptions made on the basis of language. Ockham in particular believed that much of the speculative theology espoused by their teachers was based on unwarranted generalizations. Applying his famed razor to all theological systems, the Englishman argued that plurality was not to be assumed without necessity. In other words, all objects—humans, trees, chickens— were knowable, intelligible individual entities in themselves. Universals proposed an essential relationship between some of those individuals, but these were merely mental concepts created by humans, not by God. They had no reality. And even then, these categorical names (*nomina*) represented faulty generalizations based on the resemblance of various particulars and inadequate knowledge of the whole. There was no basis for assuming that all chickens, for instance, shared a common nature or essence. Many key scholastic concepts, such as species, were thus rendered meaningless, as were the deductions made employing them. Metaphysical entities, Ockham argued, remained beyond human comprehension and were only

William of Ockham, the English Franciscan who challenged the central scholastic notion of universals and gave birth to a theological school later known as nominalism.

known to the degree that God had revealed them in scripture and church tradition.

Eckhart similarly came to believe that true knowledge of God came mainly through revelation and intuition, less so by rational deduction or induction. In that sense, he also questioned the apparent scientific certainty of some of his colleagues. But unlike Ockham and many of the other scholars later called "nominalists," Eckhart held on to the idea of universals, which he believed existed in the mind of God (but remained inaccessible to humans). This was the position he believed that his spiritual mentor Augustine had held, maintaining an essential order of the cosmos that remained implanted in the human soul but just out of reason's reach. As a "high realist," Eckhart remained convinced that his own bridge between Plato and Aristotle offered an appealing (and true) "middle way" for his fellow theologians. To his disappointment, the world of academe collectively shrugged, rendering the *Opus Tripartitum* an increasingly dubious effort.

Finding a New Voice

Eckhart's renewed devotion to popular preaching in Strasbourg returned the Parisian master to the "excellent and noble work" first proclaimed to him in his youth. Eckhart had never abandoned that calling and in fact gave sermons regularly, but during his long career he had also interpreted many other aspects of his job as ways to fulfill the Dominican duty to preach: his work as a mentor, a mediator, a scholar, a confessor, and above all, a teacher of younger friars. In his new position in Strasbourg, he was called to focus even more on preaching sermons, and this gave the forty-year veteran a renewed sense of his apostolic mission. Like Jesus and his earliest followers, he addressed all who desired to come closer to God and sought to teach them as those first apostles had done.

But what did the apostles teach? According to Bernard of Clairvaux, it was "not to read Plato and obvert Aristotle's sophisms, or to undertake an interminable course of study that never leads to the apprehension of truth. What they taught us was how we should live." Since his earliest days as a Dominican, Eckhart's ears had rung with the similar warning from former master general Humbert of Romans against "learning things curious and subtle but of little use." The conventional goal of popular sermons was to provoke a genuine sense of repentance, ideally followed by an experience of divine grace and a reinvigorated life of love and devotion. All the preaching manuals Eckhart had studied advised against raising intellectually challenging topics and instead recommended targeting the emotions of a given audience. "Useful" information led to personal conversion; all else was extraneous to the purposes of the preacher.

But to Eckhart, nothing could be more useful than helping other people experience for themselves the true happiness that was God. To succeed, however, he would have to explain sophisticated theological concepts to ordinary people, translating such notions as the divine birth from university Latin into the German of everyday life. In this respect, Meister Eckhart's understanding of his vocation as a public teacher was revolutionary. His revered mentor, Albert the Great, had scorned the use of German for theology, and fellow scholastics scoffed at the notion that uneducated common men, let alone women of any rank, were capable of grasping anything but the most rudimentary elements of the faith. Experienced preachers concurred: a successful sermon needed to be entertaining and offer a simple message, or the average listener would quickly lose interest. Scholastic theologians, they might have added, were hardly noted for their lively writing or engaging lectures. Logic and authority were the scholar's allies; humor and pathos were not. Popular, and thus effective, preaching was best left to seasoned professionals who knew how to combine diverting anecdotes with a modest, straightforward moral.

The abstruseness of academic jargon was no minor obstacle to Eckhart's preaching ambitions. Yet he faced an even greater challenge: how to describe the ineffable mystery of union with God in mere words. Virtually all Neo-platonists, since the days of Plotinus, had assumed that their way to the divine was inherently inaccessible to all but an enlightened few, and that those few would be able to unravel their dense philosophical language. Many female mystics relied heavily on allegory to address difficult concepts, but their works were mostly written accounts based on personal experience, likewise aimed at "the few" able to understand them (and still fewer able to imitate them). Conveying the unknowability of God and similar mysteries to roomfuls of ordinary people was a radically new and untested venture. How could any preacher hope to convey practical advice about divine union to a popular audience, let alone a middle-aged, celibate academic shaped by the narrow worlds of the friary and the university?

Meister Eckhart must have realized the enormity of the task he had set for himself—one that was in some ways more daunting than completion of the massive *Opus Tripartitum*. He could not deliver his philosophically complex Latin treatises on the divine birth to a church full of ordinary, German-speaking merchants, craftspeople, and peasants. To succeed in this new endeavor, he would have to make significant adjustments. The most obvious adaptation was language itself. Eckhart believed that *words*, like powerful herbs or certain precious stones, *have great power: we could work wonders with words. All words have their power from the first Word.*

Speaking in his Thuringian version of Middle High German, Eckhart the popular preacher had long ago learned to deliberately avoid Latin words as much as possible. The Luke annunciation excerpt of "Ave Gratia Plena Dominus tecum!" for example, was immediately followed by the explanation: *This text which I have said in Latin is found in the holy Gospel, and means in German, "Hail to thee, full of grace, the Lord is with thee!"* On a few occasions he

proceeded to pick apart the individual words of the day's Latin passage, ex-
positing at length (in a schoolmasterly way) on the relevance of *et* ("and")
within a certain context, or *ecce* ("behold"). Preaching on Ecclesiasticus
50:6–7 (*"Like the morning star in the mist"*), Eckhart illustrated his point about
the derived nature of human existence by singling out *the little word quasi,
which means "as" and is what the children at school call a "by-word" [adverb]. This
is what I mean in all my sermons. The truest thing that one can say of God is
"Word" [Verbum] and "Truth." God called himself a Word . . . man was a "by-word."*
Here was the grammatical equivalent of comparing humans to a face reflected in a mirror. It is hard to imagine two more eloquent or memorable
expressions of humans' fundamental dependence on God (the verb of being
itself) that still preserved individuals' distinctiveness.

Far more frequently, the master had to find or invent German words for
many concepts that he had, until now, only written about in Latin. Often no
German counterpart for a Latin term existed, or the one that did lacked the
richness or complexity Eckhart wanted to convey. This was especially true
when Eckhart wanted to describe the relationship between God and the
soul. His solution was to use the building blocks of the German language to
construct completely new words. He became a master of neologisms, creating what philosopher Karl Jaspers called "music of abstraction." In Eckhart's
hands, theology became poetry, lending his German sermons a poignancy
and vitality not found in his Latin writings. Typically he chose to insert pre-
fixes or suffixes that allowed him to transform everyday words into abstract
concepts. By adding the suffix *–heit* ("hood"), for instance, to *Got* ("God"),
Eckhart was able to talk about the essential divinity (*gotheit*) that was much
more than the Creator Himself. Similar modifications supplied him with
words for "essence" (*wesenheit* or "beinghood"), the specific quality of objects (*isticheit* or "thisness"), "immutability" (*unwandelbarkeit* or "unchange-
fulness"), and of course, the unique quality of trusting detachment necessary
to experience God (*gelâzenheit* or "letting-go-ness"). Many of Eckhart's neologisms involved negating a known concept. *Entbilden* combined *ent* (de- or
un) with *bilden* (to form or illustrate) to convey how one must "unmake" an
idea or image. *Entwerden* combined *ent* and *werden* (to become) to describe

the spiritual state of "unbecoming" or "becoming nothing." God in His ineffability was described as "unspoken" (*ungesprochen*), "being-less" (*weselos*), "a not-God" (*ein nihtgot*).

In addition to coining new words, Eckhart made use of an evocative vocabulary to convey otherwise difficult ideas. His descriptions of divine union, for example, employed a variety of verbs of movement for the relationship between God and the soul: lying, going, falling, flowing, sinking, drifting, running, bubbling, pushing, pulling. The ultimate moment of divine experience was "breaking through" (*durchbrechen*), a word that powerfully conveyed the culminating significance and drama of the event. He frequently described encountering God, an extrasensory experience, in terms of the senses, particularly taste: *Divine love is like the salt that makes bitter food taste good*; or *it would be strange indeed if the soul that had once tasted and tried God could stomach anything else. One saint says that the soul that has tasted God finds all things that are not God repugnant and stinking.*

The imagery of Eckhart's German sermons was also distinctive from that of most contemporaries. Unlike the writings of many female mystics, there were no singing birds, flowers, dancing, lovemaking, or other conventions of courtly love literature. There were also no extended allegories of Love, God, or Wisdom. In general, Eckhart preferred stark metaphors that conveyed a sense of dehumanized and unimaginable vastness. In descriptions of the soul confronted with the limitless Godhead, the most common images were *wilderness*, *desert*, *ocean*, and *abyss*. Some of these metaphors were in fact employed by Mechthild and other female mystics, but only Eckhart made use—more than 140 times—of his innovative image of the ground (*grunt*). The one major exception to these impersonal images was his frequent reference to divine union as the *eternal birth* of God in the soul. Accordingly this metaphor led Eckhart to praise the *maternal name* of God, where the eternal Word *does mother's work, for it is properly a mother's work to conceive*. In one even more remarkable passage, he also recounted, perhaps autobiographically, how *it appeared to a man as in a dream—it was a waking dream—that he became pregnant with Nothing like a woman with child, and in that Nothing God was born; He was the fruit of Nothing. God was born in the Nothing.* Such positive associations with the female body and childbirth were nowhere to be found in contemporary theological writing, not even among women mystics.

Eckhart's penchant for paradoxical images pushed human language and imagination to their limits, pointing toward something just outside our grasp but never capturing it. One scholar has likened his frequent self-subversion to "creating a kind of metaphysical black hole." Words and concepts are no sooner presented than they are deliberately undermined and negated in paradoxical fashion. *God is a word, an unspoken word . . . a word that utters itself . . . God is spoken and unspoken.* In another sermon, listeners learned that *God is nothing . . . He is being above all being. He is beingless being.* Elsewhere, Eckhart voiced with approval the opinion of an unnamed master, who claimed that God was *a becoming without becoming, newness without renewal.* When the soul freed itself from time and space, it experienced in God *breadth without breadth, expanseless expanse.* Such attempts were the closest a negative theologian could come to describing the ineffable. How does one love the ineffable? *You should love Him as He is: a non-God, a non-spirit, a non-person, a non-image; rather as He is a sheer pure transparent One, detached from all duality.* When it came to God and the soul, only negative and inherently contradictory language could convey the utter otherness of the subject from everyday human experience.

Even with a new and colorful vocabulary, the master's translation of scholastic thinking into the common idiom was not always successful. What, for instance, would a modestly educated listener have made of this attempt to describe the timeless melding of divine union?

> *You should wholly sink from your youness and dissolve into his Hisness and your "yours" and his "His" should become so completely one "mine" that with him you understand His uncreated self-identity and His nameless nothingness. . . .*

Viewed in the context of Meister Eckhart's general teaching and as words on the page, the passage appears somewhat comprehensible; heard in a sermon, the spoken concepts of "youness" and "Hisness" must have been baffling.

As might be expected, Eckhart was also not completely consistent in his use of some terms over the course of a long preaching career, and occasionally the same word (most notably, intellect; *vernünfticheit*) was used to mean different things at different times. Conversely, only experienced listeners would have realized that the soul's "little spark" (*vünkelîn*), "little castle" (*bürgelîn*), and "soul's light" (*licht in der seele*) all referred to the same thing. And not all scholarly concepts, despite Eckhart's inventiveness, could be made accessible. Niceties such as the distinctions between the active intellect, the passive intellect, and the potential intellect were especially difficult to convey to a popular audience. Fortunately, he didn't have to try. The former academic was no longer compiling a *summa* and he wasn't interested in offering a crash course in scholastic theology to a popular audience. He cared only about what was useful and necessary for them to understand in order to know God directly.

Waking the Audience

The format of Meister Eckhart's sermons remained the same throughout his career. After reading the day's scriptural passage in Latin and German, the preacher offered multiple interpretations of the verse in question. Sometimes he laid out the plan for his subsequent homily, following the conventional Dominican exegesis format of four different senses of a passage: literal, allegorical, moral, and anagogical. After reciting Acts 9:8, for instance, he proceeded to explain:

> *The text which I have quoted in Latin is written by St. Luke in Acts about St. Paul. It means "Paul rose from the ground and with open eyes saw nothing." I think this text has a fourfold sense: One is that when he rose from the ground with open eyes he saw Nothing, and the Nothing was God; for when he saw God he calls that Nothing. The second: when he got up he saw nothing but God. The third: in all things he saw nothing but God. The fourth: when he saw God, he saw all things as nothing.*

The remainder of the sermon proceeded to address each of the four senses in depth, which in the hands of Eckhart became a powerful exposition on the unknowability of God, the soul's hunger for the divine, detachment from the world, and the birth of God in the soul. Often the master veered from his youthful training and did not enumerate his points in advance, instead offering a succession of readings.

A medieval preacher speaks to a diverse audience of laypeople.

As always, Eckhart was aggressive in his interpretations of scriptural passages, convinced that any reading conveying an essential truth was a valid reading. This exegetical approach, common among contemporary scholars, gave him considerable thematic flexibility. In Eckhart's hands, Peter's exclamation upon being released from prison ("Now I know truly that God has sent me His angel"; Acts 12:11) served merely as a launching point for the master's usual topic: *Now let us turn this phrase round and say, "Because God has sent me His angel, therefore I know truly." Peter is as much as to say "knowledge." I have said before, knowledge and intellect unite the soul with God.*

As a lecturer, Meister Eckhart regularly drew on five types of authority. Most obviously, scriptures themselves provided the starting point for all his vernacular sermons as well as the internal structure of many of them. Here his reputation as a famous theologian would help assuage any doubts among listeners about some of the interpretive liberties he took with biblical passages. As in his academic writings, he also made open reference to many other thinkers. Christian figures—particularly Augustine, but also Pseudo-Dionysius, Albert, and Aquinas—were usually cited by name. Non-Christian authors, most notably Aristotle and Plato, but also Avicenna and Maimonides, received mostly indirect mention, usually as *a master* or *a pagan master*. The same was true of fellow scholastics, who were often grouped together as *our masters* or *our best masters*. Occasionally, Eckhart wished to stress the freshness of an idea, such as *yesterday a question was debated in the schools among the great theologians*.

But indisputably Meister Eckhart's favorite authority—other than Augustine—was Meister Eckhart. Dozens of times he prefaced a remark with *I have also said before (and it is a certain and true saying)*, or *sometimes I have said, as I said the day before yesterday in my last sermon*, or *I said in Paris*. Only a preacher of such an elevated scholarly status could get away with such frequent self-invocation. Yet in Eckhart's defense, his strategy was as much to establish an ongoing dialogue with his individual listeners as to proclaim his own superior knowledge—building on his own authority but also drawing each person in the room into a more intimate relationship. "I" appears several hundred times in Eckhart's surviving vernacular sermons, but almost always in the explicit or implicit sense of a conversation. Often that dialogue is with the listener, created by Eckhart's rhetorical use of *you*. *You often ask*, for instance, *how you ought to live. Now pay close attention*. Describing the utter stillness preceding a personal experience of God, Eckhart anticipated his listener's question: *But sir, you ask, where is the silence, and where is the place where the Word is spoken?* Again and again, he answered his own questions—not unlike in a scholastic *summa*—but with the justification that *I was once asked, I was recently asked, people say*, or similar formulations.

One of Meister Eckhart's most disarming tactics was the semblance of intimacy he created with his listeners. Often, he appeared to be thinking out loud in the pulpit, sharing his own emerging thoughts. Many seemingly irrelevant asides in fact served to establish a level of trust with the audience. *Last night I thought . . . as I said at St. Margaret's* created a sense of communal striving, as did *I used to wonder (it is many years ago) . . . I used to think sometimes, when I came here*. Such devices simultaneously reinforced his own teaching status while flattering his listeners that they were all involved in the same journey of discovery. *I was thinking last night that there are so many heavens,* he shared, semi-confidentially, or another time in the same sermon, *I was thinking last night that all likeness is a preamble. I cannot see anything unless it has likeness with me; I cannot know anything unless it has likeness with me.*

Like his inspiration Augustine, Eckhart the preacher was not afraid to share personal feelings and doubts with his audience: *Often I feel afraid, when I come to speak of God, at how utterly detached the soul must be to attain to union with him.* He conversationally confided from his own experience in detachment, *I will tell you how I think of people. I try to forget myself and everyone and merge myself for them, in unity.* Eckhart the man spoke openly of his love for his father, his close friends, and his fellow brothers, and confided at the beginning of one sermon that *I was thinking on the way, when I was supposed to come here, that I did not want to come here because I should become wet with love. Perhaps you too have been wet with love, but we shall not discuss that.* Were these tears of sorrow or of joy? Eckhart observed that both emotions *come from love,* but he did not disclose his own state of mind at the time.

Again, only a preacher of the master's scholarly status could have indulged in such apparent familiarities without jeopardizing his own authority. A younger friar or a parish priest, let alone a woman of any rank, could never have betrayed such vulnerability. Eckhart's challenge, by contrast, remained both making himself accessible and engaging with a general audience, and here it was to his advantage to acknowledge his own struggles in communicating essential truths. *As I was coming here today,* he confided, *I considered how to preach to you clearly so that you would understand me properly, and I hit upon an analogy. If you can understand it, you will be able to grasp my meaning and get to the bottom of all that I have ever preached about.* He then proceeded to compare the perception of a piece of wood by his own eye with the intersubjective experience of the soul's spark with divinity itself. Ironically, the analogy is in fact more confusing than the straightforward account of divine union that follows it.

One of the most striking tendencies throughout Eckhart's vernacular sermons is his fervent and almost desperate desire to connect with his audience, to be understood. Most preachers of the day sought to achieve this goal at an emotional, visceral level, with simple expectations. Eckhart wanted his words to resonate personally as well, but his message went far beyond the need for repentance. Yet often the ideas he was trying to convey remained difficult and intangible, with Meister Eckhart employing multiple metaphors and examples within single sermons in an attempt to make his main point.

Such earnestness was apparently another aspect of his intentionally disarming candor. *Dear children*, he pleaded, *I beg you to note one thing: I pray you for God's sake, I beg you to do this for my sake and carefully mark my words. Just listen to one word more*, he promised elsewhere, *and then no more*. To his credit, Eckhart good-naturedly mocked his own relentlessness: *I will say one word— or two or three!*; or another time, *This is a sermon for All Saints. Now it is over. Now all sit still, I want to keep you longer. I am going to preach you another sermon. God preserve us from peril!* Like many academic lecturers, Eckhart had a hard time confining his ideas to the allotted time (or theme).

Again, the risks in Meister Eckhart's popular preaching project were considerably greater than in typical mendicant sermons with much more modest goals. He knew that the truths he spoke often remained elusive. He charmingly conceded that *Here some folk will say, "You are telling us wondrous things, but we perceive them not." I regret that too.* In part this confusion was an inevitable shortcoming of human language. *Since our understanding is a changing thing, it cannot give birth to a perfect Word. The word you hear from me is not a perfect word: it betokens the Word that is in me.* Preaching was an imperfect art at best, but explicating matters that Eckhart himself acknowledged were often "subtle" posed an especially frustrating challenge, occasionally giving way to moments of despair: *Whoever has understood this sermon, good luck to him. If no one had been here I should have had to preach it to this offertory box.*

Frequent incomprehensibility was also a problem of the master's own making. Along with neologisms and striking metaphors, Meister Eckhart was known for outrageous statements that appeared to be dangerous, especially when taken out of context (as later inquisitors would do). In seeking to emphasize the Creator's attraction to the divine part in every human soul, Eckhart provocatively proclaimed that *God loves nothing but Himself.* Of course he went on to explain that this fact *is to our supreme advantage, for therein He has in view our highest bliss. He intends thereby to lure us into Himself and to get us purged so that He can take us into Himself, so that with Himself He may love us in Him and Himself in us.* Yet no sooner was the master safely back in the realm of conventional thought than he boldly proclaimed that *I will never give thanks to God for loving me, because He cannot help it, whether He would or not: His nature compels Him to it. I will give Him thanks because by His goodness He cannot cease to love me.* (One can only imagine the semi-attentive husband returning home to tell his wife that, according to Meister Eckhart, thanksgiving to God was unnecessary.)

Intentionally jarring statements of this nature were similar to Zen koans, meant to shake the listener out of the constraints and complacency of conventional thinking. When Eckhart preached *If God gave me anything outside of His will, I would disregard it,* he was not disparaging God or His will but rather making the point that nothing existed outside of God's will. Here the same self-confidence that led the famed scholar to make personal asides prompted him to make incautious theological remarks that could be misunderstood or later be used against him. Eckhart was prone to forget that most of society did not know the open atmosphere of intellectual exchange common to the friary and the university. In one sermon on his most difficult subject, the primordial *ground* of divinity, the master appeared to sense that he was in perilous territory. After declaring that *I am the cause of God's being God: if I were not, then God would not be God,* Eckhart immediately added, *[b]ut you do not need to know this.* Later in the sermon he reiterated, *If anyone cannot understand this sermon, he need not worry. For so long as a man is not equal to this truth, he cannot understand my words, for this is a naked truth which has come direct from the heart of God.*

Disclaimers of this nature were rare in the vernacular sermons. Instead Eckhart typically had high estimations of his listeners' powers of comprehension and attempted to remain attuned to his audience's potential concerns. *St. Augustine says, what a man loves, that he becomes in love. Should we now say that if a man loves God he becomes God? That sounds as if it were contrary to faith,* Eckhart conceded, *[and] strange . . . but so it is true in the eternal truth, and our Lord Jesus Christ possesses it.* Another statement, that *the soul is made of all things, sounds stupid, but it is true,* as was still another teaching from Augustine, that on the surface *sounds trite and commonplace.* Skeptical listeners, unswayed by the master's scholarly credentials, could at least count on his solemn word: *If you could know with my heart, you would understand, for it is true, and Truth itself declares it. . . . I call Truth as a witness and offer my soul as a pledge.*

Eckhart knew from his youthful training in Erfurt that a preacher's preceding reputation gave him a considerable advantage in the pulpit, but even here he preferred the pedagogical dialogue of the classroom to ensure that the listener was following him. *Mark this well!* he would say at one point, *now observe,* or *pay attention here!* Listeners at Eckhart's vernacular sermons also got to witness the combativeness of a university professor entertaining students with dismissive remarks about his fellow theologians. Typically, the disagreement came as an aside: *Some masters would hold that the soul is only in the heart. That is not so, and some great masters have erred in this.* Comments of this nature, delivered to a nonacademic audience, reflected an entrenched scholarly habit, less a means of self-aggrandizement than an irresistible by-product from years of lecturing and disputing. In defending more controversial assertions, Meister Eckhart could become more forceful. *I have been asked to make my meaning clear. I will do so, although it is in opposition to all masters now living,* he all but barked during one sermon. He then proceeded to give a lengthy and difficult discourse on good works and time, before concluding, *See, thus we have proved the truth of my assertion, as it truly is. And all those who contradict it, I contradict them and care not a jot for them, for what I have said is true, and truth itself declares it.*

This contentious side of the master has remained mostly hidden from modern readers. Yet it would have been no surprise to his contemporaries, particularly within the order and at the university. One did not rise to prominence in both institutions without some degree of self-assurance and forcefulness of character. But Eckhart did not use the pulpit to settle scores: he never mentions any living person by name and consistently attempts to keep the focus on his description of divine union. He was fond of clarifications—*[a]s I once said before and was not properly understood*—but generally assumed sincere confusion rather than intentional misconstrual of his words. References to *slow-witted persons* were principally aimed at fellow theologians or clerics.

> *I marvel how some priests, learned men with pretensions to eminence, are so easily satisfied and are misled by these words that our Lord spoke, "All that I have heard from my Father, I have revealed to you." They want to take it this way and declare that he has revealed to us "on the way" just so much as is needful to our eternal bliss. I do not accept this interpretation, for it is not the truth.*

While clearly benefiting from his own status as both a Dominican and a theologian, Eckhart claimed it was the truth he proclaimed, not his reputation, that was worthy of respect. Indeed among his fellow scholastics

> *there are some people who consider themselves very holy and perfect, they make a great parade and use big words, and yet they seek and desire so many things, and want so many possessions and pay so much regard to themselves and to this and that; they claim to be contemplatives, and yet they can brook no contradiction. You can be sure they are far from God and have not attained that union.*

Pitting himself and his pious listeners against hypocritical clerics was a dangerous game, and Eckhart knew it. In the *Book of Divine Comfort*, he accurately predicted that

> *many a dull-witted man will declare that a lot of things I have said in this book and elsewhere are not true. To this I reply with what St. Augustine says in the first book of his Confessions. . . . How can I help it if anyone does not understand this? . . . I am satisfied if what I say and write is true in me and in God.*

The master of learning, in other words, clearly lived on in the master of living. Eckhart's disappointing academic impact and his embrace of an intuitive path to God did not lead him to turn his back on philosophy or reason.

Intellectual and teaching habits formed in the classrooms of Paris continued to shape the popular sermons of the Dominican preacher, even as he labored to find a new, jargon-free, spiritual language. The "wayless way" that emerged was a marriage of reason and intuition, paradoxically combining an "imageless" approach to the divine with stunning metaphors and analogies. Although Meister Eckhart couldn't have known it at the time, it was these sermons that would carry his message forward—much further in time and to far, far more people than his doomed *Opus Tripartitum* ever could have.

CHAPTER TEN

The Wayless Way

Whoever is seeking God by ways is finding ways and losing God,
who in ways is hidden. But whoever seeks for God without ways
will find him as he is in Himself, and that man will live
with the Son, and he is life itself.

GERMAN SERMON 5B

Making Room for God

During Meister Eckhart's ten years in Strasbourg and subsequent four years in Cologne, he preached his "method" of divine union to thousands of people—nuns, beguines, and fellow friars, but also craft workers, bankers, merchants, lawyers, soldiers, parish priests, farmers, servants, widows, manual laborers, and assorted travelers, including pilgrims. He spoke to congregations in the Dominican churches of both cities, as well as male and female cloisters and other churches up and down the Rhine that invited him. He also counseled interested individuals privately, often as a confessor. The German sermons that have survived from this period, in fact, were meticulously transcribed by some of his devoted followers and in some instances edited by the master himself before circulation.

In recasting his religious philosophy for an audience of average men and women, Meister Eckhart distinguished himself from other preachers in some notable ways. Unlike the typical Dominican or Franciscan friar, he did not dwell in his sermons on sin and its eternal punishment in the torments of hell. He did not tell colorful anecdotes about the saints, like Berthold of Regensburg, or entertaining morality tales about religious scoffers who get their comeuppance in the end. There is, in fact, little drama or humor in the sermons that have survived. Nor were there any prophetic visions or descriptions of eternal bliss in an extended description of heaven. For those listeners seeking sensations of remorse or joy, let alone diversion of any sort, Eckhart would have been an acute disappointment.

At the same time, the Dominican master had one major draw that few if any of his contemporaries could match: he offered to show people how to directly experience God. The hunger for authentic and unmediated experience of the divine remained as strong in the early fourteenth century as it had been a hundred years earlier. People of all backgrounds continued to seek out God in the midst of their lives and in the religious options before them. Thanks to his impeccable scholarly credentials, Meister Eckhart enjoyed the authority to describe in poetic language the practical steps that led to divine union, or what he sometimes daringly called "becoming God." Seekers had to be willing to engage with his intellectually challenging—some might say impenetrable—way of speaking. But for those who persevered, the usual stories from the pulpit about dismembered martyrs paled in comparison.

Not that Meister Eckhart was the first preacher of his day to discuss *ways into God*. In his own sermons he identified two widely acknowledged methods, which he contrasted with his own "third way." *One [way] is to seek God in all creatures with manifold activity and ardent longing.* The most famous recent advocate of this *via positiva* was St. Bonaventure, like Eckhart a learned theologian and admirer of St. Augustine as well as a mendicant administrator. Bonaventure, though, was a Franciscan who embraced the affective piety of his order's founder, in which one began by loving the created world and other humans and progressed to loving the Creator Himself. In his *Soul's Journey to God*, Bonaventure described—in Latin and chiefly for his fellow Franciscans—six successive levels of illumination, beginning with the apprehension and perception of beauty in nature and fellow humans by the physical senses, followed by intellectual and spiritual contemplation up the ladder of creation, and culminating in an encounter with the divine source of all. This approach appealed to many Christians of the day and was expanded upon in such instructional works as David of Augsburg's *Seven Stages of Prayer* and Rudolf of Biberach's *Seven Roads of Eternity*. Dante Alighieri was its most famous contemporary proponent and his *Divine Comedy* the most enduring dramatization of the pathway to God through ever-expanding love.

While never impugning Bonaventure or any of his fellow Franciscans by name, Meister Eckhart rejected seeking God through the external world and senses. The Creator was in all things, he agreed, but He could not be directly encountered in this way. Human will, as he had argued against the Franciscan Gonsalvo in Paris, too readily attached itself to images and intermediaries, preventing genuine access to the divine. Even poverty, the supreme virtue of the Franciscans, could become an idol. Preaching on the feast of St. Francis, Eckhart directly challenged his rival mendicants on this score, arguing, *I used sometimes to say (and it is quite true) that whoever truly loves poverty is so desirous of it that he grudges anyone having less than he has. And so it is with all things, whether it is purity, or justice, or whatever virtue he loves, he wants to have to the highest degree.* Rather than look to the created world, *He who would see God must be blind.* Rather than seeking God's voice in the conversation of men, *anyone who wishes to hear God speaking must become deaf and inattentive to others.*

The second way into God was through an ecstatic episode, such as the rapture of St. Paul, who wrote of "a man [who] was caught up and heard such words as may not be uttered by men" (2 Corinthians 12:2). Experience of this nature was a rare gift, bestowed only on a select few throughout the Church's history, perhaps including certain contemporary nuns and beguines. This way, however, like that of Bonaventure, yielded only an external and partial view of God. *You should understand*, explained Eckhart, that in a similar ecstatic experience *St. Peter stood on the circle of eternity, but was not in unity beholding God in His own being.* In other words, there was no full union between the seeker and the divine, no direct experience of God's essence.

The third way, the master concluded, *is called a way, but is really being at home, that is: seeing God without means in His own being. . . . Outside of this way all creatures circle and are means. But led into God on this way by the light of His Word and embraced by them both in the Holy Spirit—that passes all words.* This third way—*not really a way*—offered much more than either affective piety or special revelations could ever promise, and, unlike those two paths, Eckhart's third way was accessible to all seekers. *How marvelous, to be without and within, to embrace and be embraced, to see and be the seen, to hold and be held— that is the goal, where the spirit is ever at rest, united in joyous eternity!* Such complete immersion in the Godhead, according to Eckhart, was the ultimate transformative experience sought by all humans.

But how could the seeker *be at home* in this way? *Is it better to do something toward this, to imagine and to think about God?—or should he keep still and silent in peace and quiet and let God speak and work in him, merely waiting for God to act?* Here Meister Eckhart is at his most innovative, providing genuine instruction but at the same time arguing against a formulaic striving for God. He depicts, rather, a kind of anti-striving, in which the individual progressively lets go of all the impediments to divine union and then awaits *the divine birth*, an event of pure grace. This is the process of *letting-go-ness*, the approach that Eckhart first identified as prior in Erfurt and refined over the course of the next twenty years.

Where Bonaventure and other Franciscans wrote of gradually elevating the soul to God, Eckhart preached of stripping the soul down to its bare essence. God was not to be found "out there," but within. As in his reading of the Bible, Eckhart worked as a spiritual excavator, going deep below the surface of things to get at the core truth that was God. When Jesus preached "Blessed are the poor in spirit" (Matthew 5:3), he did not just mean the physically destitute but the internally liberated individual *who wants nothing, knows nothing, and has nothing.* The ultimate preparation for an experience of the divine birth was not the accumulation of good deeds and knowledge but rather a self-emptying of all images and desires—even the desire for God—a radical letting-go of virtually every aspect of individual identity that verged on self-annihilation.

Such complete *detachment* or *cutting away* (MHG *abgescheidenheit*) had been the goal of Christian monks and nuns for over a millennium. Tradition dictated that achieving it required many years of sacrifice and suffering, and the inexhaustible resilience to rebound from countless personal setbacks. Yet Meister Eckhart reassured his listeners that to reach this state of total detachment *all you need is right intention and free will.* With such a pronouncement, he seems to embrace the kind of easy piety that foes of the new apostolic movements feared and condemned. *No one should think it is hard to come to this, even though it sounds hard and a great matter. It is true that it is a little difficult in the beginning in becoming detached. But when one has got into it, no life is easier, more delightful or lovelier.* Moreover, Eckhart claimed, any sincere believer, regardless of status, could succeed:

> *And so I say again, as I said before, there is no one here so coarse-grained, so ignorant, or unprepared but if, by the grace of God, he can unite his will purely and totally with the will of God, then he need only say with desire, "Lord, show me your dearest will and strengthen me to do it!" and God will do so as truly as he lives.*

But what Meister Eckhart assumes—though he clarifies it less frequently—is that his listeners have already internalized the teachings of conventional piety and conformed their lives accordingly:

> *Now I say, as I said before, that these words and this act are only for the good and perfected people, who have so absorbed and assimilated the essence of all virtues that these virtues emanate from them naturally, without their seeking; and above all there must dwell in them the worthy life and lofty teachings of our Lord Jesus Christ.*

Before one can transcend traditional piety, one must have absorbed its values as second nature. Nonetheless, seekers should never confuse the means of piety with its ends. *If anyone were to ask me, Why do we pray, why do we fast, why do we do all our works, why are we baptized, why (most important of all) did God become man?—I would answer, in order that God may be born in the soul and the soul be born in God. For this reason all the scriptures were written and for that reason God created the world and all angelic natures.*

The advanced seeker has already completed three of *the four steps into*

God described by Eckhart. *The first is that fear, hope, and desire grow in [the soul].* *In the beginning of the good life,* the master concedes, even *fear is useful to a man and gives him access to love.* Similarly, *for a man to have a peaceful life is good, but for a man to have a life of pain in patience is better; but that a man should have peace in a life of pain is best.* Only then can the soul take the second step, where *fear and hope and desire are quite cut off,* before coming to *the third stage . . . a forgetfulness of all temporary things.* In that sense, all—or virtually all—conventional Christian teachings and practices formed the prelude to the divine union Eckhart preached. The ultimate goal of these preliminary stages, as he had stressed to Dominican novices, was humility, which *makes a man greatest of all: whoever has this most deeply and perfectly has the possibility of gaining all perfection.* His sermons were aimed at those people who had already attained this deep level of humility, individuals who considered themselves pious Christians but hungered for more. For such men and women, he promised, divine union was a short step away; for those still immersed in selfish lives, Eckhart offered no quick fix. Unfortunately this was a key distinction that a casual listener—or inquisitor—might miss.

The remaining challenge for advanced believers, according to Eckhart, was letting go of their own piety, at least as a source of pride or self-esteem. The only acceptable objective is to know God, and this must be a pure and selfless desire. *The just man seeks nothing in his works: for those who seek anything in their works or work for any "why" are thralls and hirelings. . . . Indeed, even if you create an image of God in your mind the works you do with that in view are dead and your good works are ruined.* At one point Eckhart explicitly addresses the self-identified godly in his audience, *all those who are bound with attachment to prayer, fasting, vigils, and all kinds of outward discipline and mortification,* pleading with them to sever

> all attachment to any work that involves the loss of freedom to wait on God in the here and now, and to follow Him alone in the light wherein He would show you what to do and what not to do, every moment freely and anew, as if you had nothing else and neither would nor could do otherwise . . . for otherwise you will have no peace.

The same purity of intention applied to prayer. *Anyone who desires something from God is a merchant*—the ultimate put-down for his pious listeners.

> *If one prays for [anything] but God alone, that can be called idolatry or unrighteousness. . . . When I pray for nobody and for nothing, then I am praying most truly, for God is neither Heinrich nor Conrad. If we pray to God for [anything] else but God, that is wrong and faithless and a kind of imperfection, for it is to set up something beside God.*

Petitionary prayer, in Eckhart's eyes, was both foolish and selfish: *If you are sick and pray to God for health, then health is dearer to you than God, and He is not your God.* From the divine perspective, Eckhart preached, the great majority of individual requests were also ridiculously petty, as he illustrated with a contemporary analogy:

> *Suppose I came to the pope a hundred or two hundred miles and when I came into his presence I were to say, "My lord, Holy Father, I have traveled about two hundred miles with great difficulty and expense, and I beg you—and this is what I came for—to give me a bean;" truly, he and whoever heard it would say, and rightly, that I was a great fool.*

Even noble requests, ostensibly bringing one closer to God, stumbled over themselves and became substitutions for what should be the sole objective.

> *Anyone who seeks anything in God, knowledge, understanding, devotion, or whatever it might be—though he may find it he will not have found God: even though he may indeed find knowledge, understanding, or inwardness, which I heartily recommend—but it will not stay with him. But if he seeks nothing, he will find God and all things in Him, and they will remain with him.*

Letting go of the image of God as a heavenly wish granter was no easy matter, especially given how deeply ingrained this idea was in the

Christianity of the day. Yet according to Eckhart, this prevailing attitude constituted a fundamental misunderstanding of the nature of both God and prayer. *Looking for something with God [is] treating God like a candle with which to look for something; and when you have found what you were looking for, you throw the candle away.*

The most powerful prayer, he revealed, *one well-nigh omnipotent to gain all things, and the noblest work of all is that which proceeds from a bare mind.* Only when the seeker had made his or her mind *free* (MHG *ledic, vri, lûter, blôz*) of all images, literally *un-pictured (entbildet)*, could he or she *learn, firstly, how to pray to God . . . for God is above names and ineffable.* In other words, the seeker should pray for union with a mysterious, imageless God, not the anthropomorphized old man with a beard or any other imagined being. Yet ironically, the master provides one particularly memorable image to convey the imageless encounter: *Strip God of all his clothing—seize Him naked in his robing room, where He is uncovered and bare in Himself. Then you will "abide in Him."*

The gap between this God of the scholastics and the God of most people was considerable. Transcending the divine images that saturated fourteenth-century Christianity represented a formidable challenge that was probably beyond the average churchgoer. Yet according to Meister Eckhart only those seekers who were willing to let go of all the conventional structures of religion—to let them fall away like obsolete scaffolding—could be truly open to the divine birth within. *Whatever is familiar to you is your foe*, he warned. Even the focus on "God" Himself prevented the seeker from experiencing the infinite *ground of being* beyond the human idea of the Creator, leading Eckhart to make the seemingly shocking proclamation, *therefore I pray to God to make me free of God, for my essential being is above God*, where God is understood *as the origin of creatures.*

The final and perhaps greatest barrier to the divine birth within was the self, what we would today call the ego. *Cease to be this or that*, he advised, *and to have this and that.* Our Lord, Eckhart reminded his listeners, *says, "He who would be my disciple must abandon self;" none can hear my words or my teaching, unless he has abandoned self.* Yet how few otherwise pious seekers were able to accomplish this feat! *It is lamentable how some people think themselves very lofty and quite one with God, and yet have not abandoned self, and cling to such petty things in joy and sorrow. They are a long way from where they imagine themselves to be.* Eckhart compared a seeker who continued to hold on to his or her personal identity to a sick man with a thick coating on his tongue, who is unable to really taste food or wine: *As long as you mind yourself or anything at all, you know no more of God than my mouth knows of color or my eye of taste.*

When some of his listeners expressed frustration to Meister Eckhart that they had practiced worldly detachment yet received *no inwardness nor devotion nor rapture nor any special consolation from God,* he admonished them that they were still not letting go of all that is not God. *If you would know truth clearly,* Boethius had counseled, *you must cast off joy, and fear, and expectation, and hope, and pain.* Each of these attitudes, Eckhart explained, was a means, and thus an impediment to experiencing the divine directly. Similarly, *memory, understanding, and will, they all diversify you, and therefore you must leave them all: sense perceptions, imagination, or whatever it may be in which you find or seek to find yourself. After that, you may find this birth, but not otherwise—believe me!* Do not imagine, the master added, *that your reason can grow to the knowledge of God. If God is to shine divinely in you, your natural light cannot help toward this end.* Human reason, to the contrary, often posed additional barriers to the divine experience.

The way to reach God, in short, was to stop pursuing Him, at least with the intellect and all its desires, *for as long as you want more and more, God cannot dwell or work in you.* Occasionally Eckhart seemed to approach the heretical self-annihilation described by Marguerite Porete: *therefore a man must be slain and wholly dead, devoid of self and wholly without likeness, like to none, and then he is really God-like.* But "destroying the old man" was a perennial Christian theme. What was novel was the apparent prioritizing of a radical internal "poverty" over external poverty—a difficult goal but one accessible to all seekers. Meister Eckhart sympathized with popular reactions to such greater spiritual demands but was unwavering on their necessity:

> *A man once came to me—it was not long ago—and told me he had given up a great deal of property and goods, in order that he might save his soul. Then I thought, Alas! How little and how paltry are the things you have given up. It is blindness and folly, so long as you care a jot for what you have given up. But if you have given up self, then you have really given up.*

The true seeker must therefore be intrepid and continue forward in the midst of doubts.

> *In all a man does he should turn his will Godward and, keeping God alone in mind forge ahead without qualms about its being the right thing or whether he is making a mistake. If a painter had to plan every brush-stroke with the first, he would paint nothing.*

The Divine Birth

Meister Eckhart's mature understanding of *letting-go-ness* was comprehensive. Not only must the sinner let go of the world and sin, but also of all the traditional remedies proposed by the Church: pious acts of devotion and petitionary prayer aimed at flawed human notions of "God." The seeker had to let go of all images, desires, and thought itself. Only then was he or she ready for the final step in Eckhart's way to God, which *is to be silent and let God work and speak within.* Typically, the seeker was *more aware of God . . . in a quiet place,* but that requirement, Eckhart clarified, reflected human imperfection more than divine nature, *for God is equally in all things and places.* Most important, he continued,

> *all your activity must cease and all your powers must serve [God's] ends, not your own. . . . No creaturely skill, nor your own wisdom nor all your knowledge can enable you to know God divinely. For you to know God in God's way, your knowing must become a pure unknowing, and a forgetting of yourself and all creatures.*
>
> *Now you might say, "Well sir, what use is my intellect then, if it is supposed to be empty and functionless? Is that the best thing for me to do—to raise my mind to an unknowing knowledge that can't really exist? For if I knew anything at all it would not be ignorance, and I should not be empty and bare. Am I supposed to be in total darkness?"*
>
> *Certainly. You cannot do better than to place yourself in darkness and in unknowing.*

Eckhart knew well the potential terror of such an internal state, without rules, directions, goals, or other points of reference. *Sir, you place all of our salvation in ignorance!* But the master remained adamant, demanding the leap of faith that would allow God to enter.

> Now you might say, "Oh sir, is it really always necessary to be barren and estranged from everything, outward and inward . . . if a man is in such a state of pure nothingness, is it not better to do something to beguile the gloom and desolation, such as praying and listening to sermons or doing something else that is virtuous, so as to help himself?"
>
>   No, be sure of this. Absolute stillness for as long as possible is best of all for you. You cannot exchange this state for any other without harm. That is certain. You would like to partly prepare yourself and partly let God prepare you, but this cannot be.

There was no turning back from this ultimate letting-go, the culminating point of existence, *and if you give way to the impulse to turn back, you are bound to lapse into sin, and you may backslide so far as to fall eternally.*

These are unexpectedly harsh words from the normally encouraging master. How could he be so certain that such self-emptying would lead to the desired divine union? The answer lay in Eckhart's understanding of the very nature of the soul and its intrinsic link to the divine.

> I have a power in my soul which is ever receptive to God. I am as certain [of that] as that I am a man, that nothing is so close to me as God. God is closer to me than I am to myself: my being depends on God's being near me and present to me.

This power is variously named by Eckhart as *the divine light of the soul, the head of the soul, the husband of the soul, the guardian of the spirit, the light of the spirit, the imprint of divine nature, a citadel, a tiny drop of intellect, a twig,* and, most famously, *a little spark. The masters,* he notes, *say this [power] is nameless,* and indeed Eckhart concedes *that it is neither this nor that; and yet it is something that is more exalted over "this" and "that" than are the heavens above the earth. It is uncreated and uncreatable, a piece of divine and celestial nature.* This power *alone is free,* and *it touches neither time nor flesh, flowing from the spirit, remaining in the spirit, altogether spiritual.* Like its divine source, this power knows neither time nor other human distinctions, such as *here* and *now.*

Eckhart's descriptions of *the divine spark* harken back to his longtime search for a universal religious philosophy. Pagan and Christian sages alike, he believed, particularly those influenced by Neoplatonism, had long recognized this elusive spiritual core in all human beings and struggled to pin down its nature.

> *There is a fine saying of one pagan master to another about this. He said, "I am aware of something in me which shines in my understanding; I can clearly perceive that it is something, but what it may be I cannot grasp. Yet I think if I could only seize it I should know all truth." To which the other master replied, "Follow it boldly! For if you could seize it you would possess the sum total of all good and have eternal life! St. Augustine spoke in the same sense: 'I am aware of something within me that gleams and flashes before my soul; were this perfected and fully established in me, that would surely be eternal life!'"*

The entire point of radical self-emptying and letting-go was to eliminate the mental noise and other distractions that obscured this power, which naturally sought out *the sweetest, the highest, the best.* The theological term for this power, Eckhart explained, was *synteresis* (Greek "careful watching"), what we today might call the moral compass, or more simply the conscience. It was the part of the soul that always pointed toward God but was often drowned out by selfish desires. Eckhart compared the liberated *divine spark* to the flame of a candle, burning brightly and more clearly the farther it springs from the wick.

Ironically, the "imageless" preacher relied on several metaphors to convey the ideal precondition of the soul necessary for the divine spark to achieve its end. One was the absolute silence necessary to hear the Word, the creative work of God.

The heavenly Father speaks one Word and speaks it eternally, and in the Word He expends all His might and utters His entire divine nature and all creatures in the Word. The Word lies hidden in the soul, unnoticed and un-heard unless room is made for it in the ground of hearing, otherwise it is not heard; but all voices and all sounds must cease and perfect stillness must reign there, a still silence.

The nature of a word is to reveal what is hidden, Eckhart preaches, which is why the author of the book of Wisdom (18:14–15) wrote, *"In the middle of the night when all things were in a quiet silence, there was spoken to me a hidden word. It came like a thief by stealth."* This *secret and hidden word (verbum abscon-ditum)* is in fact *the* Word, the divine logos of creation embodied in Christ, which when "heard" joins the Creator and creature in complete union. It is the *voice crying out in the wilderness* (Matthew 3:3), the sole source of hope in the *inner desert* generated by the seeker.

Another favored representation of the soul before union was the image of complete darkness. Only when the soul is deprived of all images can the *simple, pure light* of the divine spark be perceived. Here Eckhart sides with the description of divine illumination offered by Pseudo-Dionysius:

Anything you see, or anything that comes within your ken, that is not God, just because God is neither this nor that. Whoever says God is here or there, do not believe him. The light that God is shines in the darkness. God is the true light: to see it, one must be blind and must strip from God all that is "something."

For Eckhart, this "blindness" was more than simply shutting one's eyes to creation, it was emptying one's mind of all images, *so that the divine light can shine into that place I have often spoken of: this is so pure and transcendent and lofty that all lights are darkness and nothing compared with this light.*

By far Eckhart's favorite metaphor for the divine spark's work in the soul was the *divine* (also *eternal*) *birth.* The birth of the Son in the ground of the soul of the believer had been a theme of early Christian teaching, dating back to the second century CE. Clement of Alexandria, Hippolytus, and especially Origen all wrote of Jesus being "born again" in the heart of the believer. For Origen, this event was based on acquired knowledge of the Word, while in the works of Maximus the Confessor the divine birth was the product of a virtuous life. Eckhart either knew these teachings directly or via contemporaries such as Albert or Bonaventure. But his own understanding of the divine birth was distinctive, stressing instead the internal silence and emptiness that made it possible.

Like the Blessed Virgin herself, the soul of the seeker had to be pure and uncorrupted. Only the higher power of the divine spark remained unpolluted by creaturely thinking, yet even here some unwanted alloys needed to be stripped clean. *I have often said that the soul cannot be pure unless she is reduced to her original purity, as God made her, just as gold cannot be made from copper by two or three roastings: it must be reduced to its primary nature.* Like the alchemist's elixir, the distilled essence of the divine spark makes possible the very act of creation, of birth.

To be *ready to receive God's most beloved will and to do it continually*, Eckhart clarified, *I would be a virgin, untrammeled by any images, just as I was when I was not. . . . Since according to the masters union comes only by the joining of like to like, therefore a man must be a maiden, a virgin, who would receive the virgin Jesus.* As in his embrace of spiritual poverty, Eckhart distinguishes between external virginity and chastity—as in the case of those under religious vows—and internal purity, a complete *letting-go* of all mental attachments.

The stillness and darkness of the desert night, the utter emptiness of a virgin mind, all made a direct encounter with God inevitable. And here, Eckhart revealed, was the greatest irony of the long quest for God: the ultimate role reversal of seeker and sought. The final step for the human seeker was in fact pure passivity, a total *letting-go-ness* that Eckhart called *potential receptivity*. The ultimate *breaking through*, he explained, was not made by the seeker coming to God, but by God coming to the seeker.

> *You need not seek Him here or there, He is no further than the door of your heart; there He stands patiently awaiting whoever is ready to open up and let*

Him in. No need to call to Him from afar: He can hardly wait for you to open up. He longs for you a thousand times more than you long for Him.

The divine spark provided the gateway, but the initiative came from the divine creator Himself.

The seeker who has fully let go of all images and thoughts is irresistible to God. *Whenever a man humbles himself, God is unable to withhold His own goodness; He is obliged to sink Himself, to pour Himself out into that humble man, and to the meanest of all He gives Himself most and gives Himself wholly.* Some of Eckhart's fellow theologians recoiled at the notion of limiting divine freedom in this way, but the master insisted on underscoring the divine compulsion to love:

God's comfort is pure and unmixed: it is perfect and complete, and He is so eager to give it to you that He cannot wait to give you Himself first of all. God is so besotted in His love for us, it is just as if He had forgotten heaven and earth and all His blessedness and all His Godhead and had no business except with me alone, to give me everything for my comforting. And He gives it to me complete, He gives it to me perfectly, He gives it to me most purely, He gives it all the time, and He gives it to all creatures.

Eager to press home his point, Eckhart reaches for some of his characteristic hyperbole.

If anyone were to rob God of loving the soul, he would rob Him of His life and being, or he would kill God, if one may say so; for the self-same love with which God loves the soul is His life, and in that same love the Holy Ghost blossoms forth, and that same love is the Holy Ghost.

The divine birth, after all, was *God's chief aim. He is never content till He begets His Son in us. And the soul, too, is no way content until the Son of God is born in her.* This, Eckhart explained, was the true meaning of the gospel text, "God sent His only-begotten Son into the world." *You should not take this to* mean the external world, as when he ate and drank with us, but you should understand it of the inner world. In other words, *we are an only son whom the Father has been eternally begetting out of the hidden darkness of eternal concealment.*

Eckhart's astonishing expansion of the Incarnation of Christ does not deny the historically unique identity or mission of the Savior but rather makes a distinction between Jesus's *carnal birth—about [which] you have been told plenty—*and *the eternal birth or the eternal Word . . . spring[ing] from the essential mind of [God] the Father.* In this latter respect, *God is ever at work in the eternal now, and His work is the begetting of His Son. He is bringing him forth all the time.*

> And so, if a man is to know God—and therein consists his eternal bliss—he must be, with Christ, the only Son of the Father. . . . True, you remain clearly distinguished in your carnal birth, but in the eternal birth you must be one, for in God there is no more than the one natural spring.

And so, he attempted to clarify, *if you ask me, since I am an only son whom the heavenly Father has eternally begotten, whether I have eternally been that son in God, my answer is: Yes and no. Yes, a son in that the Father has eternally begotten me, not a son by way of being unborn [i.e., eternal].*

Eckhart was treading on dangerous ground here, risking that some of his listeners might not appreciate his fine distinction between the way that Jesus was the unique Son of God and the way that the righteous seeker was also God's son. Still the preacher pursued his point with abandon: *For between your human nature and his there is no difference: it is one, for it is in Christ what is in you. That is why I said in Paris that in the righteous man all things are fulfilled that holy scripture and the prophets ever said of Christ: for, if you are in a right state, then all that was said in the Old and New Testaments will be fulfilled in you.*

These were heady words for any simple seeker in the audience. Was Meister Eckhart actually saying that experiencing the divine birth in the soul made one divine? This was far more than any other way to God promised—but could it actually be true?

Becoming God

For Eckhart, the eternal birth was the seeker's return to his or her true nature. But what was this true nature and how was it affected by the divine union? The divine birth, the master explains, is a profoundly intimate and intersubjective experience, in which the boundaries between the self and God become blurred. The actors and the act become indistinguishable from one another. The divine birth in the seeker's soul is a mutual event: *the opening and the entering are a single act.* The resulting self-awareness is likewise shared, to the extent that there is but one perspective. *You must know,* Eckhart explains, *that this is in reality one and the same thing—to know God and to be known by God, to see God and to be seen by God.* Or in his more famous—and provocative—formulation: *The eye with which I see God is the same eye with which God sees me: my eye and God's eye are one eye, one seeing, one knowing and one love.*

The state Eckhart described was more than immersion. One should not think of the soul as a piece of wood in a tub of water, he cautioned, for these were *united but not one with one another . . . where there is water there is no wood, and where there is wood no water.* Nor, conversely, was the soul like a vessel in the conventional sense: *Spiritual vessels are different from physical vessels . . . whatever is received in that is in the vessel and the vessel in it, and it is the vessel itself. Whatever the spiritual vessel receives, is its own nature.* The soul *in God,* Eckhart underscored, is *nothing like God,* but instead is *of the same essence.* Just as God is everywhere, the transformed soul is everywhere. *Whatever is in God, is God, it cannot drop away from it.*

Thus the seeker does and doesn't *become God* in a conventional or literal sense. It would be more accurate to say that the divinized soul participates in God, while keeping its own distinctive and derivative identity. Human existence, after all, is borrowed from God, who is the face causing the reflection in the mirror. *It is a question difficult to answer,* Eckhart concedes, *how the soul can endure it without perishing when God presses her into Himself.* Yet the distinction between Creator and created does not totally disappear. Eckhart also carefully distinguishes between *the inner man,* who experiences divine union, and *the outer man*, who continues to live in the world. The inner man, or *bare substantial being*, coexists with God *in the ground*; the outer man, or *personal being*, shares of this substance but remains a worldly creature, reliant on divine grace throughout its earthly existence.

For Eckhart, divine union was not some optional upgrade; it was the very purpose of human existence. *I have said before and say again that everything our Lord has ever done he did simply to the end that God might be with us and that we might be one with Him, and that is why God became man. It would be of little value for me,* he proclaimed elsewhere, *that "the Word was made flesh" for man in Christ as a person distinct from me, unless he was also made flesh for me personally so that I too might be God's son.* Yet the idea that such a union could be achieved on earth remained a controversial claim, especially among theologians and church leaders. The universal accessibility of such a state posed even more troubling questions about the roles of clergy and sacraments. And what were the consequences for an individual who achieved such union— were they truly "free in the spirit," as some contemporaries claimed St. Paul had promised? Meister Eckhart's *wayless way* to God obviously came out of a deep Christian tradition, but where it was headed was less obvious to his audiences, and perhaps even to the master himself.

CHAPTER ELEVEN

Living Without a Why

*The just man has such need of justice that he cannot love anything
but justice. If God were not just—as I have said before—he would care
nothing for God.... If the devil were just, he would love him
insofar as he was just, and not a hair's breadth more.*

GERMAN SERMON 41

The Seeker Transformed

The divine birth represented for Meister Eckhart what the chivalric romances of his youth would have called his Holy Grail. Like a questing knight,
after many years of journeying he had at last discovered the pure and shin-
ing prize he sought. This treasure, he realized early on, lay not in the wider
world he had shunned at the age of sixteen, nor, he eventually decided, in the
daily discipline or good works of a pious friar. Like Parzival and other great
seekers, he looked increasingly within himself for answers, gradually letting
go of all images and notions of his divine quarry, until the only way left to
"know" the God he sought was in a direct encounter. The God Eckhart
found was not reached by the intentional suffering and ecstatic visions of
mystical nuns or beguines, but by his final letting go of the pursuit itself,
whereupon that spark of divinity within broke through and filled his being.
The result was a divinized person (*homo divinus*), what Eckhart called the
"just" or the "noble" person.

But at what cost this prize? Had the Parisian master unwittingly strayed into the heretical territory of religionless spirituality, the "auto-theism" of Marguerite Porete? Worse yet, was he unwittingly leading scores of the trusting faithful to their own perdition? Whatever his private reflections, Eckhart the public preacher showed no doubts that *the divine birth* constituted the fundamental truth of the gospels and of all Christianity. It was his pastoral duty to share this version of the good news with the world. Yet at the same time he was no isolated naïf. As a longtime administrator with some degree of worldly experience, Eckhart knew that he was presenting a novel and potentially hazardous interpretation of the quest for salvation. Out of some combination of conviction and self-confidence he regularly courted danger with his provocative exclamations. Preaching the divine birth to "the common people" was daring enough, but Eckhart went still further, attempting to convey his unconventional notions of God and the Godhead and of an active spirituality based not on the quest for salvation but on the "why-less" nature of creation itself. The *just man* transformed by the divine birth became in that sense not just *like* God but God Himself—a seemingly heretical notion by any traditional theological standard.

Without full knowledge of the master's taste for hyperbole or of the way Eckhart qualified his most outrageous statements, his contemporaries might be forgiven for seeing more than a passing resemblance to the notorious Free Spirit heresy and its talk of self-divinization and freedom from conventional morality. Eckhart was aware of this risk and tried to head it off by invoking his theological hero Augustine, who claimed that *when a man accommodates himself barely to God, with love, he is un-formed, then in-formed and transformed in the divine uniformity wherein he is one with God.* "One with God" was a familiar and sufficiently vague phrase that kept his sermon safely within the bounds of orthodoxy, but Eckhart seemed intent on pushing his luck, adding, *when [that man] is one with God he brings forth all creatures with God, bestowing bliss on all creatures by virtue of being one with Him.*

What were the moral obligations of an individual who had been thus transformed by the *divine birth*? Here too the master treads perilously close to the alleged "spiritual liberty" of Marguerite Porete. *The truly humble man,* according to Eckhart, *has no need to pray to God for anything.*

This man now dwells in unhampered freedom and pure nakedness, for he needs undertake and take on nothing small or great—for whatever belongs to God belongs to him. . . . This humble man has as much power over God as he has over himself, and all the good that is in all the angels and all the saints is as much his own as it is God's own.

The spiritual perfection resulting from the *divine birth* in the soul, according to Eckhart, was not a rejection of human nature but a fulfillment of its true potential.

Some contemporaries heard in Eckhart's words an endorsement of the Free Spirit heresy, the idea that those who had experienced union with God could never lose divine status and were thus at liberty to live as they chose, eschewing good works and Christian ritual—and even committing sin—without consequence. But once again, Eckhart's penchant for shocking statements made things unnecessarily hard for him. His teachings on the effects of the divine birth were in fact among his most orthodox beliefs. Contrary to adherents of the Free Spirit heresy, the liberty preached by Eckhart did not make Christian virtues superfluous but rather inevitable. *Some people, Eckhart preaches, hope to reach a point where they are free of works, [but] I say this cannot be.* The individual transformed by the divine spark does not *need* to do any good works to reach heaven, but *chooses* to do them because of his or her new divine nature. Nor do sexual promiscuity or other sins suddenly become blameless—quite the opposite.

In very truth I believe, nay, I am sure, that the man who is established in this cannot in any way ever be separated from God. I say he can in no way lapse into mortal sin. He would rather suffer the most shameful death, as the saints have done before him, than commit the least of mortal sins.

As if to anticipate the accusations of future inquisitors, the master explicitly refutes any antinomian interpretation of his words.

Some people say, "If I have God and the love of God, then I can do what I like." They have not grasped this aright. So long as you are capable of doing

anything that is against God and His commandment, you have not the love
of God, though you may deceive the world into thinking you have. . . . just
like a man whose legs are tied so that he cannot walk, so a man who is in the
will of God can do no wrong.

Did this mean that transformed seekers became spiritual automatons or
puppets? Not so, Eckhart responded, explaining that *the divine birth* allowed
seekers to know God and God's will so intimately that they were strongly
inclined to do good works and live morally, but they still lived within the
world and were subject to its temptations. Still possessed of free will, they
had to choose moment by moment to follow the righteous path, and for
most, missteps were inevitable. In other words, the inner experience of
union with God *is the highest perfection of the spirit to which man can attain*
spiritually. Yet, this is not the highest perfection that we shall possess forever with
body and soul.

In Catholic tradition that ultimate experience is limited to those few extraordinary individuals known as saints. Only the saints, Eckhart proclaimed, experienced the divine birth to such a degree that the outer person
was transformed as completely as the inner spirit. Only the saints were capable of living a purely holy life. Most just people, and here Eckhart clearly included himself, could but aspire to such perfection in this life.

It may well be that those who are on the way to the same good but have not
yet attained it, can recognize these perfected ones of whom we have spoken,
at least in part. Indeed if I knew one such man, I would give a minster [large
church] full of gold and precious stones, if I had it, for a single fowl for that
man to eat . . . but note, you must pay good heed, for such people are very
hard to recognize.

For those saints, individual identity, what Eckhart calls *personal being*, is
preserved but *the outer man* has been completely subsumed by *the inner man*,
which shares the same essence as God. For most people who have experienced *the divine birth*, however, *the outer man* continues *to live by his own sup-*
port, albeit benefiting from *the influx of grace from the personal being in many*

manifestations of sweetness, comfort, and inwardness, and that is good: but it is not the best. The *just man* still remains separated from the Godhead by his worldly external nature. Sanctification may not come until much later in life or after death. In other words, for the great majority of spiritual seekers, *the divine birth* marks not the end of the individual's journey to God, but its true beginning.

Living and Loving

What will the rest of that journey look like? Meister Eckhart's long association with the contemplative tradition has frequently obscured his advocacy of the active Christian life. Yet in his preaching, the aftermath of the divine birth is even more significant than all of the preparation that made that experience possible. Take his characterization of the soul, which in both Latin and German is a feminine word (*anima; Seele*). In Eckhart's hands, that seemingly random lexicological fact is transformed into an extended metaphor on the birth of Christ in the soul, which depends on the soul first becoming pure and virgin, like the Blessed Mother herself. In his freewheeling translation of Luke 10:38, he preaches: *Our Lord Jesus Christ went up into a citadel and was received by a virgin who was a wife. Now mark this word carefully*, he stresses, *it must of necessity be a virgin, the person by whom Jesus was received.* (In German this last word, *empfangen,* can also mean "conceived," an intentional pun on Eckhart's part.) *"Virgin" is as much as to say a person who is void of alien images, as empty as he was when he did not exist.* The master is referring, of course, to his central teaching of *letting-go-ness*, whereby the individual's soul becomes "naked" and "empty," ready to receive the Word of God via the divine spark. Only a completely detached and pure soul can experience the divine birth.

The resulting union is ineffably wondrous, Eckhart agrees, but it is far from the end of the seeker's journey.

Now attend, and follow me closely. If a man were to be ever virginal, he would bear no fruit. If he is to be fruitful, he must be a wife. "Wife" is the noblest title one can bestow on the soul—far nobler than "virgin." For a man to receive God within him is good, and in receiving he is virgin. But for God to be fruitful in him is better, for only the fruitfulness of the gift is the thanks rendered for that gift, and herein the spirit is a wife, whose gratitude is fecundity, bearing Jesus again in God's paternal heart.

This is my commandment, Eckhart invokes John 15:12, *that you love one another as I have loved you.* Yet Christians should not see love as a duty or as a means to salvation: *Properly considered, love is more a reward than a behest.* Good works—the master again stresses—are the natural fruits of the divine birth, not its prerequisites. Of course the faithful seeker will attempt to lead a life of love before union, but it is only that direct encounter with the Godhead that makes such a life truly possible. Having experienced the depths of God's love, the transformed individual now avidly seeks opportunities to express that love.

In explaining the proper relationship between the contemplative (inner) life and the active (outer) life, Eckhart turned again to a contrast between two women, this time historical figures from the gospel of Luke (10:38–42; also John 11:1–2):

In the course of their journey [Jesus] came to a village, and a woman named Martha welcomed him into her house. She had a sister called Mary, who sat down at the Lord's feet and listened to him speaking. Now Martha, who was distracted with all the serving said, "Lord, do you not care that my sister is leaving me to do the serving all by myself? Please tell her to help me." But the Lord answered: "Martha, Martha," he said, "you worry and fret about so many things and yet few are needed, indeed only one. It is Mary who has chosen the better part; it is not to be taken from her."

To most fourteenth-century Christians, this translated into a biblical endorsement of the monastic life over the distracted life of a layperson. Eckhart himself voiced a version of this reading in his Latin commentary on the gospel of John: *As long as we are not like God and still undergoing the birth by which Christ is formed in us, like Martha, we are restless and troubled by many things.*

In a later vernacular sermon, however, Eckhart dramatically reversed the traditional exegesis of the passage, claiming that Martha was in fact more deserving of our admiration and imitation. Mary, he argued, embodied the first phase of the spiritual life—young, innocent, open, full of *unspeakable longing*. Martha, by contrast, was *mature* and full of *wise understanding, which knew how to do outward works perfectly as love ordains.* Her words about Mary were no angry retort, Eckhart explained, but more like teasing. *She saw how Mary was possessed with a longing for her soul's satisfaction. Martha knew Mary better than Mary knew Martha, for she had lived long and well, and life gives the finest understanding.*

As Eckhart had advised his novices back in the Erfurt priory to do, Martha came to know herself first, before she came to know God. She knew the world and its temptations, as well as her own internal struggles. She also knew *the eternal light*, and the compunction to serve others, hence her annoyance with her sister who *sat there a little more for her own happiness than for spiritual profit.* Jesus's response to Martha's plea was not a rebuke but a reassurance *that Mary would become as she desired. . . . She was filled with joy and bliss and had only just entered school, to learn to live.* Martha, on the other hand, *was so well grounded in her essence that her activity was no hindrance to her: work and activity she turned to her eternal profit.* And this, Eckhart reveals, is why the Lord named her twice ("Martha, Martha"): *He meant that every good thing, temporal and eternal, that a creature could possess was fully possessed by Martha.*

For a lay audience accustomed to accepting an inferior spiritual status, Eckhart's words must have come as an unexpected but welcome validation. The cloistered life of chastity, poverty, and obedience had its place in preparing for the divine birth, but ultimately it was a life lived for others that mattered most. The divine path he preached not only didn't denigrate the active life but raised it up as the ultimate goal of all contemplation. Just people went forth and performed good works not to earn God's favor or for any other reason, but because having experienced the divine birth within their souls and attained unity with God, they could not do otherwise. This was the meaning of *living without a why*, a phrase Eckhart did not invent but likely picked up from Beatrice of Nazareth or Marguerite Porete. *In the same way as God acts, so the just [person] acts without why; and just as life lives for its own sake and asks*

for no why for which to live, so the just [person] has no why for which to act. Following the divine birth, the seeker merely expresses the divine nature that has
become his or her own: *God and I are one. Through knowledge I take God into
myself, through love I enter into God.*

The just person—unlike the scholastic—had learned to stop questioning
everything: Why life? Why God? Why me? The just person no longer
thought of the world in instrumentalist terms, doing something in order to
achieve or receive something. Like God, he or she acted without thinking of
justification.

> *If someone asked [the just man]: "Why do you love God?" [he would re-
> spond]—"I don't know, for God's sake."—"Why do you love the truth?"—
> "For truth's sake."—"Why do you love righteousness?"—"For righteousness'
> sake."—"Why are you living?"—"Indeed, I don't know! [but] I like living."*

Love itself has become an irresistible force. The just person no longer has
any attachments whatsoever, but rather loves all of creation equally and in-
discriminately, in conformance with his or her divine nature. *You must love
all men equally, respect and regard them equally, and whatever happens to another,
whether good or bad, must be the same as if it happened to you.* Eckhart realized
that such a state of equanimity (*gelîchkeit*) seemed virtually impossible, but
for the truly transformed individual it was completely natural. Jesus himself,
Eckhart reminded his listeners, preached: *"He who leaves father and mother
and sister and brother, farm and fields or anything else, shall receive a hundred
fold and eternal life"* (Matthew 19:29; Mark 10:29–30). The transformed individual can accept a friend's death or his own eyes being plucked out without resistance or protest. *Though it should entail all the pains of hell, of purgatory,
and the world, the will in union with God would bear all this eternally, forever in
hellish torment, and take it for its eternal bliss.* One need only look to the example of the Savior Himself. When Jesus is led before Pilate, *like a lamb led to
the slaughter, he does not open his mouth* (Isaiah 53:7), despite the governor's
repeated accusations. Like the *just man,* the mute "King of the Jews" simply knows that he is the Son of God and feels no compunction to assert
this truth.

The person who had experienced the divine birth also came closer to experiencing *the Eternal Now* of God. Freed from the why of cause and consequence, the *just man* no longer lived between "before" and "after," between past and future. He lived in the instant, or as Eckhart calls it, *in this present now*. This was not an ecstatic flight from the world, as described by many Neoplatonists, but to the contrary a full immersion in the cares and suffering of the world. Since the transformed inner man was still encased in the outer man, this experience was not completely freed from the temporality of the world. But it did permit the just person to appreciate the essential shared being with fellow humans and other creatures, freed from the tyranny of time.

In some ways, the just person's state of equanimity is reminiscent of Stoic apathy—the complete eradication of all emotions from the inner self, robbing pain and misfortune of their ability to distress us. But Eckhart did not seek to eliminate a powerful emotion such as empathy so much as to universalize it. For the *just man*, love was an overwhelming and unifying force. Certainly the self-knowledge advocated by Stoics had helped prepare him for the divine birth, but it was the divine essence that now filled him that overcame all suffering. The serenity he displayed might look like that of the accomplished Stoic on the surface, but it sprang from the certainty of unity with all fellow humans, not willful separation from them. Eckhart compared the abiding guidance of the divine birth to a nearby lightning strike that we intuitively turn toward.

> So it is with all in whom this birth occurs, they are promptly turned toward this birth with all they possess, be it never so earthy. In fact, what used to be a hindrance now helps you most. Your face is so fully turned toward this birth so that, no matter what you see or hear, you can get nothing but this birth from all things.

The bond between the divine essence and active love was so strong because "God is love," in the words of 1 John 4:8. *God is love because he is totally lovable and total love. God is all the best that can be thought or desired by each and every person—and more so.* The active Christian life that followed the divine birth was not the logical outcome, but rather the inevitable outcome. This was the good news of the Scriptures, Eckhart proclaimed, and in preaching a life of joyous action he was merely serving as a guide for others on how to become *an authentic person*.

Reimagining Salvation

Living without a why is undoubtedly a noble goal, but how attainable is it for the average seeker? Even more fundamentally, how understandable was Meister Eckhart's description of it for the ordinary Christian of his day? The master frequently contradicted himself on this question, suggesting that he himself remained of two minds about the accessibility of his message (occasionally reassuring listeners *if you can't understand it, don't worry, because I am going to speak of such truth that few good people can understand*). It's possible that certain sermons were aimed at more advanced members of his audiences, but his Dominican training would have recoiled at any hint of elitism. More typically, Eckhart made universally high demands on all his listeners, assuming adequate training in basic Christian doctrine, the ability to distinguish when the master was employing hyperbole or metaphorical language, as well as an open heart motivated by genuine and pious intentions. For such individuals, who also shared his desire for a profound experience of God, all talk of the divine birth and its aftermath remained safely within the boundaries of church orthodoxy.

But what about the rest of his audience? Were most people able to understand the master's words, much less carry them out in their own spiritual journeys? What guidance did the master offer the less spiritually adept? This was the basis of later criticisms of Eckhart's preaching that he made little accommodation to "simple and uneducated" listeners, who were prone to misunderstand many of his ideas. It's possible, of course, that the master dedicated some of the hundreds, perhaps thousands, of sermons he delivered over the course of his long life to the usual topics of sin and repentance, aimed at the lowest common denominator in his audiences. In that respect, the collection of some 150 examples that survived might in fact be a nonrepresentative sample, preserved only because of their treatment of "higher" questions such as divine union. But Eckhart's provocative discussion of such questions was in fact the basis for his popular reputation as well as his own identity as a teacher. His message may have been obscure at times, but he sought to spread it as widely as possible. It was not secret knowledge in the sense of the ancient Gnostics, but his version of "the good news" preached by Jesus.

Eckhart's confidence in the spiritual capabilities of his audience also helps account for his apparent uninterest in addressing any ethical questions in his sermons. He speaks of "good works" and "love" for the most part as general concepts, only rarely describing them more specifically in terms of "dos" or "don'ts." Yet this is exactly the type of direction sought by average Christians raised to avoid sin, accumulate merit, and thus get to heaven. Perhaps Eckhart believed that the basics of Christian morality were so universally understood that he need not devote any attention to rearticulating them. And certainly those who experienced the divine birth he described did not require direction on how to love, given that they were filled with the divine essence. His calling, like that of John the Baptist, was to prepare the way of the Lord, to teach his fellow Christians how to experience God. The rest, he apparently believed, would take care of itself.

And yet Eckhart's preaching had some profound implications for Christianity as understood in his day. Unquestionably the most fundamental shift in the master's salvation scheme was his reconceptualization of good and bad deeds alike. Like his hero Augustine, Eckhart viewed evil as simply the privation, or absence, of good. As the bishop of Hippo had written against the dualist Manicheans, evil has no substance of its own, any more than does darkness (the absence of light). Eckhart concurred: *Do you want to know what sin is? Turning away from felicity and virtue, that is the origin of all sin.* And in so turning away from God, he preached, the sinner moved outside of the divine field of vision. God cannot know sin or evil any more than the light can know the darkness. *God knows nothing outside of Himself; His eye is always turned inward into Himself. What He sees, He sees entirely within Himself. Therefore God does not see us when we are in sin.* So while *God makes merry and laughs at good deeds . . . all other works which are not done to God's glory are like ashes in God's sight.*

This was a shocking revelation for fourteenth-century Christians who came of age amid incessant jeremiads and ubiquitous artworks portraying an angry, vengeful God, one who seemed unambivalently obsessed with punishing the multitude of human sins committed against Him. Eckhart's God—pure being, pure love—seeks out only those parts of Himself to be found within His creation, including the *divine spark* in every person. He is not oblivious to human transgressions, but is the very essence of mercy: *God always rewards more than he should and punishes less than he should.* Stressing the magnitude of divine forgiveness, Eckhart even declares that *God likes forgiving big sins more than small ones. The bigger they are, the more gladly and quickly He forgives them.*

In a religious culture centered on the overcoming of sin and evil, Eckhart sounded a singularly optimistic note about the human potential for reaching God. But his approach remained essentially metaphysical rather than pastoral, focused more on the cosmic big picture than on immediate needs for moral guidance. The objective of most of his fellow Dominican preachers was to provoke in their listeners visceral pangs of overwhelming remorse for personal sins, emotions that would lead to confession, penance, and reformed lives. Eckhart the Parisian master, by contrast, spoke of evil in a more abstract manner, as a necessary part of human nature but more a mistaken detour than a vicious rejection of God. Sin, he believed, was simply a perversion of humans' natural inclination toward good: *If a man slays another, he does so not in order to do evil: he thinks that as long as the other lives, he will not be at peace with himself: accordingly he will seek his desire in peace, for peace is something we love.* Even original sin could not obscure the divine light that shone in every individual, regardless of character or circumstances. *In every work, even in an evil, I repeat, in one evil both according to punishment and guilt, God's glory is revealed and shines forth in equal fashion.* Eckhart's discussions of sin and evil all share this lofty perspective, relying on scholastic theorems rather than the concrete examples most listeners were accustomed to:

> Should anyone ask what God is, this is what I should now say, that God is
> love, and in fact so loveable that all creatures seek to love His loveableness,

whether they know it or not, whether they wish to or not. . . . There is no
creature so worthless that it could love anything evil.

Obviously Eckhart believed in Satan and hell, but just as obviously his
images of both—like his descriptions of God and heaven—were dramatically different from those of other preachers.

The question is asked, what burns in hell. The masters generally say it is
self-will. But I declare in truth: nothing burns in hell . . . just because God
and all those who stand before His face have on account of their true blessed-
ness something which they who are separated from God have not, this very
not torments the souls in hell more than self-will or any fire.

This unquenchable desire to be united with God for all time, Eckhart
preached, was a worse punishment than any of the torments that artists or
poets could dream up. (Of course he had not read his contemporary Dante's
Inferno.) So too in life, choosing evil provided its own punishment:

Now you might say, "Bad people have a good time, they get their way more
than other people." Solomon says, "The evil man should not say, 'What
harm will it do me if I do evil and it does not hurt me?' or 'Who would do
anything to me on that account?' The very fact that you do evil is to your
great harm and causes you enough pain." . . . And if God were to give [the
sinner] all the sorrow in the world, He could not afflict him more harshly
than he is afflicted by being a sinner.

Just as sinning was its own punishment, Eckhart preached that performing good works was its own reward. This too was a jarring message for pious listeners who aspired to attain the rewards and avoid the punishments
of the afterlife. In some ways, the master's attitude toward good works presaged that of Martin Luther two centuries later. Both believed, for instance,
that conventional acts of piety could only indirectly affect the soul's progress
toward true union with God. In Eckhart's view, acts of asceticism and detachment might assist in the self-emptying required to make way for the

divine birth. For Luther, the seeker's frustrated attempts to achieve salvation by practicing such works might reveal the radically corrupt nature of all humans and the absolute necessity of divine help. Similarly, both men believed that the subsequent transformative moment—what Eckhart calls *the divine birth* and Luther refers to as justification by faith—was made possible only by divine grace, by God coming to the seeker. Finally, both Luther and Eckhart saw the good works that follow that moment as the natural outpouring of the soul's transformation. But while Luther characterized the resulting pious life as a form of gratitude (and quickly became wary of talk about "becoming God"), Eckhart insisted that the truly pious life lacks any cause, any "why"—even gratitude—and instead flows forth as the inevitable product of God's divine nature now dwelling within the soul. All good works, he seems to say, belong to God, since it is the divinity within that makes them possible, transforming the individual seeker into an active vehicle for God's love.

Again, Meister Eckhart does not provide his listeners with much guidance on what genuinely good works based only on divine love might look like. He does, however, explicitly discourage many so-called good works intended to help the seeker accumulate merit, namely *fasts, vigils, prayers, and the rest*. If such officially ordained activities aid in *letting-go-ness*, then they might be valuable, but Eckhart rejects all popular notions of "achieving" salvation through external acts of piety. Pilgrimages to venerate shrines and their sacred relics presumably fell into this ambivalent category, as the master at one point asks, *People, what is it you are seeking in dead bones?* If visiting a shrine helped a seeker get *in the right state*, then it was acceptable; otherwise it risked being idolatrous.

This was Eckhart's general rule: any external act that prepared the way for the divine birth was good; any act that sought something other than God was bad. Thus the master praised Holy Communion, God's entering into human beings through the sacrament of the altar, as a prefiguring of the divine birth and castigated those *unworthy [and] unbelieving people who do not believe that this bread on the altar can be transformed, that it can become the gracious body of our Lord and that God can bring this about.* Eucharistic devotions were becoming increasingly prominent in the fourteenth century, and in this sense Eckhart was perfectly in tune with his times.

Eckhart's position on that other staple of medieval piety, petitionary prayer, was a different matter entirely. Nearly all of Eckhart's contemporaries believed in the efficacy of petitionary prayer, prayer that asks God for something—to heal a sick loved one or safeguard crops or strengthen the petitioner's faith. And nearly all those who uttered such prayers believed that enlisting the help of a heavenly intermediary—be it an esteemed saint, the Blessed Virgin, or Christ Himself—increased the likelihood that God would hear and grant their requests. Eckhart, by contrast, saw no need for intermediaries but held that the divine spark within each human, eager to be reunited with its Creator, put every soul in direct contact with God. This divine union, moreover, was the only acceptable objective of any prayer; all others were not only petty and selfish but ultimately pointless, since everything that happens is part of God's plan.

On the Edge of Orthodoxy

The Christianity of fourteenth-century Europe was built on fostering a clear understanding of what constituted sins and what constituted good works. Meister Eckhart sincerely believed his preaching to be orthodox, yet his apparent disregard for external acts of piety understandably confused, frustrated, and even angered some listeners. If preparing for the divine birth was the only legitimate work of a devout seeker, then many conventional forms of devotion—such as going to mass or practicing various penitential acts—seemingly became pointless or even dangerous, as they might contribute to a false sense of spiritual progress. More troubling still, the rewards Eckhart promised were far greater than those proclaimed by most preachers. Not only heaven, the master seemed to imply, but divinity itself lay within the grasp of any genuine believer, no matter how lowly or simple. It's inconceivable that a man of Eckhart's intelligence and experience could not have expected significant resistance, from laypeople and clerics alike.

And indeed, his apparent rejection of petitionary prayer and aversion to many external acts of devotion would eventually cause Eckhart difficulties. Far more controversial, though, were his teachings about "becoming God." In large part, as usual, these problems were of his own making. To the trained theologian, it was obvious that all beings were at their core divine, since most scholars agreed with him that God was equivalent not only to love but to existence itself. As he attempted to explain to a no doubt flummoxed, non-scholarly audience, *God knows nothing but being, He is conscious of nothing but being: being is His circumference. God loves nothing but His being. He thinks of nothing but His being.* This was merely a circumlocutory way of saying that all existence was from God and thus all creatures shared in His divinity, a not unorthodox view. Yet the master could not refrain from incautiously adding, *I say all creatures are one being*—a statement that, when he was later confronted with accusations of pantheism, Eckhart admitted *sounds bad and is wrong in this sense.*

Still, he argued, both being and love—aka God—were undeniably universal, shared by all creatures. *Feeling I have in common with beasts and life even with trees. Being is still more innate in me, and that I share with all creatures. . . . Love is noble because it is universal.* This is what Eckhart means when he says that *whatever is in God, is God,* even animals and stones. All things have the same origin, what he calls the same primal outflowing (MHG *ursprunc*; Latin *ebullitio*): *God gives to all things equally, and as they flow forth from God they are equal: angels, men, and all creatures proceed alike from God in their first emanation. . . . Now all things are equal in God and are God Himself.*

Again, Eckhart's position is not pantheist (all things are God), but panentheist (God is *in* all things)—not necessarily a heretical view. And *seeing that God transforms such base things into Himself,* he asks, *what do you think he does with the soul, which He has dignified with His own image?* For while all creatures share in existence through God, only humans (and angels) have the capacity to share in God's essence through thought. This transformation was the very fulfillment of human existence. *Why did God become man?,* he asks rhetorically, answering: *That I might be born God Himself.* The incarnation was *the greatest good God ever did for man,* allowing humans to know God's being and love directly and thereby become God: *St. Augustine says, what a man loves, that he becomes in love. Should we now say that if a man loves God he becomes God? That sounds as if it were contrary to faith . . . but so it is true in the eternal truth, and our Lord Jesus Christ possesses it.*

Eckhart insisted that these and his other statements on God as being stayed well within the limits of orthodoxy, even if they weren't always comprehensible to average listeners. He could not make the same claim, however, for his teachings on *the ground* or *the Godhead*. This novel doctrine went beyond the bounds of Catholic doctrine and into the realm of controversy, possibly even heresy. *The ground*, as Eckhart conceived of it, was beyond even God. It was the primordial place of origin, the state of ultimate nonexistence, from which God—and by extension all human souls—sprang into being. The divine birth, for all its importance, was merely a preliminary step toward the soul's ultimate goal: to return to the *Godhead* or *ground*, a process Eckhart called *breaking through*.

> *In fact I will say still more, which sounds even stranger: I declare in all truth, by the eternal and everlasting truth, that [the divine spark] is not content with the simple changeless divine being which neither gives nor takes: rather it seeks to know whence this being comes, it wants to get into its simple ground, into the silent desert into which no distinction ever peeped, of Father, Son, or Holy Ghost . . . for this ground is an impartible stillness, motionless in itself.*

In this sense, both soul and Creator share the same ultimate purpose—to return to their origin in the Godhead, *to unbecome*. They meet and unite in that *strange and desert place [which] is rather nameless than possessed of a name, and is more unknown than it is known.* This is the *mysterious and secret ground* of existence, deep within the nature of both God and the human soul.

In Neoplatonic terms, *the ground* was the place of origin to which the enlightened soul must inevitably return, *the hidden darkness of the eternal Godhead.* It is this belief in a common origin and point of destination—*the ground*—that leads Eckhart to make some of his most startling assertions. *A great master says that his breaking-through is nobler than his emanation (or creation) and this is true,* the master confirmed from his own experience. As a creature, Eckhart preached, even after experiencing the divine birth, he could merely declare "there is a God,"

> . . . but in my breaking-through, where I stand free of my own will, of God's will, of all His works, and of God himself, then I am above all creatures and am neither God nor creature, but am that which I was and shall remain for evermore. . . . Then I am what I was, then I neither wax nor wane, for then I am an unmoved cause that moves all things.

These were bold—and to some listeners potentially heretical—words. At the moment of *break-through*, both the individual soul and its Creator are stripped naked of all their distinctions and properties, down to the ground of being they share. The soul is *transported* (literally "translated") *into the naked being of God*. Notions of "self" and "God" seem to melt away as God Himself is *uncreated*. To aim for total self-annihilation, in the manner of Plato's *henosis*, was indisputably heretical in the eyes of the Church. Eckhart studiously avoided talking about the process of *breaking-through* in such terms, but his *un-creation* of both soul and God treads perilously close. Even more daringly, Eckhart also seems to imply that man himself is the origin of God:

> In my birth all things were born, and I was the cause of myself and all things: and if I had so willed it, I would not have been, and all things would not have been. If I were not, God would not be either. I am the cause of God's being God: if I were not, then God would not be God.

This is as far as the master will go in this seemingly heterodox direction. Aware that his words might be so construed, he quickly adds, *but you do not need to know this*, and he concludes the same sermon with a reassurance: *If anyone cannot understand this sermon, he need not worry. For so long as a man is not equal to this truth, he cannot understand my words.* Yet Eckhart himself clearly believed this *naked truth which has come direct from the heart of God*. The concept of *the ground* or *the Godhead*—with its apparently heretical implications—lay at the heart of all his other teachings. And it was here, beneath the surface of his supposedly traditional theology, that subsequent inquisitors would rightly detect a direct challenge to several fundamental Catholic teachings. Eckhart would have denied this, of course, but the radicalism of his approach to spirituality went far beyond occasional references to *the ground*. If the path to divine union was essentially a private, internal one, what need was there for religion itself? Again, if the master considered such a dangerous query, he never expressed it explicitly. But some of his listeners clearly did. Formulating a credible answer to this legitimate question would dominate what remained of Meister Eckhart's life as well as his legacy to this day.

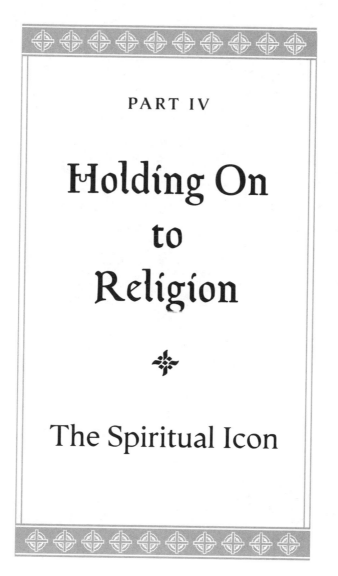

PART IV

Holding On
to
Religion

❖

The Spiritual Icon

CHAPTER TWELVE

Devil's Seed

*And some will say that such teachings should not be uttered or written
to the unlearned. To this I reply, if one may not teach the unlearned,
then no one can teach or write. For we teach the unlearned so that
from being unlearned they may become learned. If there were nothing
new there would be nothing old. "Those who are well," says our Lord,
"have no need of medicine" [Luke 5:31]. The physician is there to heal
the sick. But if anyone misinterprets this saying, how can he help
it who rightly teaches this saying, which is right?*

BOOK OF DIVINE COMFORT

Specters of Heresy

The years of Eckhart's stay in Strasbourg coincided almost exactly with the
demographic crisis of 1315–22 known to survivors as the Great Famine. Beginning with the ominous appearance of a new comet in November 1315,
northern Europeans experienced a series of bitter, extended winters followed by severe and sustained spring and summer downpours. During the
winter of 1315–16, the Baltic Sea froze over; two years later, subfreezing
temperatures lasted from late November 1317 to April 1318. Widespread floods
and windstorms during the warmer months devastated crops across the continent, leading to famine, uncontrollable inflation, malnutrition, epidemics,
and massive starvation. Mortality rates surpassed those of any other time

during the entire Middle Ages—except those of the cataclysmic Black Death thirty years later. Hordes of hungry, homeless beggars roamed the land, while theft and other crime skyrocketed. Chroniclers reported multiple cases of cannibalism and infanticide. Religious processions of barefoot, self-flagellating penitents pleaded with God to restore normal weather and prosperity. Many people, invoking the 1315 comet and other celestial signs, believed that the days of the Last Judgment were at hand.

These were also the days of Meister Eckhart's popular sermons on the divine birth. While the master himself never once spoke in apocalyptic terms, surely some of his listeners felt a new sense of urgency in their own spiritual quests. Certainly, as is usually the case, the environmental crisis aggravated existing social tensions. Parish priests and other members of the secular clergy of Strasbourg renewed their campaign against beguines, once more pleading with their bishop, Johann I, to take action against the religious women and their mendicant supporters. Johann, one of the earliest opponents of the religious women's movement, needed little convincing that something particularly dangerous was under way in his diocese. In August 1317, he published an impassioned condemnation of "so-called religious beghards and sisters [i.e., beguines]," some of whom he accused of belonging to the underground Free Spirit sect. Among the forty-two errors listed, the bishop began with the charge of pantheism, their claim that "God is everywhere and this makes them perfect. . . . They say that a person can be so united with God that all his power, will, and activity is the same as God's." They believe, he continued, "that they are God by nature without distinction," and "that with God they created all things." And since "they are so free in the spirit, whatever they do with the body, they do not sin."

The resemblance of such statements to Eckhart's own preaching is unmistakable, yet Johann never once refers to the influence of the famed Dominican or any of his fellow friars. Some modern historians have suggested that the bishop even sought out Eckhart's help in dealing with the beguines in particular. Still, the master must have been struck by the similarity to many of his own words, particularly when he heard that the accused heretics "likened themselves truly by nature to Christ himself" and claimed that they should trust their "heart" or "interior instinct" more than anything else. According to Bishop Johann, many of these "dangerous people" considered the Christianity of their day "utter foolishness," rejecting the sacraments, fasting, and petitionary prayer, as well as purgatory and hell. All such individuals, he ordered, should immediately stop wearing penitential garb, forfeit all possessions, and live conventionally pious lives or face excommunication. All laypeople were to stop listening to their songs and to their preaching.

Was there truly such an organized sect as the Free Spirits? Almost certainly not. But there were small networks of individuals who proclaimed some of these beliefs and who challenged the existing Church hierarchy. Were some of these people misunderstanding or appropriating Meister Eckhart's words? Possibly, although none of the surviving documents makes such a direct association. Many of these beliefs had been in circulation for a while, and not just in Strasbourg. Half a century earlier, Albert the Great was asked to comment on several similar heretical statements collected by contemporary church authorities in southern Germany. His final compilation of twenty-nine articles included one that he derided as "Pelagian foolishness": "Where it says that a person is not good unless he leaves God for God's sake"—an early formulation of one of Eckhart's most famous statements (*Therefore I pray to God to make me free of God*)!

Like most of his fellow theologians, Albert classified all false teachings in terms of ancient heresies, in this instance the teaching of St. Augustine's rival Pelagius that individual salvation was largely a matter of self-mastery and willpower. He also detected in his own time a common populist tone: "They say they ought not to reveal the grace they possess to learned men because [such men] would not know what it is. The learned only know what is on the page, but these folk know through experience by means of which they say they suck from the divine sweetness." Finally, Albert found that the self-enlightened of his day tended toward moral lawlessness, usually meaning sexual libertarianism, for example, "what is done below the belt by good people is not a sin."

Fifty years later, Eckhart could not have avoided recognizing the frequent affinity of his own preaching with such still current heterodox ideas. While his sermons vehemently refuted any antinomian interpretations of

his own self-divinization project, he remained aware of the persistent danger of misinterpretation. He also unaccountably made things worse for himself. Either the master was not aware of the heretical origins of some of his
most flamboyant sayings—such as "leaving God for God's sake"—or he intentionally appropriated them, supplying a new meaning. Certain of his
own orthodoxy and divine calling, he was incautious at best and reckless at
worst. There is no evidence that his continued preaching put Eckhart in any
direct jeopardy during his time in Strasbourg, but the apparent immunity
provided by his status as a Dominican vicar general and Parisian master
would not last forever.

The beguines he ministered to, by contrast, enjoyed no such reputational
protection. Only their Dominican and Franciscan confessors stood between
them and the bishop's wrath. Johann claimed that his most recent clamp-
down was based on the *Ad Nostrum* decree of the Council of Vienne, which
he subsequently published to all his clergy on October 25, 1317. Early the
next year he circulated his edict among other German bishops, hoping to
gather support for complete suppression of the beguines. Most of Johann's
peers remained ambivalent about such extreme measures, however, except
in the instances where heresy could be indisputably established. Pope
John XXII, despite multiple pleas from the Strasbourg bishop, likewise worried about unjust accusations against many pious women and charged
Johann to distinguish between good and bad beguines within his own
diocese. Instead, under intense pressure from his own clergy, the bishop defied the pope and repeated his outright ban of the beguine status in January
1319, ordering all houses to disband and their inhabitants to return to their
own parishes. A month later he threatened Dominicans and other mendicants with punishment if they failed to back him up. Only a settlement later
that year—negotiated in part by Vicar General Eckhart—diffused the crisis,
with the bishop agreeing to refer all beguine-related conflicts to independent
procurators of the papal curia. The immediate danger to Strasbourg's beguines and their mendicant backers—including Meister Eckhart—had been
averted.

Brotherly Accusations

Sometime in 1323, when he was in his early sixties, Eckhart was transferred to the city of Cologne. Though never the seat of an emperor, Cologne was the preeminent German metropolis. Its population of more than forty thousand was the largest of any city in the land and its lord, the prince-bishop of Cologne, one of the most powerful princes of the realm. The Dominican priory of the city also served as a headquarters of sorts for the order, housing about ninety brothers and boasting the most famous *studium generale*, or university school, in Europe. Scholars dispute whether Meister Eckhart formally assumed the lecture chair occupied nearly a half century earlier by his mentor, Albert the Great. Certainly he lectured regularly within the priory as well as in surrounding churches, including those of Dominican, Cistercian, and Benedictine nuns.

Cologne was also home to the largest concentration of beguines in the empire, with 169 houses and between two and four thousand religious women. The archbishop, Heinrich II of Virneburg, had been Bishop Johann of Strasbourg's closest ally in his attempt to identify and punish heretical beguines and to disband the rest. Like Johann, Heinrich detested the women's movement and remained wary of mendicants in general. He was personally familiar with the Marguerite Porete case and had been the only German archbishop in attendance at the Council of Vienne when *Ad Nostrum* was proclaimed. Like Johann, Heinrich had issued several statutes attempting to close down beguinages, only to become bogged down in conflicts with the city council and local Dominicans. Still his campaign against dangerous preaching continued. The year before Eckhart's arrival in the city, one beghard priest named Walter had been defrocked and condemned to death; shortly afterward, another priest, six beguines, and several laymen were imprisoned for life.

Heinrich of Virneburg was the type of venal and authoritarian church leader that religious reformers loved to hate. As the second son of a ducal family in the Rhineland-Palatinate, he was destined early on for a career in ecclesiastical leadership. Over the course of a long life, he gradually

assembled multiple church offices, skillfully deploying both political maneu-
vering skills and family connections. In 1298, his chief patron, King Albrecht I,
helped him obtain an archdeaconry in Trier and just two years later got him
elected to the powerful office of archbishop of Trier. When Pope Boniface
VIII ordered Heinrich to step aside for the pontiff's preferred candidate, he
obeyed and bided his time. Four years later, when the archbishopric of Cologne became available, Heinrich embarked on a two-year lobbying campaign with the new pope, Clement V, succeeding only once he agreed not to
support the French king, Philip the Fair, and to pay the curia 2,000 silver
marks, a considerable sum. He also made private financial arrangements
with the cathedral canons of Cologne.

As prince-bishop of Cologne, Heinrich subsequently not only oversaw
the church personnel and property of four dioceses (Utrecht, Lüttich, Münster, and Trier), but also ruled an expansive secular territorial state. In addition, he was one of the seven electors of the Holy Roman Emperor, a position
of tremendous influence in determining the legitimacy of any would-be
leader. By the time Eckhart encountered Heinrich in Cologne, the latter was
an old man of nearly eighty. Like the master's previous bishop in Strasbourg,
the archbishop was primarily a politician operating at the highest level who
saw his pastoral duty in terms of maintaining good order and discipline
among his clergy and their parishioners. He had not attended university, nor
was he a theologian. It's highly improbable that he ever heard one of Meister
Eckhart's sermons, let alone read any of his tracts. The prince-bishop rarely,
if ever, preached and delegated to his subordinates all matters of doctrine
and religious ceremonies. Historians have not been kind to Heinrich, variously characterizing him as selfish, crotchety, and a prodigious drinker. Yet
he was also surprisingly energetic, despite many illnesses, and above all very
pragmatic.

The "beguine problem" in Cologne, in Archbishop Heinrich's eyes, was
primarily a matter of applying his authority to satisfy his various constituen-
cies. For years he had listened to complaints from his clergy about how beguines and beghards regularly undermined their own authority vis-à-vis
their parishioners. Genuine concern about heresy undoubtedly also played a
role in Heinrich's response to the beguines, as did misogyny, exacerbating

Heinrich's apparently deep resentment of such independent women, unaccountable to any Church official. Local Dominicans and Franciscans—likewise unaccountable to the archbishop—further contributed to the potential chaos through their continuing support of such women and intentional humiliation of the city's secular clergy. Forceful actions against unpopular beguines also likely pleased members of the city council, who were enmeshed in arguments with the prince-bishop over the city's rights and privileges.

Heinrich also knew that he could count on papal support for his campaign. John XXII, elected in 1316, was involved in a monumental power struggle with Ludwig of Bavaria (Louis IV), the putative Holy Roman Emperor. Since his defeat of Friedrich the Fair in 1322, Ludwig claimed support of virtually all the German princes and cities. But because Ludwig backed some of the pope's defiant clergy and sought a larger role in ecclesiastical politics, John remained opposed to the new emperor and eventually, in July 1324, excommunicated him and all his followers. While the conflict raged on, the pope was desperate for allies in Germany and turned to Archbishop Heinrich, who agreed to back John—in opposition to much of his clergy—if Cologne's toll rights in the Rhineland were restored. On August 15, 1324, the compliant archbishop sent the papal bull excommunicating Ludwig to the Dominican priory, demanding that it be read aloud in all their churches at Sunday high mass (and that notaries attest this was done). But maintaining the prince-bishop's crucial support, the pope would learn, would not be so simple.

By this time, Heinrich and his advisers had concluded that certain local Dominicans in Cologne—perhaps including Eckhart—played a more active part than previously thought in fostering dangerous ideas among the beguines and their supporters. Complaints to high-placed Dominican officials, with the backing of the pope, eventually surfaced in the order's general chapter of May 1325. Originally scheduled to take place in Eckhart's home priory of Erfurt, the meeting had been moved to the more neutral site of Venice. There the assembled brothers listened as the papal bull of excommunication was read out and all provinces were ordered to follow suit in publicizing the pope's pronouncement. The prior of Regensburg was deposed for his previous failure to comply. The chapter also criticized unnamed "friars in Teutonia [Eckhart's province] who say things in their sermons that can easily lead simple and uneducated people into error." Provincial Heinrich of Grünigen, a strict Thomist who perhaps had instigated the complaint himself, assured the assembly that he would take appropriate action.

Four months later, Pope John XXII decided to take the matter into his own hands. Here too it is likely that the complaints of Archbishop Heinrich and his clergy prompted the pope's unusual intervention into a religious order's internal discipline. On August 1, 1325, the pontiff unilaterally appointed two Dominicans—Nicholas of Strasbourg and Benedict of Como—as his vicars to the province of Teutonia. The master general, Barnabas de Vercellis, was merely informed by an accompanying letter "that some dishonest and indecent [acts] have been committed by friars of your order in the region of Germany, and what is honest behavior is left aside or not cared for, on which a suitable remedy has to be supplied quickly." The pope appears to be referring to cases of inadequate observance of the order's Rule or perhaps worse misbehavior; there is no explicit reference to dangerous preaching. Still, the vicars had to conduct a thorough investigation of the entire province, beginning with the priory in Cologne.

Before the visitation even began, Eckhart and his Cologne brothers were rocked by a bombshell delivered at the September provincial chapter in Zurich. One or more unidentified friars accused Hermann of Summo, a previous *visitator* (inspector), of spreading "inflammatory rumors" about other friars in the province, and writing "notorious pamphlets" accusing Meister Eckhart and others of heresies. This is the first written record of any such charges against Eckhart. Apparently Hermann declined to confront any of those defamed in person, preferring to rely on gossip and innuendo. False accusation of a brother was a serious offense among Dominicans. Upon return to Cologne, the vicar Nicholas of Strasbourg found still more troubling charges against Hermann: unjustly sentencing two friars while *visitator*, attempting to rig a priory election, frequently vanishing at night from the priory in civilian clothes, and consorting with several lewd people, including a notorious priest's concubine. Another brother, Wilhelm of Nideggen, was similarly accused of socializing with a disreputable crowd and maintaining especially close ties to one particular nun, even after his superior had forbidden him to see her anymore.

Faced with certain punishment, both friars immediately turned on Meister Eckhart, offering to provide incriminating statements of his multiple heretical statements. The brothers' assumptions that such charges might gain a sympathetic audience suggests that there was already some whispering or even grumbling about Eckhart within the order. Nicholas, a respected theologian, remained skeptical and wrote to Eckhart, who responded promptly and satisfactorily to the accusations brought against him. Empowered by the pope to punish as well as investigate, Nicholas pronounced both Wilhelm and Hermann false accusers, transferred Wilhelm to Aachen, and incarcerated Hermann in the Cologne priory's jail. The papal vicar continued to inspect the province on behalf of the pope, but considered the Meister Eckhart matter closed.

Wilhelm of Nideggen, however, did not accept his exile gracefully. Upon arriving in Aachen he became allied with "a certain lewd and suspect friar and began to move around to different places." In the spring of 1326, though forbidden to travel, he attended the Dominican general chapter in Paris and unsuccessfully attempted to stir up trouble for Eckhart. Wilhelm then returned to Cologne and repeated his previous accusation against Meister Eckhart to the archbishop. His timing was perfect, as Heinrich had just launched a new general investigation, or inquisition, of lay and clerical heresy within his jurisdiction. Inquisitorial procedure, unlike most criminal law, permitted a great deal of secret testimony, thus depriving the accused of the full range of evidence assembled against him or her. The papal vicar Nicholas of Strasbourg, according to Wilhelm, could not be trusted and was himself an abettor of heresy. Intrigued, the archbishop arranged for the release of Hermann, who joined Wilhelm as open accusers of Eckhart. He also appointed two theologians, Reinhard of Friesland and Petrus de Estate (a Franciscan), as investigators. Together, the inquisitors compiled a total of forty-nine supposedly heretical statements drawn by Eckhart's accusers from various published works and sermons.

The Master Responds

Most of Eckhart's brethren in Cologne, including the prior, Johann of Greifenstein, were outraged by what they considered scurrilous attacks on a great man. The master himself appears to have been alternately stunned and furious that he should be questioned in such a way. On September 26, 1326, Eckhart defended himself before the inquisitors. He began with a direct (and legitimate) challenge to the authority of the archbishops' inquisitors: *according to the exemption and privileges of my order, I am not held to appear before you or to answer charges. This is especially true,* he continued, *since I am not accused of heresy and have never been denounced overtly, as my whole life and teaching testify, and as the esteem of the brethren of the whole order and men and women of the entire kingdom and of every nation corroborates.* The *false suggestion* made against him, Eckhart claimed, was based on professional jealousy: *indeed, if I were less well known among the people and less eager for justice, I am sure that such attempts would not have been made against me by envious people.* After several invocations of scriptural passages praising patient suffering, the master proudly noted that *in my own lifetime, the masters of theology at Paris received a command from above to examine the books of those two most distinguished men, Saint Thomas Aquinas and Brother Albert [the Great], on the grounds that they were suspect and erroneous.* Like these revered fellow Dominicans, Eckhart predicted, he too would be vindicated.

Throughout his defense, Eckhart relied overwhelmingly on his reputation and his abilities as a preeminent theologian. Acknowledging his authorship of all the articles compiled against him, he went further, arguing, *I hold that they are all true, although many are uncommon and subtle. If there is something false I do not see in them or in my other remarks and writings I am always ready to yield to a better understanding.* This simultaneous assertion of superior intellect and obedient humility was followed by an especially clever distinction: *I can be in error, but I cannot be a heretic, because the first belongs to the intellect, the second to the will.* Prove me wrong, the scholastic challenged, and I will concede, but be sure that you have the abilities to hold forth on my level.

Meister Eckhart then proceeded to lecture the two inquisitors as if they were students attending one of his courses in Paris, intentionally employing abstruse philosophical terms and concepts. *To clarify the objections brought against me, three things must be kept in mind,* all of them scholastic distinctions. *The first is that the words "insofar as"* [in quantum]—an important qualifier of seemingly sweeping statements—*that is, a reduplication, exclude from the term in question everything that is other or foreign to it even according to reason.* Several examples follow, including *although in God the Father essence and paternity are the same, He does not generate insofar as He is essence, but insofar as He is Father, even though the essence is the root of generation.*

These and other prefatory remarks, however sincere, were clearly intended as intellectual intimidation. It was an understandable but not attractive emotional reaction from Meister Eckhart, who expressed disdain for the inferior minds who had deigned to challenge him. After responding to each of the articles before him, the master railed against the *ignorance and stupidity* of those who had condemned him.

> *They think that everything they do not understand is an error and that every error is a heresy, when only obstinate adherence to error makes heresy and a heretic, as the laws and the doctors hold . . . although they say they are inquisitors in search of heresy, they turn to my books and object to things that are purely natural truths [and] they object to things as heretical that Saint Thomas openly uses for the solution of certain arguments and that they either have not seen or remembered.*

In their ignorance, Eckhart charged, his critics failed to realize that most of what they questioned had been expressed by the Church Fathers or *is the common opinion of the doctors.* To imply *that man cannot be united with God . . . is against the teaching of Christ and the Evangelist.* After citing several more examples, an exasperated Eckhart finally concluded: *that is enough for now.*

When a second list of fifty-nine articles was produced, the master again methodically provided the orthodox interpretation of each excerpt, but this time he implied that his accusers had intentionally misconstrued his teachings:

Know that these articles that follow, just like the earlier ones, are always or almost always false and erroneous in the sense in which my opponents take them, but reasonably and devoutly understood they contain excellent and useful truths of faith and moral teaching. They demonstrate the mental weakness and spite of my adversaries, and even their open blasphemy and heresy, if they obstinately defend the following points, which are against the teaching of Christ, the Evangelist, the saints and the doctors.

People who denied that humans could be united with God were the heretics, he fulminated, not those who upheld centuries of Catholic tradition.

Eckhart's response was more than a clever maneuver; it was a heartfelt declaration about the very truth of the gospel. In the charged environment of Cologne, though, any hint of heresy was an exceptionally serious matter. Few beyond the master's local Dominican brothers were willing to risk the wrath of Archbishop Heinrich by opposing the Eckhart investigation. Nicholas of Strasbourg, who himself now stood accused as an abettor of heresy, made at least three appeals to Dominicans outside the province for assistance, but received no response. On January 14, 1327, he himself was summoned to appear before the inquisitorial court, formally charged by Wilhelm of Nideggen as a *fautor haeresiae* ("favorer of heresy"). Accompanied by ten of his brethren, Nicholas rejected the court's authority and made a direct appeal to the Holy See, currently residing in Avignon. Ten days later, Eckhart followed suit.

When he came before the two inquisitors on January 24, Eckhart was accompanied by an impressive group of character witnesses: the Carmelite provincial of lower Alemannia, three Carmelite scholars, two Augustinians, two Franciscans, and other unnamed "trustworthy witnesses, who had asked to be present." In his rejection of the court's competency, Eckhart repeated many of his complaints about intentional misinterpretations, and added that the unusual duration of the investigation had resulted in great damage to his own reputation and that of the Dominicans in general. While he had promptly replied to every request, the inquisitors had *willfully or even more with criminal intent* prolonged the procedure, *lead[ing] me around in a circle, ambushing me, trying to trap me, and with the greatest scandal . . . prej-*

udicing the state of my person and my order. Eckhart no longer had any faith whatsoever that a fair decision could be reached by the current judges, who seemed readier to listen to disreputable troublemakers such as Wilhelm and Hermann than the many more brethren who came to his defense. Careful never to criticize the archbishop himself, the alleged heretic claimed that no one other than the Holy Father himself had the right or the wisdom to judge his case.

While waiting for the outcome of his appeal, Meister Eckhart made one especially passionate public defense of his innocence, the equivalent of the traditional Germanic oath of purgation. Since ancient times, this public refutation of any criminal or other accusations had served to restore the reputation of an aggrieved member of the community. Accompanied by ten of his brethren (oath-helpers, or character witnesses), he rose to the pulpit of the Dominican church in Cologne on Sunday, February 13. While his associate Conrad of Halberstadt read out a prepared Latin document, the master translated "point by point" into German and commented. The speech began with an emotional declaration of innocence.

> *I Meister Eckhart, doctor of sacred theology, declare before anything else, invoking God as witness, that I have always detested any error in faith and all deviant behavior . . . if something erroneous may be found in the foresaid [matters] having been written or said or preached by me, openly or privately, in what time or place whatsoever, directly or indirectly, out of less good understanding or to be reproved, I expressly revoke publicly all and every single sentence of this in front of you who are present, because I from now on want to have it held as not said or written by you because I hear I have been understood wrongly.*

Eckhart's appearance before the church's congregation, presumably including many of his lay and clerical supporters, was not an attempt to start a popular movement in his support. He knew that neither the archbishop nor his inquisitors would be swayed by such means. This was Eckhart the man defending his honor and by extension his reputation. This time, the tone of the defense was not that of the haughty scholastic but of the wounded friar, who had dedicated his life to spreading God's word. Many of the statements attributed to him, he claimed, were not even accurate transcriptions. At times the normally commanding preacher sounds frantic, incoherent, even equivocating:

> . . . and I also never said, as far as I know, nor meant, that something would be in the soul, something of the soul that would be uncreated and cannot be created, because then the soul would be pieced together out of [what is] created and [what is] uncreated. I have written and taught the contrary, unless somebody would like to say "uncreated," or "not created," that is, "not created by itself," but rather concreated.

Whatever the accusation, the clearly shaken master vowed *to correct and revoke whensoever and as often as this would be appropriate everything that could be found as having a less good understanding.* Eckhart's diffident willingness to recant any "erroneous" statements was a notable reversal of his previous defiant attitude. Perhaps only at this moment did he realize the determination and resources of the enemies assembled against him. With such a concession, he could still pursue his cause but without any danger to his person as a condemned heretic.

Nine days later, on February 22, Meister Eckhart, accompanied by his prior and two other companions, reported to the library of the archbishop's palace. Upon his arrival, the inquisitor Master Reinhard greeted him, then immediately delivered the unwelcome news: "We have arrived at the decision not to concede the [right] to appeal . . . because this is evidently frivolous, as follows manifestly from the acts of the inquisition because of heresy pending against the same Meister Eckhart." In other words, the Cologne investigation would continue. Two notaries recorded the pronouncement, then accompanied Eckhart and his group to the Franciscan house next door, where Albertus of Milan, who had replaced Petrus de Estate as the second inquisitor, repeated the same decision and handed the accused heretic a copy. Everyone present at both meetings knew, however, that the lower inquisitional court did not have the ability to prevent Eckhart from carrying through his appeal to the pope. As soon as winter passed, the master set out with his provincial Heinrich of Cigno, Nicholas of Strasbourg, and three other brethren to make the six-hundred-mile journey to Avignon, the new home of the Holy See.

Looking for Justice in the New Rome

There could have been few starker contrasts to Meister Eckhart's interior spirituality than the Avignon of 1327. One longtime resident, the famed humanist Petrarch, called it "unholy Babylon, thou sink of iniquity, thou cesspool of the world." Within the space of two decades, a picturesque town of 5,000 on the banks of the Rhone had been transformed into the headquarters of western Christendom, a metropolis of more than 25,000, teeming with various ecclesiastical, political, and business dignitaries and their retinues. When Pope Clement V established residency there in 1309, the stay was meant to be temporary, not unlike the other extended absences from Rome of his predecessors. Since 1100, popes had spent more than half of their reigns outside the Eternal City, most of them decamping to one of their palaces in the Italian countryside to avoid Roman politics and any threats to their own power. For his part, Clement chose to relocate to Avignon because of violent conflicts between his own backers, known as Guelphs, and supporters of the emperor, known as Ghibellines. But after Clement's death in 1314, his successor, John XXII, decided it was still best to maintain a distance from his proxy battles with the emperor. What John did not anticipate was that he and his successors would remain in Avignon for another sixty-four years, a period subsequently known—thanks to the excoriations of Petrarch, Dante, and others—as the "Babylonian Captivity of the Church."

When Eckhart and his companions passed through the city's gates in the spring of 1327, two months after setting forth from Cologne, what they encountered was one enormous construction site. Once it became clear that the papacy might stay in Avignon indefinitely, certain cardinals and other church dignitaries had begun tearing down the ramshackle housing of the old city and constructing opulent palaces of their own. Papal ambassadors from across Europe refused to stay in the city and joined most of the cardinals in developing property outside Avignon's massive walls. In 1316, the newly installed Pope John XXII attempted to forestall the building frenzy and forbade his cardinals from retaining retinues of more than ten squires. Even so, once the necessary clerks, artisans, and other workers were added, each of roughly one hundred cardinals maintained a household (*familia*) of at least twenty or thirty people. Consequently, the market for luxury items in Avignon surged, attracting numerous dealers in fine fabrics, jewelry, and rare delicacies.

Meanwhile, Pope John had begun to renovate the existing episcopal residence to be worthy of the many dignitaries he would entertain. Visitors were received in a magnificent grand hall, fitted with silk and taffeta tapestries and luxurious carpets. Bankers and ambassadors were feted with sumptuous banquets on par with those of a king or emperor, where they ate off silver plates with gold utensils. At least five hundred people were employed in the papal court alone, including some two hundred knights and squires as well as the chamberlain who cared for the pontiff's vestments and uncovered the papal slipper that visitors were expected to kiss. Maintaining this level of magnificence required a substantial budget, with the pope annually spending more than 8,000 gold florins (more than US $1 million in modern terms) on clothing alone. Six years earlier, John had bought a country villa, a short distance north of the city, with a stunning pleasure garden leading down to the River Ouvèze, as well as a newly constructed nearby castle (Châteauneuf) with a sizable vineyard (which still produces a grand cru today under the name Château Pape-Clément). The year 1327 saw the peak of private and public construction, with the erection of many new monuments, the opening of a papal zoo (with animals from all parts of the known world), and the creation of early blueprints for what would eventually become the famed Palais des Papes. At night the pope slept in silk bedclothes on a feather mattress and laid his head on a pillow lined with ermine.

It's not difficult to imagine what Eckhart and his fellow friars thought of such pomp. Yet they were men of experience and knew the face of worldly power. Even the Dominican priory in Avignon was grand, with a colossal Gothic church containing not one but three naves. The Order of Preachers had been established in the city for over a century by the time Eckhart and his party arrived, and many of the priory's members had become powerful leaders in the Church, most recently Guillaume Pierre Godin (ca. 1260–1336), who was serving at the time as dean (president) of the College of Cardinals. Just four years earlier the Avignon Dominicans had celebrated the canonization of Thomas Aquinas, a tremendous achievement for the entire order, but especially here, in the heart of papal power. Eckhart would apparently not want for well-connected allies when his case came before the pontiff.

News of Eckhart's ordeal preceded his arrival in Avignon. Hermann of Summo, one of the master's chief accusers, had arrived before him and denounced Eckhart to the master of the Avignon Dominican priory, Barnabas de Vercellis. The archbishop's inquisitors had also decided to withdraw their rejection of Eckhart's appeal and had sent two delegates with all the relevant documents to the papal consistory in Avignon. In response, Nicholas of Strasbourg traveled on to the Dominican spring chapter in Perpignan (in the Pyrenees) and persuaded the assembled brethren to reinstate the punishments against Eckhart's accusers. The master's backers in Avignon then sent a letter to Pope John, demanding that both men be arrested and handed over to their superiors for punishment. Hermann was in fact subsequently imprisoned by the papal curia; whether Wilhelm ever arrived in Avignon is unknown.

The case against Eckhart, however, did not die with the disappearance of his two chief accusers. Archbishop Heinrich, out of genuine concern about heresy or simple mistrust of Eckhart, insisted that the investigation continue. Given Eckhart's public oath of purgation back in Cologne, there was no danger to his person, only to his reputation. In effect, it was now a censure case, a procedure in which a commission of theological experts would determine whether the various statements Eckhart acknowledged making were in fact within the realm of Catholic orthodoxy. At no time was there a possibility of Meister Eckhart's being burned at the stake, the fate of those unfortunate individuals who clung obstinately to their errors. Still, his reputation as a preacher, as well as his personal honor, lay in real jeopardy.

The man to whom Eckhart appealed for justice had little interest in what he considered mere theological niceties. Pope John XXII, born Jacques Duèze in the Occitain region of southwest France, was a civil lawyer who had shrewdly served as court chancellor for Charles II, king of Naples. Historians have judged him an astute jurist, a prudent financier, and a rigid despot. A small, delicate, pale man of eighty-three, he nonetheless demonstrated great energy and willpower, with an astounding capacity for work. Subordinates found him exceptionally demanding and occasionally harsh, but rarely cruel. Like Eckhart, he was a man of vision and determination, almost single-minded in his sense of vocation.

But that vision could not have been more different. Above all, John sought to establish an imperial papacy, the greatest power—secular or religious—in all of Christendom. Like all state builders, he knew the importance of money, and immediately upon assuming the papacy in 1316, he began revolutionizing the finances of his office. Tightening central control of benefices—church offices such as bishop, archdeacon, pastor—was the key. Under John's leadership, his Camera Apostolica began collecting annual taxes of 10 percent on the income of all benefices, as well as an *annate* (the total revenue of the first year) from newly bestowed benefices, fees for dispensations from canon law (such as permission for second cousins to marry), and various other administrative charges. He also took more direct control over appointments to benefices, eliminating the election of bishops by cathedral chapters and appointing all high clerics himself, including twenty-eight new cardinals (twenty-six of them from southern France and three of them his nephews). By the time of Eckhart's arrival in Avignon, John had quintupled the annual income of the papacy, to more than half a million florins, equal to that of the kingdoms of France or England. One eyewitness wrote that "every time I went to the apartment of the Lord Pope's chamberlain, I inevitably found bankers, money changers, tables loaded with gold, and clerks weighing and counting florins." Contemporaries nicknamed him "the Midas pope."

The greatest obstacle to John's ambitions for the papacy was the Holy Roman Emperor, Ludwig of Bavaria, who refused to kowtow to the pontiff on the question of benefices and ecclesiastical oversight. Two-thirds of the pope's expanded income was devoured by the costs of proxy wars with Ludwig in Italy. The conflict also consumed most of John's attention, although battles against heresy always invigorated him, given their threat to the

orderly functioning of the Church. John was no fan of the beguine movement and probably shared some of Archbishop Heinrich's misgivings about
Eckhart and other Dominican enablers, but the central doctrinal controversy of his reign was his struggle with certain Franciscans over the definition of apostolic poverty—a return to the very issue Pope Innocent III
thought he had resolved a century earlier.

The dispute over members of the clergy owning property reached a head
in 1327, the same year Eckhart arrived in Avignon, when the pope summoned the minister general of the Franciscans, Michael of Cesena (ca. 1270–
1342), to appear before him in Avignon. Michael enjoyed wide support
among his brethren, particularly in Italy, where Ludwig of Bavaria had just
invaded. The potential of an alliance between the Holy Roman Emperor and
the Franciscans greatly distressed the pope. As the emperor made his way
steadily to Rome, John scrambled to ostracize his enemy, making new proclamations against him and fortifying existing alliances, including that with
the archbishop of Cologne. It's not clear how much the pope knew about the
specifics of Eckhart's case or wanted to. Given the master's apparent willingness to recant and the much greater matters of state at stake, a censure case
against a German theologian was at most an afterthought to the preoccu-
pied lawyer-pontiff.

Pruning the Field of the Lord

The papal investigation of Meister Eckhart was thus primarily an academic
exercise, albeit one with lasting consequences for the master's good name
and his teachings. Sometime in the second half of 1327, a panel of theologians examined the evidence forwarded from Cologne. The commission
could not ignore the accusations and replies of the previous twelve months
but neither were they bound by the previous inquisition's conclusions. Beginning with four or five lists of more than 150 suspicious articles, the investigating theologians winnowed the charges against the Dominican master
down to twenty-eight questionable propositions. Two-thirds of the articles
appear to have been drawn from Latin works, mainly the commentaries on

Genesis and John and the *Book of Divine Comfort*. The remaining quotations seem to come from German sermons, although the wording is too imprecise to be sure. There is no apparent order to the excerpts, which to the contrary often repeat or return to earlier subjects in the list.

The articles singled out by the theological commission fell into five general groups: comments on creation, characterizations of sin, criticisms of external acts, statements about God, and descriptions of the divine man. Many can be attributed to Eckhart's hyperbolic exuberance. The fifteenth article, for example, sounds just like the master exaggerating to make a point: *If a man had committed a thousand mortal sins, if such a man were rightly disposed he ought not to will that he had not committed them*. God's merciful forgiveness, in other words, is beyond measure and in that sense all human sin is part of the providential plan. Other articles are misquotes or are taken out of context.

The articles concerning good works, by contrast, are direct quotations from sermons and do not seriously distort the general tenor of Eckhart's teaching. *He who prays for anything particular prays badly* (article seven) is a fairly accurate representation of the master's rejection of petitionary prayer, as are articles sixteen through nineteen on the internal nature of salvation:

> *God does not properly command an exterior act. . . . The exterior act is not properly good or divine, and God does not produce it or give birth to it in the proper sense. . . . Let us bring forth the fruit not of exterior acts, which do not make us good, but of interior acts, which the Father who abides in us makes and produces. . . . God loves souls, not the exterior work.*

As with Eckhart's statements about sin, such comments themselves were insufficient to have triggered an investigation, but proved useful given the inquisitors' already established charge.

Much more serious for the papal commission were Eckhart's various claims about God, including the first three articles dealing with God's existence and the supposed eternity of the world. In his reply, Eckhart maintained that these statements needed to be understood in terms of *the eternal Now*, the moment outside of time where God existed. Invoking this concept to justify his teachings was a tactical misstep on Eckhart's part. The *eternal Now* was a tenet of Neoplatonic philosophy, but the master's judges were, to a man, adherents of Aristotelian philosophy and thus rejected his argument out of hand. A similarly scholastic difference of interpretation is evident in articles twenty-three and twenty-four, where Eckhart argued that *no distinction can exist or be understood in God Himself.* In stressing the unity of "the One," Eckhart seemed to be challenging the doctrine of the Trinity, which held that the Father, the Son (Christ), and the Holy Spirit are three aspects or manifestations of the same one God—although the master vehemently insisted that he was not. Such fine distinctions were the stuff of academic disputations, except that Eckhart was not permitted to defend himself with oral arguments, only written ones.

The most dangerous articles were those excerpts describing the effects of the divine birth on an individual, for these came closest to sounding like endorsements of the Free Spirit heresy. Predictably, Eckhart's equating of the *divine man* with Christ caused the biggest stir, accounting for a quarter of the twenty-eight excerpts. Article ten, for instance, slightly tweaked and artfully arranged quotations from one German sermon to devastating effect:

> *We shall all be transformed totally into God and changed into him. In the same way, when in the sacrament bread is changed into Christ's Body, I am so changed into him that he makes me his one existence, and not just similar. By the living God it is true that there is no distinction there.*

The next four articles more faithfully reproduced Eckhart's words, but the impact was just as incriminating: *Whatever holy scripture says of Christ, all that is also very true of every good and divine man.* The master's penchant for surprising and even shocking his audience had never met with greater success.

As in Cologne, Eckhart claimed that virtually all of the assembled articles had been taken out of context, and he proceeded to defend their orthodoxy by arguing in typical scholastic style and terms. But his inquisitors were not interested in the master's greater philosophy or his subtle justifications. Their concern was the impact of such "heretical" or "evil-sounding" words on the simple laypeople who attended Eckhart's sermons. To a degree, this claim was disingenuous, since more of the excerpts in question in fact came from his Latin writings, but the principal danger remained not Eckhart's intent but what other people might have heard. This distinction seems to have eluded the master, who continued to battle in the way he knew best, with the scholarly weapons of the *disputatio*.

The next step in the procedure would have been for the case to come before a cardinal's tribunal, where Eckhart would finally have a chance to defend himself before a judge. But early in the new year, most likely on January 28, 1328, Meister Eckhart died. No details about his death or burial survive, and only very recently has an enterprising historian determined the time and place of the master's death. Eckhart was in his late sixties and far from both Tambach and Erfurt. Our only commemoration from the time is Pope John XXII's claim that before Eckhart left this world he drew up a public document,

> profess[ing] the Catholic faith at the end of his life and revok[ing] and also deplor[ing] the twenty-six articles, which he admitted that he had preached, and also any others, written and taught by him, whether in the schools or in sermons, insofar as *[in quantum]* they could generate in the minds of the faithful a heretical opinion or one erroneous and hostile to the true faith.

How fitting that Eckhart ended his argument (and his life) with his favorite scholastic qualifier—*insofar as*—in effect maintaining to the end that he knew his words were orthodox but regretted if anyone misunderstood them. And how typical that his evasion of guilt fell on deaf ears among his accusers.

Normally, according to Roman law, an inquisition or other process ended with the death of the accused. Two factors kept Eckhart's case alive after his own demise. The less significant one came from an outside evaluation prepared by the theologian Jacques Fournier (ca. 1285–1342). Fournier had studied and taught in Paris, likely worked on the Marguerite Porete case, and received his master's degree in 1314, during Meister Eckhart's second magisterium. The Cistercian had climbed quickly up the ecclesiastical ladder, becoming an abbot in 1311, at the age of twenty-six, then serving as chief inquisitor against the last Cathars in Languedoc from 1318 to 1322. In the end, only five heretics were burned at the stake, but the experience—which he described in a 1323 book—earned Fournier a reputation as an extremely punctilious, tenacious, and conscientious foe of heresy in all forms. Pope John congratulated him with a sheaf of indulgences and the bishopric of Mirepoix in 1326 and the next year with a cardinal's hat.

The man subsequently known as the White Cardinal (because of his Cistercian robes) was a rising star in the curia of John XXII (and seven years hence would succeed his patron as Pope Benedict XII). He had already written extensively for the pope in the Franciscan controversies of the past few years, including learned criticisms of Peter Olivi, William of Ockham, and Michael of Cesena, the head of the order. Shortly before Eckhart's death, Fournier compiled an expert outside assessment of the articles against the Dominican. He displayed no sentimentality in judging his former Parisian colleague. Most articles were condemned as "false and heretical," another as "blasphemous and insane," still another as "laughable among all intelligent people." A few items, the cardinal granted, were merely wrong (such as *that all creatures are pure nothing*). Fournier's report became part of Eckhart's still-open case file.

The pope clearly valued his new cardinal's opinion, but it was the continued urging of Eckhart's Cologne persecutor, Archbishop Heinrich, that ultimately persuaded the pontiff to move forward with the censure case. Shortly before the Dominican's death, on January 17, Ludwig had himself crowned emperor in Rome; three months later he declared John deposed for heresy, and on May 12, the emperor appointed his own pope, Nicholas V (Pietro Rainalducci of Corvaro). Within a few weeks, the Franciscans Michael of Cesena and William of Ockham both slipped out of Avignon and joined Ludwig in Rome and later in Munich. Pope John's call for a crusade against the emperor was met with derision and he was again desperate for allies, especially in Germany. If Heinrich of Virneburg insisted that the pope pursue Eckhart's case, it was a small price to pay for the archbishop's crucial loyalty.

Still, it was not until March 27, 1329—fourteen months after Meister Eckhart's death—that the eighty-five-year-old pope issued the condemnation known as *In agro dominico* ("In the field of the Lord"). In the bull, John lamented the "evil weeds" and "devil's seeds" that had recently taken root among "the good crop of Catholic truth." Specifically,

> we are indeed sad to report that in these days someone by the name of Eckhart from Germany, a doctor of sacred theology (as is said) and a professor of the Order of Preachers, wished to know more than he should, and not in accordance with sobriety and the measure of faith, because he turned his ear from the truth and followed fables. The man was led astray by the Father of Lies . . . [and] he presented many things as dogma that were designed to cloud the true faith in the hearts of many, things which he put forth especially before the uneducated crowd in his sermons and that he admitted also in his writings.

The pope takes a harsh tone, possibly to reassure Archbishop Heinrich, but at no point does he condemn Eckhart himself as a heretic. He also mentions the deathbed "recantation," and censures only fifteen of the twenty-eight articles as heretical "as the words sound," two others as heretical but not authenticated, and eleven more as "quite evil sounding, very rash," and likely to be misunderstood, "though with many explanations and additions they might take on or possess a Catholic meaning." The pope did not order any books to be burned, but warned that if anyone presumed "to defend or approve the same articles in an obstinate manner, we desire and order a process of heresy."

Three weeks later, on April 15, 1329, Pope John sent a copy of his bull to Archbishop Heinrich in Cologne, ordering him to have it proclaimed throughout the diocese and city of Cologne, "so that through such publication the hearts of the simple people, who are easy to mislead, and to whom Eckhart during his lifetime preached the afore-mentioned articles, might not be infected by the erroneous teaching contained in them." This—both pope and archbishop fervently hoped—would be the end of the story for the man who "wished to know more than he should."

CHAPTER THIRTEEN

The Man from Whom God Hid Nothing

If anyone cannot understand this sermon, he need not worry.
For so long as a man is not equal to this truth, he cannot
understand my words, for this is a naked truth which
has come direct from the heart of God.

GERMAN SERMON 52

Our Sweet and Sainted Teacher

In 1356, the Benedictine monk Oswald of Brentzahusen translated into Latin a work that he mistakenly attributed to the late Meister Eckhart. *Sister Katie (Schwester Katrei)*, originally composed in the Alemannic dialect, did in fact date from the master's time in Strasbourg four decades earlier. It also contained many familiar Eckhartian elements. In the treatise, a beguine penitent, Sister Katie, has become impatient with the spiritual counseling of her Dominican confessor and asks him to teach her the most expedient way to salvation. When he demurs, she leaves to pursue a life of detachment "in foreign lands," guided only by the Holy Spirit. After a time, she returns to Strasbourg, so transformed by her experience that her confessor can barely recognize her. Yet even in her new angelic form, she has not yet attained divine union. Her confessor advises her (in good Eckhart fashion) to let go even of her desire for God, and after a great deal of praying and meditation she exclaims to him, "Sir, rejoice with me, I have become God!" Skeptical that her new state can last, the confessor observes as she withdraws to a corner of the church and becomes completely still, seemingly dead to all observers. After three days of frozen ecstasy, she comes back to life and claims that she is now in a permanent state of union with God, having "achieved by grace what Christ is by nature." Astounded, the confessor becomes the pupil, learning from his former "daughter" how to become God. In the course of her instructions, she confirms the reality of heaven, hell, and purgatory and denies the freedom from moral constraints proclaimed by some Free Spirit followers. At the same time, she minimizes the necessity of priests and sacraments, preferring individual guidance from the Holy Spirit.

For more than a century after Meister Eckhart's death, a variety of sermons and apocryphal stories like this one vied to define the master's legacy. The humiliated theologian of the 1329 papal condemnation was gradually forgotten; in his place emerged the venerable sage who gently guided spiritual seekers along the path to divine union. In folk poetry and fictive dialogues, "the man from whom God hid nothing" offered learned (if frequently obscure) aphorisms and encountered many would-be disciples, including "The Naked Boy," a youthful beggar who turned out to be God himself in disguise. Many spurious sermons circulated, as did many genuine works, most famously in the collection known as *The Paradise of the Intellectual Soul*, a compendium of sixty-four sermons, half written by Meister Eckhart, the rest by fellow Dominicans. Almost all of the portrayals of the departed master were positive, even reverential.

But what was this spiritual legacy? In works such as *Sister Katie*, the teachings of Eckhart are conflated with some more radical Free Spirit ideas, seemingly justifying Pope John XXII's concerns. A 1353 Dutch treatise, *Meister Eckhart and the Unknown Layperson*, even more directly appropriates the Dominican for a pro-beguine criticism of saints' cults and the church hierarchy. Like other religious icons, Meister Eckhart—officially discredited but more popular than ever—risked becoming a multipurpose literary figure, who seemingly endorsed a wide range of ideas and practices, some far from his actual teaching.

Immediately after the master's death, control of the Eckhart "brand" fell to the people who had the most to lose from its tarnishing—his fellow Dominicans. Their initial reaction was one of fear and caution. Few friars openly criticized the late master, but following the pope's condemnation in early 1329, the Dominican general chapter, meeting in Sisteron, near Avignon, underscored the order's enthusiastic support for the teaching of its most orthodox and newly canonized theologian, Thomas Aquinas. Within the next two years, virtually all of Eckhart's most vocal supporters, including his provincial Heinrich of Cigno, were purged from their leadership positions within the order. Whatever copies of the master's writings that were destroyed appear to have suffered this fate at the hands of his fellow Dominicans, eager to mollify the pope and prove their dedication to orthodoxy.

At the same time, some of Meister Eckhart's followers within the order took it upon themselves to defend the master's legacy, although they took care to avoid any associations whatsoever with heretical belief. Heinrich Suso (ca. 1295–1366), who had studied under Eckhart in both Strasbourg and Cologne, was outraged by the investigation and condemnation of his master. As a young friar, Suso had undertaken the path of self-torment common to many nuns and beguines, fasting for long periods, wearing a spiked crucifix under his habit, and at one point even carving Christ's name into his own flesh above his heart. Profoundly depressed by his own unworthiness, Suso claimed that only the intervention of the "saintly Meister Eckhart" had freed him "from the hell in which he had existed for so long a time."

During the period before and after Eckhart's condemnation, Suso published two works. In the *Little Book of Truth*, he singles his master out as "one of the most learned and experienced human beings to whom God has revealed his hidden wisdom." A series of dialogues between Truth and its disciple presents a succinct primer of Eckhart's main teachings: the unfathomable nature of being, distinctions between God and the Godhead, the origins of multiplicity and of evil, the nature of true detachment and self-surrender, breakthrough, and becoming one with the divine will. Suso apparently had access to the condemned twenty-eight articles, and skillfully uses such authorities as Aquinas and Bernard of Clairvaux to convey the true understanding (and orthodoxy) of Meister Eckhart's words. Finally he explicitly distinguishes his revered master from those people with "a mistaken idea of freedom," who "live completely according to [their] impulses, heedless of all else, without looking ahead or behind." Such people are reckless, disorderly, and selfish, since "a person never becomes so completely annihilated in this [eternal] nothing that his senses are not aware of the difference of their origin or his reason is not aware of its free choice." Consequently, "some uneducated but intelligent people have falsely understood their teachers with respect to the lofty meanings of sacred scripture, twisting it according to their own undisciplined nature and even writing things down, but not according to the true sense of scriptures."

Yet even Suso's understanding of Eckhart's teachings deviated from his "sweet teacher" in some important ways. The younger man is dismissive of dry academic learning, which he claims nurtures vanity and egotistical pedantry. Speculative theology, which he learned from his late master, does not interest him, but rather "good actions are, without a doubt, more instructive and uplift one's heart somehow more than words alone." His book, consequently, "describes by many examples many holy deeds that really happened as depicted." Contrary to Meister Eckhart, Suso avoids metaphysical discussions (particularly anything that smacks of pantheism) and focuses on concrete and specific ascetic instruction.

The *Little Book of Truth* was aimed at "anyone who would like to become a good and blessed person and share a special intimacy with God," to which Suso added, "or whom God has singled out by severe suffering—as he is accustomed to do with his special friends." Like many of the nuns Eckhart counseled, his disciple reveled in corporal and psychological tribulations, enduring them in what he saw as an explicitly chivalric quest for divine wisdom. Suso's descriptions of his own agonies, many of them self-inflicted, are in fact reminiscent of the very path to God that Eckhart explicitly rejected. And while the master had been likewise wary of ecstatic visions and images in general, Suso recounts with relish his own "very painful" experiences, including an apparition of Meister Eckhart himself.

A short time later, Suso produced the *Little Book of Eternal Wisdom*, probably published not long after the pope's official condemnation of his master. This work similarly combines Eckhartian elements of letting-go-ness and the divine birth with conventional ascetic practices. "The more bitterly you have suffered," Suso writes, "the more worthily you will be received." Unlike Eckhart, who generally eschewed specific instructions and preferred to allow for multiple paths to God, Suso's book includes four chapters teaching the reader how to live inwardly, how to receive the Eucharist, how to have a good death, and how to praise God always. While Eckhart avoided most Christ-centered devotions, Suso devotes twenty chapters to the wonder of the Passion, the supreme manifestation of God's love for the world. So too with meditation, which the master had treated as a profoundly personal experience; Suso, by contrast, provides one hundred accessible meditative exercises with instructions.

For all his caution, Suso was one of those friars rebuked in the immediate aftermath of the papal condemnation. In 1330, he was summoned to the provincial chapter at Maastricht on charges of heresy and subsequently dismissed from his lector position in Constance. Humiliated, but unrepentant, Suso returned to Constance and began an extended period of itinerant preaching in the southern Rhine region. Here his version of Meister Eckhart's teaching enjoyed an enthusiastic reception among many beguines, nuns, clerics, and laypeople. Calling themselves the Friends of God (based on John 15:14–15), this loosely knit network of mystical seekers gradually expanded to many cities along the Rhine, all the way up to the Netherlands. Some later historians have gone so far as to consider the Friends of God a proto-Protestant sect, but in fact it appears to have been more of an extended reading group with local chapters—and a completely orthodox one at that. All the group's discussions of Eckhart carefully steered clear of the condemned twenty-eight articles.

It was in one of these Rhineland cities, Basel, that another Dominican and former pupil of Eckhart, Johannes Tauler (1300–1361), first encountered the Friends of God. Like Suso, Tauler had been an enthusiastic student of the master during his final years in Cologne and had continued to spread Eckhart's "theology of the ground" as a preacher in Strasbourg. When the pro-emperor city council expelled all backers of the pope in 1339, Tauler traveled to Basel, where he reconnected with Suso and other admirers of the late Meister Eckhart. Four years later, Tauler returned to Strasbourg and soon persuaded a wealthy banker, Rulman Merswin, to devote his life and fortune to the growing movement. Merswin funded many ventures and twenty years later bought an abandoned monastery on the island of Grünwörth near Strasbourg to serve as a retreat center for the Friends of God.

Together, the two protégés attempted to take custody of the master's popular legacy, Suso through his elegant prose, Tauler with his powerful preaching. In 1334, Suso wrote the *Clock of Wisdom*, a Latin book of mystical teachings that was eventually translated into eight vernacular languages and became one of the most popular spiritual writings of the Late Middle Ages. Toward the end of his life he published *The Exemplar*, combining revised versions of his earlier "little books" with some pastoral letters and an autobiography, the *Life of the Servant*. In many ways, his books are more similar in style to the works of female writers such as Mechthild of Magdeburg and Hadewijch of Antwerp than to the scholasticism of Meister Eckhart. But Suso's work served his master's memory well. Now purged of obscure and dangerous statements and encased in a lyrical literary style, the teachings of the master enjoyed greater popularity than they ever had during his own lifetime.

Johannes Tauler also worked hard to make Eckhart more accessible to the average person. The eighty-one of his sermons that have survived share most of the master's Neoplatonist vision of divine union but present his philosophy in very practical terms. According to Tauler, every human is divided into three parts: external, internal, and highest, or most inward. The external person lives by sensory perception and is compared by Tauler to a donkey. The internal person, or servant, is guided by reason. But only the noblest part of the person—what Eckhart called *the divine spark of the soul*—is capable of uniting with God. Unlike his master, Tauler thoughtfully describes how the first two persons struggle to take control and offers practical methods of letting-go one can use to allow the third to prevail. Temptations by the seven deadly sins—completely absent in Eckhart's sermons—also receive detailed attention. Tauler's explanation of the steps to divine union is true to Eckhart, but he presents it in clear, jargon-free terms that avoid any hint of pantheism. In short, Tauler produced a less original, more conventional, but also far more accessible version of his master's teachings. Implicitly, Eckhart's backers seem to have agreed with his critics that the master's words alone were too often confusing to the average Christian. Not surprisingly, the sanitized versions of Eckhart offered by Suso and Tauler quickly overshadowed the extant sermons and writings of their "noble master."

A Light in the Medieval Darkness

Over the course of the fourteenth century, the movement later known as Rhineland mysticism gradually gave way to a new form of lay apostolic piety known as the Modern Devotion. Like the beguines, small groups of laypeople, together with some clerics, established houses that cultivated a deeper spiritual life, through communal prayer and Bible reading. Also known as Brothers and Sisters of the Common Life, these intentional communities along the Rhine represented a powerful merger of the active and contemplative ideals. Many of the Modern Devotion's insights and practices were conveyed in the most popular book of the later Middle Ages—*The Imitation of Christ*, published anonymously in the early fifteenth century. The mysticism of the movement, however, had been thoroughly domesticated and purged of any controversial Eckhartian ideas, further contributing to the master's eventual disappearance as a spiritual authority.

Meister Eckhart's gradual fade into the background of Rhineland mysticism was understandable from another perspective. Despite the efforts of Suso and Tauler, his name remained dangerous throughout the fourteenth century. This was the period of greatest persecution for German beguines and beghards, who were often conflated with the Free Spirit sect, which in turn had been linked to Eckhart. Both Tauler and Suso went to great pains to distance their master from any heretical associations, but the stigma of the papal condemnation remained in the collective memory of Dominicans and other clergy.

Theologians who appropriated the master's work consequently did so only with great caution and even then usually without attribution. The one major exception to this tendency came in 1449, over a century after Eckhart's death. In his *Apology for Learned Ignorance*, Nicholas of Cusa (1401–64), a celebrated theologian and bishop, openly praised Meister Eckhart for his intelligence, creativity, and erudition. Nicholas was a fellow proponent of negative theology and was in awe of many of the insights garnered by his predecessor. Eckhart's mistake, he wrote, had been to preach to common people, who "are not able to understand these matters, with which he often dealt differently from other teachers, even though intelligent men will find in [his writings] many subtle and profitable things." Even then, 120 years after the papal condemnation, Nicholas was attacked by the Heidelberg theologian Johannes Wenck of Herrenberg for his "curious and vain" reintroduction of pantheism and other past heresies. The famous bishop brushed aside such accusations and a few years later commissioned a complete copy of Eckhart's Latin works. Nicholas took the precaution, however, of making the resulting manuscript accessible only to scholars.

By the early sixteenth century, the Friends of God were a distant memory, Meister Eckhart was mostly forgotten, and only the writings of Suso and Tauler preserved some of the master's teachings. Some Dominican chronicles vaguely referred to Eckhart as a past friar of great holiness; others omitted him altogether. Still, Eckhart's vision of an unmediated experience of God, wherein the selfish human will was replaced with divine will, did manage to reach some of the early proponents of what would become the Protestant Reformation. In 1516, the thirty-three-year-old theology professor Martin Luther was entranced by a late fourteenth-century mystical tract which he edited and published with the new name of the *Theologia Deutsch*. Luther especially liked the anonymous author's description of the passive nature of conversion, although neither Luther nor the text referred explicitly to Eckhart's letting-go-ness. The future reformer's greatest objection was that the *Theologia Deutsch* minimized the radical nature of original sin and thus denied God full credit for the divine birth within the soul (a transformation Luther would later call "justification"). Believing that Johannes Tauler was in fact the author, Luther asked his friend Georg Spalatin to send him a collection of Tauler's sermons, which the future reformer carefully annotated.

It would be misleading, however, to assign more than a peripheral influence to Eckhart or his disciples in the subsequent Protestant Reformation.

Luther likely read at least a handful of Eckhart's sermons but preferred a "domesticated mysticism," remaining wary of spiritual "enthusiasts" throughout his life. The famed prophet of *sola scriptura* and "a priesthood of all believers" was no fan of untutored, individualistic interpretations of the Bible or expressions of the spirit. Protestant publications of Tauler's sermons did acknowledge Meister Eckhart as "a highly learned man," but most readers' encounters with his teaching remained indirect, via Tauler or Suso. A 1522 publication on mysticism included around seventy of Eckhart's sermons, but even then the master's impact was strongest at the margins of the new Protestant reforms, particularly among the radical reformers Andreas Bodenstein from Karlstadt, Valentin Weigel, and Sebastian Brant.

In the early seventeenth century, the Strasbourg poet Daniel Sudermann (1550–1631) rediscovered the master through Tauler and published the first partial collection of Eckhart's works, albeit to little effect. Sudermann also composed more than a thousand spiritual songs based on the writings, including "I rely on a groundless ground" and "Man, sink into your nothingness." About the same time, the "shoemaker theologian" Jakob Böhme (1575–1624) conducted a deeper exploration of Eckhart's teachings, which he interwove with other Neoplatonist, alchemical, and astrological concepts in his mystical masterwork *Aurora* (1612). But an Eckhart revival subsequently attempted by the bestselling Catholic convert Johann Scheffler (better known as Angelus Silesius, 1624–77) found no audience.

Perhaps the greatest indicator of Eckhart's obscurity during the sixteenth and seventeenth centuries is his exclusion from the *Index of Prohibited Books*, the Catholic list of censored writings created in 1559 and regularly updated thereafter. The Counter-Reformation Catholic Church remained inordinately suspicious of mysticism, as the troubled careers of subsequently sainted Teresa of Ávila and John of the Cross testify. Protestant embrace of some medieval mystics as reformers before their time—"lights in the thick darkness of medieval Christianity"—only solidified concern among church leaders. Thus while many of Meister Eckhart's contemporaries were placed in the *Index*—Mechthild of Magdeburg, Heinrich Suso, Johannes Tauler, Jan van Ruusbroec—the master himself remained conspicuously absent.

Intellectual Hero of the Fatherland

The modern rediscovery of Meister Eckhart began chiefly as a response to Enlightenment rationalism. At the dawn of the nineteenth century, many German intellectuals sought a new philosophy that would approach the great truths of human existence with a combination of reason and feeling, or sensibility. The "soulless materialism" and "hyper-rationalism" coming from France left such artists and poets cold, demanding in response a profound spiritual regeneration drawn from the distinctive *Geist* (spirit) of the German people. Poet Friedrich von Hardenberg (1772–1801), better known as Novalis, captured the new "Romantic" spirit of the age in celebrating the "beautiful splendid times, when Europe was a Christian land, when *one* Christendom inhabited this humanely structured continent, *one* great communal interest united the far-flung provinces of this vast spiritual empire." A mystical quest for life's fulfillment was still possible in the modern world, Novalis averred, but first one had to overcome the legacy of the Enlightenment, which had "branded as heretical all imagination and feeling, placed man with difficulty at the top of the order of natural being, and turned the infinite creative music of the universe into the monotonous clattering of a gigantic mill."

Novalis's call for "a new humanity" was answered by the Catholic intellectual Franz von Baader (1765–1841), who came to Meister Eckhart via Tauler and the *Theologia Deutsch*, both considerably better known at the time. Perusing Eckhart's surviving German sermons, Baader discovered a profound speculative and mystical thinker, superior even to Jakob Böhme, who enjoyed a high reputation among Romantics. "Eckhart is rightly called the Master," he wrote. "He surpasses all mystics" and had been tragically underappreciated until then. It was Baader who introduced Eckhart to the great Georg Wilhelm Friedrich Hegel (1770–1831), who in turn incorporated the master into his 1824 lectures on the philosophy of religion. Hegel especially loved the master's famous words on divine intersubjectivity (*The eye with which I see God is the same eye with which God sees me*), which the philosopher considered the supreme expression of self-consciousness without distinction between subject and object.

Scholarly interest in Meister Eckhart spread rapidly over the next three decades. Hegel's student Karl Rosenkranz (1805–79) dubbed him "the forefather of a specifically German philosophy" and "herald of a philosophy of the future." Rosenkranz's praise of "German mysticism" was further promulgated by Joseph von Görres (1776–1848) in his four-volume *Christian Mysticism*, published between 1831 and 1842. Von Görres's fourth volume coincided with the appearance of the first major work devoted to Meister Eckhart by the Danish Lutheran H. L. Martensen (1808–84). Martensen not only viewed the great master as the patriarch of all German mysticism and modern idealist philosophy, but judged German mysticism itself as the highest expression of mysticism in the entire Christian tradition. In 1857, Germanist Franz Pfeiffer (1815–68) published the most complete edition ever of Eckhart's German works, including 111 sermons, 18 treatises, numerous sayings, and odd fragments. The intellectual world was abuzz with the new edition's various implications for all modern thought. Within half a century, Meister Eckhart had gone from obscure honorary Protestant to one of the most important thinkers in German history.

Meanwhile, Eckhart's new identity as the world's first idealist philosopher was quickly complicated by allegations of pantheism and even atheism. Protestant philosophers such as Karl Steffensen (1816–88) differed only on what kind of pantheism Eckhart embraced, yet extolled the medieval master's heroic resistance to the church authority of his day. In his *History of Mysticism*, Wilhelm Preger (1827–96) conceded that "the word mysticism is already its own condemnation," but similarly acknowledged that Meister Eckhart's teachings were necessary preparation for the later Protestant Reformation. Accusations of atheism actually attracted the philosopher Arthur Schopenhauer (1788–1860), who considered Eckhart the founder of transcendental idealism and was among the first admirers to note similarities to many Hindu and Buddhist ideas.

Of course admiring Catholic intellectuals rejected such heretical characterizations, but still celebrated the distinctive German identity of Eckhart and his philosophy. In his *German Mysticism in the Mendicant Orders from 1250–1350*, church historian Carl Greith (1807–82) welcomed Eckhart's approach as an antidote to the materialism of the modern era, but also cautioned against the master's "daring claims, inappropriate images, and ambiguous expressions that border on false doctrine." In 1886, the Dominican Heinrich Suso Denifle (1844–1905) began publishing the Latin works of Meister Eckhart, hoping to counter any pantheist undertones in the German sermons and to present the master as an orthodox scholastic and "one of the most original thinkers of the Middle Ages." Eckhart made some errors, Denifle conceded, but he remained "the father of Christian philosophy"— far from the pantheist heretic portrayed by Protestant admirers.

The one thing that Protestant and Catholic writers could agree upon was that there was something distinctively German about Meister Eckhart's brilliance. In the newly unified Second Empire (1871–1918), which had brought together twenty-six formerly independent German entities, the theologian from Thuringia became a source of great national pride. An influential 1904 article by Leopold Ziegler praised Eckhart as a genius who started a sort of German Renaissance, long before the better-known Italian version. Pantheist, heretic, proto-Protestant—the master was now a hero to a new generation of early twentieth-century German writers. Greatly embellished portrayals of his trials in Cologne and Avignon provided the dramatic focus for novels. Popular poems and songs further promoted the anti-Catholic image of a lone warrior for truth in the benighted past. New Catholic accounts of the master's orthodoxy were dismissed by Protestant critics as "unsustainable rescue efforts" for a figure undeniably closer to Luther and all things truly German.

Only by bearing such nationalist effusions in mind can we understand the incongruous and grotesque appropriation of Eckhart by the National Socialists on the eve of their ascension to power. In 1930, thirty-seven-year-old Nazi propagandist Alfred Rosenberg published *The Myth of the Twentieth Century: An Assessment of the Spiritual-Psychological Paradigm Struggles of Our Time*. Deemed unreadable even by the party faithful, Rosenberg's *Myth* nonetheless provided an intellectual fig leaf for the most egregious Nazi policies once Hitler came to power. It described a Manichean conflict among modern Germans between two worldviews: the "Roman-Syrian-Jewish-Alpine" myth of Christianity and the new German myth of blood. Mixing in degraded elements of Darwin and Nietzsche, Rosenberg singled out the papacy as the architect of an insidious ideology that had enfeebled the German people for centuries but was about to be conquered by a new cosmic order based on racial supremacy. Over the next ten years the book would sell more than a million copies.

In Rosenberg's fantasy, Meister Eckhart was "the greatest apostle of the Nordic west," embodying "the greatest soul power, the most beautiful dream of the German people." All of the propagandist's information on Eckhart was second- or third-hand, with direct quotations carefully edited and inserted amid Rosenberg's rants against the Roman Church's historic attempts to poison and "Judify" the Aryan race. Eckhart was a heroic follower of Jesus who preached the freedom of the soul and will, not the sacrificial doctrine of Jewish prophecy. His work was continued by Martin Luther and other Protestant reformers, who were eventually succeeded by the Romantic poets and their cult of the individual soul—and of course the National Socialists, who would empower the German *Volkgeist* to finally conquer its alien foes.

Historians and other academics ruthlessly mocked Rosenberg's shabby scholarship, including his oversight of the seemingly pertinent fact that Eckhart had relied heavily on the teachings of the Jew Maimonides. In 1935, the Jesuit theologian Otto Karrer (1888–1976) publicly condemned Rosenberg's ahistorical portrayal of Eckhart—the *Myth* itself had been placed on the Catholic Church's *Index of Prohibited Books* the year before—then immediately fled to Switzerland, where he remained until 1945. By contrast, Josef Quint (1898–1977), whose project to publish all of Eckhart's German works had just received government funding, prudently toed the party line. In 1937, Quint joined the Nazi party and two years later, in a speech as professor at the University of Breslau (Wrocław), he rejoiced that "the name Eckhart has become a very familiar sound in all the German lands," with the "undeniable credit" going to Rosenberg and his masterwork. Now all Germans knew this "deepest and most German thinker of the past" who possessed "the unrestrained Faustian-Nordic drive for depth." Quint continued to oversee the authoritative edition of Eckhart's German works until his death nearly forty years later, while the German Dominican Josef Koch (1885–1967) assumed responsibility for the Latin works.

The Universal Sage

Fortunately for Meister Eckhart, most serious thinkers ignored his appropriation by German nationalists, so that his reputation suffered no harm in the eventual collapse of the Third Reich. Already in the nineteenth century, philosophers such Schopenhauer had begun to celebrate Eckhart as a universal figure of human enlightenment, far beyond a parochial source of national pride. The Dominican master's championing of intuition as a necessary complement to reason particularly resonated with Schopenhauer's interpretation of "metaphysical will." Similarly, Eckhart's description of subjectivity during the divine birth for many twentieth-century philosophers anticipated the "modern discovery of the self," evident in the antipositivist systems constructed by René Descartes (1596–1650), Immanuel Kant (1724–1804), and Karl Jaspers (1883–1969). His just man, *living without a why*, is the embodiment of the authentic life embraced by existentialists such as Jean-Paul Sartre (1905–80). The postmodern deconstructionist Jacques Derrida (1930–2004) wrote at length about the themes of *letting-go-ness* and *living without a why*, exploring the limitations of language even in Eckhart's own negative theology. In short, virtually all modern continental philosophers acknowledged some debt to the revolutionary approach of Meister Eckhart six centuries earlier.

No twentieth-century philosopher drew more directly on Eckhart than Martin Heidegger (1889–1976), one of the founders of phenomenology. Heidegger believed that reality was best understood through the individual subjective experience of the world's phenomena and that "representationalist" thinking was itself delusional. Scientific calculative approaches to being and reality consistently favored their own technological agendas, simultaneously revealing and hiding the world. Meister Eckhart's *letting-go-ness*, by contrast, opened up the thinker to a transcendent, direct experience of reality ("Being") itself. The "old Master of Learning and of Living" had long ago perceived the limitations of human reason and developed an alternative, contemplative access to the mystery of existence.

Of course the unspoken assumption among Heidegger and other twentieth-century philosophers, all of them agnostics or atheists, was that Eckhart's insights needed to be extracted from their original and outdated religious context. The master's unknowable God had been categorized by Sigmund Freud (1856–1939) as an infantile human projection, at best "the dark self-perception of the realm beyond the ego, of the id." Freud and his fellow psychiatrists typically considered mystics as neurotic individuals suffering from morbid or hysterical personalities, accentuated by self-hypnosis. Some modern admirers of Eckhart have consequently resisted characterizing the master as a mystic and instead, like their nineteenth-century predecessors, pay Meister Eckhart the ultimate compliment of treating him like a secular contemporary, freed from the shackles of medieval religiosity.

Yet as the scholars Amy Hollywood and Ben Morgan have pointed out, modern theoretical appropriations of Eckhart's teachings have invariably interpreted them as manifestations of something other than what their author intended. This approach does not necessarily invalidate these theorists' arguments, but it does distort the historical Eckhart, who was in fact motivated by a religious vision. It also tends to patronize the man, suggesting that he apparently did not appreciate the true significance of what he was saying. How can it be that the prophet of "modern subjectivity" displayed so little concern about questions of individual autonomy and agency in describing the effects of the divine birth? It appears that Eckhart's appeal as a universal philosophical figure has less to do with the totality of his approach than with the useful parts contained therein.

Even Meister Eckhart's greatest admirer among twentieth-century theorists believed that the master's religious language could be misleading. Contrary to his former mentor Freud's dismissal of all so-called religious experiences, psychologist Carl Gustav Jung (1875–1961) proclaimed that "it is to the mystics that we owe what is best in humanity." When searching for inroads to the "deep psyche," Jung found that "only in Meister Eckhart did I feel the breath of life." "The art of letting things happen," he wrote, "action through non-action, letting go of oneself, as taught by Meister Eckhart, became for me the key opening the door to the way." For Jung, Eckhart's fathomless abyss of the Godhead was nothing other than the unconscious, the soul, what he called the libido (not in the modern sexual sense), and the divine birth "a state of intense vitality," during which "God disappears as an object [and becomes] a subject which is no longer distinguishable from the ego." This intersubjectivity, also appreciated by Heidegger, was the focus of a chapter in Jung's influential *Psychological Types* (1921), where he described Eckhart's pivotal insight of "a reciprocal and essential relation between man and God, whereby man can be understood as a function of God and God as a psychological function of man." Jung's secular adaptation of Eckhart's religious philosophy is certainly among the most coherent modern interpretations—but is it one that the master himself would have appreciated?

Of course Eckhart's greatest appeal should be to modern Christians, but this has not always been a straightforward matter. Roman Catholics have always been attentive to the "dangerous" parts of the master's teaching, particularly those sermons on the Godhead that appear pantheistic. Eckhart's brief appropriation by the Nazi regime did him no favors among Catholics in the Reich or abroad, despite the Vatican's consistent rejection of such an association. Only in recent decades, especially since the endorsement of the famous monk Thomas Merton (1915–68), have Eckhart's writings gained a broader public among Catholics, including the last three popes. In 1986, an Eckhart commission set up by the Dominican master concluded that "on the basis of our studies it is already clear to us that a reconsideration of the teaching of Meister Eckhart is justified." The order's 1992 request to the then head of the Congregation for the Doctrine of the Faith, Cardinal Joseph Ratzinger (later Pope Benedict XVI), was not answered until 2010, when Master Timothy Radcliffe explained:

> We tried to have the censure lifted on Eckhart . . . and were told that there was really no need since he had never been condemned by name, just some propositions which he was supposed to have held, and so we are perfectly free to say that he is a good and orthodox theologian.

This response, if accurate, is a far cry from rescinding *In agro dominico*, let alone proclaiming Meister Eckhart a Doctor of the Church. Perhaps the magisterium still considers the master's dramatic language too vulnerable to misinterpretation by the faithful.

Despite Eckhart's longtime reputation as an honorary Protestant and his enthusiastic reception among nineteenth-century Romantics and Idealists, mainstream Protestants, particularly German Lutherans, have been slower to embrace the master fully because of his association with "Catholic" mysticism. The great church historian Adolf von Harnack (1851–1930) proclaimed that "mysticism can never be made Protestant without slapping history and Catholicism in the face." As theologian Karl Barth (1886–1969) argued, mysticism propagates a path to salvation "that completely bypasses the biblical history of salvation and the Last Days." Since the 1960s, Protestant believers have been worried less by the Catholic context of Meister Eckhart and other mystics than by the latter's growing association with several New Age—and presumably unscriptural—approaches to enlightenment. That cautiousness continues today, although many American Protestants, including evangelicals, are increasingly discovering worthwhile spiritual insights in the words of the medieval master.

Most commonly since the mid-twentieth century, the master has been praised as a bridge to Asian religions and philosophies. In his correspondence with Thomas Merton, Japanese scholar D. T. Suzuki (1870–1966) called Eckhart "the one Zen thinker of the West." The just man's inner Christ nature described by the medieval master looks remarkably similar to the internal Buddha nature of Mahayana tradition, as does Eckhart's combination of the contemplative-active life of love. Letting-go-ness lines up nicely with the Zen "no-mind" (*wuxin*) as well as the Taoist "no action" (*wuwei*). The Buddha also remained wary of human God-talk and aspired to a unity with the ultimate similar to Eckhart's deification. The many resemblances are indeed striking.

Several modern observers have also noted Meister Eckhart's kinship with parts of the Hindu tradition, particularly the Advaita Vedanta school. The Tamil writer Ananda K. Coomaraswamy (1877–1947) exclaimed that "Eckhart's Sermons might well be termed an Upanishad of Europe," noting the master's "astonishingly close parallel to Indian modes of thought; some whole passages and many single sentences read like a direct translation from

Sanskrit." Here too, some Eckhartian terms seem to have other religious equivalents, such as Brahman for the ground, and *neti neti* (not this, not this) for the ineffability of the divine mystery. Above all, both Eckhart and the Vedanta school emphasize the necessity of intuition to experience the entirety of reality, which then leads to loving kindness.

Both Islam and Judaism also have their own strong mystical traditions, and here too many notable similarities to Meister Eckhart's teachings emerge. Like Eckhart, his near contemporary, the great Sufi master Ibn Arabi (1165–1240) sought a religious philosophy that would above all be practical for genuine spiritual seekers. His Perfect Human, like Eckhart's Just Man, has realized the divinity within—the inseparableness from the divine essence in the eternal Now—and has dedicated himself or herself to a life of perfect love. The fantastically popular Sufi poet Jalāl ad-Dīn Rūmī (1207–73) prefigures his Christian counterpart's language and message even more strikingly. With evocative images and meticulously crafted phrasing, Rumi describes his own relentless pursuit of union (*fanā*) with "the Beloved." The experience of this mystery, which most non-Sufis reject as heretical, is like no other. Coincidentally, a Jewish contemporary of Eckhart and Rumi, the mystic and philosopher Abraham Abulafia (1240–91), taught a similar kind of divine union, known as meditative Kabbalahism, which remains likewise controversial among modern Jews.

Meister Eckhart's seemingly universal applicability among virtually all the world's religions accounts for his particular popularity in the rapidly growing belief in religious syncretism, also known as perennialism (and sometimes religious pluralism). This is the conviction that all the world's religions share a common essential truth, which has since been fractured into various rituals, doctrines, and other structures. Given that Meister Eckhart in fact sought such a universal religious philosophy, it's little surprise that he has proven such a superstar among its adherents. The Neoplatonist Agostino Steuco (1497–1545) coined "perennial philosophy" to describe a common, transcendent truth evident in both classical Greek philosophy and later religious traditions. Steuco's idea lay largely dormant until spreading among the Deists of the eighteenth century and even more spectacularly among the Transcendentalists, Universalists, and Theosophists of the nineteenth century. In 1945, Aldous Huxley (1894–1963) published *The Perennial Philosophy*, in which Eckhart plays a prominent role, taking the universalist perspective into popular culture. Since then, perennialism has become closely associated with various New Age writers as well as some ecumenists among Christian denominations.

At least on the surface, Eckhart could qualify as the patron saint of the perennial movement. Like its modern advocates, he rejected the materialism of human society to seek a hidden, spiritual truth. He was also remarkably inclusive in his sources for past wisdom, consulting not just Christian thinkers, but also Jews, Muslims, and ancient pagans. Although a Christian (and member of the clergy!), he stressed individual, internal transformation over external rituals or doctrines. His approach was egalitarian, not requiring a high degree of learning or other special gnosis. And above all, his sermons were practical and encouraging, full of colorful metaphors, memorable aphorisms, and answers to anticipated questions. There was but one goal, union with God, which modern followers refer to as ultimate reality—and Eckhart would not disagree with the characterization.

Was Meister Eckhart a perennialist before his time? At first glance, the resemblance to a modern spiritual teacher, such as his namesake Eckhart Tolle (b. 1945), is quite striking. Tolle's earliest mystical influence was the prolific German writer Joseph Anton Schneiderfranken (aka Bô Yin Râ; 1876–1943), a profound admirer of Jakob Böhme, who in turn was of course shaped by his reading of Meister Eckhart. Although Tolle only explicitly mentions the master a few times, the influence of the medieval sage is pervasive. In *The Power of Now* (1999), Tolle writes at length of both mindfulness and surrendering (letting go of) the "false self," so as to experience "the Source" (ground) and "the Unmanifested" (silent, apophatic God) in "the eternal Now." "The One" who existed before the Big Bang similarly is present in the "isness" of all things, including of course humans. Like the master, Tolle teaches that experiencing the divine essence within will transform the seeker, leading to a life of joy and compassion. He also skillfully anticipates a reader's potential questions within the text and provides reassuring answers.

But appearances can be misleading. Tolle's main goal—and this accounts in large part for his popular success—is therapeutic: healing the "pain body" of its "negativity," typically manifested in addictions and unhappy relationships. His "timeless wisdom" draws on an impressive all-star cast—the Buddha, the Tao Te Ching, Jesus, Rumi, the Tibetan Book of the Dead, Marcus Aurelius, the Gnostic Gospel of Thomas, and so on. His prose is straightforward, conversational, and mixes in contemporary references from movies and popular music. At times he translates his points into "theistic language," but he carefully avoids—in good perennialist fashion—endorsing any specific religious doctrines. "Salvation" consists of freedom from "the psychological need of the past for your identity and future for your fulfillment." In language reminiscent of Meister Eckhart, Tolle explains:

> You find God the moment you realize that you don't need to seek God. So there is no only way to salvation: Any condition can be used, but no particular condition is needed. However, there is only one point of access: the Now. There can be no salvation away from this moment. You are lonely and without a partner? Enter the Now from there. You are in a relationship? Enter the Now from there.

Not only will such a transformation bring inner peace, we are told, it will strengthen the immune system and slow down the aging process.

To be fair, Tolle never claims to be the modern incarnation of Meister Eckhart. But his indirect, secularized, self-help application of the master's insights is currently making more inroads than any other representation, particularly among the growing number of "spiritual but not religious" individuals in the West. Like the philosophers of the twentieth century, contemporary spiritual teachers such as Tolle unquestionably bring the teachings of Meister Eckhart to a wider audience, but also like these predecessors, they extract him from his original religious context, intentionally disregarding or reconfiguring some of his distinctly Christian interpretations.

Appropriation of this latest nature is an inherent risk to every public thinker, although Eckhart seems to have endured more than his fair share of diverse interpretations and applications over the years. An optimist could say that this result is a tribute to the rich, transcendent nature of his teaching. A pessimist might counter that it is the frequent ambiguity and obscurity of the master's words that have condemned him to such a fate. A historian can concede that while both views have merit, Eckhart died convinced that he had neither said nor written anything contrary to the Catholic faith—"insofar as" he understood it. The fate of those teachings, he believed, was in the hands of a just God, just like the outcome of his own lifelong quest to be united with that God in eternity.

Epílogue

In whatever way you find God most, and you are most often aware of Him, that is the way you should follow. But if another way presents itself, quite contrary to the first, and if, having abandoned the first way, you find God as much in the new way as in the one that you have left, then that is right. But the noblest and best thing would be this, if a man were to come to such equality, with such calm and certainty that he could find God and enjoy Him in any way and in all things, without having to wait for anything or chase after anything: that would delight me! For this, and to this end all works are done, and every work helps toward this. If anything does not help toward this, you should let it go.

THE MASTER'S LAST WORDS

The story of Meister Eckhart's life and legacy leads us to question certain basic assumptions about his impact. Was he, for instance, ever really that dangerous? Remember that in his own day, Eckhart's number of listeners, let alone avid followers, remained small, perhaps a few thousand at most. While many Christians shared his goal of a more spiritually authentic life, only those relative few who regularly heard him preach in the churches of the Rhineland could have fathomed his "highly subtle" philosophy and attempted to put it into practice. Because Eckhart lived more than a century before the advent of the printing press, copies of the master's sermons and writings—all painstakingly written by hand—appear to have circulated only among a small number of admirers in monasteries and convents. He repeatedly rejected radical interpretations of "spiritual liberty" and was never once accused of openly challenging the clerical hierarchy of the church or denigrating its sacraments. When, toward the end of his life, Eckhart became caught up in the beguine and Free Spirit maelstrom, he was never considered a heretical leader or abettor. Rather, he fell victim to a convergence of toxic circumstances, where the desperate accusations of two renegade friars caught the interest of a zealous archbishop, who happened to enjoy the backing of his political ally, the pope. Even after Meister Eckhart's death and the papal condemnation of the twenty-eight articles, the Friends of God and other disciples continued their discussions of his teachings without threat of persecution. The only genuine danger Meister Eckhart seemed to pose during his time was to his own reputation—which eventually recovered in the modern era.

In some ways, given our advanced means of communication, he poses a greater threat today. Many twenty-first-century people would consider any "mystic" dangerous, or at least seriously misguided. As William James already observed a century ago, "the words 'mysticism' and 'mystical' are often used as terms of mere reproach, to throw at any opinion which we regard as vague and vast and sentimental and without a base in either facts or logic." One of the reasons Kurt Flasch and other modern philosophers have waged a sustained campaign to "de-mysticize" Meister Eckhart is that they worry no one other than "spiritual fringe groups" will take him seriously unless this modern stigma is removed. Or—worse yet—that the master will be appropriated by such groups and his words used to support their dubious agendas. In the rationalist paradigm that currently dominates Western thought, there is no reality beyond that which can be measured "objectively." In the eyes of many contemporary educated people, bestowing credibility on a so-called medieval mystic would be a dangerous intellectual step backward.

Yet despite modern suspicion of "mysticism" (a term Eckhart himself never used), the great majority of the world's population recognizes the essential ambiguity and uncertainty—the mystery—of human existence. Whether religiously oriented or not, many people remain open to the possibility that some combination of reason and intuition might provide direct access to "something more" than what we can experience with our five senses, imagine with our limited reason, and describe with our language.

This is the possibility that Meister Eckhart speaks to in his teachings. This is one of the reasons he has become so popular in the modern era, where totalizing ideologies of all stripes have become increasingly suspect.

There are other reasons as well, most of them not that different from the reasons Eckhart's contemporaries found him compelling. He presents the way to spiritual fulfillment as a common journey accessible by many paths. He offers a direct, unmediated experience with the oneness of existence, accessible to anyone with sincere intentions. His profoundly egalitarian approach does not privilege anyone by outward religious or social status and does not require any special powers. Above all, Meister Eckhart's path to the God within, as we have seen, is compatible with virtually every major religious tradition and many secular philosophies as well.

This nearly universal religious compatibility, however, potentially makes Eckhart dangerous in another way, particularly to members of certain Christian faith communities. If, as Eckhart seems to suggest, this personal transformation is all that really matters in life and it can be pursued individually, what is the need for the doctrines, rituals, and communal experiences of a particular religion or denomination? Especially for some members of evangelical churches, the universalist (and panentheist) nature of the master's preaching—his apparent embrace of "religionless spirituality"—can work against him. So-called hard exclusivists vehemently resist the inroads of "soft" perennialism and religious pluralism embodied in the New Age enthusiasm for many of Eckhart's controversial statements. In these believers' eyes, there is no further interpretation required for the salvation specifically preached by Jesus and the apostles in the Bible.

Other more ecumenically minded Christians welcome the teachings of Eckhart. Franciscan Richard Rohr, for example, believes that his own wisdom tradition (in this case Roman Catholicism) is deep and strong enough to withstand the doctrinal challenges of Eckhart's approach. Some admirers, such as the former Dominican Matthew Fox, go still further, veering into perennialist territory while supposedly staying anchored in a religious tradition. In Fox's *Creation Spirituality*, Eckhart is a "Mystic-Warrior" who "touches the depths of Western culture's wisdom, which connects to the depths of Eastern wisdom."

Of course Meister Eckhart encountered the same range of reactions among the Christians of his own day, from those who thought him an abettor of the Free Spirit heresy to those who accepted his own repeated assertion that everything he preached was entirely compatible with Catholic doctrine. Whatever Eckhart's Christian orthodoxy, it would be a profound mistake to treat him as a feel-good, "different strokes for different folks," modern relativist. There is real intellectual and spiritual substance at the heart of his teachings, not just a message of "do as you will."

* * *

I began and completed this journey with Eckhart as a historian, intrigued by the evolution of his thought as well as by his teachings' impact on both his world and ours. Over the course of our time together, I have come to have a profound admiration of Meister Eckhart's persistent striving not just for knowledge but for useful understanding. In that spirit, I offer three particularly valuable insights that I believe the master provides to all seekers of wisdom and meaning in our own frequently loveless and chaotic world.

First, Eckhart argues that every quest for greater understanding of existence must begin in humility, an acceptance of our own extremely limited knowledge and intellectual powers in the face of an infinite universe. In his own life, he ultimately rejected his fellow scholastics' attempts to capture God with rational formulations and language. Even when he himself stripped away images and mental constructs of "God" down to "being itself," Eckhart realized that his words still distorted the truth. Profound humility regarding the intellect's limitations did not come easily to the gifted scholar but it has been a hallmark of all great thinkers from Socrates and the Buddha on. He would have agreed with the great Enlightenment figure John Locke, who openly acknowledged "what a darkness we are involved in, how little it is of Being and the things that are, that we are capable to know." We must, Locke concludes, "sometime be content to be very ignorant." For Eckhart this meant resisting the worldly tendency to equate intellectual humility with weakness, and certainty with strength.

Second, Meister Eckhart offers a sophisticated defense of intuition, providing a useful complement to our inadequate rational understanding. As the author Marilynne Robinson has pointed out, "We know only what we know in the ways that we know it or can know it. It is only reasonable to assume that the physical world is accessible to other modes of perception than we are capable of." Eckhart believed, on the basis of his own experience, that in fact humans possess another way of knowing God or reality, an internal recognition, which church tradition calls mystical but might just as aptly be called intuitive. The *divine spark* within each person, the master teaches, is what links us to one another and to all creation, and intuitive awareness of that unity is accessible to anyone through his contemplative process of *letting-go* of all desires and images. Whereas science relies on representing the multiplicity of things in language, intuition allows a person to "know" the unity of things through direct experience.

In that respect, Meister Eckhart presents a holistic vision of existence—not a skewed (and unsustainable) division of phenomena into "natural" and "supernatural." It's all natural, he teaches, just not all understandable in the same way or to the same degree. At the university, Eckhart attempted to construct a philosophical bridge between the transcendent Plato and the empiricist Aristotle, but he found few takers. Obviously today's self-described new atheists and other radical materialists would also reject his model of the universe, yet for many modern people Eckhart's approach to the vast unknown is at least plausible. At the very least, it offers an alternative perspective to many religious people who remain captive to the Enlightenment's natural/supernatural dichotomy, in which God and spirituality have been assigned to an ever-shrinking role in our understanding of existence.

Eckhart's combination of rational and intuitive ways of knowing God or reality is not a unique approach, although few have portrayed the resulting "divine birth" in such evocative terms. In fact, if we remove the label "mysticism," many of the modern world's greatest philosophers and scientists have embraced it. Immanuel Kant argued that "thoughts without intuition are empty; intuitions without concepts are blind." In pondering the universe, Albert Einstein urged young researchers to resist the "god of intellect" for "intuition and feeling," arguing that "there is no true science which does not emanate from the mysterious." Some contemporary brain scientists have even identified "two fundamentally opposed realities, two different modes of experience" residing respectively in the brain's two hemispheres. While conceding that some "rationalist" and "intuitive" processes occur in both halves, psychiatrist Iain McGilchrist argues that the left hemisphere "tends to deal more with pieces of information in isolation, and the right hemisphere with the entity as a whole, the so-called *Gestalt*." McGilchrist in fact attributes Western culture's prevailing materialism to a historical imbalance of left brain dominance over the right brain—the primary source of wonder, interconnectedness, and compassion.

Eckhart's third valuable insight for current spiritual seekers of all varieties involves the consequences of what he calls human divinization. In essence, Eckhart cracked the active/contemplative conundrum of Christianity for laypeople long before Protestant or other modern attempts. Going deep within oneself and reaching out to the world in service were two sides of the same coin for him, not an either/or choice. Without a profound appreciation of what he called the divine unity of existence, good works easily lend themselves to a transactional, commercial way of thinking about salvation. Without participation in the world, the supposedly enlightened person risks slipping into solipsistic selfishness—a state Eckhart compares to a tree that never bears fruit. The just person who has truly experienced *the divine birth*, the direct intuitive encounter with the unity of existence, does not withdraw from society, free from any obligation toward other human beings. Instead, experiencing God means becoming one with God and thus acting as God does—by which Eckhart means living an active life of love and service *without a why*, or any thought of justification or compensation. Acts of personal kindness or contributions to social justice are not means to spiritual enlightenment or salvation but natural effects of the inward experience preached by Meister Eckhart (and many other religious figures). Again, the master describes a holistic approach to the good life, where the perceived divisions between the self and the world, between the individual person and others, dissolve.

This is an important distinction for non-Christian or nonreligious admirers of the master who wish to follow his model of contemplation and personal enlightenment for purposes of self-fulfillment. New Age adherents and other perennialists in particular who desire to learn from Eckhart must acknowledge his grounding in basic Christian principles of neighborly love and mutual obligation. He does not preach a quietist message of self-improvement and escapism, but one of joyful immersion in the needs and suffering of other people, all of whom are created in the image of God (*imago dei*). In this respect, the doctrinal traditions and congregational nature of organized religion offer a useful counterbalance to the potentially individualistic nature of *the divine birth*.

Neglecting such core aspects of Eckhart's message would indeed constitute the act of "hermeneutical violence" that philosopher Kurt Flasch condemns in his screed about the master's appropriation by "the mysticism industry." But Flasch is wrong when he criticizes all attempts by contemporaries—religious or not—to make Eckhart "useful" in their own pursuit of God. The master himself did not live in a religiously pluralistic society in the modern sense, but he was no stranger to spiritual diversity. Just as his own definition of "catholic" wisdom included many non-Christian sources, his approach to divine union consistently recognized individual differences in spiritual experience.

Meister Eckhart's *wayless way* deliberately remained general and nonprescriptive, allowing for countless subjective variations. It would be ahistorical and presumptuous to predict his opinion of either religious exclusivism or perennialism. But based on his long life of service, we can conclude with conviction that nothing would have pleased the master more than to be considered still useful in his fellow seekers' journey to the God within.

Acknowledgments

I came to this project as an interloper from the sixteenth century, the period of European history most familiar to me. It would have been impossible to even conceive of this book without the pioneering work of the last two generations of Eckhart scholars. This debt is acknowledged in the endnotes, but I would like to underscore the pivotal contributions of several individuals, particularly Caroline Walker Bynum, Oliver Davies, Kurt Flasch, Alois Haas, Jeremiah Hackett, Niklaus Largier, Alain de Libera, Dietmar Mieth, Kurt Ruh, Reiner Schürmann, Walter Senner, Loris Sturlese, Frank Tobin, Winfried Trusen, and Richard Woods. As I mentioned in the prologue, I also benefited from the meticulously produced editions of Eckhart's German and Latin works, as well as the English translation of most of Eckhart's German sermons by the late Maurice O'C. Walshe. I'm very grateful to Crossroad Publishing and its editor, Chris Myers, for permission to make such extensive use of quotations from this last work. Finally, the acclaimed Eckhart scholar whose work has most guided my own presentation, Bernard McGinn, graciously agreed to read my penultimate draft, making several invaluable suggestions and saving me from many embarrassing errors. I take full responsibility for any remaining misrepresentations and remain deeply indebted to Professor McGinn for his generosity of spirit on a subject he knows so thoroughly. My sincere hope all along has been that the advantages I bring as an outsider to the topic have outweighed the inevitable shortcomings.

For financial support and other encouragement, I am indebted to the Vanderbilt Provost's Office, headed successively by Richard McCarty and Susan Wente, as well as my two deans in the College of Arts and Science, John Sloop and Lauren Benton. All of us laboring in the humanities at Vanderbilt have been very fortunate in the consistent backing of our administrative leadership, starting at the top with our chancellor, Nick Zeppos, a genuine champion of the liberal arts. May such farsighted support for the humanities continue here and elsewhere!

I researched and wrote the book while chairing the Department of History at Vanderbilt, a task made considerably lighter by the long-standing culture of collegiality we enjoy. For moral and emotional support through various challenges, I am especially grateful to Celia Applegate, Michael Bess, David Blackbourn, Jeff Cowie, Dennis Dickerson, Marshall Eakin, Jim Epstein, Peter Lake, Jane Landers, Helmut Smith, Arleen Tuchman, Frank Wcislo, and Eddie Wright-Rios. Our outstanding departmental staff— Christen Harper, Tiffany Giese, Susan Hilderbrand, and Heidi Welch—have kept things running smoothly and helped me personally in too many ways to count (although I would like to single out Heidi Welch's assistance with some of the illustrations). Many Vanderbilt colleagues in other departments have made helpful suggestions for the book over the last four years, particularly Dan Sharfstein, Paul Stobb, Holly Tucker, and Lenn Goodman (who urged me to own the term "mystic"). I'm also grateful for advice from Bill Caferro, Volker Leppin, Tom McGinn, Lyndal Roper, and Francesca Trivellato. Once again, Jim Toplon and his interlibrary loan colleagues have cheerfully fulfilled every request I've sent their way.

The final version of the book has benefited greatly from the careful reading of my team of trial readers who kindly reviewed the entire manuscript, namely Michael Bess, Joan Dayton, Paul Freedman, Bob Grabman, Laura Huff Hileman, Deirdre Reidy Horton, Barry Hudgin, Madeleine Philbin, Jonathan Scruggs, and Phil Soergel. Translating Meister Eckhart's ideas into accessible (and hopefully engaging) prose would have been much harder without these friends' many thoughtful suggestions. The congregation of Second Presbyterian Church in Nashville likewise provided me with a forum for exploring Eckhart's teachings among interested nonspecialists.

My ever astute and supportive literary agent Rafe Sagalyn had confidence in this project from early on and succeeded in finding the ideal publisher for the book. Ginny Smith Younce, my editor at Penguin Press, has likewise been a consistently enthusiastic supporter. She has helped me pare down the text considerably and otherwise provided me with many insightful suggestions. Megan Gerrity repeatedly went above and beyond the call of duty as production editor. I am grateful to Darren Haggar for the beautiful dust jacket, and to Gene Thorp for his usual cartographical virtuosity and good humor. Katie Martin and Maggie Corbett assisted me with preliminary research, and Jessica Lowe gracefully performed the grinding task of securing high-resolution images and permissions. Charlotte M. M. Harrington expertly converted nearly eight hundred endnotes to blind notes.

As always, my family has kept me happily anchored in the Now and provided much joy. My father, Jack Harrington, passed away during the course of the book's composition but up until his final two weeks continued to discuss the project with me and offer encouragement. I continue to rely on the generosity and kindness of my mother, Marilyn Harrington, as well as that of the Filloons of Lebanon, the Harringtons of Tampa, and the Monins of Jonesborough and Tulsa. My children, George and Charlotte, are on the verge of beginning their adult lives, and I am daily grateful for my remaining time with them. Above all, my greatest debt—and I apologize for the cliché—is to my wife, Beth Monin Harrington. Beth read every part of the book, some parts more than once, and gently reshaped (or cut) my "least effective" sentences or passages. The final product is immeasurably better because of her wise and generous contributions, and my life is immeasurably richer for having her as my partner.

Recommended Reading

Writings by Eckhart

For those readers willing and able to consult the original versions of Eckhart's writings, there are two meticulously edited collections of primary sources that have been published since 1936. All widely accepted Latin works are contained in *Meister Eckhart, Die lateinischen Werke*, ed. Ernst Benz et al., vols. I–V (Stuttgart: Kohlhammer, 1936–2007). All authenticated writings in Middle High German have been assembled in *Meister Eckhart, Die deutschen Werke*, ed. Josef Quint and Georg Steer, vols. I–V (Stuttgart: Kohlhammer, 1936–2007). There are many translated selections of the Latin and German writings available in English. The most complete and accessible English collection of Eckhart's German sermons and other vernacular writings is *The Complete Mystical Works of Meister Eckhart*, trans. Maurice O'C. Walshe (New York: Crossroad, 2009). Eckhart's commentaries on Genesis and John, as well as documents from the investigation of his orthodoxy, are excerpted in *Meister Eckhart: The Essential Sermons, Commentaries, Treatises, and Defense*, trans. and ed. Edmund Colledge and Bernard McGinn (New York: Paulist Press, 1981). Excerpts from various Latin commentaries and sermons are found in *Meister Eckhart: Teacher and Preacher*, ed. Bernard McGinn (New York: Paulist Press, 1986). Surviving samples of Meister Eckhart's disputations are presented in *Parisian Questions and Prologues*, trans. Armand A. Maurer (Toronto: Pontifical Institute of Mediaeval Studies, 1974).

Books About Eckhart

The bibliography on Eckhart is vast, and grows significantly every year. The most up-to-date and comprehensive scholarly overview on Eckhart is *A*

Companion to Meister Eckhart, ed. Jeremiah M. Hackett (Leiden: Brill, 2013). My favorite biographical approach to Eckhart, albeit with some lapses, is Kurt Ruh, *Meister Eckhart: Theologe—Prediger—Mystiker* (Munich: C. H. Beck, 1989), unfortunately not yet available in English translation. Oliver Davies, *Meister Eckhart: Mystical Theologian* (London: SPCK, 1991), provides less social and cultural context but is quite good on Eckhart's influences and main teachings. The recently translated Kurt Flasch, *Meister Eckhart: Philosopher of Christianity*, trans. Anne Schindel and Aaron Vanides (New Haven, CT: Yale University Press, 2015), has much interesting material, although Flasch's long-standing attempts to "de-mysticize" Eckhart can be distracting. For a broader view of Eckhart within the religious thinking of his own time, there is no better guide than Bernard McGinn, *The Harvest of Mysticism in Medieval Germany*, vol. IV of *The Presence of God: A History of Christian Mysticism* (New York: Crossroad, 2005). The German Meister-Eckhart-Gesellschaft maintains an annually updated bibliography of works published about Eckhart at http://www.meister-eckhart-gesellschaft.de/bib liographie.htm. Readers may also wish to view the recommended reading at the Eckhart Society based in England: http://www.eckhartsociety.org /resources/resources.

Books About Eckhart's Times

There are many surveys of medieval Europe available. One outstanding recent work is Chris Wickham, *Medieval Europe* (New Haven, CT: Yale University Press, 2016). Other commendable overviews include: Johannes Fried, *The Middle Ages*, trans. Peter Lewis (Cambridge, MA: Belknap Press of Harvard University Press, 2015); Barbara Rosenwein, *A Short History of the Middle Ages*, 3rd ed. (Toronto: University of Toronto Press, 2009); and Robert Bartlett, *The Making of Europe: Conquest, Colonization and Cultural Change, 950–1350*, reprint ed. (Princeton, NJ: Princeton University Press, 1994). For a reliable overview of Eckhart's Germany, see F. R. H. Du Boulay, *Germany in the Later Middle Ages* (New York: St. Martin's Press, 1983). A richer (and longer) account of the German nobility is found in Joachim Bumke, *Courtly Culture: Literature and Society in the High Middle Ages*, trans. Thomas Dunlap

(Berkeley: University of California Press, 1991). The most engaging account of everyday life in Eckhart's day, albeit in England, is Ian Mortimer, *The Time Traveler's Guide to Medieval England: A Handbook for Visitors to the Fourteenth Century* (New York: Touchstone, 2011).

My favorite introduction to late medieval Christianity is R. N. Swanson, *Religion and Devotion in Europe, c. 1215–c. 1515* (Cambridge, UK: Cambridge University Press, 1995). I also like the classic Francis Oakley, *The Western Church in the Later Middle Ages* (Ithaca, NY: Cornell University Press, 1979), as well as the recent Kevin Madigan, *Medieval Christianity: A New History* (New Haven, CT: Yale University Press, 2015). There is no more comprehensive or enjoyable survey of medieval saints than Robert Bartlett, *Why Can the Dead Do Such Great Things?: Saints and Worshippers from the Martyrs to the Reformation* (Princeton, NJ: Princeton University Press, 2013). Two scholarly works are essential for a reader interested in the first century of Dominican life: William A. Hinnebusch, *The History of the Dominican Order*, 2 vols. (Staten Island, NY: Alba House, 1966 and 1973), and M. Michèle Mulchahey, *"First the Bow Is Bent in Study": Dominican Education Before 1350* (Toronto: Pontifical Institute of Mediaeval Studies, 1998). For a broad introduction to religious dissent, see Malcolm D. Lambert, *Medieval Heresy: Popular Movements from the Gregorian Reform to the Reformation*, 2nd ed. (Cambridge, MA: B. Blackwell, 1992). For a stimulating and more polemical take on the background of the attempts to enforce orthodoxy, see R. I. Moore, *The Formation of a Persecuting Society: Authority and Deviance in Western Europe 950–1250*, 2nd ed. (London: Wiley & Blackwell, 2007). Edwin Mullins, *The Popes of Avignon: A Century in Exile* (New York: Blue Bridge, 2007), offers a highly readable, non-scholarly approach to the subject, while Geoffrey Barraclough, *The Medieval Papacy* (New York: Norton, 1968), provides an older but still insightful overview of the institution itself during this crucial period.

A good, brief introduction to scholastic culture is Jacques Verger, *Men of Learning in Europe at the End of the Middle Ages*, trans. Lisa Neal and Steven Rendall (Notre Dame, IN: University of Notre Dame Press, 1997). I have benefited greatly from the careful and clear overview of Richard Cross, *The Medieval Christian Philosophers: An Introduction* (London: I. B. Tauris, 2014). For a broader survey, see also *The Cambridge History of Later Medieval Philosophy:*

1100–1600, ed. Norman Kretzmann et al. (Cambridge, UK: Cambridge University Press, 1982; reprint 1988).

The best overview of thirteenth- and fourteenth-century female mysticism is Bernard McGinn, *The Flowering of Mysticism: Men and Women in the New Mysticism—1200–1350*, vol. III of *The Presence of God: A History of Western Christian Mysticism* (New York: Crossroad, 1998). The pioneering work in this area is Herbert Grundmann, *Religious Movements in the Middle Ages*, trans. Steven Rowan (Notre Dame, IN: University of Notre Dame Press, 1995). The scholarship of Caroline Walker Bynum on late medieval religious women has been path breaking; see especially *Jesus as Mother: Studies in the Spirituality of the High Middle Ages* (Berkeley: University of California Press, 1984) and *Holy Feast and Holy Fast: The Religious Significance of Food to Medieval Women* (Berkeley: University of California, 1987). Readers interested in late medieval women mystics will wish to consult Amy M. Hollywood, *The Soul as Virgin Wife: Mechthild of Magdeburg, Marguerite Porete, and Meister Eckhart* (Notre Dame, IN: University of Notre Dame Press, 2000), as well as her more recent collection of essays, *Acute Melancholia and Other Essays: Mysticism, History, and the Study of Religion (Gender, Theory, and Religion)* (New York: Columbia University Press, 2016). For the key primary sources discussed, see *Mechthild of Magdeburg: The Flowing Light of the Godhead*, trans. Frank Tobin (Mahwah, NJ: Paulist Press, 1997), and *Marguerite Porete: The Mirror of Simple Souls*, trans. Ellen Babinsky (Mahwah, NJ: Paulist Press, 1993). A broader sampling can be found in *Medieval Writings on Female Spirituality*, ed. Elizabeth Spearing (New York: Penguin, 2002).

Paulist Press has published very fluid translations of important works by Heinrich Suso (1989) and Johannes Tauler (1985). For a broader historical range of selections, see the impressive collection *The Essential Writings of Christian Mysticism*, ed. Bernard McGinn (New York: Modern Library, 2006), as well as William Franke's scholarly anthology, *On What Cannot Be Said: Apophatic Discourses in Philosophy, Religion, Literature, and the Arts*, 2 vols. (Notre Dame, IN: University of Notre Dame Press, 2007).

Notes

ABBREVIATIONS

DW: *Meister Eckhart, Die deutschen Werke,* ed. J. Quint and G. Steer, vols. I–V (Stuttgart: Kohlhammer, 1936–2007).

ESSENTIAL ME: *Meister Eckhart: The Essential Sermons, Commentaries, Treatises, and Defense,* trans. and ed. Edmund Colledge and Bernard McGinn (New York: Paulist Press, 1981).

HACKETT: *A Companion to Meister Eckhart,* ed. Jeremiah M. Hackett (Leiden: Brill, 2013).

HARVEST: Bernard McGinn, *The Harvest of Mysticism in Medieval Germany,* vol. IV of *The Presence of God: A History of Christian Mysticism* (New York: Herder & Herder, 2005).

LW: *Meister Eckhart, Die lateinischen Werke,* ed. E. Benz et al., vols. I–V (Stuttgart: Kohlhammer, 1936–2007).

ME: Meister Eckhart

PR: *Predigt* (German Sermon), based on enumeration of *DW.*

T&P: *Meister Eckhart: Teacher and Preacher,* ed. Bernard McGinn (New York: Paulist Press, 1986).

W: *The Complete Mystical Works of Meister Eckhart,* trans. Maurice O'C. Walshe (New York: Crossroad, 2009).

EPIGRAPH

viv **There are those who seek:** *Sermones in Cantica* XXXVI, in Jacques Paul Migne, *Patrologia Latina* (1841–55), 183, col. 968–69.

PROLOGUE

1 **The contrast between the setting:** While Meister Eckhart likely preached at least once at the cathedral during his ten years in Strasbourg, there is no record of the event. The sermon in question (Pr 101) dates from this period.

3 **The biblical text that served:** As was his wont, Eckhart takes some liberties with the verse, translating it as "When all things lay in the midst of silence, then there descended down *into me* from on high, from the royal throne, a *secret* word." (Interpolations italicized).

3 *The more completely you are able:* Pr 101 (W 33).

4 *The Son of the heavenly Father:* Pr 101 (W 36–37).

5 **"In essence," writes Tolle:** Eckhart Tolle, *The Power of Now: A Guide to Spiritual Enlightenment* (Novato, CA: Namaste, 1999), 9.

6 **Many modern Christian authors:** https://cac.org/meister-eckhart-part-i-2015-07-15.

7 **He saw himself first as:** On the question of Eckhart as a mystic, see the summary in Karl Albert, "Epilogue: Meister Eckhart—Between Mysticism and Philosophy," in *Hackett,* 599–790. Kurt Flasch has been the most outspoken and persistent advocate of dropping the mystical designation of Eckhart altogether and just calling him a philosopher. See Recommended Reading, 328.

8 **Before we attempt to adapt:** I fully agree with Bernard McGinn on the importance, as well as difficulty, in fully historicizing Eckhart's teachings. See especially *The Mystical Thought of ME* (New York: Crossroad, 2001), 20–34.

8 **"The eye with which":** Pr 12 (W 298).

11 **To answer that question:** I adopt this phrase from Markus J. Borg, *Meeting Jesus Again for the First Time: The Historical Jesus and the Heart of Contemporary Faith* (New York: HarperCollins, 1994).

CHAPTER 1: THE NOBLE HEART

15 *Some people are half raised up:* Pr 25 (W 200).

17 **"There is nothing on this earth":** Thomas Aquinas, *On Charity*, trans. Lottie H. Kendzierski (Milwaukee: Marquette University Press, 1960), art. 4.

18 **Eckhart's exact contemporary:** Dante Alighieri, *The Divine Comedy, Purgatorio*, Canto 33, translated in Stephen Mitchell, *The Enlightened Heart* (New York: Harper Perennial), 68.

18 **Knight Wirnt von Grafenberg:** Joachim Bumke, *Courtly Culture: Literature and Society in the High Middle Ages*, trans. Thomas Dunlap (Berkeley: University of California Press, 1991), 15.

18 **"Formerly, the world was so beautiful":** Johannes Fried, *The Middle Ages*, trans. Peter Lewis (Cambridge, MA: Belknap Press, 2015), 242.

19 **Just within his own century:** Alfred Haverkamp, *Medieval Germany, 1056–1273* (Oxford, UK: Oxford University Press, 1992), 29, 296; Joachim Leuschner, *Germany in the Late Middle Ages* (Amsterdam: North-Holland Publishing, 1980), 3; Thomas A. Brady, Jr., *German Histories in the Age of Reformations, 1400–1650* (Cambridge, UK: Cambridge University Press, 2009), 21.

19 **Cologne, where Eckhart would end:** Leuschner, *Germany*, 5; Lester K. Little, *Religious Poverty and the Profit Economy in Medieval Europe* (Ithaca, NY: Cornell University Press, 1978), 23.

21 **"We are in desperate need":** Fried, *Middle Ages*, 237.

21 **In some German lands, feudal dues:** Peter Spufford, *Money and Its Use in Medieval Europe* (Cambridge, UK: Cambridge University Press, 1989), 242.

23 **"All over the world":** *The Book of Good Love*, cited in Norman Cantor, ed., *Medieval Reader* (New York: HarperCollins, 1995), 269.

24 **The first written mention:** Erika Albrecht, "Zur Herkunft Meister Eckharts," in *Amsblatt der evangelisch-lutherischen Kirche Thüringen*, no. 31 (1978), 28–34. The most up to date and succinct summary of Eckhart's biographical information is Walter Senner, "Meister Eckhart's Life, Training, Career, and Trial," in Hackett, 7–81. For a range of theories on Eckhart's origins, see 8–10.

24 **By this time, there were perhaps:** F. R. H. DuBoulay, *Germany in the Later Middle Ages* (London: Athlone Press, 1988), 65–69.

24 **By law it could not:** Bumke, *Courtly Culture*, 107ff.

25 **Some of the new nobles:** Ibid., 33–35.

25 **Around 1260, the knight's wife:** The latest possible birth year is 1262. Sermon of August 28, 1303 (LW V:158), refers to hometown as Hochheim. Walter Senner, "Meister Eckhart's Life," in Hackett, 9.

25 **Five years later, another document:** Johann Georg August Galletti, *Geschichte und Beschreibung des Herzogthums Gotha* (Gotha, 1780), III:263ff.; Albrecht, "Zur Herkunft," 30.

26 *Why do I love my father:* Pr 74 (W 376).

26 **[My] bodily father, in other words:** Pr 6 (W 331); Pr 28 (W 131).

27 **When the knight Eckehard hosted:** Bumke, *Courtly Culture*, 222ff.

29 **By the thirteenth century, the German:** Brady, *German Histories*, 16.

30 **In Eckhart's own Thuringia:** Steffen Raßloff, *Geschichte Thüringens* (Munich: 2010), 27.

31 **Most of the material troubadours performed:** Olive Sayce, *The Medieval German Lyric, 1150–1300: The Development of Its Themes and Forms in Their European Context* (Oxford, UK: Clarendon Press, 1978), 265.

33 **"To love wisely":** Albrecht Classen, "Courtly Love Lyric," in Gentry, *Companion*, 118; Bumke, *Courtly Culture*, 101.

33 **Many "dawn songs":** Sayce, *The Medieval German Lyric*, 12ff.

34 **Eckhart's contemporary, poet Hugo von Trimberg:** Bumke, *Courtly Culture*, 513–14; Witte Jackson, "Arthurian Material and German Society in the Middle Ages," in W. H. Jackson and Silvia Ranawake, *The Arthur of the Germans: The Arthurian Legend in Medieval German and Dutch Literature* (Cardiff, UK: University of Wales Press, 2000), 281–84.

35 **"The way I see it":** Bumke, *Courtly Culture*, 321.

36 **The order had established:** https://de.wikipedia.org/wiki/Deutschordensballei_Th%C3%BCringen.

37 *Knowledge,* he preaches: Pr 3 (W 165–66).

37 **Most strikingly, the adult Dominican friar:** On noble language, see Hermann Kunisch, "Offenbarung und Gehorsam: Versuch über Eckharts Religiöse Persönlichkeit," in *ME der Prediger. Festschrift zum Eckhart-Gedenkjahr*, ed. Udo Maria Nix and Raphaël Louis Öchslin (Freiburg im Breisgau: Herder, 1960), 122–40.

37 **Individual human beings:** Pr 25 (W 93).

37 *must leave the crowd:* Pr 4 (W 55).

37   *I extol detachment above:* On Detachment (W 566–67).
38   "There was a nobleman": Pr 15 (W 270–74); also *The Nobleman* (W 557–65).
38   *How could a man:* Ibid., 563.
38   Later in life, in his mid-fifties: *Book of Divine Consolation,* (W 552–53).

CHAPTER 2: HEROIC CHRISTIANITY

39   Nothing is so cheap as heaven: Pr 58 (W 243).
47   A new papal canonization process: Robert Bartlett, *Why Can the Dead Do Such Great Things?: Saints and Worshippers from the Martyrs to the Reformation* (Princeton, NJ: Princeton University Press, 2013), 60.
49   Satires such as: Jacques LeGoff, *Money in the Middle Ages* (Berkeley: University of California Press, 2012), 39.
49   The celebrated quotation from 1 Timothy: Little, *Religious Poverty*, 36.
51   *Who were they who bought:* Pr 1 (W 67).
52   an "axial age in spirituality": For a succinct argument, see Peter Dinzelbacher, "Die Achsenzeit des Hohen Mittelalters und die Ketzergeschichte," in Günther Franke and Friedrich Niewöhner, *Reformer als Ketzer: heterodoxe Bewegungen von Vorreformatoren* (Stuttgart: Friedrich Frommann Verlag Gunther Holzboog, 2004), 101ff.
52   And just as Arthur and his knights: Heinrich Fichtenau, *Heretics and Scholars in the High Middle Ages, 1000–1200,* trans. Denise A. Kaiser (University Park: Penn State University Press, 1998), 136.
53   The people denigrated by some: Herbert Grundmann, *Religious Movements in the Middle Ages,* trans. Steven Rowan (Notre Dame, IN: University of Notre Dame Press, 1995) 14, 69–74.
54   a "medieval Reformation": See, for example, B. M. Bulton, *The Medieval Reformation* (London: Edward Arnold, 1987).
54   One thirteenth-century critic marveled: Fried, *Middle Ages,* 256–57.
55   "We know that they suppose": Jennifer Kolpacoff Deane, *A History of Medieval Heresy and Inquisition* (Lanham, MD: Rowman & Littlefield, 2011), 24.
55   "Wolves in sheep's clothing": Christine Caldwell Ames, *Righteous Persecution: Inquisition, Dominicans, and Christianity in the Middle Ages* (Philadelphia: University of Pennsylvania Press, 2008), 30.
55   "[They] commonly say that": Karen Sullivan, *The Inner Lives of Medieval Inquisitors* (Chicago: University of Chicago Press, 2013), 129.
55   Only when the Lyons merchant: Grundmann, *Religious Movements,* 40–41. For a fuller account, see Euan Cameron, *The Waldenses: Rejections of Holy Church in Medieval Europe* (Hoboken, NJ: Wiley, 2001).
57   "dumb dogs who do not bark": Ames, *Righteous Persecution,* 35.
58   Lay apostolic groups who recognized: See R. I. Moore, *The Formation of a Persecuting Society: Authority and Deviance in Western Europe, 950–1250,* 2nd ed. (Oxford, UK: Blackwell, 2007).
60   By the time of Eckhart: Jean-Claude Schmitt, *Mort d'une hérésie: l'Église et les clercs face aux béguines et aux béghards du Rhin supérieur du XIVe au XVe siècle* (Paris: Mouton, 1978), 63.
60   Dominicans, who called themselves: M. Michèle Mulchahey, *"First the Bow Is Bent in Study": Dominican Education Before 1350* (Toronto: Pontifical Institute of Mediaeval Studies, 1998), 41.

CHAPTER 3: THE DOMINICAN WAY

63   Why am I more glad: W 377.
65   Unlike the provincial village: Brady, *German Histories,* 23.
65   By then, the Order of Preachers: *Geschichte in Daten: Thüringen,* ed. Jürgen John, Reinhard Jonscher, and Axel Stelzner (Munich: Koehler & Amelang, 1995), 95; John B. Freed, *The Friars and German Society in the Thirteenth Century* (Washington, DC: The Mediaeval Society of America, 1977), 44ff.
65   By 1270, when ten-year-old Eckhart: Freed, *The Friars,* 330.
66   The resulting pedagogical arms race: William A. Hinnebusch, *The History of the Dominican Order,* 2 vols. (Staten Island, NY: Alba House, 1966 and 1973), I:283, 322–23.
66   The life of a Dominican preacher: Humbert of Romans, *Treatise on Preaching,* trans. Dominican Students Province of St. Joseph; ed. Walter M. Conlon O.P. (http://dominicanidaho.org/humbert.pdf), 9.
66   "carpenters, stonecutters, masons": Humbert, *Preaching,* 10.
67   There are some who, endowed with: Humbert, *Preaching,* 49–50; also cited in Little, *Religious Poverty,* 202.
67   The preaching of a single friar: Humbert, *Preaching,* 64–65.
67   "Preaching is such a noble art": Ibid., 27.
67   Those few brave souls willing: Ibid., 1, 18, 99.

68   **Dominicans and Franciscans, by contrast:** Freed, *The Friars*, 132.
68   **Upon his application to enter:** The following description of initiation draws heavily on the accounts of Hinnebusch, *History*, I:290 ff., and Mulcahey, *"First the Bow Is Bent in Study,"* 75–78.
70   **Undergarments were also woolen:** Hinnebusch, *History*, I:340.
71   **The largely autonomous community:** Ibid., I:289.
71   **The remaining duties of the day:** Ibid., I:347.
72   **The focus on rote memorization:** Mulcahey, *"First the Bow Is Bent in Study,"* 99–101.
73   **During his novitiate year:** Hinnebusch, *History*, I:299.
73   **As an advanced student:** Ibid., I:351.
73   **In these early years:** Ibid., I: 355–59.
75   **"first the bow is bent":** Mulcahey takes this epigraph as the title for her excellent survey of thirteenth-century Dominican education, *"First the Bow Is Bent in Study,"* ix.
75   **All were fellow brothers:** Hinnebusch, *History*, II:20.
75   **Eckhart and his fellow students attended:** Mulcahey, *"First the Bow Is Bent in Study,"* 179, 248.
77   **The latter class was directed:** Ibid., 133–36.
77   **Lectures on Lombard's *Sentences*:** See the classic work on the topic, Henri de Lubac, *Medieval Exegesis: The Four Senses of Scripture*, 3 vols., trans. Mark Sebanc and E. M. Macierowski (Grand Rapids, MI: Eerdmans, 1998–2009); also Philipp W. Rosemann, *The Story of a Great Medieval Book: Peter Lombard's "Sentences"* (Toronto: University of Toronto Press, 2007).
78   ***teaches us very clearly:*** Commentary on Genesis in *Essential ME*, 108.
78   **"each and every sentence":** Fichtenau, *Heretics and Scholars*, 206.
79   **The most significant transformation:** R. N. Swanson, *Religion and Devotion in Europe, c. 1215–c. 1515* (Cambridge, UK: Cambridge University Press, 1995), 74.
80   **Here too, Dominicans led the way:** Mulcahey, *"First the Bow Is Bent in Study,"* 504–12.
80   **"each day they attend lectures":** Little, *Religious Poverty*, 184.
80   **"Our order is recognized":** Quoted in Mulcahey, *"First the Bow Is Bent in Study,"* 3.
80   **"Others apply themselves":** Humbert, *Preaching*, 64.
81   **In *On the Education of Preachers*:** Humbert, *Preaching*, 4–7, 19–20.
81   **The most famous preacher of Eckhart's day:** See Peter Segl, "Berthold von Regensburg und die Ketzer seiner Zeit," in *Festschrift Kurt Reindel, in Studien und Quellen zur Geschichte Regensburgs*, 4 (Regensburg: Universitaetsverlag Regensburg: 1987), 115–29.
82   **Thirteenth-century Dominican authors:** Fichtenau, *Heretics and Scholars*, 318; Little, *Religious Poverty*, 196.
82   **In addition to Humbert's own:** Little, *Religious Poverty*, 191.
83   **Jacobus da Voragine, compiler of:** Mulcahey, *"First the Bow Is Bent in Study,"* 423.
83   **Other preaching aids offered:** Ibid., 460–62.
83   **A successful preacher, he was taught:** Humbert, *Preaching*, 29ff.; Mulcahey, *"First the Bow Is Bent in Study,"* 138, 481–84, 530–40.
84   **Every good preacher should first:** Humbert, *Preaching*, 24–26.
84   **"The manner of delivery":** Ibid., 54.
85   **Finally, both Hugh of Saint-Cher:** Little, *Religious Poverty*, 185.
85   **In contrast to Franciscan preachers:** Beverly Mayne Kienzle, "Medieval Sermons and Their Performance: Theory and Record," in *Preacher, Sermon and Audience in the Middle Ages*, ed. Carolyn Muessig (Leiden: Brill, 2002), 99, 108; Augustine Thompson, "From Texts to Preaching: Retrieving the Medieval Sermon as an Event," in Muessig, *Preacher*, 25.
85   **"As the seed is planted in preaching":** Ibid., 189.
86   **"those who cannot be understood":** Humbert, *Preaching*, 32.
86   **"It is worth far more":** Ibid., 34.
87   **After more experience:** Hinnebusch, *History*, I:263–67; Little, *Religious Poverty*, 185.
87   **Like students off to college:** Humbert, *Preaching*, 89.
87   **A good preacher should not trouble himself:** Ibid., 108.

CHAPTER 4: THE RIGHT STATE

89   **We are the cause of all:** Pr 5a (W 107).
89   **"that perfect love of God":** *The Rule of St. Benedict*, trans. Anthony C. Meisel and M. L. del Mastro (Garden City, NY: Image, 1975), 61.
91   **The work, known as the *Talks of Instruction*:** See the discussion in Dagmar Gottschall, "Eckhart's German Works," in *Hackett*, 146–49.

91   **We don't know if Eckhart:** Loris Sturlese, "Eckhart as Preacher, Administrator, and Master of the Sentences: From Erfurt and Back, 1294–1313; The Origins of the *Opus Tripartitum*," in *Hackett*, 127.

92   *People should not worry so much: Talks of Instruction* (W 489).

92   *In true obedience there should be:* W 487.

92   *[God] is little concerned:* W 503.

92   *Many people think they are performing:* W 501.

93   *Skillful diligence is required:* W 512.

93   *People say, "Alas, sir":* W 487–89.

94   *as I have often said:* W 490.

95   **Drawing closer to God:** W 519.

95   *in all his acts and in all things:* W 493.

95   *This above all is necessary:* W 512.

95   *If you have a true:* W 495.

95   *If a man is not drawn:* W 495.

96   *the greater and fiercer:* W 510.

96   *However great the suffering:* W 499.

96   *People may well be daunted:* W 504–5.

96   *As I have often said:* W 505.

97   *God in His faithfulness:* W 507–8.

97   *Great hope and trust:* W 501.

97   *Wherever a man in obedience:* W 486.

97   *When a man stands right:* W 500–501.

97   *In the right state of mind:* W 497.

97   **What today would be called mindfulness:** W 492.

98   *One is when God tells a man:* W 502.

99   *As I have said before:* W 496.

99   *But you might say:* W 509.

99   *Whenever a man wishes:* W 511.

100 *There was never so close:* W 510.

100 *His passing mention:* W 512.

100 *a light shin[ing] in the darkness:* W 499.

101 *You should know that:* W 494.

101 *Inclination to sin:* W 494.

101 *Willingness to sin:* W 499.

101 **Amid the unrelenting:** W 520.

101 *Whatever God then sends him:* W 515.

102 *Do not bother yourself:* W 521.

102 *It all depends on that:* W 489.

104 *The more deeply:* LW V:142.

104 **Even the pagan Ptolemy:** LW V:146.

104 **Albert the Great, the preeminent:** LW V:145.

CHAPTER 5: THE SCIENCE OF GOD

109 *What is truth?:* Pr 25 (W 95).

110 **At most one in ten Dominicans:** William J. Courtenay, *Schools and Scholars in Fourteenth-Century England* (Princeton, NJ: Princeton University Press, 1987), 6; Hinnebusch, *History*, II:11; Mulcahey, "First the Bow Is Bent in Study," 231.

110 **Eckhart's 1293–94 stay:** Cf. reference to 1286 Parisian stay in Easter sermon of 1294. LW V:155.

110 **By Eckhart's time:** Jacques Verger, *Men of Learning in Europe at the End of the Middle Ages* (Notre Dame, IN: University of Notre Dame Press, 2000), 47; Senner, "Life," in *Hackett*, 11–12.

111 **Earlier in the century, Philip Augustus:** Alfred Fierro, *Histoire et dictionnaire de Paris* (Paris: Robert Laffont, 1996), 270.

112 **In addition to the large merchant:** Boris Bove and Claude Gauvard, *Le Paris du Moyen Age* (Paris: Belin, 2014), 24–25.

113 **Even at the graduate level:** Alan B. Cobban, *Universities in the Middle Ages* (Liverpool: Liverpool University Press, 1990), 165.

113 **Perhaps fortunately for the enhancement:** William J. Courtenay, "Study Abroad: German Students at Bologna, Paris, and Oxford in the Fourteenth Century," in *Universities and Schooling*, ed. William J. Courtenay and Jürgen Miethke (Leiden: Brill, 2000), 18.

113 **Although college statutes repeatedly condemned:** Cobban, *Universities*, 196–99.

114 **A few decades earlier, one particularly:** Kevin Madigan, *Medieval Christianity: A New History* (New Haven, CT: Yale University Press, 2015), 269.

114 **The French king Philip Augustus:** John W. Baldwin, *The Scholastic Culture of the Middle Ages, 1100–1300* (Lexington, MA: D. C. Heath, 1971), 49.

114 **Wealthy families leased entire houses:** Courtenay, *Schools and Scholars*, 82, 88; Lynn Thorndike, *University Records and Life in the Middle Ages* (New York: Columbia University Press, 1944), 118, also 88–98; Helene Wieruszowski, *The Medieval University: Masters, Students, Learning* (London: Andrews McMeel, 1966), 106–9.

115 **In theory, the Paris priory:** Hinnebusch, *History*, II:38–39.

115 **Since their arrival in the 1220s:** Cobban, *Universities*, 92–93; James A. Weisheipl, *Friar Thomas D'Aquino: His Life, Thought and Work* (New York: Doubleday, 1974), 80, 93.

116 **As in every subject, classical Roman:** Richard Cross, *The Medieval Christian Philosophers: An Introduction* (London: I. B. Tauris, 2014), 28.

116 **Given the great cost of parchment:** Verger, *Men of Learning*, 66–69; Thorndike, *University Records*, 100ff.

118 **Historians still debate:** "Albertus saepe dicebat," LW V:145.

119 **During Eckhart's formative years:** Hinnebusch, *History*, II:123, 125.

119 **In the words of a later chronicler:** "War er nit gewesen, Deutschlandt wer ein eysel bleiben," quoted in *Harvest*, 13.

119 **In 1248, despite much internal resistance:** Hinnebusch, *History*, II:27–28.

120 **Between 1250 and 1350:** https://plato.stanford.edu/entries/medieval-philosophy/.

121 **"seeking to know the incomprehensible":** Thorndike, *University Records*, 80–81.

121 **Looking for reputable allies:** Fichtenau, *Heretics and Scholars*, 318.

123 **No records survive of Eckhart's lectures:** LW, V:3–16.

123 **Typically, a lecture would focus:** *Sentences*, *Book 1*, chapters 13 and 185, 25, 230.

124 **His "Second Bachelor" status:** Hinnebusch, *History*, II:31.

124 **The university typically waived:** Ibid., II:59.

124 **"despise simple persons who know":** Thorndike, *University Records*, 171–72.

124 **Francis of Assisi thought:** John Hine Mundy, *Europe in the High Middle Ages, 1150–1309 (General History of Europe)* (Boston: Addison-Wesley, 1991), 203.

125 **How could he not feel:** Verger, *Men of Learning*, 84.

127 **By the time of Eckhart's study:** Cross, *Medieval Christian Philosophers*, 105–6.

129 **"Authority is the weakest form":** Fichtenau, *Heretics and Scholars*, 218.

130 **Certainly angels were a well-embedded part:** David Keck, *Angels and Angelology in the Middle Ages* (Oxford, UK: Oxford University Press, 1998), 4–5.

131 **"the perfection of the universe":** *Summa Theologica*, Part I, Question 50, article 1.

131 **Several later fathers:** Keck, *Angels*, 13ff.

131 **The major intellectual work:** Ibid., 23, 110.

132 **A few scholars proposed a nebulous:** Cross, *Medieval Christian Philosophers*, 159.

133 **"correcting Aristotle through a pious":** Ibid., 100.

CHAPTER 6: MASTER OF LEARNING

135 *Now a master [i.e., Aristotle]:* Pr 10 (W 335).

135 **The solemn ceremony of induction:** Weisheipl, *Friar Thomas*, 98–100.

137 **The last German to receive:** Sturlese, "Eckhart as Preacher," in *Hackett*, 128.

137 **As a Dominican, Meister Eckhart:** Courtenay, *Schools and Scholars*, 28–29; appendix in *Hackett*, 722–23; Mulcahey, "First the Bow Is Bent in Study," 379.

137 **When the archbishop of Canterbury:** Kurt Flasch, *Das philosophische Denken im Mittelalter: Von Augustin zu Machiavelli* (Stuttgart: Reclams Universal-Bibliothek, 2001), 374.

137 **The most important direct Dominican influence:** Markus Führer, "Dietrich of Freiberg," *The Stanford Encyclopedia of Philosophy* (Winter 2015 Edition), Edward N. Zalta (ed.), http://plato.stanford .edu/archives/win2015/entries/dietrich-freiberg/; Kurt Flasch, *Dietrich von Freiberg: Philosophie, Theologie, Naturforschung um 1300* (Frankfurt am Main: Vittorio Klostermann, 2007), esp. 26ff.

139 *Nature, he wrote:* Comm on Genesis, in *Essential ME*, 99.

139   *Pagan masters say that God:* Pr 13 (W 159).

140   *I used to wonder:* Pr 22 (W 281).

140   *If I were in a wilderness:* Pr 78 (W 176).

140   *The masters say all creatures:* Pr 22 (W 280).

140   **In the academic works that have survived:** Yossef Schwartz, "Zwischen Einheitsmetaphysik und Einheitshermeneutik," in *ME in Erfurt*, 279; also Alessandro Palazzo, "Eckhart's Islamic and Jewish Sources: Avicenna, Avicebron, Averroes," in *Hackett*, 271, says Eckhart mentions Averroës forty-two times.

141   **But the two non-Christian masters:** Flasch, *Das philosophische Denken im Mittelalter*, 277; Schwartz, "Zwischen Einheitsmetaphysik," 279.

141   **The most important intellectual and spiritual:** Schwartz, "Zwischen Einheitsmetaphysik," 279.

141   **By the time of his elevation:** Josef Koch, *Kleine Schriften* (Rome: Edizioni Di Storia e Letteratura, 1973), 211.

141   **"Let me know Thee who":** Augustine, *Confessions*, trans. F. J. Sheed, 2nd ed. (Indianapolis: Hackett, 2006), 189.

141   **Like Augustine, he compared:** Pr 51 (W 407–8).

141   **The Bible, according to Eckhart:** Comm on Genesis, in *Essential ME*, 92.

142   **Every passage, he believed:** Comm on John, in *Harvest*, 112.

142   **His commentary on the first line:** Comm on Genesis, in *Essential ME*, 96–107.

142   *I am astonished that Holy Scripture:* Pr 51 (W 407).

142   **In parables, virtually every word:** Comm on John (LW 3:649.3–10), in *Harvest*, 111.

142   *I do this to arouse:* Comm on Genesis, in *Essential ME*, 92.

142   *bringing honey forth:* Comm on Genesis, in *Essential ME*, 93–94.

142   **He conceded as much:** Comm on Exodus, in *Teacher and Preacher*, 41.

143   *Please note that the preceding words:* Comm on John, in *Essential ME*, 135.

143   *Moreover, since the literal sense:* Comm on Genesis, in *Essential ME*, 93.

143   *even if the [human] author:* Eckhart quoting from Augustine's *Confessions*, in Comm on Genesis, in *Essential ME*, 93.

143   **Some modern scholars have argued:** Donald Duclow, "Meister Eckhart's Latin Biblical Exegesis," in *Hackett*, 321, 326; see also *Harvest*, 111.

145   **For example, during Eckhart's previous stay:** Cross, *Christian Medieval Philosophers*, 153.

145   **Eckhart's entry into the fray:** LW V:37–54.

145   **According to Eckhart, understanding:** LW V:42.

145   *I am no longer of the [Thomist] opinion:* LW V:40. See also Kurt Flasch, *ME: Philosoph des Christentums* (Munich: C. H. Beck, 2011), 118ff.

145   **Rather he sought to reverse:** Alain de Libera, *La Mystique rhénane. D'Albert le Grand à Maître Eckhart* (Paris: Le Seuil, 1994), 166.

146   **As Thomas Aquinas explained:** *Summa Theologica*, Ia, 7a, art. 8, quoted in C. S. Lewis, *The Discarded Image* (Cambridge, UK: Cambridge University Press, 2012), 157.

147   **Sometime during Eckhart's regent professorship:** LW, V:55–71.

147   *Will and love fall on God:* Pr 37 (W 188).

147   *Goodness is a cloak:* Pr 9 (W 344).

148   *Love infatuates and entangles:* Pr 19 (208).

148   **"In this brief volume, we have":** Lombard, *Sentences*, 4–5.

149   **While his fellow Franciscans revered:** Roger Bacon, *Opus Minus*, ed. J. S. Brewer (1859), 325.

149   **Like Albert and Dietrich, Bacon:** Richard LeMay, "Roger Bacon's Attitude Toward the Latin Translations and Translators of the Twelfth and Thirteenth Centuries," in *Roger Bacon and the Sciences: Commemorative Essays, Studien und Texte zur Geistesgeschichte des Mittelalters*, No. 57 (Leiden: Brill, 1997), 40–41.

149   **Admirers and enemies alike:** Cross, *Christian Medieval Philosophers*, 163–64.

149   **Like Eckhart, Duns Scotus:** Ibid., 176.

150   **Duns Scotus, for one:** Ibid., 105.

150   *to satisfy as far as possible:* LW I:148.5–9, translated in McGinn, *Mystical Thought*, 7–8.

151   *By way of preface:* Comm on Genesis, prologue to *Opus Tripartitum*, in *Essential ME*, 82.

151   *What the philosophers have written:* LW 3:154.14–155.7, translated in McGinn, *Mystical Thought of ME*, 3.

152   **In rare instances of conflict:** Pr 9 (W 344).

152   **Eckhart conceived of his own *summa*:** See Andre Beccarisi, "Eckhart's Latin Works," in *Hackett*, 95ff.

153   **The first thesis, in Part I:** Prologue, *Parisian Questions and Prologues*, trans. Armand A. Maurer (Toronto: Pontifical Institute of Medieval Studies, 1974), 79.

153 *An image is not of itself:* Pr 14b (W 116); see also Pr 77 (W 267).

153 **This new position:** Sturlese, "Eckhart as Preacher," in *Hackett*, 132–33.

153 **As promised in the general prologue:** Maurer, *Parisian Questions*, 81.

153 *Everything that exists,* in other words: Ibid., 86–87.

154 *All of this would seem:* Ibid., 82.

154 **Since the** *Opus* **would** *simply touch:* Ibid., 105.

154 *at first glance some of the:* LW I:152.3–5, translated in McGinn, *Mystical Thought of ME*, 8.

154 **His "utterly original" attempt:** Sturlese, "Eckhart as Preacher," in *Hackett*, 131.

CHAPTER 7: KNOWING THE UNKNOWABLE GOD

157 *Where is this [hidden] God?:* Pr 79 (W 447).

157 **During the three decades:** Fried, *Middle Ages*, 21; Hinnebusch, *History*, I:376.

157 **It's possible that Eckhart:** Senner, "Life," in *Hackett*, 18.

158 **The new province contained:** *Geschichte in Daten: Thüringen*, 154.

158 **Eckhart's new position required:** Senner, "Life," in *Hackett*, 19–21.

158 **Not only were no complaints registered:** Ibid., 23–27.

160 **"Man reaches the peak":** Maurer, *Parisian Questions*, 40–41.

160 **"made everything I had written":** Weisheipl, *Friar Thomas*, 321.

160 *[God]'s knowledge is the cause:* Maurer, *Parisian Questions*, 48.

161 **If so, he nonetheless remained:** Ibid., 71–75.

162 **His inspiration, Eckhart claimed:** LW V:89–90.

163 *a man should not have:* Talks of Instruction (W 491).

164 **Eventually Eckhart agreed with Maimonides:** Comm on Exodus, in *T&P*, 56.

164 *Know that whatever you add:* Ibid., 101–2.

164 **Specifically, Maimonides posited:** Ibid., 57–58.

164 **Eckhart streamlined this list:** Pr 11 (W 347); also Pr 12.

164 **God, by contrast, exists:** Comm. on John, in *Essential ME*, 161.

165 *Nothing is so firmly opposed:* Pr 50 (W 452).

165 *Some people ask how:* Pr 39 (W 307).

165 **From the divine perspective:** Pr 20 (W 336).

165 **He recounted being asked:** Latin Sermon 45, in *T&P*, 230.

165 *all that happened a thousand years:* Pr 26 (W 95).

165 *In eternity, being and youth:* Pr 83 (W 462).

165 **The eternal Now, according to Eckhart:** Pr 38 (W 178).

166 *If I were asked where God is:* Pr 63 (W 390).

166 **Borrowing a popular Neoplatonic metaphor:** Pr 82 (W 404).

166 *Where are we to look?:* Pr 20b (W 201).

166 *Heaven is at all points equidistant:* Pr 68 (W 354); also Pr 81 (W 326).

166 *so vast and so wide:* Pr 69 (W 233).

166 **But God has no distinctions:** Comm on Genesis, in *Harvest*, 99. Eckhart is quoting Macrobius here.

167 *God is in all things:* Pr 30 (W 133).

167 *. . . the source of all numbers :* Comm on Wisdom; LW II:487, 366, 482.

167 *everything that is said or written:* Feast of Holy Trinity Sermon, in *T&P*, 210.

167 *For anyone who could grasp:* Pr 38 (W 176).

168 *God is unnameable:* Harvest, 142.

168 **All attributes we would apply:** Cross, *Christian Medieval Philosophers*, 117.

168 *God is nameless because none:* Pr 83 (W 463).

169 **Neither is God wise:** Pr 23 (W 287).

169 *No distinction,* Eckhart insists: Comm on Exodus 15:3, in *T&P*, 64.

169 **The only true proposition:** Ibid., 45–47.

169 **As Eckhart explains, "Shaddai" signifies:** Ibid., 94.

169 **In this sense, Eckhart agrees:** Comm on Wisdom, in *T&P*, 166.

169 *we should learn not to give God:* Pr 53 (W 153).

169 *every word that we can say:* Pr 36b (W 223); see a similar passage on Heraclitus in Pr 36a (W 219).

169 *whatever we say of God:* Pr 20a (W 192).

169 *. . . be silent and do not chatter:* Pr 83 (W 463).

170 *The more one tries to speak:* Comm on Exodus, in *T&P*, 82.

170 *it sometimes happened that they:* Pr 50 (W 452).

170   *the purest form of affirmation:* Harvest, 139.
170   **The existence of the One:** Pr 21 (W 466).
170   *anything we ascribe to [God]:* Pr 54b (W 254).
170   *He is as high above being:* Pr 9 (W 342).
170   **It would be better, Eckhart advised:** Pr 23 (W 287). See also Pr 10 (W 343).
170   *He is being above all being:* Pr 82 (W 316).
171   **Here the ancient authority:** Pr 28 (W 131).
171   **Scholars today debate the fidelity:** Harvest, 42–45.
171   **Proclus's ideas arrived:** Kurt Ruh, *Geschichte der abendländischen Mystik*, vol. III: *Die Mystik des deutschen Predigerordens und ihre Grundlegung durch die Hochscholastik* (Munich: C. H. Beck, 1996), 19; De Libera, *La Mystique rhénane*, 25; Harvest, 42–45.
171   **The Church Father even went:** Duclow, "ME's Latin Biblical Exegesis," 332.
172   **In 1265, Albert's disciple:** De Libera, *La Mystique rhénane*, 33; also 41–53.
172   **Even Aquinas, the supposed champion:** Flasch, *Das philosophische Denken im Mittelalter*, 323.
172   **These souls were themselves the result:** For a concise explanation, see Alessandro Palazzo, "Eckhart's Islamic and Jewish Sources: Avicenna, Avicebron, and Averroes," in Hackett, 257–62.
172   **One image in circulation:** The most notable proponents of this image were Robert Grosseteste (ca. 1175–1253) in *De Luce* (1225) and the Spanish rabbi Nahmanides (1194–1270) in his *Commentary on the Book of Genesis*, chaps. 1–6 (1250). See A. C. Crombie, *Robert Grosseteste and the Origins of Experimental Science* (Oxford, UK: Clarendon Press, 1971). In the *Paradiso* (Canto 16), Dante also described God as a single point of light.
172   *Do not imagine that God:* Pr 101 (W 34).
173   **God's intellect did indeed create:** Comm on Genesis, in *Essential ME*, 86–87.
173   *Creation is the production:* Both formulations appear in the general prologue to the *Opus Tripartitum*, Commentary on Genesis, Commentary on Wisdom, and Commentary on John, all cited in Harvest, 143.
173   **Like his spiritual father Augustine:** Pr 47 (W 157). See also De Libera, *La Mystique rhénane*, 269ff.
174   *in unity, not like in likeness:* Pr 13 (W 160); De Libera, *La Mystique rhénane*, 170.
174   *You must know that all creatures:* Pr 69 (W 235–36).
174   *God, as infinite Truth and Goodness:* Sermons and Lectures on Ecclesiasticus, in T&P, 174
174   **Maimonides, like many Aristotelian-oriented scholars:** Yosef Schwartz, "ME and Moses Maimonides," in Hackett, 389–414.
175   *Is there then,* he lamented: Pr 57 (W 170).
175   **The same reluctance was evident:** See Harvest, 118–124, on the concept Bernard McGinn considers the key to ME's theology.
175   **God the Creator, he claimed:** Pr 22 (W 283).
175   *God and Godhead are as different:* Pr 109 (W 293).
175   *When someone asked me why:* Comm on Genesis, in *Essential ME*, 85.
176   *When I yet stood in my first:* Pr 52 (W 424).
177   *Intellect forces its way in:* Pr 69 (W 237).
177   *The simple ground,* again only: Pr 48 (W 311).

CHAPTER 8: PERNICIOUS FEMALES

181   *I thought of something:* Pr 9 (W 326).
182   **In Strasbourg the master encountered:** Most scholars agree with this interpretation. For an opposing view on the beguines' influence, see Loris Sturlese, "ME und die cura monialium: Kritische Anmerkungen zu einem forschungsgeschichtlichen Mythos," in *MEs Straßburger Jahrzehnt*, eds. Andrés Quero-Sánchez and Georg Steer (Stuttgart: Kohlhammer, 2008), 1–16.
182   **In effect, they were the last remnants:** The medievalist Herbert Grundmann was the first to write of a "religious 'women's movement'" during this period, in his 1935 classic study, recently translated as *Religious Movements in the Middle Ages*, trans. Steven Rowan (Notre Dame, IN: University of Notre Dame Press, 1995). After more than two decades of neglect, his characterization has now become part of the scholarly consensus for the twelfth and especially thirteenth centuries.
183   **Numbering in the hundreds:** Oliver Davies, *ME: Mystical Theologian* (London: SPCK, 1991), 69. The early work of Dayton Phillips characterized the beguine house as primarily a social and economic institution with secondary religious interests. *Beguines in Medieval Strasburg: A Study of the Social Aspect of Beguine Life* (Ann Arbor, MI: Edwards Brothers, 1941), 159. Subsequent research has stressed the multifarious but primarily religious nature of the houses, ranging from members who still lived with their parents to quasi-convents. Amalie Fößel and Anette Hettinger, *Klosterfrauen, Beginen,*

Ketzerinnen. Religiöse Lebensformen von Frauen im Mittelalter (Idstein: Schulz-Kirchner, 2000), 50. There are many alternate explanations of the name's origin, including the beige robes that the women wore.

184   **Within twenty-five years:** Grundmann, *Religious Movements*, 130–39.

184   **By 1300, for example:** Schmitt, *Mort d'une héresie*, 147; Otto Langer, *Mystische Erfahrung und spirituelle Theologie. Zu MEs Auseinandersetzung mit der Frauenfrömmigkeit seiner Zeit* (Munich: Artemis, 1987), 21. By the early fourteenth century, there were at least fifty-seven such houses in Frankfurt, thirty-six in Basel, and twenty-two in Nuremberg. Phillips, *Beguines*, 145; Grundmann, *Religious Movements*, 135, 139, 148.

185   **The papal legate Gilbert of Tournai:** Little, *Religious Poverty*, 132.

185   **The prominent canonist Hostiensis:** Swanson, *Religion and Devotion*, 104.

185   **Like other lay apostolic movements:** They were also called lollards, *pauperes mulierculae, beatas, bizzoche, pinzochere,* poor sisters, virgins, and widows. Deane, *History of Medieval Heresy*, 159; Grundmann, *Religious Movements*, 164; Schmitt, *Mort d'une héresie*, 65.

185   **At one end of the spectrum:** McGinn, *Flowering*, 159; Kurt Ruh, *ME: Theologe, Prediger, Mystiker* (Munich: C. H. Beck, 1985), 99.

185   **Nikolaus of Bibra, a poet:** Grundmann, *Religious Movements*, 147; *Geschichte in Daten: Thüringen*, 98.

186   **Not long after assuming office:** Winfried Trusen, *Der Prozess gegen Meister Eckhart, Vorgeschichte, Verlauf und Folgen* (Paderborn: Ferdinand Schöningh, 1988), 25.

186   **The following year, the newly consecrated archbishop:** Grundmann, *Religious Movements*, 185.

186   **Marguerite, in William's view:** McGinn, *Flowering*, 245.

187   **The third reason for William's:** Robert E. Lerner, *The Heresy of the Free Spirit in the Later Middle Ages* (Notre Dame, IN: University of Notre Dame Press, 1972), 68–78. The current scholarly consensus, however, seems to be in favor of genuine beguine status.

188   **"Men of theology and scholars":** *Mirror*, prologue and chapters 9, 12, 13.

188   **"in the whole of a kingdom":** Edmund Colledge, J. C. Marler, and Judith Grant, "Interpretative Essay," in *Mirror*, il.

188   **"[annihilated] souls . . . do not make":** *Mirror*, 18.

188   **Even a hostile chronicler:** Colledge et al., *Mirror*, ix, xlvi.

189   **After first resolving the question:** Thorndike, *University Records*, 149–50.

189   **Here the text of Marguerite Porete's:** *The Essential Writings of Christian Mysticism*, ed. Bernard McGinn (New York: Modern Library, 2006), 493.

190   **One modern historian has characterized:** Richard Kieckhefer, *Repression of Heresy in Medieval Germany* (Philadelphia: University of Pennsylvania Press, 1979), 19.

190   **Twice—from 1261 to 1263:** Sandrine Turck, *Les dominicains à Strasbourg: entre prêche, prière et mendicité (1224–1420)* (Strasbourg: Société savante d'Alsace, 2002), 33–40.

192   **Two-thirds of the city's eighty-five:** Phillips, *Beguines*, 217.

192   **Educated at the University of Bologna:** Wilhelm Wiegand, "Johann, Bischof von Straßburg," in *Allgemeine Deutsche Biographie* (Leipzig: Duncker and Humblot, 1881), vol. 14: 418–19; Joseph Fuchs, "Johann I," in *Neue Deutsche Biographie* (Berlin: Duncker and Humblot, 1974), vol. 10:537.

193   **In addition to frequent interventions:** LW, V:158–181.

193   **The first, and most straightforward:** LW, V:161–163.

193   **Attempts to establish a new Dominican:** LW, V:173.

193   **The details of this monumental transition:** I strongly concur with Loris Sturlese (*ME: Ein Porträt* [Regensburg: Friedrich Pustet, 1993], 18, and Kurt Ruh (*ME*, 95ff.) on the significance of this turning point in Eckhart's life.

193   **Although he had visited the Strasbourg:** There were 110 friars resident in 1290. Turck, *Les Dominicains*, 119.

194   **Eckhart first appears in Strasbourg's:** LW V:182–83.

194   **A similar document two:** Property donation to the Dominican female cloister of St. Markus on November 13, 1316. LW V:184–85.

194   **Whenever this formal appointment:** Davies, *ME*, 71

194   **Surviving deeds and other financial records:** LW, V:184–88; Turck, Les *Dominicains*, 139–50, 260–63.

194   **Its cohorts, officially capped:** Turck, *Les Dominicains*, 128.

195   **The city of twenty thousand:** Phillips, *Beguines*, 7.

195   **His surviving German sermons:** LW V:187–89; Ruh, *ME*, 12.

196   **Most significantly, he co-resided:** Trusen, *Der Prozess*, 21; *Geschichte in Daten: Thüringen*, 155.

196   **His own German sermon:** Pr 52 (W 420–26).

196   **Eckhart's fellow theologian Godfrey:** Colledge et al., "Interpretive Essay," in *Mirror*, xl–xli.

197   **More than a century earlier:** See Bernard McGinn, *The Growth of Mysticism*, vol. II of *The Presences of God* (New York: Crossroad, 1994), 333–37.

197   **The period 1250–1350:** See especially Caroline Walker Bynum, *Jesus as Mother: Studies in the Spirituality of the High Middle Ages* (Berkeley: University of California Press, 1984).

198   **"Ah Lord," she sighed:** *Mechthild of Magdeburg: Selections from* The Flowing Light of the Godhead, ed. Elizabeth A. Anderson (Cambridge: D. S. Brewer, 2003), 48. On Mechthild, see also Amy Hollywood, *The Soul as Virgin Wife: Mechthild of Magdeburg, Marguerite Porete, and Meister Eckhart* (Notre Dame, IN: University of Notre Dame Press 2000); and Frank Tobin, *Mechthild von Magdeburg: A Medieval Mystic in Modern Eyes* (Columbia, SC: Camden House, 1995).

198   **He responded that it was her:** Anderson, *Mechthild,* 56.

198   **"Now I fear God":** Ibid., 52.

198   **"I was warned about":** Ibid., 47.

198   **Mechthild's work,** *The Flowing:* Frank Tobin, *Meister Eckhart: Thought and Language* (Philadelphia: University of Pennsylvania Press, 1986), 5.

199   **The Soul is a "full-grown bride":** McGinn, *Flowering,* 237; Anderson, *Mechthild,* 36.

200   **Whereas Marguerite envisioned:** Hollywood, *Soul as Virgin Wife,* 64.

200   **Lack of food, drink, and sleep:** Langer, *Mystische Erfahrung,* 60–79; Davies, *ME,* 74–75.

200   **As the** *Book of Twelve Beguines:* Carolyn Walker Bynum, *Holy Feast and Holy Fast: The Religious Significance of Food to Medieval Women* (Berkeley: University of California Press, 1987), 110.

201   **The beguine Hadewijch of Antwerp:** Langer, *Mystische Erfahrung,* 117ff.

201   **The liturgical calendar and nearby statues:** Ibid., 122.

202   **A century earlier, for instance:** Fried, *Middle Ages,* 267.

202   **In Eckhart's day, the Premonstratensian:** McGinn, *Flowering,* 283.

202   **Another contemporary, Christina of Stommeln:** Ibid., 177–79.

203   *Now you might ask:* Pr 103 (W 59–60).

203   *[i]t is great foolishness:* Pr 33 (W 402).

203   **About the time of his arrival:** The date of this book is contested, with composition estimates ranging from 1309 to 1324. See Dagmar Gottschall, "Eckhart's German Works," in *Hackett,* 150–51.

204   *misfortunes occurring to outward goods: Book of Divine Comfort* (W 524).

204   *There is solace for every sorrow:* Ibid. (W 526, 528).

204   *probably no one can be found:* Ibid. (W 533).

204   *a man should take all things:* Ibid. (W 527–30).

204   **Such "corporeal" and "spiritual" experiences:** Langer, *Mystische Erfahrung,* 221–22; Bernard McGinn, "Visio Dei: Seeing God in Medieval Theology and Mysticism," in Carolyn Muessig, ed., *Envisioning Heaven: An Introduction,* 16. See also Pr 72, (W 459).

204   *Some people want to see God:* Pr 16b (W117).

205   **He did not go as far:** McGinn, "Visio Dei," 18–19.

205   **According to one admiring chronicler:** From Gertrude the Great's *Legatus divinae pietatis,* translated in McGinn, *Flowering,* 267.

205   *Whoever seeks God in a special:* Pr 5b (W 110).

206   **"We think that in the Eucharist":** Bynum, *Holy Feast,* 156.

206   *Wisdom, he explains:* Pr 40 (W 320).

206   *When God made man:* Pr 6 (W 330).

206   *a woman and a man are unlike:* Pr 27 (W 101).

206   *we use the word homo:* Pr 20 (W 45).

207   **His response was not recorded:** LW V:187–188; Ruh, *ME,* 12.

207   *no earthly wisdom can grasp it:* LW V:188.

CHAPTER 9: MASTER OF LIVING

209   *Better one master of life:* Franz Pfeiffer, *ME* (1857; reproduced Göttingen: Vandenhoeck & Ruprecht, 1924), 599, 19–21, translated in McGinn, *Mystical Eckhart,* 1.

209   *[T]here is not one of you:* Pr 66 (W 301).

210   **The only Latin works:** Eckhart makes references to commentaries on Isaiah, Matthew, Romans, and Hebrews, but none has survived. Dietmar Mieth, *Die Einheit von vita activa und vita contemplativa in den deutschen Predigten und Traktaten MEs und bei Johannes Tauler* (Regensburg: Pustet Friedrich KG, 1995), 113.

210   **In a few sermons, he mentions:** Cf. references to "mîn buoch" in Pr 14 and Pr 28. I find convincing the argument of Sturlese, *Porträt,* 16. For a prominent dissenting voice, see Kurt Ruh, *Geschichte der abenländische Mystik,* vol. 3, *Die Mystik des deutschen Predigerordens und ihre Grundlegung durch die Hochscholastik* (Munich: C. H. Beck, 1996), 301–3.

210 *Humility is a root of all good:* Pr 14 (W 267).

211 *That is true humility:* Pr 49 (W 439).

211 *so long as the intellect:* Pr 104 (W 50).

211 *The light of the sun:* Pr 70 (W 231).

212 *There is no way man can know:* Pr 104 (W 50).

212 **The Neoplatonic modification:** Again, I am persuaded by the argument of Sturlese, "Eckhart as Preacher," in *Hackett*, 129.

212 **Applying his famed razor:** See the overview of Ockham's approach in Cross, *Medieval Christian Philosophers*, 189–209.

214 **According to Bernard of Clairvaux:** Sermon on the feast of SS. Peter and Paul, quoted in Fichtenau, *Heretics and Scholars*, 203.

214 **"learning things curious and subtle":** Thorndike, *University Records*, 73.

214 **His revered mentor, Albert the Great:** Grundmann, *Religious Movements*, 199.

215 **Eckhart believed that *words*:** Pr 18 (W 213).

215 **The Luke annunciation excerpt:** Pr 22 (W 279).

215 **On a few occasions he proceeded:** Pr 44 (W 143–46).

216 **Preaching on Ecclesiasticus 50:6–7:** Pr 9 (W 344).

216 **called "music of abstraction":** *Von der Wahrheit* (1947), 897. I borrow this reference from Davies, *Meister Eckhart*, 192.

216 **Similar modifications supplied him:** The most important work on Eckhart's literary innovations is Frank Tobin, *ME: Thought and Language* (Philadelphia: University of Pennsylvania Press, 1986). I am also indebted to the discussion of this topic in Davies, *ME*, 188–91.

217 *Divine love is like the salt:* Pr 22 (W 282).

217 **Some of these metaphors:** Frank Tobin, "Mechtild of Magdeburg and ME," in *ME and the Beguine Mystics: Hadewijch of Brabant, Mechthild of Magdeburg, and Marguerite Porete*, ed. Bernard McGinn (London/New York: Bloomsbury Academic Press, 1997), 46.

217 **Accordingly this metaphor led Eckhart:** No Pr, W 442.

217 **In one even more remarkable passage:** Pr 30 (W 140).

218 **One scholar has likened:** Davies, *ME*, 116.

218 *God is a word:* Pr 53 (W 152).

218 *God is nothing:* Pr 82 (W 316–17).

218 *God was a becoming without becoming:* Pr 50 (W 453); see also Pr 83 (W 462).

218 *breadth without breadth, expanseless expanse:* Pr 38 (W 178).

218 *You should love Him as He is:* Pr 83 (W 463).

218 *You should wholly sink:* Pr 83 (W 463–64).

219 *The text which I have quoted:* Pr 71 (W 137).

220 *Now let us turn this phrase:* Pr 3 (W 165).

221 **Christian figures—particularly Augustine:** E.g., Pr 80 (W 456).

221 *yesterday a question was debated:* Pr 74 (W 374).

221 **Dozens of times he prefaced:** See, for example, Pr 24 (W 450), Pr 58 (W 244), Pr 6 (W 331), Pr 74 (W 374), Pr 3 (W 166), Pr 51 (W 409).

221 *You often ask, for instance:* Pr 16b (W 116).

221 *But sir, you ask:* Pr 101 (W 30).

221 *Last night I thought:* Pr 14 (W 267); Pr 82 (W 281).

222 *I was thinking last night:* Pr 51 (W 409–10).

222 *Often I feel afraid:* Pr 73 (W 373).

222 *I will tell you how:* Pr 64 (W 393).

222 *I was thinking on the way:* Pr 74 (W 376–77); Pr 22 (W 282).

222 *As I was coming here today:* Pr 48 (W 309).

223 *Dear children, he pleaded:* Pr 64 (W 393).

223 *Just listen to one word:* Pr 74 (W 378).

223 *I will say one word:* Pr 69 (W 237).

223 *This is a sermon for All Saints:* Pr 63 (W 390).

223 *Here some folk will say:* Pr 29 (W 125).

223 *Since our understanding is a changing:* No Pr (W 441).

223 *Whoever has understood this:* Pr 56 (W 294).

223 *In seeking to emphasize:* Pr 73 (W 372).

224 *If God gave me anything:* Pr 15 (W 270).

224 *I am the cause of God's being God:* Pr 52 (W 424). Eckhart also began the sermon by noting: *I beg you for the love of God to understand this wisdom if you can; but if you can't understand it, don't worry, because I am going to speak of such truth that few good people can understand* (W 420).

224 *St. Augustine says, what a man:* Pr 5a (W 105).

224 *the soul is made of all:* Pr 3 (W 165); Pr 6 (W 329).

225 *If you could know with:* Pr 2 (W 81).

225 *Some masters would hold:* Pr 9 (W 341).

225 *I have been asked to make:* Pr 105 (W 122).

225 **He was fond of clarifications:** Pr 47 (W 156).

226 **References to** *slow-witted persons:* Comm on Book of Wisdom (W 474).

226 *I marvel how some priests:* Pr 29 (W 196).

226 *there are some people:* Pr 41 (W 241).

226 *many a dull-witted man:* Book of Comfort, Part III (W 553).

CHAPTER 10: THE WAYLESS WAY

229 *Whoever is seeking God:* Pr 5b (W 110).

229 **The German sermons that have survived:** Sturlese, "Eckhart as Preacher," in Hackett, 132.

230 *One [way] is to seek God:* Pr 86 (W 86).

231 **This approach appealed:** McGinn, *Flowering*, 115–17.

231 *I used sometimes to say:* Pr 74 (W 374).

231 *He who would see God:* Pr 72 (W 460).

231 *anyone who wishes to hear God:* Comm on Genesis, in *Essential ME*, 114.

231 **The second way into God:** Pr 86 (W 86).

231 **The third way, the master concluded:** Pr 86 (W 87).

232 *How marvelous, to be without:* Ibid.

232 *Is it better to do something:* Pr 101 (W 33).

232 **When Jesus preached:** Pr 52 (W 420).

233 *all you need is right intention:* Pr 29 (W 125).

233 *No one should think:* Pr 68 (W 355).

233 *And so I say again:* R 66 (W 301).

233 *Now I say, as I said before:* Pr 101 (W 33).

233 *If anyone were to ask me:* Pr 38 (W 177).

233 **The advanced seeker has already completed:** Pr 84 (W 415).

234 *The first is that fear, hope:* No Pr (W 380).

234 **Similarly,** *for a man to have:* Pr 68 (W 353).

234 *makes a man greatest of all:* Pr 74 (W 374).

234 *The just man seeks nothing:* Pr 39 (W 305).

234 *all attachment to any work* Pr 2 (W 78).

235 *Anyone who desires something:* Pr 1 (W 67).

235 *If one prays for [anything]:* Pr 65 (W 64).

235 *If you are sick and pray:* Pr 25 (W 91–92).

235 *Suppose I came to the pope:* Book of Divine Comfort (W 552).

235 *Anyone who seeks anything in God:* Pr 62 (W 289).

236 *Looking for something with God:* Pr 4 (W 226).

236 *The most powerful prayer:* Talks of Instruction (W 487).

236 *for God is above names:* Pr 53 (W 153).

236 *Strip God of all his clothing:* Pr 40 (W 318).

236 *Whatever is familiar to you:* Pr 102 (W 43).

236 *therefore I pray to God:* Pr 52 (W 424).

236 *Cease to be this or that:* Pr 77 (262).

236 *Our Lord, Eckhart reminded:* Pr 10 (W 337).

236 *It is lamentable how some:* Pr 11 (W 350).

237 *As long as you mind yourself:* Pr 28 (W 132).

237 **When some of his listeners:** Pr 16b (W 116).

237 *If you would know truth clearly:* Pr 69 (W 234).

237 **Similarly, memory, understanding, and will:** Pr 103 (W 55–56).

237 *for as long as you want more:* Pr 11 (W 347).

237   *therefore a man must be slain:* Pr 29 (W 127).
237   *A man once came to me:* Pr 28 (W 130).
238   *In all a man does:* Pr 62 (W 291).
238   *is to be silent and let God:* Pr 101 (W 33).
238   **Typically, the seeker was** *more aware:* Pr 68 (W 353).
238   *all your activity must cease:* Pr 103 (W 55–56).
239   *Sir, you place all:* Pr 102 (W 43).
239   *Now you might say, "Oh sir . . .":* Pr 103 (W 55–58).
239   *I have a power in my soul:* Pr 68 (W 352).
239   *The masters,* **he notes:** Pr 24 (W 449), Pr 2 (W 80).
240   **It is** *uncreated and uncreatable:* Pr 13 (W 161), Pr 48 (W 310), No Pr (W 381).
240   **This power** *alone is free:* Pr 2 (W 79).
240   **Like its divine source:** Pr 42 (W 399).
240   *There is a fine saying:* Pr 101 (W 35).
240   **The entire point of radical:** Pr 79 (W 446).
240   **Eckhart compared the liberated** *divine spark:* Pr 60 (W 248).
241   *The heavenly Father speaks:* Pr 19 (W 207).
241   *The nature of a word:* Pr 101 (W 34). See also Pr 73 (W 372).
241   **It is the** *voice crying out:* Pr 104 (W 52).
241   *Anything you see, or anything:* Pr 71 (W 140–41).
241   *so that the divine light:* Pr 45 (W 185).
241   **The birth of the Son:** For references to the ancient Fathers on this topic, see David W. T. Brattston, *Traditional Christian Ethics: Affirmative or Positive Commandments* (Nashville: WestBow Press, 2014), II:91.
242   *I have often said that the soul:* Pr 57 (W 169).
242   **To be** *ready to receive God's:* Pr 2 (W 77).
242   *You need not seek Him:* Pr 103 (W 58).
243   *Whenever a man humbles himself:* Pr 22 (W 281).
243   *God's comfort is pure and unmixed:* Pr 79 (W 446).
243   *If anyone were to rob God:* Pr 69 (W 234).
243   *The divine birth,* **after all:** Pr 11 (W 347).
243   *You should not take this:* Pr 5b (W 109).
244   *we are an only son whom:* Pr 22 (W 281).
244   **Eckhart's astonishing expansion:** No Pr (W 441–43).
244   *God is ever at work:* Pr 43 (W 394).
244   *And so, if a man is to know God:* Pr 46 (W 255).
244   **And so, he attempted to clarify:** Pr 22 (W 280).
244   *For between your human nature:* Pr 24 (W 450).
245   **The actors and the act:** Pr 103 (W 58).
245   **You must know, Eckhart explains:** Pr 76 (W 72).
245   *The eye with which I see God:* Pr 12 (W 298).
245   *united but not one with:* Pr 64 (W 392).
245   *Spiritual vessels are different:* Pr 16b (W 114).
245   **The soul** *in God:* Pr 76 (W 74).
245   **Just as God is everywhere:** Pr 63 (W 390).
245   *Whatever is in God:* Pr 3 (W 167).
245   *It is question difficult to answer:* Pr 47 (W 157).
246   **The inner man, or** *bare substantial being:* No Pr (W 359).
246   *I have said before and say again:* Pr 78 (W 175).
246   *It would be of little value:* Comm on John, in McGinn, *Harvest,* 153.

CHAPTER 11: LIVING WITHOUT A WHY

247   *The just man has such need:* Pr 41 (W 239).
248   *when a man accommodates himself:* Pr 82 (W 320).
248   *The truly humble man,* **according to Eckhart:** Pr 14 (W 267).
249   *This man now dwells:* Pr 15 (W 271).
249   *Some people, Eckhart preaches:* Pr 86 (W 89).
249   *In very truth I believe:* Pr 101 (W 37).

249   Some people say, "If I have God . . .": Pr 29 (W 125).
250   the highest perfection of the spirit: Pr 67 (W 358–59).
250   It may well be that those: No Pr (W 215–16).
250   For most people who have experienced: Pr 67 (W 359).
251   In his freewheeling translation: Pr 2 (W 77).
251   Now attend, and follow me closely: Pr 2 (W 78).
252   This is my commandment: Pr 27 (W 99).
252   Properly considered, love: Pr 4 (W 226).
252   As long as we are not like God: Comm on John, in Essential ME, 172.
253   In a later vernacular sermon, however: Pr 86 (W 84).
253   Martha, on the other hand: Pr 86 (W 89).
253   This was the meaning of living: Harvest, 188.
253   In the same way as God: Pr 41 (W 239).
254   Following the divine birth: Pr 6 (W 331).
254   If someone asked [the just man]: Pr 26 (W 96).
254   You must love all men: Pr 5a (W 105).
254   Jesus, himself, Eckhart reminded: Book of Divine Comfort (W 532).
254   The transformed individual: Ibid.
254   Though it should entail: Pr 25 (W 92).
254   When Jesus is led before Pilate: Reiner Schürmann, Wandering Joy: Meister Eckhart's Mystical Philosophy (Great Barrington, MA: Lindisfarne, 2001), 72
255   This was not an ecstatic flight: I am indebted to Reiner Schürmann, Wandering Joy, especially 14–15 and 32–36, for this insight.
255   So it is with all: Pr 103 (W 59).
255   The bond between the divine essence: "Feast of Holy Trinity Sermon," in T&P, 212.
257   Do you want to know what sin is?: Pr 32 (W 277).
257   God knows nothing outside: Pr 5a (W 104).
257   So while God makes merry: Pr 79 (W 445).
258   God always rewards: Comm on John, in Essential ME, 151.
258   God likes forgiving big sins: Pr 4 (W 225).
258   If a man slays another: Pr 63 (W 388).
258   In every work, even in an evil: Comm on John, in Essential ME, 44, n. 494.
258   Should anyone ask what God is: Pr 65 (W 62–63).
259   The question is asked, what burns: Pr 5b (W 109).
259   Now you might say, "Bad people": Pr 74 (W 375).
260   All good works, he seems to say: Pr 105 (W 120–21).
260   fasts, vigils, prayers, and the rest: Pr 1 (W 66).
260   People what is it: Spruch 8, Franz Pfeiffer, ME (1857); reproduced Göttingen: Vandenhoeck & Ruprecht 1924, 599.19–21, translated in McGinn, The Mystical Thought of ME, 1.
260   unworthy [and] unbelieving people: Pr 51 (W 410).
262   God knows nothing but being: Pr 8 (W 404).
262   Feeling I have in common: Pr 4 (W 225).
262   whatever is in God, is God: Pr 12 (W 297).
262   And seeing that God transforms: Pr 3 (W 167).
262   Why did God become man?: Pr 29 (W 126).
262   The incarnation was the greatest: Pr 22 (W 279).
262   St. Augustine says, what a man: Pr 5a (W 105).
263   In fact I will say still: Pr 48 (W 310).
263   They meet and unite: Pr 28 (W 131).
263   A great master says that his: Pr 52 (W 424).
264   In my birth all things: Pr 52 (W 424).
264   The concept of the ground: For a more extensive analysis of Eckhart's grunt, see the discussion in McGinn, Mystical Thought of ME, 114–61.

CHAPTER 12: DEVIL'S SEED

269   And some will say that such: W 553.
269   The years of Eckhart's stay: For an excellent overview of this crisis, see William Chester Jordan, The Great Famine (Princeton, NJ: Princeton University Press, 1996).

270 **In August 1317, he published:** Alexander Patschovsky, "Straßburger Beginenverfolgungen im 14. Jahrhundert," in *Deutsches Archiv für Erforschung des Mittelalters*, Bd. 30 (1974), 133–42.

270 **Some modern historians have suggested:** Martina Wehrli-Jons, "Mystik und Inquisition: Die Dominikaner und die sogenannte Häresie des Freien Geistes," in *Deutsche Mystik im abendländlichen Zusammenhang: Neu erschlossene Texte, neue methodische Ansätze, neue theoretische Konzepte: Kolloquium Kloster Fischingen, 1998*, ed. Walter Haug and Wolfram Schneider-Lastin (Tübingen: Niemeyer, 1999), 243.

271 **Half a century earlier:** *Harvest*, 59; Pr 52 (W 424).

271 **"They say they ought not to":** *Harvest*, 89.

272 **The beguines he ministered to:** Patschovsky, "Straßburger Beginenverfolgungen," 95–107.

272 **Early the next year he circulated:** Winfried Trusen, *Der Prozess gegen Meister Eckhart: Vorgeschichte, Verlauf und Folgen* (Schönigh: Schoeningh Ferdinand, 1988), 29.

273 **The Dominican priory of the city:** G. M. Lohr, *Beiträge zu Geschichte des Kölner Dominikanerklosters im Mittelalter* (Leipzig, 1920), 34–36.

273 **Certainly he lectured regularly:** Trusen, *Der Prozess*, 63.

273 **He was personally familiar with:** Ulrich Seng, *Heinrich zweite von Virneburg als Erzbischof von Köln* (Cologne: F. Schmitt, 1977), 75ff.

273 **The year before Eckhart's arrival:** Lerner, *Free Spirit Heresy*, 29–30.

273 **Heinrich of Virneburg was the type:** Seng, *Heinrich*, 17.

274 **He had not attended university:** Ibid., 41, 121ff.

275 **While the conflict raged on:** Davies, *ME*, 44; Senner, "Life," in Hackett, 42.

275 **Originally scheduled to take place:** Senner, "Life," in Hackett, 46; McGinn, *Mysticism*, 14; Trusen, *Der Prozess*, 188.

276 **"that some dishonest and indecent":** Senner, "Life," in Hackett, 47.

276 **One or more unidentified friars:** Ibid., 49.

276 **Upon return to Cologne:** Ibid., 50–51.

277 **Faced with certain punishment:** Ibid., 52.

277 **Upon arriving in Aachen:** Ibid.

278 **Most of Eckhart's brethren:** Ingeberg Degenhardt, *Studium zum Wandel des Eckhartbildes* (Leiden: Brill, 1967), 13. My description of Eckhart's trials in Cologne and Avignon draws heavily on the careful research of Senner, "Life," in *Hackett*, 44–81, and Trusen, *Der Prozess*, esp. 105 ff.

278 **according to the exemption:** *Essential ME*, 71.

279 **To clarify the objections:** Ibid., 72–73.

279 **They think that everything:** Ibid., 75.

280 **Know that these articles:** Ibid., 76.

280 **When he came before the two:** Senner, "Life," in Hackett, 66–67.

280 **While he had promptly replied:** Ibid., 65.

281 **While waiting for the outcome:** I am grateful to Senner, "Life," in Hackett, 71, for this interpretation.

281 **I Meister Eckhart:** Senner, "Life," in Hackett, 68.

282 **"We have arrived at the decision":** Ibid., 71.

283 **"unholy Babylon, thou sink of iniquity":** Guillaume Mollat, *The Popes at Avignon, 1305–78* (London: Thomas Nelson and Sons, 1963), 279.

283 **Within the space of two decades:** Bernard Guillemain, *La Cour Pontificale d'Avignon (1309–76): Étude d'une Société* (Paris: Éditions E. de Boccard, 1962), 551.

283 **Since 1100, popes:** Yves Renouard, *La papauté à Avignon* (Paris: Presses Universitaires, 1955), 37.

283 **Papal ambassadors from across Europe:** Mollat, *The Popes*, 280.

284 **Even so, once the necessary clerks:** Ibid., 307.

284 **At least five hundred people:** Ibid., 283.

284 **Six years earlier, John had bought:** Edwin Mullins, *The Popes of Avignon: A Century in Exile* (New York: BlueBridge, 2007), 52.

284 **The year 1327 saw the peak:** Guillemain, *La Cour Pontificale*, 443.

284 **Even the Dominican priory:** Paul Amargier, "Le couvent dominicain d'Avignon de ses origins à la peste noire," *Études vauclusiennes*, no. 5 (1971): 21–30.

285 **The archbishop's inquisitors:** Senner, "Life," in Hackett, 72–74; Trusen, *Der Prozess*, 114–15.

285 **In effect, it was now a censure case:** Trusen, *Der Prozess*, 118.

286 **Historians have judged him:** C. W. Previte-Orton, *The Shorter Cambridge Medieval History* (Cambridge, UK: Cambridge University Press, 1975), I:836; Mollat, *The Popes*, 23.

286 **Tightening central control of benefices:** Mollat, *The Popes*, 14; Mullins, *The Popes of Avignon*, 55.

286 **By the time of Eckhart's arrival:** Davies, *ME*, 50; Spufford, *Money and Its Uses*, 157; Mullins, *The Popes of Avignon*, 48; Ruh, *ME*, 183.

286 **Two-thirds of the pope's expanded income:** Mollat, *The Popes*, 316.

287 **Beginning with four or five lists:** Senner, "Life," in Hackett, 74–76.

288 **The articles singled out:** *Essential ME*, 78–79.

289 **The *eternal Now* was a tenet:** Ibid., 40–41.

289 **A similarly scholastic difference:** Ibid., 79.

289 **Such fine distinctions were the stuff:** Ibid., 116.

289 **We shall all be transformed:** Ibid., 78.

290 **But early in the new year:** Senner, "Life," in Hackett, 77.

290 **profess[ing] the Catholic faith:** *Essential ME*, 81.

291 **Most articles were condemned:** Koch, *Kleine Schriften*, 384.

291 **The pope clearly valued:** Senner, "Life," in Hackett, 78–79.

292 **we are indeed sad to report:** *Essential ME*, 77.

292 **censures only fifteen:** Ibid., 80.

292 **Three weeks later, on April 15:** Ruh, *ME*, 186.

CHAPTER 13: THE MAN FROM WHOM GOD HID NOTHING

293 ***If anyone cannot understand:*** Pr 52 (W 424).

293 **In 1356, the Benedictine monk:** Lerner, *Free Spirit*, 216–21; *Harvest*, 344–49.

294 **"the man from whom God hid nothing":** This is the title of the first "sayings" attributed to ME, first published in Pfeiffer, *ME*, 597.

294 **Almost all of the portrayals:** For a significant exception, see the "good cook's" criticisms in *Erroneous Teachings of ME*, in Bernard McGinn, *The Varieties of Vernacular Mysticism, 1350–1550* (New York: Crossroad, 2012), 71–76.

294 **A 1353 Dutch treatise:** Degenhardt, *Studium*, 27.

295 **Few friars openly criticized:** Trusen, *Der Prozess*, 155, 162.

295 **Profoundly depressed by his own unworthiness:** Henry Suso, *The Exemplar with Two German Sermons*, ed. Frank Tobin (New York: Paulist Press, 1989), 105.

295 **"one of the most learned and experienced":** Ibid., 308.

295 **Finally he explicitly distinguishes:** Ibid., 326–27.

296 **"some uneducated but intelligent people":** Ibid., 58

296 **Speculative theology, which he learned:** Ibid., 57.

296 **The *Little Book of Truth* was aimed:** Ibid., 59.

297 **"The more bitterly you have suffered":** Suso, *The Exemplar*, 241.

297 **It was in one of these Rhineland cities:** Josef Schmidt, "Introduction," in *Johannes Tauler: Sermons*, trans. Maria Shrady, *Classics of Western Spirituality* (New York: Paulist Press, 1985), 5.

298 **According to Tauler, every human:** See, for instance, Sermon 1 (35–40) and Sermon 19 (69–73) in *Johannes Tauler*.

299 **This was the period of greatest persecution:** Ingrid Würth, *Geißler in Thüringen: Die Entstehung einer spätmittelalterlichen Häresie* (Berlin: Walter de Gruyter, 2012), 432ff.; Lerner, *Free Spirit Heresy*, 145; Grundmann, *Religious Movements*, 245.

299 **Theologians who appropriated:** Degenhardt, *Studium*, 20; Koch, *Kleine Schriften*, 438–43.

300 **Eckhart's mistake, he wrote:** *Essential ME*, 24; Degenhardt, *Studium*, 52; Elizabeth Brient, "ME's Influence on Nicholas of Cusa: A Survey of the Literature," in Hackett, 557.

300 **Some Dominican chronicles vaguely:** Degenhardt, *Studium*, 71–73.

300 **In 1516, the thirty-three-year-old theology professor:** See *Harvest*, 392–404.

300 **The future reformer's greatest objection:** Volker Leppin, *Die fremde Reformation: Luthers mystische Wurzeln* (Munich: C. H. Beck, 2016), 31–41.

301 **Luther likely read at least:** Ibid., 204.

301 **Protestant publications of Tauler's sermons:** Degenhardt, *Studium*, 69–70.

301 **A 1522 publication on mysticism:** I am very grateful to Bernard McGinn for sharing with me his unpublished paper on the topic. See also Andrew Weeks, "ME and Valentin Weigel" in Hackett, 607–27.

301 **Sudermann also composed:** Degenhardt, *Studium*, 94.

301 **Protestant embrace of some medieval mystics:** Ibid., 85.

301 **Thus while many of:** Davies, *ME*, 215.

302 **"beautiful splendid times, when Europe":** Tobin, *Mechthild*, 18.

302 **"branded as heretical all imagination":** Ibid.

302 **"Eckhart is rightly called the Master":** See especially the enlightening discussion of Cyril O'Reagan, "Eckhart's Reception in the 19th Century," in Hackett, 629–67; also Degenhardt, *Studium*, 112–14.

303 **Hegel's student Karl Rosenkranz:** Ruh, *ME*, 14.

303 **Protestant philosophers such as:** Degenhardt, *Studium*, 146.

303 **In his *History of Mysticism*:** Tobin, *Mechthild*, 26.

303 **Accusations of atheism:** Degenhardt, *Studium*, 156–65.

303 **In his *German Mysticism*:** Tobin, *Mechthild*, 23.

304 **In 1886, the Dominican:** *ME in Erfurt*, 110.

304 **An influential 1904 article:** Kurt Flasch, *ME: Philosopher of Christianity*, trans. Anne Schindel and Aaron Vanides (New Haven, CT: Yale University Press, 2015), 161.

304 **Greatly embellished portrayals:** Degenhardt, *Studium*, 240.

304 **New Catholic accounts:** Ibid., 288.

305 **In Rosenberg's fantasy:** Ruh, *ME*, 14; also Degenhardt, *Studium*, 259.

305 **In 1935, the Jesuit theologian:** Flasch, *ME*, 195.

305 **In 1937, Quint joined the Nazi party:** Ibid., 162.

306 **The postmodern deconstructionist:** Dermot Moran, "Meister Eckhart in Twentieth-Century Philosophy," in Hackett, 697.

306 **No twentieth-century philosopher:** See especially the astute overview of Moran in Hackett, 687–96.

307 **"the dark self-perception":** Ben Morgan, *On Becoming God: Late Medieval Mysticism and the Modern Self* (New York: Fordham University Press, 2013), 152.

307 **Yet as the scholars Amy Hollywood:** Amy Hollywood, *Sensible Ecstasy: Mysticism, Sexual Difference, and the Demands of History, Religion and Post-Modernism* (Chicago: University of Chicago Press, 2003), esp. 155ff.; Morgan, *On Becoming God*, 82–87.

307 **Contrary to his former mentor:** Carl Jung, *Psychological Reflections*, eds. Jolande Jacobi and R. F. C. Hull (Princeton, NJ: Princeton University Press, 1978), 340.

307 **When searching for inroads:** Carl Jung, *Memories, Dreams, Reflections*, ed. A. Jaffe and R. and C. Winston (New York: Vintage, 1961), 68–69.

307 **"The art of letting things happen":** Carl Jung, commentary in Richard Wilhelm, trans., *The Secret of the Golden Flower* (New York: Harcourt Brace Jovanovich, 1962), 93.

308 **Eckhart's pivotal insight:** *Psychological Types*, in *Collected Works*, ed. R. F. C. Hull (Princeton, NJ: Princeton University Press, 1977), 254.

308 **We tried to have the censure:** https://en.wikipedia.org/wiki/Meister_Eckhart#cite_note-rehab-118.

309 **"the one Zen thinker of the West":** Cited in Matthew Fox, *ME: A Mystic-Warrior for Our Times* (Novato, CA: New World Library, 2014), 36.

309 **Letting-go-ness lines up:** See the intriguing comparisons of Hee-Sung Keel, *ME: An Asian Perspective* (Leuven: Peters Press/Eerdmans, 2007).

309 **The Tamil writer Ananda K. Coomaraswamy:** *The Transformation of Nature in Art* (New Delhi: Munshiram Manoharlal Publishers, 1994), 61, 201.

311 **Tolle's earliest mystical influence:** John W. Parker, *Dialogues with Emerging Spiritual Leaders*, 2nd ed. (New York: iUniverse, 2009), 93–122.

312 **"Salvation" consists of freedom:** Tolle, *The Power of Now*, 72.

312 **You find God the moment:** Ibid., 147.

EPILOGUE

315 *In whatever way you find God:* W 589.

316 **As William James already observed:** William James, *The Varieties of Religious Experience* (New York: Penguin Books, 1982), 379–80.

317 **Franciscan Richard Rohr:** See, for example, Richard Rohr, *What the Mystics Know: Seven Pathways to Your Deeper Self* (New York: Crossroad, 2015).

317 **In Fox's *Creation Spirituality*:** Fox, *ME: A Mystic-Warrior for Our Times*, xiv.

318 **"what a darkness we are involved in":** John Locke, *An Essay Concerning Human Understanding*, ed. Alexander Campbell Fraser (New York: Dover Publications, 1959), vol. 2, bk. 4, chap. 3, 222; cited in Marilynne Robinson, *The Givenness of Things* (New York: Farrar, Straus and Giroux/Picador, 2016), 189.

319 **As the author Marilynne Robinson:** Robinson, *The Givenness of Things*, 84.

319 **Immanuel Kant argued:** From his *Critique of Pure Reason*, as quoted in https://plato.stanford.edu/entries/kant-judgment/supplement1.html.

319   **Albert Einstein urged:** William Hermanns, *Einstein and the Poet: In Search of the Cosmic Man* (Wellesley, MA: Branden Press, 1983), 108.

319   **Some contemporary brain scientists:** Iain McGilchrist, *The Master and His Emissary: The Divided Brain and the Making of the Western World* (New Haven, CT: Yale University Press, 2009), 3–4.

320   **Going deep within oneself:** I especially wish to acknowledge my debt to Dietmar Mieth, *Die Einheit von vita activa und vita contemplativa,* a very thoughtful treatment of this subject.

321   **Neglecting such core aspects:** Flasch, *ME: Philosopher of Christianity,* 158.

Index

Illustration Credits